WRITING THE BLACK REVOLUTIONARY DIVA

Writing the Black Revolutionary Diva

WOMEN'S
SUBJECTIVITY
AND THE
DECOLONIZING
TEXT

Kimberly Nichele Brown

INDIANA UNIVERSITY PRESS
Bloomington and Indianapolis

This book is a publication of

INDIANA UNIVERSITY PRESS

601 North Morton Street

Bloomington, Indiana 47404-3797 USA

www.iupress.indiana.edu

Telephone orders 800-842-6796
Fax orders 812-855-7931
Orders by e-mail iuporder@indiana.edu

∞ The paper used in this publication
meets the minimum requirements of the
American National Standard for Information Sciences—Permanence of Paper for
Printed Library Materials, ANSI Z39.48-
1992.

Manufactured in the United States of
America

LIBRARY OF CONGRESS CATALOGING-
IN-PUBLICATION DATA

Brown, Kimberly Nichele.
  Writing the black revolutionary
diva : women's subjectivity and the
decolonizing text / Kimberly Nichele
Brown.
    p.   cm. — (Blacks in the diaspora)
  Includes bibliographical references
and index.
  ISBN 978-0-253-35525-6 (cloth : alk.
paper) — ISBN 978-0-253-22246-6 (pbk.
: alk. paper) 1. American literature—
African American authors—History and
criticism. 2. African American women
authors. 3. African American women
in literature. 4. African American
women—Race identity. 5. Subjectivity in
literature. I. Title.
  PS153.N5B674 2010
  810.9'928708996073—dc22

                        2010008466

1 2 3 4 5 15 14 13 12 11 10

This book is dedicated to my husband and friend,
Mohamed T. Thiaw.
Without his love and support,
the completion of this project would not have been possible.

CONTENTS

ACKNOWLEDGMENTS

First and foremost, *Writing the Black Revolutionary Diva: Women's Subjectivity and the Decolonizing Text* is dedicated to my family. I want to thank my parents, Millicent and Roger Brown, for my life and my education. I want to also show my gratitude to my surviving grandparents, Shirley and Louis Stukes; my aunts Jacqueline and Bobbi Brown and my uncle Louis Stukes, Jr., for their love and generous monetary support over the years. Without my family's pooling their resources to buy me a black computer (black to match my fashion aesthetic more than my political consciousness), because "Who ever heard of a PhD candidate who didn't have her own computer," this project would not have been possible. I also want to thank my brother, Roger L. Brown II, for making me live up to the role model he sees in me. Much thanks to my cousins, the Stukes sisters, Doris, Moni, Keisha, Ekundayo, and my other cousin, Doris, because their "invented lives" showed me other possibilities for my own.

Second, I also want to thank my friends for their support and understanding over these long years. To my undergraduate posse, Desiree Scott, Laura Varner-Norman, Tonya Norman, and Kelli Byrd-Jackson, for surrounding me with love and laughter and for making my transition into womanhood bearable. To my graduate posse, Tanya Shields, Kenyatta Dorey Graves, Virginia Bell, and Maria Karafilis, for encouraging me to reach my full potential as a human being and a scholar. To my New York posse, Milton Moy, Allen Counts, Charlene Dougall, and Mirasol Santiago, for finding me apartments, providing me computer equipment, office furniture, transportation, and companionship during my summer writing retreats to New York. And finally, to my brother- and sister-scholars, Greg Thomas, Jennifer Williams, Christina Sharpe, Finnie Coleman, and Amy Ongiri, for giving me much-needed feedback.

I would also like to thank the late Barbara A. Sizemore, whose Black Studies course and personal attention first awakened the *scholar* in me when I was an undergraduate at the University of Pittsburgh—I will always regret this book's belated publication; I don't think you ever knew how much you meant to me. To Brenda Berrian who, as an African American English professor, was my first professional role model. To Vernell A. Lillie, who has always reminded me of my potential and has never faltered in her belief in that potential. To Jack Daniel and Johnetta Davis, who showed me what it means to be committed to advancing black graduate students—without their mentorship I would not have gotten this far. I also want to acknowledge my dissertation committee at the University of Maryland, Carla L. Peterson, Sangeeta Ray, Merle Collins, Shirley Logan, and Melinda Chatauvert. Additionally, I owe a debt of gratitude to Leona Fischer, Gene Hammond, and John Lowe for their constant support. A special thanks should also go to Trudier Harris and Farah Jasmine Griffin for their advice and encouragement.

At Texas A&M University (TAMU) I would like to thank the Department of English for their continued faith in me. At TAMU, I would like to give specific thanks to Victoria Rosner, J. Lawrence Mitchell, Pamela Matthews, Mary Ann O'Farell, David McWhirter, Marco Portales, Joseph O. Jewell, Jimmie Killingsworth, Larry Oliver, and Albert Broussard, and my graduate assistants, Cherry Levin, Jennifer Haley, Christina Ashie, Bryan Gillin, and Glenn Phillips. I would also like to give a heartfelt thanks to Janis P. Stout and Karan L. Watson (former deans of faculties at TAMU, respectively) for their support and faith in me over the years. This research was supported by Texas A&M University by a Faculty Mini-Grant from the Race and Ethnic Studies Institute, under the direction of Mitchell Rice, a Scholarly and Creative Activities Enhancement Grant, and the Faculty Fellows Program of The Melburn G. Glasscock Center for Humanities Research, under the direction of James Rosenheim.

I am also indebted to Sandra Kumamoto Stanley, the editor of *Other Sisterhoods: Literary Theory and US Women of Color* (University of Illinois Press, 1998), whose persistence and feedback was life-altering in that it ushered me into the world of the academy. A special thanks to my anonymous readers at Indiana University Press, as well as Robert Sloan for his patience and for not giving up on me.

And last but not least, I would like to thank Dr. Seuss—he lit the first spark.

WRITING THE BLACK REVOLUTIONARY DIVA

PRELUDE

On July 14, 1989, Maya Angelou, Angela Davis, Ntozake Shange, Alice Walker, and Michelle Wallace appeared on the syndicated talk show *Donahue*. Their presence was a testament to the fact that black female writers had more than solidified their hold on America's publishing forefront.[1] Unfortunately, the occasion was prompted by the negative response of many African Americans to the 1985 release of director Stephen Spielberg's Hollywood adaptation of Alice Walker's novel *The Color Purple* (1982). bell hooks hotly recalls that the black women writers present were taken to task for their supposedly myopic and unflattering portrayals of black men in their novels and were made to defend their depictions of male characters rather than engage in any meaningful discussion about gender or feminist issues as they pertain to the black community. hooks writes, "As public spectacle the show gave the impression that there is a tremendous hostility between black women and men; that black women writers are responsible for disrupting solidarity between the two groups, and finally that there is little or no communication taking place" (*Yearning* 71).

It would seem that "the dilemma of the Negro artist" that James Weldon Johnson emphasized in his 1928 essay finds a resonance in this contemporary example. He writes:

> It is quite possible for a Negro author to do a piece of work, good from every literary point of view, and at the same time bring down on his head the wrath of the entire colored pulpit and press, and gain among the literate element of his own people the reputation of being a prostitutor [*sic*] of his talent and a betrayer of his race—not by any means a pleasant position to get into. ("The Dilemma of the Negro Author" 96)

As a "public spectacle," the show foreshadowed (or set the stage for) the now widespread belief that contemporary black female writers are in cahoots with the white power structure to assassinate the public image of black men. In her introduction to her revised edition of *No Crystal Stair* (1997), Gloria Wade-Gayles explains that

> Negative responses to the film, which according to some feminist crit-ics reflected Spielberg's twisting of Walker's vision, constituted a dress rehearsal for conflicts between black men and black women that would take place in the eighties; these conflicts reached a crescendo in 1991 in responses to the Clarence Thomas nomination or, more precisely, to Anita Hill's allegations of sexual harassment. (xv)

Mel Watkins's article "Sexism, Racism and Black Women Writers," published in *The New York Times* on June 15, 1986, serves as one example of the public critique of black women writers such as Walker. While he praises their skills as writers, Watkins questions the decision of many acclaimed black women who write outside the "parameters" of the Afri-can American literary tradition's unspoken rule that positive images of blacks must be presented. Citing Toni Cade Bambara, Gayl Jones, Toni Morrison, Carlene Hatcher Polite, Ntozake Shange, Alice Walker, and Michelle Wallace as prime examples, Watkins insists that "[t]heir fiction often presents brutal, barely human straw men who exist only to demon-strate the humanity of the protagonists or antagonists with whom they are contrasted. These writers have, in effect, shifted their priorities from the subtle evocation of art to the blunt demonstration of politics and propaganda" (36–37). In this instance, the "politics" in question is femi-nism and the "propaganda" is the supposed tendency of black women writers to discredit black men in their novels.

While black men like Tony Brown and Charles Johnson also pub-licly berated Walker,[2] Ishmael Reed's censure loomed the largest. In his April 1992 keynote address to the College Language Association,[3] titled "Klu Klux Klan Feminism and Its Impact on Black Male Culture," Reed accused what he called the "divas" of black feminism for cavorting with white feminists to "bash" black men (Jackson, *Images of Black Men*, 85). Such remarks are indicative of those he made on television programs like *Tony Brown's Journal* or the *Today* show that aired in 1986.[4] His most egregious statements, however, can be found in his novel *Reckless Eye-balling* (1986), where Reed satirizes Walker in the character of Tremon-isha Smarts. Described as a "crass, bitchy, single issue, racial and sexual opportunist," Tremonisha is a critically acclaimed playwright, known for her contemptuous portrayals of black men. In her play *Wrong-Headed Man*, "the lead villain has screwed his children, sodomized his missionary wife, put his mother-in-law in bondage, performed bestial acts with pets, and when the police break down the door he's emptied the fish bowl and is going after the fish" (51–52). When they learn that *Wrong-Headed Man* is scheduled to be made into a film, the "fellas," black male friends of Ian Ball, the protagonist, worry: "since the film version of *Wrong-Headed Man* was being produced, directed, and written by white males . . . they, the fellas, could look forward to a good media head-whipping. . . . They imagined that the white feminist critics were already lining up to review it" (12). But Tremonisha is effectively punished for conspiring with "the enemies of black men"; a man breaks into her apartment, ties her up, and shaves her head because "this is what the French Resistance did to those women who collaborated with the Nazis" (4).

Trey Ellis, who coined the phrase and defined the parameters of the new black aesthetic, follows in Reed's footsteps by offering his own satiric portrayal of Walker (and by extension, other established black female writers) in his novel *Platitudes* (1988) with his characterization of Isshee Ayam. Her name is as much of a pun as it is a criticism of black cultural authenticity and the supposed tendency of contemporary black women writers to romanticize black southern life. Unlike her male counterpart, Dewayne Wellington, who writes in an experimental postmodernist vein that she despises, Isshee, whose writing style Dewayne considers banal, has won numerous awards. Additionally, her academic and commercial success is attributed to her negative depiction of black men in her works. While Ellis redeems Isshee's character by having her fall in love with Dewayne (thus, metaphorically, allowing for the marriage of realism and postmodern aesthetics), he also deduces that her dubious depiction of black men as villains is the result of her own failed relationships rather than a realistic critique of sexism. Although Ellis seems to be more sympathetic to contemporary black women writers than is Reed, he ultimately decides that the way to fix Isshee is to show her love. For Reed, Tremonisha's redemption lies in admitting her faults and keeping herself proverbially barefoot and pregnant.[5] Either approach relieves Ellis and Reed from engaging in any meaningful dialogue with black feminists about sexism within the black community, while simultaneously insinuating that the texts of black women like Walker are therapeutic experiments designed to allow women to vent their sexual frustrations.[6]

Given that it was the movie, the collaborative effort of Dutch screenwriter Menno Meyjes and Stephen Spielberg, rather than Walker's novel that served as the actual cause for the backlash against black women writers of Walker's ilk, hooks may be correct when she writes, "Certainly Walker's book was not the catalyst for the discussion, but a white male's interpretation, a fact which suggests that black men are more concerned with how they are seen by white men than by black women" (*Yearning* 70). A closer analysis of Walker's original text would reveal that in her deliberation on domestic violence, her principal male characters undergo a redemptive transformation that breaks the cyclical patterns of abuse—a fact that is not translated to the film adaptation. Nonetheless, what the *Donahue* show also demonstrates is that the issues deemed germane to African Americans, as with U.S. society as a whole, are often regulated by the media. Furthermore, this talk show segment illustrates the various ways African American women are rendered both visible (as scapegoats and spectacles) and yet invisible (lacking agency) within the public sphere.

In *The Same River Twice* (1996), however, Alice Walker does not dwell on the fact that she was stripped of her agency or made into a scapegoat; her biggest lament is that her public castigation was sanctioned, to a large extent, by black audiences. Walker's torment over the negative reaction to the film leads credence to my argument that since the black aesthetic movement (BAM),[7] African American writers have become increasingly more concerned about how they are received by blacks than by whites.

I begin my project with a description of the *Donahue* scenario to tie discussions about black spectatorship by scholars like Jacqueline Bobo, Manthia Diawara, bell hooks, James Snead, and Jacqueline Stewart to the issue of decolonized black subjectivities. While I see the move from a dual audience (black and white) rhetorical strategy to the privileging of a black audience as an act of decolonization for both the author and her intended audience, I want to be careful not to present the shift I see in the priorities of black writers as idyllic. Nor do I want to disregard the effect of mainstream or public audiences on African American writers;[8] that the discussion of black female writers' supposed betrayal of black men was conducted on the *Donahue* show, a public forum, complicates my proclamation. What this example reveals is that the interior lives of blacks are always going to be subject to public consumption because the majority of African American women writers publish in mainstream venues. Therefore, black women who air our community's "dirty laundry"[9] in public run the risk of censure or ridicule.

Walker discloses that what prompted her to agree to a movie adaptation of *The Color Purple* was her desire to reach those in the black

community who would not ordinarily have read her book; more specifically, her own mother had grown too ill to finish the novel. On many
levels, making the movie was Walker's gift to her mother as well as an
homage to their shared southern heritage. Prior to the movie's release, in
a journal entry dated February 21, 1984, Walker seemingly entreats God,
the universe, the ancestors: "I want so much for this to be good. Something to lift spirts and encourage people" (*The Same River Twice* 18). In
essence, her prayer is that the movie bear the same moral/social responsibility with which she endowed her novel. *Writing the Black Revolutionary Diva: Women's Subjectivity and the Decolonizing Text* is an investigation of how African American women writers bring their interior desires
for racial/social uplift to fruition in their creative works. Rather than to
disconnect women writers like Walker from the mission of black aestheticians, I see African American women as continuing its legacy.

Even though it would appear that Walker's wish for the movie was
unfulfilled, I think it would be a mistake to conclude that the *Donahue*
show and the public controversy that surrounded the film ultimately
stripped Walker of her agency. The act of writing *The Same River Twice*
is Walker's way of critiquing the negative response she received as the
result of the movie's release. By offering her audience a glimpse into her
personal thoughts during the making of the film, Walker forces people
to rethink how they stereotyped her public persona.

While hooks primarily reads the *Donahue* program as a disastrous
public fiasco, there were moments when the writers enacted what I term a
revolutionary diva subjectivity, when they broke loose from the fixed label
of emasculators and forced the audience to re-examine their assumptions of blackness and black womanhood. For example, in response to
a white female audience member's question about whether or not she
wrote from experience, Ntozake Shange, in true diva fashion, swiveled
her neck from side to side and answered curtly, "Can't a black person
have an imagination?" It is the tone of the question, in conjunction with
Shange's body language (both of which can be construed as reflecting
her conspicuous frustration with what she presumes are the audience
member's assumptions about blackness) that has left a lasting impression upon me. This scenario serves as background narrative to this project's investigation of African American female self-definition after the
black aesthetic movement in the mire of externally imposed definitions
of African American subjectivity by the white mainstream. One could
speculate that had a black woman asked Shange the same question, her
response might have been different. With this supposition in mind, my

ultimate preoccupation is with how notions of the self change depending upon who sits in the audience.

It is what Shange potentially reads into the woman's *whiteness* that makes this exchange so interesting. The result, perhaps, of being asked that question one too many times, Shange's caustic response reflects more than her offense at the implication that blacks lack the ability to imagine; Shange takes the audience member's question as a denial of African American humanity. Upon further analysis, I see the audience member's comment as mirroring white mainstream's imagination and its impression of blackness as somehow more authentic, more *real* than the experience of whiteness—delineated as inhibited, rigid, sterile. With such an expectation, black imagination is virtually unthinkable or perhaps deemed unnecessary when, supposedly, the real life experience of blacks already provides such fertile material for writing.

It is precisely because of the historical connection that exists between texts written by blacks and "the black experience," however, that the question the audience member posed to Shange should not be construed as entirely baseless. Given that African American literature and black cognition serves as the context for this dialogue, I am reminded of older connections between the black author/black text and the presumed white audience. Shange's question inadvertently illustrates an aversion to long-standing traditions that conflate the lived experiences of black writers with their texts. David Bradley writes, "Today literature is often read, taught—and judged—as much for its experiential content as for its literary quality. But the literature produced by American blacks . . . has always been read this way."[10] In *Writing the Subject*, Gunilla Theander Kester explains that the reason people tend to link a black author's text with her or his lived experience is because of "the immersion of double-ness on all levels of African American culture" (5). Kester's point can be extended to include the dichotomous nature of African American subjectivity, a subjectivity that is both central and marginal to U.S. cultural traditions and history, one that is both American and African (i.e., Du Bois's notion of double-consciousness), and intraracially both individual and collective.

We, as readers and literary critics, have come to expect African Americans, and people of color in general, to produce experiential writings; the attention given to testimonial narratives serves as just one example.[11] The shift to autobiographical writings in the mid- to late 1990s by novelists like Charles Johnson and Alice Walker, and literary critics like Michael Awkward, Henry Louis Gates, Jr., bell hooks, and Deborah McDowell, serves as yet another example.[12] This link between text and subject is perhaps so pervasive and perduring because black writers have historically achieved textual authority as a result of their lived experience. The very credibility of slave narratives depended on narrators depicting themselves as authentic members of and spokespersons for an oppressed caste—persons who had firsthand knowledge of the atrocities of slavery. For example, Frederick Douglass exclaimed in an 1841 speech that he had "been engaged in pleading the cause of [his] brethren,"[13] while Harriet Jacobs, in the preface to *Incidents in the Life of a Slave Girl* (1861) wrote, "Neither do I care to excite sympathy for my own sufferings. But I do earnestly desire to arouse the women of the North to a realizing sense of the condition of two millions of women at the South, still in bondage, suffering what I suffered, and most of them far worse" (1).

Frances Smith Foster states that in order to appeal to a predominantly white audience, slave narrators had to comply with white standards of humanity.[14] To obtain freedom for themselves and their enslaved brethren, the narrators had to articulate the text in a language that would be acceptable to their white readership while also confronting the widespread myth that blacks lacked basic cognitive abilities and the aptitude to be self-reflective about their lives and situations. Therefore, the question at hand was not so much "Can't a black person have an imagination?" but "Can't a black person think?"

Sudhi Rajiv demonstrates that slave narrators suffered from double-consciousness in attempting to comply with the demands of the white audience. Rajiv asserts that "the conflict in their psyche was between the master's definition of their reality . . . and the knowledge of their separate existence" (*Forms of Black Consciousness* 153). The master's definition of the slave's reality cast the slave in the role of a mechanical being or an unthinking brute, while the slave was, of course, aware that the depths of her or his humanity ran much deeper. Rajiv further states that the conflict, which finds its earliest literary manifestation in the slave narrative, "forced [slave narrators] to lead a kind of double-existence which tore their personalities apart" (153). This psychic rupture resulted from the slave narrators' constant attempts to prove their humanity to their white constituency. The tension between the tendency to act as an exemplar in order to make a living and the emancipatory endeavor to be representative of a collective is further complicated given that, for the slave narrator, the very act of writing was in many respects performative. In essence, the slave narrator had to perform her or his humanity by donning the roles of both author and character for a predominantly white audience. Therefore, it is because of the role the perceived white audience played in the creation of the slave narrator's autobiographical subjectivity that the slave narrative genre serves as a literary marker of the beginning of William Edward Burghardt (W. E. B.) Du Bois's concept of "double-consciousness" and what James Weldon Johnson terms the "dilemma of the Negro artist."

In his seminal 1903 text, *The Souls of Black Folk,* W. E. B. Du Bois borrowed the term "double-consciousness" from the psychology lexicon to describe what it felt like for American-born blacks to be classified as "other" (meaning something other than or different from whites) and therefore labeled as inferior by mainstream white society. In *The Souls of Black Folk,* Du Bois describes the psychological trauma that racism produces in the U.S.-born black. Within the paradigm of double-consciousness, the African American is essentially born *colonized,* born into a set of unequal social, economic, and political circumstances that renders the black subject subordinate to that of the white. According to Du Bois, "measuring" one's very soul by standards that code one's existence as a problem promotes a false sense of self that the Negro American must strive to counter. Double-consciousness occurs, then, when the black subject internalizes negative definitions of blackness.

What Du Bois delineates is the paradoxical existence of the African American who is born into "a world which yields him no true self-consciousness, but only lets him see himself through the revelation of the other world" (11). This double-existence produces what Charles Johnson labels "a crisis of identity," which Johnson believes extends even into modern-day imaginative texts. He writes, "The black American writer begins his or her career with—and continues to exhibit—a crisis of identity. If anything, black fiction is *about* the troubled quest for identity and liberty, the agony of social alienation, the longing for a real and at times mythical home" (*Being and Race* 8). These tropes are analogous to the desire for wholeness (the wholeness of the African American text, as well as that of the African American subject) and indirectly call for a remedy for the split Du Bois initially saw in the American Negro.[15]

Like Du Bois, James Weldon Johnson also envisioned U.S. society as one that was composed of two predominant yet distinct cultures. In "The Dilemma of the Negro Author," Johnson explains that Negro artists, unlike white American artists, must always remember that she or he has two audiences with which to contend—one black, one white. Johnson's solution to ending this dilemma was for the "Aframerican" author to simultaneously write to both audiences. Ironically, his solution ultimately calls for the creation of texts that actually reflect the double-consciousness Du Bois sees in African Americans—a dual-text. As a derivative of James

Weldon Johnson's discussion of the double audience, a dual-text is one that, often by political necessity, participates in double-voiced discourse primarily between the black writer and her or his white audience. Examples include slave narratives like those by Frederick Douglass and Harriet Jacobs, William Wells Brown's novel *Clotel* (1853), Charles Chesnutt's book of short stories, *Conjure Woman* (1899), as well as protest literature like Richard Wright's *Native Son* (1940) and *White Man Listen!* (1957). What is problematic about such texts is that, in varying degrees, they must cater to white audiences by making clarifications and justifications, or by being extremely tactful in how they communicate emotions like anger and depict sensitive issues such as the rape of slave girls and women by white men on plantations. Thinking specifically of how slave narrators used double-voiced discourse, the slave narrative serves as a material manifestation of the narrator's split subjectivity and as such can be viewed as a colonized text.

In this book, I argue that most contemporary scholarship on African American literature continues to focus on Du Bois's concept of double-consciousness and the James Weldon Johnson–influenced notion of the structural doubleness of African American texts. I see these concepts as problematic because they ultimately privilege white audiences, and by extension white interpretations of blackness, over black audiences and how blacks often construct conceptions of blackness that exist outside of (or at least as alternatives to) prescribed stereotypes. Equally problematic is the continued preoccupation with the psychosomatic effects of racism on African Americans and our creative products, rather than analyses of black texts that have a decolonizing imperative.

In this project, I present an alternate theoretical paradigm for reading the texts of contemporary African American women. Rather than the continued focus on the psychic and structural doubleness of African American subjects and texts, I propose analyzing the decolonizing properties and initiatives prevalent in the traditions of African American culture. In lieu of the contemporaneous development of black studies programs and black and Third World journals and publishing houses, I argue that the black aesthetic movement fostered a new collective black consciousness that privileged black audiences, and that the shift from white aesthetics and the white gaze served as a linchpin to a program of decolonization for African Americans and their creative artistry. My assertion is that many critics have ignored the indebtedness to black aesthetics that much contemporary African American women's writing reflects.[16] Using the figure of the "revolutionary diva" as both a moniker for women such as Toni Cade Bambara, Jayne Cortez, Angela Davis,

Toni Morrison, and Alice Walker as well as a trope for revolutionary and feminist agency, I contend that the majority of contemporary African American women authors continue the legacy wrought by BAM by writing with an imperative to decolonize their black reading constituencies. In the section that follows, I expound upon my use of the diva trope as a vehicle for black feminist agency.

"LET ME CLEAR MY THROAT": THEORIZING THE REVOLUTIONARY DIVA

In *The Diva's Mouth: Body, Voice, Prima Donna Politics,* Susan J. Leonardi and Rebecca A. Pope discuss the "wanton proliferation" of the word "diva." They state that the term "has been debased from its origin in the female pantheon to its current mundaneness"; virtually any woman (or even a gay man)—from the stage, to the boardroom, and even the trailer park—has the potential to don the title (1). In addition to its excessive and indiscriminate usage, the label of diva has often been used to placate women. Speaking specifically of female vocalists who also produce and write their own material, Lauryn Hill states, "They will never throw the 'genius' title to a sister. They'll just call her diva and think it's a compliment. It's like our flair and vanity are put before our musical and intellectual contributions."[17] Moreover, labeling a woman a diva has often been a way to imply that a woman is a ruthless bitch, as Lisa Jones's clarification of her use of the phrase "Bulletproof Diva" suggests: "A Bulletproof Diva is not, I repeat, not that tired stereotype, the emasculating black bitch too hard for love or piety" (*Bulletproof Diva* 3). The term "diva," then, has been granted a great deal of caché in contemporary popular parlance; it has come to encompass everything and nothing at all.

Within its original operatic context, it would seem that the diva fares no better. Masculinist characterizations of the diva mirror the Judeo-Christian correlation of darkness with evil and the grotesque. Wayne Koestenbaum writes, "The diva is demonized: she is associated with difference itself, with a satanic separation from the whole, the clean, the contained, and the attractive. Mythically, she is perverse, monstrous, abnormal, and, ugly" (*The Queen's Throat* 104). Additionally, Leonardi and Pope see the diva's vilification as the subsequent debasement of the ethnic Other: "[the diva] is consistently othered . . . along ethnic rather than racial lines. She is most often constructed, especially in the masculinist tradition as Italian, as, in other words, a dark Caucasian who is excessive, transgressive, stupid, loud-mouthed" (*The Diva's Mouth* 17). Though the diva is ethnically Othered, I submit that in this instance the diva is still essentially *niggerfied*—rendered spectacle and defined using racial stereotypes traditionally associated with blacks that mark blackness as antithetical to whiteness. Concurrently, Koestenbaum reminds his audience that although women of color are now more commonplace in the operatic scene, the genre has a very long history of demonizing the diva by using costuming and vocal manipulations to signify racial Otherness:

> Color is one of the primary metaphors for the qualities of vocal tone. Singers are taught to avoid the "white" sound and to cover the tones to make them darker. Roles like Carmen rely on the notion of the diva's "Latin blood." When divas have been made up to appear Asian or African for such roles as Aida, Selika, Cio-Cio-San, and Iris, they were expressing opera culture's insistence on the dark nature of the diva, as well as underscoring, in a problematic masquerade, the white diva's separation from the women of color she portrays. (*The Queen's Throat* 106)

Given the explications of Leonardi, Koestenbaum, and Pope, I see that a parallel can be made between their readings of the historical place the diva has held in the opera and one of the themes underscoring my own project: the diva suffers from her own form of double-consciousness. Although she is often cast in roles of empowerment, her agency is undermined when her ineffectiveness as a ruler is meant to be interpreted as directly resulting from her deviance. For example, Koestenbaum writes that "[t]hough divas have been firmly associated with queens and with the perpetuation of empire, they have been considered deviant figures capable of ruining an empire with a roulade or a retort" (*The Queen's Throat* 104). A further duality is implicit in her charade as an ethnic or racial Other; by masquerading as a woman of color, the white diva is able to maintain her supposed racial superiority by manipulating the audience's impressions of her dark character (pun intended)—impressions that are largely based on conventions set by mainstream society that code women of color as negative polar opposites to white women.

An added parallel can be drawn between masculinist renditions of the diva and the proverbial Sambo of the American stage. Joseph Boskin writes:

> Sambo the performer was a major event in the long course of entertainment, whose unfolding requires . . . a high degree of suspended disbelief. Image and reality were often theatrically interwoven. In this particular

instance the theatricality was compounded by the fact that what the audience often saw was not only an actual performance but at times their own imaginations projected and enacted. (*Sambo* 42)

Like earlier renditions of the diva, Sambo, then, was a performance of blackness that not only blurred the lines between stereotype and reality, but was also a re-enactment of the racist beliefs of the white audience members. In instances where white men donned blackface, they were not just *performing* blackness but *constructing* it. Boskin further asserts that Sambo, as a primarily male manifestation, was a form of social control exerted "to render the black male powerless as a potential warrior, as a sexual competitor, as an economic adversary" (14). Similarly, the defamation of the diva can be interpreted as a form of social control intended to label women of color as unfeminine and therefore not only powerless as "sexual competitors," but as ineffective when exhibiting mannerisms and inhabiting spaces traditionally reserved for men.

When I first viewed the *Donahue* talk show segment and heard Ntozake Shange's acrimonious remark, I was amused and thought to myself, "You go, diva." I read Ntozake Shange's sarcasm as an act of decolonization. I saw her as performing a new type of radical subjectivity for African American women and wondered if there was a way to imbue the term "diva" with the revolutionary potential I saw evident in the swivel of Shange's neck and in the roll of her eyes. Unlike instances of blackface minstrelsy in which black actors literally applied black greasepaint to effect a "falsely smiling face"[18] and used these same gestures as an act of buffoonery or to enact accommodationist performances of blackness, Shange's movements connoted defiance—her anger and annoyance was unmasked.

According to Catherine Clément, however, a feminist application of the diva is impossible. She writes:

Opera concerns women. No, there is no feminist version; no, there is no liberation. Quite the contrary: they suffer, they cry, they die. Singing and wasting your breath can be the same thing. Glowing with tears, their décolletés cut to the heart, they expose themselves to the gaze of those who come to take pleasure in their pretend agonies. Not one of them escapes with her life, or very few of them do. (*Opera, or the Undoing of Women* 11)

Clément equates the diva with other marginal figures like tricksters, jesters, madmen, and Negroes. She surmises that within the world of the opera, these liminal figures are destined for defeat and will forever remain victims "because the world represented there cannot put up with any social transgression." Therefore, "Madmen are doomed to asylums, blacks doomed to racism, and clowns doomed to everyone's ridicule" (120). Koestenbaum also blames the repressive nature of the opera for preventing the diva from using her voice to gain any real power. According to Koestenbaum, the diva's rhetoric, which he calls "divaspeak," is actually a facade in that, as a language of "vindication and self-defense," her rhetoric only works because the audience is already aware of the story's moral and because the diva "assumes [the audience] share[s] her interpretation of the events" (*The Queen's Throat* 132). Divaspeak, then, is a somewhat delusional mode of discourse in that the diva "utterly believes in the effectiveness of these gestures—or pretends to" (133).

Unlike Clément, Koestenbaum seems to suggest that the opera is a microcosm of the larger society when he informs his readers that divaspeak also finds a home in gay dialect. Using Jennie Livingston's film *Paris Is Burning* (1990) as his frame of reference, Koestenbaum equates divaspeak with techniques like throwing "shade" and "reading people" (i.e., signifying) done by African American and Latino drag queens. For him these gestures, like divaspeak, are ineffective; they are "a way of asserting power, preeminence, and invulnerability through language alone, of speaking strong though one is really weak" (132). While his logic is definitely liberal-minded, it is faulty on at least three levels.

First, Koestenbaum inadvertently emasculates gay men of color. When straight men play the dozens, though we may understand the act as posturing, we do not question the threat. He fails to recognize that while gay men may be marginal figures, there is no direct correlation between gayness and the lack of physical strength. Since "throwing shade" and "reading" someone can lead to physical violence, participating in such actions can be dangerous in itself. Randall Kenan destroys the myth that gay men lack physical prowess with his depiction of Gideon in his 1989 novel *A Visitation of Spirits*. Although he characterizes the teenage version of Gideon as someone who "cultivated a dainty, feminine air, delicate and girllike [*sic*]" and explains that "his hands formed flowery gestures in midair, and he had something of a mincing walk," he also makes it clear that Gideon is as mean as he is smart (98). In a scene in which other black youths tease him about his sexuality, Gideon remains unfazed. When one of his classmates asks him what it feels like to kiss another man, Gideon responds, "I don't know. . . . Your daddy ain't much of a man" (99). And while his classmate bristles and "ball[s] up his fist," Gideon continues to calmly berate the others that also participate in the teasing. In the end, it is the youths that are left rattled.

Second, Koestenbaum seems to have little belief in the power of words and the damage words can do regardless of any supposed power dynamic (straight/gay, man/woman). Take for example the way *Oprah Winfrey Presents: Their Eyes Were Watching God,* which aired on ABC on March 6, 2005, deviates from Zora Neale Hurston's 1937 novel. The fundamental problem with the made-for-television version, starring Halle Berry, is its rewriting of the novel's pivotal scene of Janie's emancipation from her second husband. In the original version, Janie responds to her husband's ridicule of her supposed fading beauty by announcing to all present that "[w]hen you pull down yo' britches, you look lak de change uh life" (75). In the novel, Janie publicly emasculates Jody with her words, forever shaming and silencing him until his death. In the television version, however, Jody slaps Janie, thus re-inscribing his patriarchal power over her—rendering Janie mute and publicly humiliated. The moral of the original scene is lost in this version: words can wield power; they can anger, humiliate, and silence as effectively as a balled fist.

Third, Koestenbaum does not take into account his own underlying perceptions of black gay men. It could be that it is inconceivable to him that black gay men could be anything *but* victims. In his play *The Colored Museum* (1986), George C. Wolfe introduces his audience to Miss Roj, a black drag queen. In her vignette, Miss Roj educates her audience about another subversive tool used by gay men of color, "snapping." Wolfe states, "Snapping comes from another galaxy, as do all snap queens. That's right. I ain't just your regular oppressed American Negro. No-no-no! I am an extraterrestial [*sic*]. And I ain't talkin' none of that shit you seen in the movies! I have real power" (14–15). True to her statements, in the stories she tells about her life, Miss Roj refuses to be a victim to either her homophobic father, whom she indefinitely locks in a closet after he has "baptized [her] with the 'faggot' over and over" (15), or the macho white men she encounters one day at Jones Beach who insult her race and her sexual orientation when they blurt out, "Hey look at da monkey coon in da faggit suit" (16).

On the surface one might read Miss Roj's vignette as a clear example of Koestenbaum's divaspeak. For example, it might be a coincidence or a downright lie when Miss Roj implies that she literally snaps to death the most boisterous of the macho assailants. But what does it matter? In the end, what is important is that Miss Roj does not allow others to define her: "We don't ask for approval. We know who we are and we move on it!

I guarantee you will never hear two fingers put together in a snap and not think of Miss Roj. That's power, baby. Patio pants and all" (17–18). Incidentally, one wonders if all Koestenbaum's knowledge about "shade" and "reading" comes from the movies. Has Koestenbaum, for instance, ever been actually "read" by a drag queen? And if so, did he rest on his laurels, secure in his own white male privilege, or was he publicly disgraced like anyone else might be?

In "Black Macho Revisited: Reflections of a Snap! Queen," Marlon T. Riggs views the terrains of the Hollywood, television, and rap industries as just as repressive as Clément and Koestenbaum view opera culture. Interestingly, Riggs equates "majority representations" of the Snap! Queen persona with that of the Sambo. He states, "In the Sambo and the Snap! Queen, sexuality is repressed, arrested. Laughter, levity, and a certain childlike disposition cement their mutual status as comic eunuchs" (392). It is also significant that Riggs further explains how both conventions are connected to the double-consciousness of American blacks in that all embody aberrant subjectivities when compared to the white mainstream. He writes:

> Behind the Sambo and the Snap! Queen lies a social psyche in torment,
> a fragile psyche threatened by deviation from its egocentric/ethnocentric construct of self and society. Such a psyche systematically defines
> the Other's "deviance" by the essential characteristics which make the
> Other distinct, then invests those differences with intrinsic defect. Hence,
> Blacks are inferior because they are not white; Black Gays are unnatural
> because they are not straight. Majority representations of both affirm
> the view that Blackness and Gayness constitute a fundamental rupture
> in the order of things, that our very existence is an affront to nature and
> humanity. (391)

To add insult to injury, Riggs explains that those spearheading the proliferation of what he calls the "Negro Faggot identity" are blacks in the entertainment industry. Within the parameters of this identity, the black gay man is neither *truly* black or a man because authentic blackness and maleness do not allow for the possibility of homosexuality.

What I would like to highlight in regards to Riggs's article is that, like Wolfe's character of Miss Roj, he does not allow mainstream or Hollywood representations of black gay men to dictate how he should define himself, nor does he allow either to strip him of his agency. Both Clément and Koestenbaum restrict the diva within the operatic tradition. Koestenbaum goes even further in his extrapolation of the diva by confining gay men of color to their racist and homophobic stereotypes. Riggs's article is instructive for the purposes of this project because he offers a space to interpret black gay subjectivity that lies outside of the parameters of both the black and white mainstream. He writes:

> Within the Black Gay community . . . the Snap! contains a multiplicity of coded meanings—as in SNAP! "You *fierce!*" or SNAP! "Get out of my face!" or SNAP! "Girlfriend, pleeeease." The Snap! can be as emotionally and politically charged as a clenched fist; can punctuate debate and dialogue like an exclamation point, a comma, an ellipsis; or can altogether negate the need for words among those who are adept at decoding its nuanced meanings. (392)

Additionally, it is significant to note that when he is specifically talking about the black gay community, in his very description of the various meanings of snapping, he does not depict black gay spaces as utopian. What is important is that even when interactions are negative in these spaces, free expression is allowed and the speaker has agency because his anger or annoyance is taken seriously, rather than as a caricature.

Given that he chose to publish his article in *Black American Literature Forum*, Riggs almost assuredly hoped to convince homophobic blacks, and those who unwittingly laugh at caricatures of black gay men, that there is a direct correlation between how black gay men are stereotyped in the media and long-standing stereotypes of black men in general. He offers a valid critique of claims of black cultural authenticity that exclude homosexuals and thereby insists that black gays are by rights a part of the black community. Therefore, I read Riggs's act of writing this article as one of decolonization for both himself and his intended black audience. Likewise, when the diva is unbound, freed from the stifling parameters of traditional opera, she might also serve as a model for feminist agency.

In *Global Divas: Filipino Gay Men in the Diaspora*, Martin F. Manalansan IV uses the trope of the diva as a way to discuss how Filipino gay men perform identities that counter clichéd filmic depictions that strip them of their sexual agency. Manalansan writes:

> Performance in this book, therefore, is not only a matter of just "acting," but rather is about the aesthetics of Filipino gay men's struggles for survival. They are agentive sexual subjects who defy their representations in either mainstream films or in gay male porn. They move beyond the stereotypes of houseboys, farmers, feminized sexual vessels, innocent waifs, or other "Oriental" icons in both genres. (*Global Divas* 16)

For my project, I emulate Manalansan in his interpretation of "performance" as a survival technique, rather than as make-believe, to show how donning a revolutionary diva subjectivity can be an act of black feminist agency. Culled from colloquial and feminist usages, I have established four characteristics the diva possesses, when removed from masculinist operatic representations, that make her an apt metaphor of black female empowerment: (1) her voice, (2) her transgressive co-option of a public space usually designated for men, (3) her style, and (4) her familial connection to her audience.

In feminist traditions, Leonardi and Pope remind us that the diva's voice can be interpreted as a political instrument because it functions as "a metaphor of and vehicle for female empowerment both on stage and off" (*The Diva's Mouth* 18). For scholars like bell hooks, the *act* of speaking or gaining voice is a decolonizing gesture—one that transforms from object to subject. She writes that "only as subjects can we speak. As objects, we remain voiceless—our beings defined and interpreted by others" (*Talking Back* 12). Additionally, it is the feminist usage of the term that "unsettles gender oppositions" because the diva serves as "the exception to feminine silence and powerlessness and by the fact that she performs both femininity and masculinity" (*The Diva's Mouth* 21). The diva, then, serves as the ultimate archetype of the assertion of the female voice in the public sphere. Her staged androgyny partially derives from her position on the stage—the diva occupies the public domain usually reserved for men. Therefore, I find the term appealing because the presence and subsequent performance of the revolutionary diva challenges the assignment of the public sphere as a male realm and thereby demonstrates that revolution and liberation are not just male issues. Evoking the diva as a theoretical tool in this manner enables me to discuss how the women analyzed in this project challenge assertions that black women have no place in struggles for liberation or in general discourses of black revolution.

Referring to its colloquial usage, Geneva Smitherman defines the "diva" as "1) a stately grand woman, a 'trophy' who may or may not be a beauty; 2) a female rapper or other musical entertainer who is superbly talented; 3) by extension any accomplished woman in any walk of life" (*Black Talk* 94). The most defining characteristic of the diva, however, is her style—whether it be represented in her fashion sense or by the skill with which she turns a phrase. For my project, I want to delineate three interrelated ways the diva's style functions as a metaphor of black feminist agency: style as a survival strategy, style as performance, and style as subjectivity.

Nikki Giovanni believes that African Americans have used style as a survival mechanism that serves as a testament to the human spirit:

> Style has a profound meaning to Black Americans. If we can't drive, we will invent walks and the world will envy the dexterity of our feet. If we can't have ham, we will boil chitterlings; if we are given rotten peaches, we will make cobblers; if given scraps, we will make quilts; take away our drums, and we will clap our hands. We prove the human spirit will prevail. We will take what we have to make what we need. (*Racism 101* 154–155)

Giovanni's words remind us that being functional, a key component of the black aesthetic, is imbedded in our tradition of survival. Giovanni also seems to be saying that not only have we survived, we have made survival into an art form.

As a postsegregationist text, Lisa Jones's urban trope of the "Bulletproof Diva" is spawned from the same tradition of style Giovanni posits. Jones defines the Bulletproof Diva as "[a] woman whose sense of dignity and self cannot be denied; who, though she may live in a war zone like Brownsville, goes out everyday greased, pressed, and dressed. . . . She is fine and she knows it. She has to know it because who else will?" (*Bulletproof Diva* 3). Thinking herself "bulletproof," immune to external definitions of the self, the Bulletproof Diva is not living merely to dodge the bullet one more day. To go out in the "war zone" perfectly coiffed shows that the diva possesses a love of self that is prioritized over those who seek to vilify her or, at the very least, imprison her in definitions of their own making.

Dealing with another "war zone," the Roxbury section of Boston, sociologist Janet K. Mancini provides her readers with the case studies of five adolescent black males to demonstrate how they use style as a coping mechanism to deal with the psychological conflict stemming from both the external pressures of urban life in the 1960s and the internal pressure to be their own individuals. For Mancini, "Strategic style is the way a person deals with the definitions prevailing in the cultures most salient to him. It includes the way he defines situations in his own right, and the information about himself he expresses or 'gives off'" (*Strategic Styles* 23). Therefore, using style in a strategic manner can be seen as a way to deal with double-consciousness.

For the purposes of this study, I want to place Mancini's comments in the context of audience. I have chosen to use the term "subjectivity" rather than "identity" in my title because I want to highlight that performances of the self are ever-shifting rather than static. For example,

Amina Mama regards subjectivity "as being continuously constituted and changing, as being locked in a recursive relationship of mutually advancing production and change" (*Beyond the Mask* 1). Likewise, Mancini also seems to suggest that style is situational and therefore can be seen as a function of subjectivity. She writes, "Style is not simply a reaction to cues given by others in a particular interaction, but is a person's way of acting, creating, and redefining his self *in relation* to others" (*Strategic Styles* 23). I am interested in the ways African American writers use style "in relation" to their African American audiences rather than in relation to white audiences, as had been the norm prior to the black aesthetic movement. I want to discuss how the prioritizing of an African American audience is a decolonizing act for both the writer and her audience in that the context for discussion allows both greater agency, an agency that is stunted, at best, in mainstream contexts.

I assert that the revolutionary diva's attention to style has a direct correlation to the connection she feels to her audience. Janice D. Hamlet sees style (she uses the vernacular "stylin'") as an inherent component of African American oration. Hamlet states, "Stylin' refers to the conscious or unconscious manipulation of language or mannerisms to influence favorably the hearers of a message. By using language common to the audience, a speaker is not merely understandable but credible" ("Understanding African American Oratory" 96). Stylin', then, refers to the ways we communicate with each other as African Americans. Unlike Sambo, whose audience consists of racist whites, the revolutionary diva seeks a black audience and has as her primary goal the upliftment of that audience. For many black singing divas, their first audience was the black church, and therefore the black audience was given priority from the beginning. Additionally, since the majority of black divas first found voice in the church, working their way up to fame like Tina Turner or Diana Ross, it therefore becomes easier for the folk to identify with these divas.

Considering the diva as "of the folk" also disrupts class distinctions in a way the operatic usage does not. Lisa Jones states, "It's safe to assume that a Bulletproof Diva is whoever you make her—corporate girl, teen mom, or the combination—as long as she has the lip and nerve, and as long as she uses that lip and nerve to raise up herself and the world" (*Bulletproof Diva* 3). In carving spaces for black women (and quite often for black men) where none had existed before, the diva becomes revolutionary not only because she embodies struggle and survival, but because her desire for uplift extends beyond herself to making a positive difference in the world. A revolutionary diva is not just representative of the folk, she embodies *the potential* of the folk. A revolutionary diva, like Alice

Walker's womanist, uses her strengths for the betterment of her people. She lyrically marks her audience—her voice is both the manifestation of black pain and redemption.

In a chapter titled "Third World Diva Girls," bell hooks explains that she conferred this label to a group of young women of color that she was mentoring at the time as a title "which gives expression to their uniqueness and importance. . . . And we use the term 'diva' because of the special role women have had in opera" (*Yearning* 100). And yet, embedded in the title is a warning to these women, having been spurned by the diva-like behavior of older female (and male) academics of color who ridiculed rather than nurtured their budding scholarship, about the dangers associated with acting like a diva: "It both names specialness but carries with it the connotation of being just a bit out of control, stuck on oneself. We wanted it as a reminder of how easy it is to imagine we are superior to others and therefore deserve special treatment or have the right to dominate" (100). It is precisely because of the danger in developing a superiority complex once one becomes a diva that induces me to use the adjective "revolutionary" as a modifier. In my estimation, the revolutionary diva believes that it is an imperative to guide others who have yet to reach her stature, or have not been privileged or empowered to speak in the public sphere. In an academic setting, what it would mean to be a revolutionary diva would mean to provide mentoring for younger scholars of color, as hooks suggests, that would better prepare them for the rigors of academia and teach them to work in cooperation with other scholars of color rather than see them as ready competitors.

Despite hooks's cautionary advice, however, I see the benefits to "being just a bit out of control, stuck on oneself" in a society that has placed severe restrictions on black female mobility and has systematically sought to besmirch our image. I have always been amused by the admonitory phrase "Don't make a spectacle of yourself" and its specific significance for black women. It has always occurred to me that for African American women, making a spectacle of oneself, or being unruly, has meant doing anything outside of what is expected—which might encompass almost anything. Like Alice Walker's womanist, characterized in part by her audacious behavior, I see the figure of the revolutionary diva as one who makes a successful career out of being a spectacle.

There are, however, even socially expected, stereotypical ways for a black woman to make a spectacle of herself. The eye-rolling, neck-swiveling ancestors of Sapphire that currently dominate mainstream media have made expressions of black female anger a joke, an act of buffoonery.

Sapphire, Sambo's female counterpart, then, is antithetical to the figure of the revolutionary diva, not so much because the revolutionary diva's anger is more controlled or less ostentatious, but because her anger is executed in response to social malaise rather than for the amusement of a white audience. The figure of the diva offers a stark contrast to that of Sambo and Sapphire; the revolutionary diva is a figure of agency, where Sapphire and Sambo are reactionary figures that are acted upon. The revolutionary diva, then, is synonymous with what Kevin Everod Quashie calls "diva subjectivity": "an undeniably self-righteousness and self-regarded temperament that imposes itself on the world rather than the opposite" (*Black Women, Identity, and Cultural Theory* 161).

Given my earlier discussion concerning how slave narrators performed their humanity for white audiences, as theatrical concepts both the diva and Sambo present two very different performances of blackness. If Sambo symbolizes the powerless black male, the revolutionary diva is a symbol of empowerment that can have implications for blacks of both sexes. I envision the revolutionary diva as a warrior stance, an act of erotic empowerment (in Audre Lorde's use of the phrase),[19] but more importantly as a trope of transformation. Unlike Sambo, the concepts of "presence" and "voice" associated with the diva combat the idea of invisibility normally affiliated with the black subject. With Sambo, blackness is not only emphasized, but exaggerated. The high visibility of his skin coloration, though, is just another variation on the invisibility motif because the blackness depicted is not only fake, but degrading. In comparison, the diva is not merely visible, she is adored and idolized, people aspire to be like her. In contrast to Sambo, her performance is of her own choosing rather than an external and imposed conception of her racial identity. Therefore, the analogy of the diva's voice is alluring because it can be seen as a vehicle through which black subjects may become self-actualized. Ultimately, what I like about the term "revolutionary diva," in all its manifestations, is that it thwarts the image of the victimized black woman. The revolutionary diva is not just surviving, but truly *living* in all senses of the word.

ESTABLISHING PARAMETERS: WRITING THE BLACK REVOLUTIONARY DIVA

In *Writing the Black Revolutionary Diva* I analyze the literary and cultural production of African American women from 1970 to the present to determine the ways black women's texts demonstrate a reconfiguration of Du Bois's original concept of double-consciousness and offer various methodologies toward decolonization. I assert that the women in this study offer alternative models of black subjectivity that seek to transform their audiences into radical/revolutionary agents. I argue that these women perform not only a particular type of blackness (one wedded to the black aesthetic), but a type of womanhood as well (one that sees revolution as natural rather that antithetical to femaleness). I posit the women analyzed here as the successors of the black aesthetic movement. I examine the extent to which each woman's text can be labeled "functional, collective, and committed"—Maulana Karenga's definition of the black aesthetic. Throughout the project, I demonstrate each woman's connection with the black aesthetic, as well as how each woman offers programs for revolution that extend beyond the sometimes essentialist and misogynist limitations of black aesthetic ideology.

The first chapter establishes the parameters of my project by discussing the discourses of double-consciousness and decolonization as they relate to African American subjectivity. In this chapter, I trace the decolonizing properties found in texts from the slave narrative to those of the black aesthetic to underscore the black aesthetic movement as one in which the concept of double-consciousness changes from the conflicting nature of being a marginal person (of being both "Negro" and American) to that of being both an individual and part of a larger black community.

In the second chapter, I shift the project's focus from double-consciousness to multiple-consciousness as I more closely examine how African American women dealt with the added pressures of sexism and often class oppression during the 1970s, as evidenced in their writings. Using *The Black Woman: An Anthology* and *Essence* magazine's inaugural year as my primary texts, I analyze how each negotiate black nationalist and feminist discourses and provide forums for black women to discuss issues pertinent to their own experiences. I pay particular attention to how each publication champions female participation in the struggle for black liberation and deals with the debates surrounding the Moynihan Report, which unwittingly casts black women in the unflattering role of emasculating matriarchs.

To answer bell hooks's call to study women who have chosen to be "radical subjects," in chapter 3 I discuss how Angela Davis's manipulation of her public persona classifies her as a revolutionary diva. While chapter 2 demonstrates how both commercial and political women-centered texts serve as consciousness-raising tools for blacks, this chapter explores the ways an individual makes use of her own public image to act as a model for those who would follow in her footsteps. In this chapter I juxtapose media images that construct Davis as an enigmatic figure with an analysis of how she counters such portrayals and consciously recasts herself as "one of the folk."

The fourth chapter situates Cortez as a revolutionary diva that uses poetry to construct a model of healthy black subjectivity (one that places "blackness" as its central concern rather than "whiteness") for her audience. I analyze an assortment of Cortez's earlier work to explain how they are products of the black aesthetic movement and yet serve as theoretical models for revolution in their own right. I therefore discuss how Cortez uses what she calls "supersurrealism"—a visceral use of anatomy as a metaphor for the global oppression of blacks—as what I call "scarification aesthetics." I introduce the concept of "scarification aesthetics" as Cortez's revolutionary agenda to utilize the black body in pain as a unifying device for blacks worldwide.

The fifth chapter necessarily follows because in it I assert that with her novel *The Salt Eaters* (1980), Toni Cade Bambara presents an alternate way of dealing with the black body in pain and additional traumas associated with African American subjectivity. In this chapter I discuss how *The Salt Eaters* presents a "new world order," or paradigm shift for her audience, and therefore serves as a penultimate example of a decolonizing text in multiple ways: authorial intent, plot, and structure. I contend that Bambara uses the theme of the apocalypse as a dual metaphor for both revolution and decolonization. Throughout the novel we confront the notion of duality in terms of the textual structure, setting, and character development. But it is through the character of Velma Henry, her failed suicide attempt and subsequent healing ritual, that Bambara's audience is ultimately able to use her example to map out their own pathways to self-actualization.

Throughout this project I will demonstrate how the revolutionary diva acts as a model for female empowerment by discussing the following: (1) how women publicly invent and reconstruct their identities in the arenas of the academy, politics, and publishing in order to counter racist and sexist depictions of black women; and (2) the intrinsic connection the revolutionary diva (as a performer/writer) sees between herself and her black audience, or "the folk." In the succeeding chapters, I will analyze the ways African American women construct texts that move beyond mere survival and therefore serve as revolutionary blueprints to renovate the soul. I focus on the genres of anthology, autobiography, poetry, magazines, and the novel to examine the extent to which women use the black aesthetic to construct their own revolutionary ideologies. *Writing the Black Revolutionary Diva* is also concerned with how women use characterization and structure to enable their readers to become radical subjects. And finally, this project will examine how African American writers work with notions of difference (both racial and gendered) to introduce and highlight denied subjectivities and to subvert imposed stereotypical definitions of black women.

One

FROM SOUL CLEAVAGE TO SOUL SURVIVAL

Double-Consciousness and the Emergence of the Decolonized Text/Subject

> I still think today as yesterday that the color line is a great problem of this century. But today I see more clearly than yesterday that in back of the problem of race and color, lies a greater problem which both obscures and implements it: and that is the fact that so many civilized persons are willing to live in comfort even if the price of this is poverty, ignorance and disease of the majority of their fellow men; that to maintain this privilege men have waged war until today war tends to become universal and continuous, and the excuse for this continues largely to be color and race.
>
> —W. E. B. DU BOIS

In 2005, the Contemporary Arts Museum of Houston showcased an exhibition titled "Double-Consciousness: Black Conceptual Art Since 1970," which featured the multigenerational work of artists Terry Adkins, Edgar Arceneaux, Sanford Biggers, Charles Gaines, Ellen Gallagher, David Hammons, Lyle Ashton Harris, Maren Hassinger, Jennie C. Jones, Senga Nengudi, Howardena Pindell, Gary Simmons, Lorna Simpson, Adrian Piper, Nari Ward, and Fred Wilson. This exhibition is specifically appealing to me because its contributors approached Du Bois's theory in much the same way that I do in this project. Not only does its period selection suggest a shift in black artistic expression since the 1970s, the publisher's review of the corresponding art book explains that "[t]he exhibition's concept is an aesthetic contribution to the rethinking of Du Bois's 'double consciousness' theory that asserts that African-Americans are no longer relegated to looking at themselves through the eyes of others, but rather through their own gaze."[1] In general the museum is an appropriate metaphoric site to describe my own ambivalence concerning the continued applicability of double-consciousness in describing postmodern black-ness—is it a concept to be memorialized as a remnant of modernity, or is it still a significant component of black postmodernity? These questions should also be read through the context of the epigraph; what Du Bois wrote in 1953 was true in 1903 and remains true today. Therefore, if the parameters of the color line have remained fairly stable, what about our strategies to deal with these divisions, do they remain unchanged as well?

Given that 2003 marked the centennial anniversary of the publication of William Edward Burghardt Du Bois's *The Souls of Black Folk,* the same questions I pose have been asked and answered in various ways in both academic and popular books, conference panels, and commemorative ceremonies that explore the text's millennial significance. Du Bois has even found a home in the annals of hip-hop culture, the 2004 release of *Double Consciousness* by Ghanian-born, yet U.S.-university-educated rapper Blitz is one such example. The cover art on the compact disc features a slave woman spinning turntables in the middle of a cotton field while her fellow/sister workers pick cotton in the background. This image suggests a link between slavery's past and the future while it begs the question: How far *have* we come as a people?

Written in 1903, *The Souls of Black Folk* has been extolled as the defin-itive text on black modernity. Not only does *Souls* articulate the psy-chological ramifications of racist discrimination on the black psyche, it also expresses Du Bois's aspirations for the turn of that century—that newly freed African Americans would one day rise above the stigma of blackness and be accorded the privileges of U.S. citizenship. Using the metaphor of a cathartic journey through America's racist terrain, Du Bois conceived of the development of a new consciousness that would change the "child of Emancipation" into the "youth with dawning self-consciousness, self-realization, self-respect" (*The Souls of Black Folk* 14).

Souls was bicultural in its structure and in Du Bois's perception of audience. Structurally, each chapter is headed by an epigraph by a white poet and an excerpt of a "sorrow song," or rather a Negro spiritual. In addressing his text to both blacks and whites, Du Bois was strategic in that he hoped to persuade his audience to mimic his literary integra-tion in the real space of the nation. By focusing on the *souls* of American blacks, Du Bois emphasized their humanity to his white readers in an attempt to counter negative stereotypes. The text also held a particular significance for his black readers. Saunders Redding states that the pub-lication of *Souls* "may be seen as fixing that moment in history when the American Negro began to reject the idea of the world's belonging to white people only, and to think of himself, in concert, as a potential force in the organization of society" (Introduction vii). Redding further acknowledges that *Souls* also served to validate the experiences of "Negroes of training and intelligence, who had hitherto pretended to regard the race problem as of strictly personal concern and who sought individual salvation in a creed of detachment and silence"; in *Souls* they "found a bond in their common grievances and a language through which to express them" (viii). Indeed, *Souls* articulates what I have oftentimes experienced—the feeling of being Othered. While I agree that double-consciousness is a condition through which every U.S.-born black must eventually encounter and come to terms, I object to its use as the principal measure of postmodern African American subjectivity and question the extent to which it dominated black subjectivity during the modern era.

While I am convinced that the problem of the twenty-first century, as Du Bois said of the twentieth century, continues to be the color line, I am less persuaded that double-consciousness is as persistent as a disabling feature of African American identity formation. For example, Henry Louis Gates proclaims:

> Today, talk about the fragmentation of culture and consciousness is a commonplace. We know all about the vigorous intermixing of black culture and white, high culture and low—from the Jazz Age freneticism of what Ann Douglas calls "mongrel Manhattan" to hip-hop's hegemony over America [I would say the world's] youth. . . . Today, the idea of wholeness has largely been retired. And cultural multiplicity is no longer seen as the problem, but as a solution—a solution of the confines of identity itself. Double consciousness, once a disorder, is now the cure. ("Both Sides Now" 31)

Although Gates seems a bit overly optimistic in pronouncing double-consciousness as the cure, surely one needs to take into account that the globalization of African American culture has intensified. And although such visibility has yet to be translated into real power, such integration into the global market has done much to boost the self-esteem of darker people and marginal cultures the world over. It is not my intention, however, to argue that racism has been eradicated or plays no part in the development of contemporary African American psyches; quite the contrary, racism is often more subtle and therefore arguably more lethal.[2]

Arnold Rampersad writes that "[a]mong black intellectuals, above all, *The Souls of Black Folk* became a kind of sacred book, the central text for the interpretation of the Afro-American experience" ("Slavery and the Literary Imagination" 296). Dolan Hubbard concurs when he proclaims the text to be "the Old Testament of twentieth-century African American letters" (1). Adolph L. Reed, Jr., speculates that it is Du Bois's articulation of double-consciousness that accounts for the text's endurance. According to Reed, the paragraph in which Du Bois first defines double-consciousness is not only the most widely known in his "entire corpus," but may also be the "most familiar in all of Afro-American letters" (*W. E. B. Du Bois and American Political Thought* 91). The passage reads as follows:

> After the Egyptian and Indian, the Greek and Roman, the Teuton and Mongolian, the Negro is a sort of seventh son, born with a veil, and gifted with second-sight in this American world, a world which yields him no true self-consciousness, but only lets him see himself through the revelation of the other world. It is a peculiar sensation, this double-consciousness, this sense of always looking at one's self through the eyes of others, of measuring one's soul by the tape of a world that looks on in amused contempt and pity. One ever feels his two-ness, an American, a Negro, two thoughts, two unreconciled strivings; two warring ideals in one dark body, whose dogged strength alone keeps it from being torn asunder. (*The Souls of Black Folk* 10)

Reed surmises, "The passage's enduring resonance derives from its verisimilitude in expressing a core lament of the Afro-American condition" and as such has served as a "distinctly attractive template for the articulation of both interpretive and substantive, academic and hortatory arguments concerning the race's status" (*W. E. B. Du Bois and American Political Thought* 91).

Scholars from various disciplines—such as Harold Cruse, Shanette M. Harris, Adolph L. Reed, Jr., and Shamoon Zamir—offer alternate readings of double-consciousness that counter its reign as a universal signifier of African American identity. While Harris characterizes Du Bois as a "filtering agent through which whites could learn what it means to be black," rather than just offering a treatise on life "beyond the veil," she contends that the text should also be read as Du Bois's personal attempt to come to grips with U.S. racism ("Constructing a Psychological Perspective" 218). Harris explains that while his mission was to promote "socio-behavioral change" among his black audience and empathy among his white audience, "[Du Bois's] own understanding of and empathy toward 'black folk' was rather limited because of his few experiences with other African Americans until college" (218).

While Harris commends Du Bois for being courageous enough to bare his own soul (so to speak) and show his vulnerability by personalizing his text, Harold Cruse uses this same argument, that Du Bois had little contact with blacks prior to attending Fisk, to condemn Du Bois. In an interview conducted by Van Grosse, Harold Cruse charges that the centrality that Du Bois continues to enjoy in African American studies, largely due to his concept of double-consciousness, is a "manufactured" one: "Du Bois is a philosophical phony. That double-consciousness thing is a phony. It's *his* double-consciousness. It's philosophical romanticism" ("Interview with Harold Cruse" 297). Although he concedes that Du Bois is an important intellectual figure, Cruse believes it is problematic to overidealize Du Bois given that he was a northern and a "near-white mulatto" (297). Perhaps because he was light-complected and was accorded privileges based on his appearance, Cruse explains that "blackness" was Du Bois's choice, but he maintains that for Du Bois to make that choice he had to recreate blackness over in his own image and according to his own experiences with racial discord. It is the combination of Du Bois's father's lineage and his own northern upbringing that serves as an indicator for Cruse of Du Bois's detachment from black southerners and reveals his fashioning of double-consciousness to be one of "egotistical idealism." While Cruse views double-consciousness as the reflection of Du Bois's own racial anxieties, he also zealously discredits double-consciousness as an accurate portrayal of the black elite Du Bois met when he attended Fisk University:[3] "[Double-consciousness has] been handed down as a verity, and it's not. It had nothing to do with those blacks he met when he went to Fisk University, nothing. They had no goddamn double-consciousness, they knew who they were" (297).

Zamir, however, challenges Du Bois's claim that he had little contact with blacks while growing up in Massachusetts. He writes, "Du Bois's silences about his own experience of poverty in his childhood, about living on Railroad Street, a particularly wretched part of town, or about his having had a broader knowledge of black life in his childhood than he admits in later life are, in *Souls* at least, aids to an unmasking rather than a masking of certain aspects of his politics" (*Dark Voices* 138). Zamir argues that these silences "highlight" the differences between Du Bois and the black southern majority "rather than disguise it," and therefore Du Bois consciously "problematizes his own status as guide to the black world for the white reader" by making the motif of a journey into life behind the veil a "central theme" of the work from the very beginning (139).

Zamir does, however, concur with Cruse that double-consciousness's centrality in African American studies is manufactured. He believes that while double-consciousness is widely "accepted as a universally and transhistorically true analysis of a tragic aspect of African-American self-consciousness," it should more accurately be considered as both class-specific and historically specific (116). He writes, "The account of 'double-consciousness' . . . represents the black middle-class elite facing the failure of its own progressive ideals in the late nineteenth century, in the aftermath of failed Reconstruction and under the gaze of a white America." Therefore, according to Zamir, "'Of Our Spiritual Strivings' [the first chapter of *Souls* and the one in which Du Bois defines double-consciousness] is intended as a psychology of the Talented Tenth in crisis, not of the 'black folk' as a homogenized collectivity" (116).

Adolph Reed also charges that the double-consciousness motif has been used transhistorically in that scholars from various disciplines appropriate the concept for their own usages. Because these appropriations seem to exist irrespective of Du Bois's own desire to see double-consciousness eradicated by the full integration of blacks into the U.S. socioeconomic strata, Reed laments that the resolution of double-consciousness does not seem to be an urgent objective anymore; instead "double-consciousness tends to be seen naturalistically, as an essential fact of Afro-American existence in the here and now" (*W. E. B. Du Bois and American Political Thought* 94). In the preface of the 1953 edition of *Souls*, Du Bois apparently views the text as a document circumscribed by history when he explains how he resisted the urge to revise it: "Several times I planned to revise the book and bring it abreast of my own thought and to answer criticism. But I hesitated and finally decided to leave the book as first printed, as a monument to what I thought and felt in 1903" (*Souls* [Blue Heron Press] x). Additionally, what is often forgotten in contemporary discussions concerning double-consciousness is that even in Du Bois's first use of the term he simultaneously envisioned a future time in which black psyches would not be solely predicated on white definitions of blackness.

Saunders Redding explains that *The Souls of Black Folk* differs from *The Philadelphia Negro* (1899) in that its publication marked a "revolution" in Du Bois's thinking regarding his belief that scientific inquiry alone would be adequate in effecting social reform. By the time *Souls* was published, Du Bois could be said to have experienced another revolution of thought; he had already begun to rethink the original strategy he employed in the text—lifting the "veil" to demonstrate to whites how racism impeded black progress in the hopes that whites would feel morally compelled to curtail racist behavior. I would also like to believe that Du Bois had also begun to rethink the effectiveness of employing double-consciousness as a strategy against racism at the expense of the so-called black psyche.

In the first chapter of *The Souls of Black Folk,* "Of Our Spiritual Strivings," Du Bois labels double-consciousness the "gift of second sight" because living in a society dominated by whites enables blacks to have an insight into the white psyche that is seldom true in the inverse. Therefore, many scholars have interpreted double-consciousness in a somewhat positive manner because it can be used as a strategic tool in the battle against racism. Yet despite its effectiveness as a strategy against racism, typically double-consciousness can be disabling to African Americans because it relies on external conceptions of blackness that have historically been negative.[4]

Racist whites have found support for racial inequality in sources from scientific examples including phrenology, to social Darwinism, to the bell curve; labeling blacks as something other than human provided many whites with the proper justification for inhumane and unequal treatment of blacks. Double-consciousness occurs when the black subject internalizes negative definitions of blackness and involuntarily substitutes the dominant white societal definitions of black subjectivity or definitions that exist as antithetical to white aesthetic values. According to Du Bois, "measuring" one's very soul by standards that code one's very existence as a "problem," then, promotes a false sense of self that the African American subject must seek to counter.

In the preface to the Norton 1999 reprint edition of *The Souls of Black Folk,* Henry Louis Gates, Jr., and Terri Hume Oliver write that "Du Bois's use of [the veil] suggests, among other things, that the African American's attempt to gain self-consciousness in a racist society will always be impaired because any reflected image coming from the gaze of white America is necessarily a distorted one, and quite probably a harmful one as well" (xxvi).[5] Given the illogical nature of racism, strategies of assimilation that rely on the morality of racist whites, or on their acceptance of blacks, have historically proven to be ineffectual.

The epigraph that begins this chapter further exhibits a revision in Du Bois's thinking; he had come to realize the extent to which people will go to protect their privilege, even at the expense of the suffering of others (and what he writes in 1953 is as much a critique of white privilege as it is of the West). Given his longevity as a public intellectual, one can infer that Du Bois changed his position on various issues several times; double-consciousness is one such example. When thinking about the centrality that double-consciousness holds in most discourses concerning black identity and subjectivity, what is perplexing is that "the double-consciousness notion by and large disappeared from Du Bois's writing after 1903—he does not even mention it in subsequent reflections on *Souls.*" (Reed, *W. E. B. Du Bois and American Political Thought,* 124).

In his investigation of the enduring popularity of Du Bois's "double-consciousness" in *W. E. B. Du Bois and American Political Thought: Fabianism and the Color Line,* Adolph Reed locates the impetus of the motif's current infamy in racial discourses that abounded in World War II. Reed explains that Gunnar Myrdal's 1944 text *An American Dilemma: The Negro Problem and Modern Democracy* spearheaded a re-articulation of the so-called "Negro Problem" as "both a matter for national moral (and pragmatic) concern and an appropriate object for enlightened social engineering at the hands of national policy elites" (7). He identifies two factors indicative of the postwar climate that helped to shift the discourse of race in the United States: (1) the increase in black migration to the North served to undermine the commonly held belief that blacks were a southern problem, and (2) the cold war rhetoric that cast the United States as the "leader of the 'free world'" was seen as a blatant contradiction given the existence of racial segregation. According to Reed, these two factors helped to solidify the image of African Americans as "appendage[s]" to U.S. society, as well as "objects of administration"; both approaches served to further the belief that blacks have the goal of "race relations management" as their sole concern (7). Not only does this belief blind even "well-intentioned racial liberal[s]" to the "relatively autonomous dimensions of black thought and action," it also reinforces black marginalization and "implies that the black experience exists only insofar as it intersects white American concerns or responds to white initiatives" (7). To further punctuate this last point, Reed evokes Ralph Ellison's review of Myrdal's work as a study that exemplifies the tendency to see blacks "simply as the creation of white men."[6]

Reed's work underscores a crucial problem with the continued focus on double-consciousness as the central signifier of African American identity formation. African American subjectivity is almost always seen as intrinsically bound to whiteness, while whiteness is often free from such a constraint; it seems curious that we rarely talk about the hybrid nature of 'whiteness' and white cultural productions.[7] Tiffany Ruby Patterson and Robin D. G. Kelley make a similar point that African identity is seen only in terms of whiteness: "The idea of a 'European' culture or even 'English' culture is often taken for granted and hardly ever problematized in the way that 'African' is constantly understood as a social construction" ("Unfinished Migrations" 18). Viewing African and African American identity as social constructions and double-consciousness as a static condition of African American subjectivity reinforces the widespread belief that black identity cannot exist independent of its link to whiteness, thus privileging racism over all other factors that might influence identity formation, which inadvertently reinforces white superiority and curtails discussions of black agency.

The canonizing of double-consciousness can therefore be credited for the pervasive association of black subjectivity with pathology and eternal victimization. Amina Mama states that by the mid-1960s blacks were viewed as "damaged by racist society," and although this perception was an improvement over prevailing thoughts that blacks were somehow innately inferior, it still "meant taking white racism to be the sole factor in black identity formation and ignoring the existence of the diverse cultural referents available to many black people" (*Beyond the Mask* 52). bell hooks suggests that the rhetoric of victimization gained momentum after the revolutionary fervor of the 1960s had settled and many blacks had become disillusioned about the possibility of revolution after the assassination of many black male leaders. She states, "Suddenly a spirit of resistance that had been grounded in an oppositional belief that white power was limited, that it could be challenged and transformed, had dissipated. In its place was a rhetoric that represented that structure as all-powerful, unchanging" (*Killing Rage* 57).

The second problem with double-consciousness serving as the principal signifier of African American subjectivity is that it was conceived within a Eurocentric paradigm. C. W. E. Bigsby suggests that in his earlier years Du Bois had a predilection toward Western culture. He writes:

> Du Bois accepted, all too readily, Western pretensions. He believed that the Shakespeares, Michelangelos, Platos, and Kants were not isolated examples but metaphors of the strength of Western culture. This led him to believe in integration, in the merging of black and white cultures. Only later in his life was he to realize . . . that one does not make bargains with the devil, that the devil honors no bargains, will effectuate no meaningful compromise. (*The Second Black Renaissance* 56)

I find Joy James's rationale that W. E. B. Du Bois was both profeminist yet nevertheless "influenced by a masculinist worldview which de-radicalized his gender progressivism" as instructive for explaining my second objection to the rampant privileging of Du Bois's double-consciousness in contemporary discussions of African American subjectivity ("The Profeminist Politics of W. E. B. Du Bois" 142). James's characterization of Du Bois's gender politics is not contradictory given that, as she explains, his antisexist stance was constricted because he remained wedded to a "masculinist framework." To prove her point, James substitutes gender for race: "For instance, anti-racist stances that are contextualized within a larger Eurocentric worldview present European American culture as normative; consequently, they inadvertently reinforce white dominance despite their democratic positions on racial politics" (142). Although James does not have Du Bois in mind with this example, I submit that double-consciousness is an antiracist stance that "inadvertently reinforce[s] white dominance" because, in *Souls* at least, Du Bois is unable to conceive of U.S. black subjectivity other than in relation to whiteness or outside of a Eurocentric framework. Since double-consciousness is by its very definition intrinsically bound to a Eurocentric paradigm, its canonization in African American studies obscures other traditions that do not hold Eurocentric aesthetic values and, by extension, white audiences in such high esteem.

I want to argue that other psychological or sociological models of identity formation, as well as more historically specific analyses of African American texts, might yield alternative methodological approaches and unearth writing traditions that do not foreground white audiences. For example, psychological and sociological research offers a myriad of ways to look at black subjectivity outside of double-consciousness, which positions black subjectivity in relation to that of whites. But there is very little corresponding scholarship in cultural and literary studies concerning how African American literature reflects concepts deriving from racial identity development theorists like William E. Cross, Wade Nobles, Alexander Thomas, Kinnard P. White, and Marvin D. Wyne, who suggest alternative ways of looking at how black identity and subjectivity develops.[8] Approaches stemming from the work of racial identity development theorists would therefore address the ways blacks relate to one another outside of the paradigm of racism. For example, bell hooks's concept of "self-recovery" essentially mirrors the aims of racial identity theorists in that she views black subjectivity as relational, meaning that in many cases black subjectivity is informed by the larger black community.[9]

It is no coincidence that the shift in discourses on racial identity in the field of psychology parallels the rise of the black aesthetic movement. Attempts to canonize African American literature by more contemporary literary theorists, however, tend to argue that all African American texts, by nature, have a dual audience or tend to favor African American authors who envision a dual audience. Therefore, for the purposes of this study, what I find most useful about Adolph Reed's research on Du Bois is his analysis of how double-consciousness has been appropriated for "a purely academic program" as articulated in the works of Henry Louis Gates, Jr., in his attempt to link the concept of double-consciousness to the double-voiced discourse prevalent in the eighteenth- and nineteenth-century canonical African American texts. Reed emphasizes Gates's desire to focus on the hermeneutic aspects of black texts and distance himself from the black aesthetic movement and other literary movements that saw social activism as an imperative in their critiques of black texts. And even though Gates would balk at the accusation that his appropriation of Du Bois is an essentialist one, given that his desire to distance himself from black aestheticians is partially predicated on his reading of BAM as an essentialist movement,[10] Reed criticizes Gates, among many others, for "presum[ing] an unchanging black essence and . . . [for failing to] consider the possibility that Du Bois's construction [double-consciousness] bears the marks of historically specific discursive patterns, debates, and objectives" (*W. E. B. Du Bois and American Political Thought* 97–98).

At the time of this manuscript's writing, there are currently three books in the field of literary studies that concentrate on Du Bois's concept of double-consciousness as the central mode of inquiry, Denise Heinze's *The Dilemma of "Double-Consciousness": Toni Morrison's Novels* (1993), Sandra Adell's *Double Consciousness/Double Bind: Theoretical Issues in Twentieth-Century Black Literature* (1994), and Devon Boan's *The Black "I": Author and Audience in African American Literature* (2002).[11] These three texts are emblematic of the prevailing mode of discourse that views double-consciousness as a fixed condition of African American subjectivity and cultural production.

Heinze argues that "[i]n a somewhat radical shift from a strictly indigenous concept of aesthetics, Toni Morrison's writings suggest that it is insufficient—indeed naïve—to define a black aesthetic independent of white aesthetics" (15). What confuses me about Heinze's argument is what she sees as constituting a black or white aesthetic. Heinze points to Morrison's position as a faculty member at an elite school and her acceptance by the white literary establishment as proof that she has "transcended the 'permanent condition' of double-consciousness that afflicts her characters" (7). Such logic affixes black aesthetics to the working class and white aesthetics to the wealthy, while it also assumes that acceptance into predominantly white institutions means that Morrison no longer has to deal with the racism that makes double-consciousness possible in the first place. Heinze's quotation also negates Morrison's expressed longing to create a black aesthetic of her own. Morrison's interview with Nellie McKay not only demonstrates her attempt to create such an aesthetic, but her desire to distance herself from white male canonical writers. Morrison exclaims, "I am not *like* James Joyce; I am not *like* Thomas Hardy; I am not *like* Faulkner. I am not *like* in that sense . . . My effort is to be like something that has probably been fully expressed in [black] music. . . . Writing novels is a way to encompass this—this something" ("An Interview with Toni Morrison" 426). Later in this chapter I argue that Morrison's shift in marketing strategies (which began in 1997 with *Paradise,* after the publication of Heinze's book) demonstrates a desire to cultivate a larger black audience among her reading constituency. This shift suggests that white mainstream acceptance is not Morrison's motivation for writing.

Adell convincingly argues that "black literary criticism and theory, like literary criticism and theory in general, relies heavily on the Western philosophical tradition" (*Double-Consciousness/Double Bind* 1). According to Adell, the dependency on this tradition calls into question the possibility of black-specific theories of writing. She contends that until there is a better understanding of how this double-consciousness manifests itself, "the field of black literary studies will not advance beyond these disputes over the presumed opposition between the social and political and the aesthetic or beyond the great Afrocentric/Eurocentric divide" (3–4). But Adell's focus is on modernism and the texts of Léopold Senghor, Aimé Césaire, Richard Wright, James Baldwin, and Maya Angelou— her methodology appears sound because she has selected texts that easily fit into the double-consciousness paradigm. Additionally, while the critical practices of the black aesthetic come under fire, Adell neglects to test her methods on its texts.

In his book *The Black "I,"* Devon Boan deals with the multiple manifestations of double-consciousness in African American literature in regards to the challenge of writing to a dual audience, one black and one white. Boan maintains that "a reader should never forget that to divorce the discourse of black literature from its context, black *and* white, is to risk misunderstanding it" (6–7). Like Heinze, Boan participates in furthering a well-worn binary that insists on the interconnectedness of blacks and whites. Boan is successful in his argument because he deals with male writers who have written canonical African American texts that take place during slavery or the era of Jim Crow and therefore easily lend themselves to an analysis that sees black texts in a dialectic debate with an oppressive (or ambiguous) white audience. It is significant that while he ends his book on an optimistic note that charts the successes African Americans have made toward integrating into mainstream society, he still envisions that "double-conscious black writers will be forced to continue balancing the racial expectations of a dual audience" (106). Although the mention of a "double-conscious black writer" implies that there are different types of black writers, Boan makes no attempt to tackle the work of younger writers who might not neatly fit into his study. For example, Trey Ellis's 1989 proclamation of a "new black aesthetic" whose vanguards, according to Ellis, are cultural mulattos that effortlessly navigate between black and white worlds and therefore see themselves as neither restricted by black identity or tragically caught between two worlds, is conspicuously absent from his text.

In her seminal text, *"Doers of the Word": African-American Women Speakers and Writers in the North (1830–1880)*, Carla L. Peterson argues for the need to "ground literary scholarship in historical specificity" (4). Although what she writes is in the context of the nineteenth century, Peterson's work is useful in reading more contemporary texts in that her approach to literature supplants the generalizing impulses of other contemporary scholars of black literature. Implicating Gates and Houston Baker, among others, she writes:

> I would argue that since so much of our history has yet to be recovered, we are not yet in a position to theorize in a totalizing fashion about black literary production, either by constructing a literary canon of masterpiece texts, by formulating a black aesthetic based on the cultural matrix of the blues, the vernacular, or folk expression, or more narrowly, by insisting upon the existence of a transhistorical black feminist aesthetic. (4)

In *Doers of the Word*, Peterson offers, or unearths, an alternate black literary tradition that serves to counter the prescribed reading—one that privileges the slave narrative as the "metonym for nineteenth-century African-American literary production," and thus favors "texts produced under the direction of white sponsors for the consumption of a white readership" (5). By investigating how African Americans in the nineteenth century defined the parameters of a literary text to include sociological texts, journalism, history, religious tracts, poetry, and spiritual autobiographies, she is able to include writing produced with a black readership in mind. Peterson's work can serve as a model by which African American writers (and the critics that study them) can break free of the Eurocentric double-consciousness paradigm that Du Bois constructs in *Souls*.

What is problematic about many of the arguments that Heinze and Boan make about black authors is that they often rely on the easy conflation of an author's perceived audience and her reading constituency.

In this project, I am privileging the audience that the writer keeps in her head when she's constructing the story—an invisible "girlfriend," to use Kevin Quashie's metaphor for black female friendships.[12] In this chapter, through an investigation of the decolonizing elements found in the texts of earlier African American writers, I also offer an alternate theoretical view to that of double-consciousness by defining what constitutes a "decolonizing" text for African American writers. My goal is to examine canonical black writing in a continuum and to envision it as an evolutionary process, moving from the preoccupations of the dual text (a text that, by political necessity, participates in double-voiced discourse between black writer and white audience) to the creation of texts that are decolonized or decolonizing. Viewing the black aesthetic as the most emblematic example of a decolonizing moment in African American history, I revisit the 1960s to discern what is salvageable and useful from the program of black aesthetics. Despite valid charges of sexism and homophobia, the black aesthetic movement is largely responsible for the types of texts produced today. This chapter, therefore, explores the ways the black aesthetic movement serves as a pivotal point in African American literary traditions, one that, to a greater extent than any other literary movement before, helped usher in the present era of the decolonizing text. Finally, I will discuss how contemporary women writers go beyond the limits of the black aesthetic and create war plans for galvanizing their black readership toward either personal or collective revolution.

RETALIATORY VIOLENCE AND THE RHETORIC OF SELF-CONSCIOUS MANHOOD

Sidonie Smith writes that "[t]he theme of violent self-expression, in which manhood is predicated on resistance to society and in which the individual's violent self is a product of violence directed to that self by society, is prominent in the slave narrative" (*Where I'm Bound* 50). However, when looking at African American literary traditions, the rhetoric of violent self-defense and self-conscious manhood also often alludes to attempts to develop decolonized subjectivities on the part of African American characters. Descriptions of violence against white oppressors usually serve to illustrate psychic metamorphoses or revolutionary transformations that catapult the black protagonist from the lowly status as bestial slave to that of "altruistic man."[13] Typically, this violence is meted out in retaliation for past injustices suffered by the black character. Retaliatory violence, or violent self-defense, has been seen by many

African American authors as the ultimate step, and most expedient one, in the process of decolonization.

The rhetoric of manhood is intrinsically bound to the issue of violent self-defense and is prevalent in most discourses of revolution, nationalism, and decolonization. The concept of manhood is perhaps so pervasive within these discourses because, traditionally speaking, masculinity is often equated with agency and power. The example of Frederick Douglass's first narrative best demonstrates the process by which one transforms from bestial slave to altruistic man. Frederick Douglass writes, "A man without force is without the essential dignity of humanity" (*Narrative* 142–143). In the scene in Douglass's first narrative where he confronts Covey, the man to whom his master sends Douglass to make him behave like a proper slave, Douglass succeeds in trouncing the self-proclaimed "nigger breaker." Douglass is not punished or killed, as one would normally expect, because Covey must protect his reputation. Ronald T. Takaki writes that "Douglass' act of violence liberated him psychologically. It completed his rebellion against his slavish hatred of himself and his slavish fear of the white oppressor. It enabled him to repudiate the definition of property imposed on him by the master class and to affirm his identity as a human being and his right to be free" (*Violence in the Black Imagination* 22). In this violent confrontation with Covey, we see Douglass attempting to destroy his own double-consciousness, which also includes his shame in being black. Douglass, like Du Bois, sees retaliatory violence and the expression of anger in general as essential to the human character. More specifically, Douglass sees retaliatory violence as an initiation into manhood.

Not so surprisingly, Du Bois coins the term "self-conscious manhood" to express what he hopes will be the evolving consciousness of the American Negro. Du Bois uses the rhetoric of self-conscious manhood in two ways: (1) as a metaphor for a black subjectivity not subsumed by racism, and (2) as a call for self-defense. For Du Bois, the remedy for double-consciousness is for the American Negro to "attain self-conscious manhood, to merge his double self into a better and truer self" (*The Souls of Black Folk* 11). This merging of two antithetical selves (the American and the Negro) in order to achieve self-conscious manhood, however, is not to be read as succumbing in total to either side of the African American psyche. Du Bois is not advocating that the American Negro become totally African or totally American, nor is it Du Bois's desire that either side lose its distinctiveness.

One can therefore infer that Du Bois also rejects the solution to the "dilemma of the Negro artist" proposed by James Weldon Johnson (that the writer address both audiences in her or his work).[14] For Du Bois, the real conflict is not necessarily the hybridity of the African American subject, but rather the disenfranchisement and stress brought about by America's pervasive racist character and its own double-consciousness—the raging conflict between American rhetoric and its actual practices. According to Du Bois, the American Negro "simply wants to make it possible for a man to be both a Negro and an American, without being cursed and spit upon by his fellows, without having the doors of Opportunity closed roughly in his face" (11). Felipe Smith explains that Du Bois felt that he could influence "the course of the prolonged struggle over the inclusion of black Americans in the imagined community only if blackness lost its stigma of inferiority" (*American Body Politics* 206). "Self-conscious manhood" can therefore be defined as individual or collective historical attempts made by African Americans to actively better conditions for blacks in the United States regardless of gender, despite the implicit sexism embedded in the term "manhood."

An illustration of how self-defense or retaliatory violence can be used as a way of obtaining self-conscious manhood can be best illustrated in "Of the Coming of John," a fictional exploration of Du Bois's concept of double-consciousness. The short story, the only one included in *The Souls of Black Folk,* is set in the Jim Crow South. Its plot is developed around two Johns, one black and one white, who have been sent off to college to become men while both halves of the community eagerly await their return. The narrator states:

> Thus in the far-away Southern village the world lay waiting, half-consciously, the coming of two young men, and dreamed in an inarticulate way of new things that would be done and new thoughts that all would think. And yet it was singular that few thought of two Johns,—for the black folk thought of one John, and he was black; and the white folk thought of another John, and he was white. And neither world thought the other world's thought, save with a vague unrest. (144)

This quotation demonstrates the division (the veil) that exists between the black and white worlds. Both characters therefore afford Du Bois the opportunity to personify the color line.

Having grown up in an environment that saw and treated blacks as unequal, both men meet again in the supposedly racism-free terrain of the North. When they meet by happenstance in a theater, white John is unaware that he has been seated next to his childhood 'friend' and demands that black John be removed from the theater—he is offended by his presence. Caught in the rapture of the music, black John is awakened from his dream state by white John's actions and moved to return to the South to work toward racial uplift because he realizes that there is no place on U.S. soil free of racism. With a northern academic education in tow, black John begins to realize that the world is unjustly unequal—no longer does he view Jim Crow restrictions as something natural. Upon returning to the South, black John attempts, unsuccessfully, to educate his fellow blacks about the unjustness of the southern social strata.

The technique of doubling characters enables Du Bois to use each to personify the promise of a "new world order." I use this phrase with all of its apocalyptic potentialities precisely because neither world's vision can be fulfilled without the death of the other's (hence the "vague unrest" each side feels). For example, when the white John's father learns of black John's going to college, he comments that college would spoil him, thereby echoing Frederick Douglass's master when he states that "[l]earning would *spoil* the best nigger in the world . . . if you teach that nigger . . . how to read, there would be no keeping him. It would forever unfit him to be a slave. He would at once become unmanageable, and of no value to his master" (*Narrative* 57).

At the end of the story, black John kills white John for attempting to sexually assault his sister Jennie, and then he calmly waits for the lynch mob. Gates and Oliver state that the story's dismal ending, the killing that essentially kills both Johns, suggests that "[b]oth of their houses are cursed; neither black nor white survives" (*The Souls of Black Folk* [Norton] xxvii). Chester J. Fontenot, Jr., in his exceptional reading of the short story, explains that black John is not only a representation of a new type of "race man," he also represents "the danger of literacy that stands at the center of racial discourse in the South" ("Du Bois's 'Of the Coming of John'"148). For Fontenot, the ending, with black John waiting for the lynch mob, demonstrates how black achievement and sense of being can be curtailed by "a violent and repressive social text" (148). I, however, read the ending slightly differently. First, what Gates, Oliver, and Fontenot seem to overlook is that John's sister Jennie does survive. Through a conversation between Jennie and black John, we learn that she too is developing a desire to be "self-conscious"—meaning that she also seeks to place herself and her people in a centralized position within her own psyche. She seeks to eliminate her double-consciousness and fight for the equality of blacks. Reading the death of both men as the destruction of both worlds suggests that revolution, both of the nation and of the African American psyche, is only possible through the actions of men.

Given that black John kills his white counterpart to protect his sister (whose character can also serve to stand for black womanhood), and given that Du Bois was influenced by Frederick Douglass, I also read the killing of white John as a call for violent self-defense. By having black John kill his white antithesis, black John also, in effect, eradicates his double-consciousness. The act of killing white John destroys the suggestion of passive responses to dehumanization and serves as a veiled entreaty to blacks to act in violent self-defense. We can therefore read white John's killing as black John's decolonizing moment.[15] Because we are told that the hopes of both worlds rest respectively with both Johns, I read the killing of white John as a destruction of the hope of the white world to forever keep blacks subservient through the use of racial intimidation.

"Of the Coming of John" is a literary antecedent to Richard Wright's novel *Native Son* (1940), which serves as the most extreme example of self-conscious manhood and offers a chilling look at what might happen when dreams are deferred. Max, Bigger Thomas's lawyer, warns the reader to "remember that men can starve from a lack of self-realization as much as they can from a lack of bread!" (399). Wright first attempted to depict the consequences of the "lack of self-realization" in *Uncle Tom's Children* (1938), a collection of short stories, but Wright was disappointed by the text's sentimental reception by his white readership. In his essay "How 'Bigger' Was Born," he writes:

> When the reviews of that book began to appear, I realized that I had made an awfully naïve mistake. I found that I had written a book which even bankers' daughters could read and weep over and feel good about it. I swore to myself that if I ever wrote another book, no one would weep over it; that it would be so hard and deep that they would have to face it without the consolation of tears. It was this that made me get to work in dead earnest. (*Native Son* 454)

By pitying the downtrodden black characters in the stories, Wright's white audience could essentially feel freed from any responsibility to work actively toward changing the status quo. Pity became enough; sympathy afforded the reader a sort of cathartic release from assuming any real responsibility or taking action.

Native Son centers on the actions of a murderous urban black youth who more readily embodies the image of blackness feared by many of Wright's white readers. The character of Bigger Thomas does not allow Wright's white readers the benefit of pity because Bigger becomes self-actualized by murdering Mary Dalton, a woman with whom many of his white readers could empathize. For Bigger, Mary is the representation of all that is rich, white, beautiful, and forbidden. We learn that although Mary's murder was accidental, Bigger takes responsibility for the crime because it seemed inevitable, predestined, and "because it made him free, gave him the possibility of choice, of action, the opportunity to act and to feel that his actions carried weight" (396).

Through Mary's murder, Bigger essentially recreates himself. Prior to killing Mary, Bigger ashamedly sees himself as a Sambo figure in the presence of her father, Mr. Dalton, to whom he is applying for a job: "his knees slightly bent, his lips partly open, his shoulders stooped; and his eyes held a look that went only to the surface of things" (*Native Son* 48). Murdering Mary, and the subsequent actions he takes to conceal his crime, enables Bigger also to murder the socially imposed image of himself as Sambo. Bigger interprets his actions as bold—he has dared to do something taboo and in planning his escape, he believes that he demonstrates an intellectual capacity of which many whites would think him incapable.

Addison Gayle writes that in comparison to *Uncle Tom's Children*, *Native Son* "succeeds on a much more fundamental level, undoing the work of black novelists heretofore, pointing out the dangerous consequences of romanticism and unlimited faith in an America of the future, and calling for a total restructuring of the society along egalitarian lines" (*The Way of the New World* xvii). Therefore, the threat of violence becomes a better tool than relying on the pity or morality of white readers. Bigger Thomas, like the composite "bad niggers" from which he was spawned,[16] acts as a prophet and would-be executor, predicting and enacting a future where the oppressor reaps what he or she has sown at the hands of the oppressed. *Native Son* demonstrates that poverty and racism can pose a bodily threat to those of a more privileged caste.

If Bigger Thomas is the quintessential "bad nigger," then Pecola, of Toni Morrison's *The Bluest Eye* (1970), is the quintessential victim. Although, as I state earlier, the term "self-conscious manhood" is problematic because of its sexist implications, many twentieth-century writers create women characters who use violence as a tool for self-actualization.[17] Pecola, however, symbolizes the violated black female body, the silenced black female voice, the invisible girl, as well as the schizophrenic and damaged black psyche—all resulting from American racism. Pecola's belief system, like that of her entire family, relies heavily on white standards of acceptable beauty that are imposed from all facets of U.S. society. These images have been disseminated as Truth, and Pecola has accepted the "master narrative" that reads her blackness as something less than, as something inferior to, white standards of beauty. Victimized also by her own community, an Other and an outsider even to blacks because she embodies an extreme digression from the American ideal of beauty, Pecola hungers for blue eyes.

Morrison, like Wright, admits to being unsatisfied with the public reaction to her novel. In the afterword to a later edition of *The Bluest Eye,* Morrison writes:

> One problem was centering: the weight of the novel's inquiry on so deli-
> cate and vulnerable a character could smash her and lead readers into the
> comfort of pitying her rather than into an interrogation of themselves
> for the smashing. My solution—break the narrative into parts that had to
> be reassembled by the reader—seemed to me a good idea, the execution
> of which does not satisfy me now. Besides, it didn't work: many readers
> remained touched but not moved. (211)

In this instance, the difference between being "touched" and "moved" is highly significant. Here Morrison is using the term "moved" in a more radical sense. Like Wright when he states his desire to write something "hard and deep," Morrison had hoped to incite readers, to move her readers to action. Morrison also believes that pity diminishes the reader's ability to see her or his own culpability for Pecola's condition. Morrison seems to suggest that by allowing anger to be an undercurrent, second-ary to Pecola's story, pity is ultimately the result. Interestingly, bell hooks codes Pecola as a "dehumanized *colonized* black girl." hooks espouses Fanonian logic when she suggests that Morrison's problem (the senti-mental reaction of her black and white readers) would have been elimi-nated had Pecola been able to express her rage. hooks quotes the novel: "anger is better, there is a presence in anger." From this quotation, hooks concludes, "Perhaps then it is that 'presence,' the assertion of subjectivity colonizers do not want to see, that surfaces when the colonized express rage" (*Killing Rage* 12).

It is in the character of Claudia, however, that Morrison demonstrates this sense of presence and rage. Morrison uses Claudia as an alternative to Pecola and her plight. Michael Awkward suggests that "the dual voices of narrator [Claudia] and protagonist [Pecola] are also, in fact, coded inter-texts of W. E. B. Du Bois's discussion of a Black 'double-consciousness'" (*Inspiriting Influences* 12). Both characters symbolize the seemingly con-tradictory factors present in the black consciousness; Pecola falls victim to the "Othering" of her self while Claudia rebels against this Othering. But, although Claudia has been born into a set of circumstances that posit double-consciousness as an inevitable psychological development of the African American, she has yet to develop a double-consciousness (Claudia explains that she would later acquiesce once she grew older). Claudia is instinctively repulsed by and even resentful of white beauty. She finds white baby dolls to be cold and their plastic flesh "unyielding." Claudia essentially deconstructs whiteness by tearing apart her white dolls because she wants "to see what it was made of, to discover the dearness, to find the beauty, the desirability that escaped [her]" (*The Bluest Eye* 20).

Claudia's dismembering of white baby dolls can be compared to Bigger's decapitation of Mary in Wright's *Native Son*. While Bigger's murder of Mary actually heightens the historic national importance conferred upon the white female body, Claudia's dismemberment critiques it. Felipe Smith uses the example of the visiting card episode found in *The Souls of Black Folk*, in which a white girl refuses Du Bois's card because he is black, to explain how historically the white woman's body has been a contested site. Smith writes that "the visiting card episode shows Du Bois's sensitivity to the way that American body politics sited the boundary between white and black social space on the white woman's body, and despite the seeming innocuousness of the encounter, it obviously stands for a whole range of experiences of social exclusion" (*American Body Politics* 201). Given Smith's comments, it is telling that for Bigger Thomas, Mary's death serves as his initiation into self-conscious manhood. The death of a privileged white woman, represents not only the death of privilege itself, but a dismantling of the veil or "the boundary between white and black social space." The murder of Bessie, even though it is deliberate and more brutal, ultimately counts for less. Bessie's body, the body of an underprivileged black woman, is used as a "body of evidence" to support the prosecutor's case concerning Bigger's propensity for murder.

In contrast, Claudia's dismemberment of white baby dolls and her violence toward girls who embody and project the ideal of American beauty should not be read as an act of self-actualization. Instead, Claudia's rage should be seen as an affirmation of an existing propensity toward self-actualization. Additionally, Claudia's unmasked rage prefigures the collective unmasking that takes place during the black aesthetic movement. In her afterword to *The Bluest Eye*, Morrison credits "the reclamation of racial beauty in the sixties" and its "wide public articulation" as being one of the impetuses for the novel (210). The character of Claudia, a child of the 1950s, challenges the master narrative that fosters white privilege and devalues blackness. Claudia's awareness of the subreption inherent in the master narrative speaks to a shifting collective consciousness among blacks. Because she refuses to mask her anger, Claudia's budding consciousness is emblematic of the generation that came of age during the 1960s and eventually participated in the black liberation struggle, which included the black power and black aesthetic movements.[18]

THE BLACK AESTHETIC MOVEMENT AND DECOLONIZATION

The introduction to the black arts section of the *Norton Anthology of African American Literature* sets the black aesthetic movement as falling between 1960 and 1970. James Smethurst, though, suggests that the black aesthetic movement began in 1965 when LeRoi Jones (Amiri Baraka) founded the Black Arts Repertory Theatre/School. Smethurst also asserts that "it is after 1965 that one can talk about a Black Arts Movement in a cohesive sense" because of the proliferation of black journals and anthologies, as well as national conferences devoted to black aesthetic thought.[19] Although I agree with Smethurst, I additionally assert that the black aesthetic becomes solidified as a movement when a major shift occurs from civil rights to black power. This shift from what Houston Baker labels "post-integrationist poetics" to black aesthetics and black power is marked by historical events such as Stokely Carmichael replacing John Lewis as the chairman of the Student Nonviolent Coordinating Committee (SNCC) in 1966 and adopting the platform of black power.[20] The death of Martin Luther King, Jr., in 1968 marked this shift on a mass level; many became disillusioned by the nonviolent platform, as evidenced by the riots that erupted once King was assassinated.

Bigsby writes that this shift from the civil rights strategy of nonviolence to that of a black aesthetic occurred because many felt the initial strategy to be "increasingly demeaning, not only because it took as its premise the desirability of integration and the implicit passivity of the black, but because, as a movement, it lacked any coherent vision of social and political realities, any analysis that went beyond a simple wish to inherit the American dream" (*The Second Black Renaissance* 23). Proponents of the black aesthetic movement rejected this notion of the American dream (integration) as an unattainable goal and one not conducive to promoting a healthy African American psyche.

In 1964, the Organization of Afro-American Unity called for a cultural revolution to "unbrainwash an entire people [and to] embark on a journey to rediscover ourselves" (Bigsby, *The Second Black Renaissance*, 427). The organization saw culture as an essential "weapon in the freedom struggle." Black aestheticians evoked, unearthed, and gave voice to their forgotten literary and revolutionary predecessors, as well as came into voice in their own right. With the archival enterprise also came the desire to conceive of and recuperate theories that would offer an alternative to European ways of being and creating. Leftist factions of the black liberation struggle were committed to the decolonization of African Americans; the black aesthetic created an alternative to European criteria of art and beauty, while the resurgence of black nationalism called for a black nation within, yet separate from, the dominant white American nation. Because the African American subject was not colonized in the traditional sense, militant factions of the black liberation struggle sought to expose the internal colonization of African Americans. Their analysis of slavery and black attempts at assimilation as detrimental to the African American psyche can be compared to Ngũgĩ wa Thiong'o's view of imperialism as a "cultural bomb" whose effect "is to annihilate a people's belief in their names, in their languages, in their environment, in their heritage of struggle, in their unity, in their capacities and ultimately in themselves" (*Decolonising the Mind* 3).

Proponents of the black aesthetic and black power movements, as well as the Black Panthers, embraced internationalist rhetoric of decolonization and resistance literature. For example, Nikhil Pal Singh writes that the Panthers defined themselves as revolutionary nationalists and true internationalists. Singh further states that to make a distinction between the affinity they felt to nationalism elsewhere and their aversion to U.S. nationalism, which they saw as intrinsically connected to American oppression, the Panthers "self-consciously redefined their own quasi-nationalist politics in terms of anti-colonialism by fashioning themselves in the flamboyant image of anticolonial revolutionaries like Che Guevara and Ho Chi Minh—[and read] resistance literature from the *Red Book* to *The Autobiography of Malcolm X*" ("The Black Panthers and the 'Undeveloped Country' of the Left" 67). Leftist factions of the black liberation movement were also influenced and encouraged by a series of Third World anticolonial movements from 1959 to 1975, such as in Ghana (1957), Cuba (1959), Republic of Congo (Zaire 1960), Ivory Coast (1960), Nigeria (1960), Senegal (1960), Algeria (1962), Kenya (1963), Guinea-Bissau (1974), and Mozambique (1975).

The affinity to Third World nationalist movements by the leftist factions of the black liberation struggle was reciprocal. Singh reminds us that in *The Wretched of the Earth* (1961), Frantz Fanon made several connections between the Algerian revolution and the situation of blacks and other minorities in the United States. In her essay "Back to Africa: The Evolution of the International Section of the Black Panther Party (1969–1972)," Kathleen Neal Cleaver demonstrates this reciprocity when she talks about African American participation in the 1969 First Pan African Cultural Festival in Algiers. Additionally, countries like Algeria and Cuba offered asylum to many black revolutionaries; Eldridge Cleaver sought refuge in Algeria in 1969, the Panthers were waiting in Algeria to receive Angela Davis before her 1970 capture by the FBI, and Assata Shakur escaped from prison to Cuba in 1979, where she remains to this day.

Although I argue that the black aesthetic movement serves as the defining literary movement that marks a generational shift in the collective consciousness of African Americans, I am not suggesting that black aestheticians were the first to push for decolonization, nor am I suggesting that earlier texts written by African Americans could not also be labeled as having a decolonizing imperative.[21] In the context of the United States, Valerie Smith reminds us that, as a massive program to re-appropriate negative images of blacks, the black aesthetic movement did not differ much from the Harlem Renaissance, the era to which the black aesthetic movement is most compared. Of the participants of the Harlem Renaissance, Smith writes that "they began to take pride in elements like folk culture, spirituals, blues, jazz, etc., that gave them a distinct culture. They also came to realize that whiteness was not simply skin color in America but a set of mythologies inherited by white writers with which they interpreted the universe" (*Self-Discovery and Authority* 17). During the Harlem Renaissance specifically, elements of decolonization as a mode of discourse was exhibited in Marcus Garvey's speeches as well as in Zora Neale Hurston's act of putting Eatonville, an all-black incorporated town, on the African American literary map as a model of folk culture at work and as a model of black self-sufficiency and nationalism. Garvey's back-to-Africa movement and Hurston's statements about Eatonville both offered African Americans spaces—in Africa and the United States—in which blacks could function outside the double-consciousness paradox on a more literal level. For Hurston, living in such spaces where whiteness is at the periphery results in the development of psyches that are not split or "tragic." In "How It Feels to Be Colored Me," Hurston flippantly comments, "But I am not tragically colored. There is no great sorrow dammed up in my soul, nor lurking behind my eyes. I do not mind at all. I do not belong to the sobbing school of Negrohood who hold that nature somehow has given them a lowdown dirty deal and whose feelings are all hurt about it" (153).[22]

While I maintain that decolonizing texts have always been a part of the African American literary tradition, I assert that there are three interrelated decolonizing components of the black aesthetic movement that catapulted African American literature into an entirely different phase:

(1) the collective unmasking of anger, an act that valorizes the African American subject's right not only to be angry, but to express that anger, (2) the deconstruction of whiteness, which attempts to thwart constructions of Western ideology as both naturalized and universal, and (3) the creation of a larger black reading audience as its intended constituency; the writers are concerned with addressing an audience that more resembles them racially rather than speaking to whites either to appeal to their sense of morality or in protest.

As I discuss in the prelude, the idea of unmasking is a key component in the process of decolonization because it means a rejection of the mask of Sambo that many African Americans were forced to don. Roger D. Abrahams writes, "It seems clear that in most cases, blacks have found it convenient to wear the mask of Sambo; they have developed upon numerous traditional techniques by which they may successfully aggress in both covert and overt fashion. The Sambo, then, often was not a personality-type as much as a convenient mask to wear; in assuming this role consciously or reflexively, blacks could achieve aggression and protection at the same time" (*Positively Black* 7). Masking, a term that originally derives from Paul Laurence Dunbar's poem "We Wear the Mask" (1895), can be defined as the ability to hide one's true emotions and thoughts from whites. During slavery, blacks acted as if they were happy or enacted subservient mannerisms, often to protect themselves[23] or as an act of resistance—to disguise plans of escape or rebellion from their owners. Janet K. Mancini explains that

> Regardless of class, blacks knew that donning the masked role was the safest course. . . . Children learned early to suppress their natural feelings of fear, hatred, or confusion. Fitting on the mask was a part of growing up black and an extension of the instinct to survive. Faked friendliness, aloof obedience, and Uncle Tom solicitousness were responses to the casting calls of slavery period whites. Whites wanted the blacks to live and work close to them to play one role—affable compliance—and to play it well. Those expectations wove a persistent thread through interracial relations in this country. (*Strategic Styles* 60)

As is implied by my discussion of *Native Son* earlier in this chapter, instances of masking and other accommodationist behaviors that suggest black subservience existed far beyond slavery. For example, Bigger Thomas (*Native Son*) found himself involuntarily acting as Sambo during his initial meeting with his white employer, Mr. Dalton; he had been socially conditioned to play the role of Sambo in the presence of whites.

The collective unmasking practiced in the black aesthetic movement is essential to the ongoing process of decolonization. bell hooks explains its importance as follows:

> Collective unmasking is an important act of resistance. If it remains a mark of our oppression that as black people we cannot be dedicated to truth in our lives, without putting ourselves at risk, then it is a mark of our resistance, our commitment to liberation, when we claim the right to speak the truth of our reality. (*Sisters of the Yam* 26)

In the specific case of African Americans, unmasking means revealing a self that is unfettered—one that is not governed by the anticipated reactions of white people. Unmasking can also be equated with the notion of gaining voice—the act of being empowered to speak out against injustice, for example. Unmasking on a broader level can also mean the unveiling of certain truth-claims as fallacies or myths created in the interest of the status quo. The resulting literature of the black aesthetic participated in the deconstruction of whiteness by unmasking the anger originally suppressed by the black writer in her or his portrayal of the black literary subject and by directly attacking (and often demonizing) the supposed white audience and dominant white culture.[24]

African American literature between 1954 and the late 1960s is peppered with examples of unfettered anger and the metaphoric use of unmasking as a collective act of resistance. James Baldwin's "Going to Meet the Man" (1965) is one such example. Told through the eyes of a racist white sheriff, this story depicts his reaction to this shifting consciousness from ready accommodation to open defiance. The very title of the story alludes to a shifting paradigm. The phrase "the Man" usually refers to the white establishment or, more precisely, the white patriarchal power structure. However, the tension of the story revolves around the sheriff's preoccupation with going to meet a young black revolutionary, "the Man," whom he has locked up in his jail. With the youth's open defiance and the growing support gathering outside his jail cell, the sheriff is literally rendered impotent, his own manhood stripped.

Baraka's play *Dutchman* (1964) serves as the most prominent example of metaphoric usage of the trope of unmasking. In the closing scene of *Dutchman*, Clay removes his mask of a bourgeois Negro in front of his would-be white seductress, Lula. Lula, with a skill that would rival any psychic, adeptly plays on Clay's insecurities as a middle-class black and his level of identification with the so-called black masses. Lula, as a "liberated" white woman, feels that she understands his plight as a black man in the United States and chastises him as she might if she were also black, and sees his need to assimilate and integrate into white society as counterrevolutionary. Lula calls him an "Uncle Tom" and mocks the vestiges of white culture he holds dear (e.g., his conservative manner of dress, his penchant for Baudelaire). By possessing black men sexually and living in a predominantly black neighborhood (a tangible representation of life behind "the veil"), Lula believes she can somehow look through the metaphoric veil Du Bois sees dividing the black world from the white and see under the masks blacks have historically had to wear for protection, survival, and often resistance.

Clay, unnerved and therefore unmasked by Lula's goading, gives the phrase "verbal assault" a new meaning. With a misogynistic threat, "I'll rip your lousy breasts off," Clay threatens the symbols of white womanhood that white men have historically killed to protect.[25] Additionally, through the character of Lula, Baraka is able to harshly critique and figuratively punish "liberated" white feminists. In his lengthy closing diatribe, Clay denounces Lula and the arrogance of whiteness that allows her to speak on issues and judge actions about which she knows little. Clay demands the right to define himself as he sees fit, even if it is out of sync with present-day notions of blackness: "You telling me what I ought to do. . . . Well, don't! Don't you tell me anything! If I'm a middle-class fake white man . . . let me be. And let me be in the way I want. . . . Let me be who I feel like being. Uncle Tom. Thomas. Whoever. It's none of your business" (34). Lula's instructing him how to be black, even if it falls in line with the current rhetoric on blackness, is just another way for her (and all of white America) to assert power over his own definition of himself as a black man. Clay believes that his subjectivity is none of her concern. Clay states that all she sees is the mask, "an act. Lies," not the reality. She sees the "device" and not the undisclosed mechanisms, "not the pure heart, the pumping black heart." Under the mask, Clay warns, are a " whole people of neurotics, struggling to keep from being sane. And the only thing that would cure the neurosis would be your murder. Simple as that" (35). But in disclosing what lies behind the mask, Clay gives Lula access to the heart of blackness. Once she has access to something he accuses her of not being able to possess, she destroys it by stabbing Clay in the heart twice, until he is dead.

We can read Clay as having some complicity in his own murder because he allowed himself to be unmasked; in this instance to remove the mask proves to be just as deadly in the early 1960s as it did during slavery. Or perhaps Baraka makes the authorial decision to kill Clay because he refuses to *stay* unmasked and instead retreats; Clay says, "Ahhh. Shit. But who needs it? I'd rather be a fool. Insane. Safe with my words, and no deaths, and clean, hard thoughts, urging me to new conquests" (35). Clay's monologue speaks to a hidden consciousness that lies just beneath the surface. Clay retreats back into what Baraka considers to be his insanity, but not before he allows himself to be the embodiment of a foreshadowed destiny of black resistance in America.

The collective unmasking addressed in the examples above demonstrates the second stage in the process of decolonization—the removal of white values that blacks have attempted to emulate. Sudhi Rajiv writes that Frantz Fanon saw the removal of the "white mask" as the second phase of decolonization: "The second state arises when the oppressed begins to feel locked within a definition and realize that the white mask does not satisfy their basic human needs. In order to overcome this estrangement from their real selves, they begin to discard the superimposed Western values" (Rajiv, *Forms of Black Consciousness*, 151). Black aestheticians participated in the deconstruction of whiteness; they believed that a massive paradigm shift in collective thinking on the part of U.S. blacks could only be reached if there was a change in the ways blacks talked about "blackness" *and* "whiteness." Instead of focusing on the similarities between the races in the hopes of integration and to end the second-class treatment of blacks, black aestheticians focused on the differences between blacks and whites. W. Lawrence Hogue explains that "[t]his stress on differences defamiliarized the dominant American society's practices, thereby showing the American public, and especially Afro-Americans, that what had been presented as 'natural' was in fact a construct, a production" (*Discourse and the Other* 52).

The deconstruction of whiteness often meant the Othering or "counterstereotyping" of the white subject.[26] There are five iterrelated advantages that I see to counterstereotyping of whiteness. First, it demonstrates that "difference" is subjective. Second, viewing difference as subjective usurps the white subject from the authoritative position as absolute definer of difference and measure of normality.[27] Third, counterstereotyping undermines white privilege by critiquing the use of European cultural traditions as the ultimate measure of art, beauty, and the model of correct behavior in general. Fourth, counterstereotyping also acknowledges that the self-actualization of oppressed peoples can occur *in spite of* racial oppression; to see "white" as Other rather than to see oneself as the "black Other" might mean a move beyond double-consciousness. Finally, counterstereotyping acknowledges the existence and importance of audiences other than the white majority status quo.

The final method of decolonization that black aestheticians employed was to eradicate the control whites traditionally held over black texts by discouraging white patronage and opting instead for black self-sufficiency in the arena of publishing. Bigsby writes:

> The second renaissance was not only an explosion of new literary talent, but a rediscovery of the past. It relied, therefore, on the reprinting of books long-since out of print, the publication of anthologies of black writers, past and present, and ultimately the introduction of black studies courses in universities, whose job was both to teach this material and to provide the context for the new sense of black identity. (*The Second Black Renaissance* 52)

By creating black and Third World publishing houses and journals, establishing Black Studies programs, and recovering texts that had long since gone out of print, the black aesthetic movement participated in the development of a wider black reading audience that had been in existence on a smaller scale since Frederick Douglass first published *The North Star* and had been growing larger ever since the Harlem Renaissance. However, the black aesthetic movement differed from the Harlem Renaissance in its desire to speak to "the folk," and to cultivate working class blacks as a reading constituency.

Disillusioned by the early attempts of the slave narrative authors and later by the efforts of the nonviolent factions of the black liberation struggle, black writers opted to write solely for the benefit of blacks. Bigsby writes, "The Black Arts Movement was an attempt to destroy what, in another context, Du Bois referred to as the double-consciousness, by simply denying one element of a dialectical process" (51). African American writing and African American subjectivity has traditionally been viewed as being informed by a white constituency—one with whom we are in constant dialogue. Bigsby is suggesting that the black aesthetic movement sought to sever the communicative relationship between blacks and whites. In *Souls,* Du Bois also contemplated the problems associated with the dual audience:

> Here in America, in the few days since Emancipation, the black man's turning hither and thither in hesitant and doubtful striving has often made his very strength to lose effectiveness, to seem like the absence of power, like weakness. And yet it is not weakness, it is the contradiction of double aims. The double-aimed struggle of the black artisan—on the one hand to escape white contempt for a nation of mere hewers of wood and drawers of water, and on the other hand to plough and nail and dig for a poverty-stricken

horde—could only result in making him a poor craftsman, for he had but half a heart in either cause. . . . This waste of double aims, this seeking to satisfy two unreconciled ideals, has wrought sad havoc with the courage and faith and deeds of ten thousand people,—has sent them often woo- ing false gods and invoking false means of salvation, and at times has even seemed about to make them ashamed of themselves. (11)

In this quotation, Du Bois prefigures James Weldon Johnson's 1928 dis- cussion of the dual audience in his essay "The Dilemma of the Negro Author." While Bigsby is correct to locate the "two-ness" of the African American as the dilemma, again one must remember that for Du Bois the solution was not to eradicate the two-ness, but to eliminate the rac- ism and the stigma attached to being black. Therefore, for Du Bois the problem with being both a Negro and an American was that blacks in the United States had to deal with institutionalized racism that denied them access to the full privileges of citizenship.

Bigsby suggests that ending double-consciousness by forgoing a rela- tionship with a white audience "was perhaps not a credible method in a cultural sense since the dilemma of the black American, after all resides precisely in the fact that he is both black and American" (51). And although several critics agree with Bigsby, I submit that to suggest that the eradication of double-consciousness cannot occur without involv- ing whites in the dialogue places too high a premium on whiteness and implies that a black subjectivity that supports a communicative relation- ship among blacks is somehow less valid. Additionally, as I have said before, we do not ordinarily determine the validity of whiteness by this same communicative process.

Bigsby seems to downplay the importance of the creation of a larger black audience at this juncture. Envisioning a reading public that mir- rors the author's racial or sexual components seems an essential fac- tor in the process of decolonization, according to bell hooks: "To make the liberated voice, one must confront the issue of audience—we must know to whom we speak . . . the way in which the language we choose to use declares who it is we place at the center of discourse" (*Talking Back* 15). Subjectivity is informed by who we, as African Americans, envision as our community. It was important for black writers to voice their intention to write for a black audience instead of a white audience in order to transform their subjectivity. Francis Jacques writes that "our self is a function of the communicative interaction which occurs in dia- logue. This interaction takes place on the level of 'utterance,' a term that expresses the fact that what the speaking subject is saying depends on the interlocuting context of communication" (*Difference and Subjectivity* xii). If the self is informed by one's "communicative interaction," the eradication of double-consciousness must entail a change in one's interactions. I see the removal of the white audience from the "dialectical process" as a very credible method because it recognizes that there are other audiences for African American writers and artists to address, the most logical being their own. The black aesthetic movement forever changed both "communicative interaction" and the "context of communication."

In addition to shifting intended audiences, black writers during the black aesthetic movement also attempted to change the relationship between writer and audience. Instead of the writer assuming a hierarchical or authoritative position over her or his audience, many endeavored to establish a symbiotic relationship—one in which the writer's freedom was dependent upon the freedom of her or his intended audience. Gayl Jones writes, "Decolonization of the African American audience is only possible with the possibility of an African American audience, and the decolonization of the African American novel depends on the decolonization of the African American audience" ("From the Quest for Wholeness" 513). This practice correlated with the African idea of "nommo," in which "traditional African philosophy cannot make the distinction of 'speaker' and 'audience' to the same degree found in rhetorical traditions of Euro-American society" (Hamlet, "Understanding African American Oratory," 66). Additionally, "nommo" implies a reciprocal relationship between the writer and the audience. As with earlier traditions of black writing, writers of this era sought to be representative of the larger masses. In terms of the black aesthetic, however, this desire to be representative did not mean that the writer should use her or his work to exemplify the humanity of blacks for a white audience. For black aestheticians, being representative meant there was a greater chance to build a movement—to unify under the rubric of sameness, of identification—to push for revolutionary change on a national and international level. It is this reciprocity between the African American writer and her or his African American (or black) audience that seems to be the most important quality of a decolonizing text.

Given that the intended audience for black writing has changed, I contend that the black aesthetic movement produces a shift in the original meaning of double-consciousness. While the Du Boisian concept of double-consciousness saw a contradiction between being both Negro and American, the double-consciousness that currently takes precedence is the contradiction between being both an individual and part of a larger perceived black collective. On some level, Toni Morrison alludes to this dilemma in her 1984 article "Rootedness: The Ancestor as Foundation." In this article, Morrison points to a conflict between an author's public and private lives. She muses, "There must have been a time when an artist could be genuinely representative *of* the tribe and *in* it; when an artist could have a tribal or racial sensibility and an individual expression of it. There were spaces and places in which a single person could enter and behave as an individual within the context of the community" (339). I tend to agree with Morrison, but I proffer that the ways contemporary scholars have traditionally approached the study of African American literature, coupled with the realities of mainstream publishing, tends to occlude such an analysis, and instead critiques that preference the black artist's connection to white audiences have loomed large.

Morrison alludes to a rationale for why critics and scholars often overlook the attempts made by black artists to connect to a black audience or their depictions of characters who are dependent on a black community. She reasons that the academy envisions the artist's role differently; the tendency is to view the artist as "the supreme individual" and one who is forever in conflict with society (343). For Morrison, this distinction leads to differences in how literature is interpreted. She uses her own novel *Sula* (1974) as an example: "Whether or not Sula is nourished by the village depends on your view of it. I know people who believe that she was destroyed by it. My own special view is that there was no other place where she could live. She would have been destroyed by any other place; she was permitted to 'be' only in that context, and no one stoned her or threw her out" (343).

For my own purposes, I am interested in black writers who, even if they do not call it as such, believe in "nommo" and in a reciprocity with and responsibility to their intended audience. I submit that the African American writer's psyche now exhibits a division between her or his individual self and her or his identity as part of the racial group, which would include a feeling of obligation to and responsibility for that group as its primary referent. The writer, therefore, becomes less concerned with how the white world views her or his text, and by extension her or himself, and more concerned with maintaining a balance between being both an individual and a part of a larger black collective. Such a responsibility to one's audience does not, however, mean that the black audience will automatically confer its acceptance.

Alice Walker's reaction to black public response after the December 1985 film release of *The Color Purple* and Toni Morrison's marketing decisions concerning *Paradise* in 1998 serve as two key examples of this alternate view of double-consciousness. Since I have already discussed, in the prelude to this project, Alice Walker's distress over the overwhelmingly negative response to the filmic version of *The Color Purple,* here I would like to focus solely on Morrison. In Morrison's case, I submit that she consciously targeted a black audience for *Paradise* even though she already has a large following in the academic community. Although Morrison is widely taught in the academic arena, students and people outside of English departments often complain to me that Morrison's novels are just too difficult. Possibly in anticipation of this sort of response, A. J. Verdelle prefaced an interview with Morrison concerning *Paradise* by telling *Essence* magazine readers that "[y]ou may have to read carefully, but if you persist you'll be richly rewarded." In addition to submitting to an interview in *Essence,* a magazine geared toward black women, Morrison also toured prestigious black churches and community colleges in urban neighborhoods, reading sections of *Paradise* to packed houses conceivably to garner a larger black following.

Perhaps I am more aware of this attention to black audiences, this new double-consciousness, because of the flak many black female writers have gotten because their books are considered feminist (i.e., antimale) or too highbrow (i.e., catering to whites). In the black community, and in other marginalized communities in which unifying against the larger population is stressed, feminism is often seen as something divisive to group cohesiveness. Often in these instances, the concerns of men are universalized—they are viewed as speaking for the black community as a whole, while the concerns of women are seen as particular, and therefore self-serving. As a result of this eschewed perception, I suggest that African American women feel more pressure to prove their loyalty to the black community than do male writers.

Because of the potential of new dilemmas emerging as a result of catering to the expectations of the black audience, I believe it is important to talk specifically about the current era of writing and the extent to which African American female writers rely upon the tenets of the black aesthetic as a way of expressing the symbiotic connection they feel to their black audience.

CONTEMPORARY AFRICAN AMERICAN WOMEN WRITERS: THE ERA OF THE REVOLUTIONARY DIVA

Sylvia Wynter identifies four "major developments" that caused the demise of the black aesthetic movement. The first development was the reduction in black middle-class participation in social activism and uprisings, partially due to the creation of affirmative action programs that incorporated "the black middle and socially mobile lower-middle classes into the horizons of expectation of the generic white middle classes" ("On How We Mistook the Map for the Territory" 109). According to Wynter, this incorporation led to the division between the black middle and lower middle classes from the black lower and under classes. The second development was what Wynter characterizes as Amiri Baraka's "defection . . . from Black Power Nationalism to the Maoist wing of Marxism-Leninism as a universalist counter to the universalism of Liberalism" (110). Although she recognizes that black women equally participated in the black aesthetic movement, Wynter credits the rise of black feminism and the publication of black women's fiction as the third reason for the demise of BAM. The final development was the "hegemonic rise of a black (soon to be 'African-American') poststructuralist and 'multicultural' literary theory and criticism" (110). Wynter sees Henry Louis Gates, Jr., as instrumental in the displacement of black aesthetics and the reformation of the "African-American literary canon to complement the Euro-American one" (110).

While I agree with much of what Wynter says, I also believe that this hegemony has effectively obscured that there is a disconnect between the aims of black postructuralism and that of contemporary black women's fiction in general. And while I am not suggesting that one forgo using poststructuralist theory in analyses of African American texts, I am suggesting that the heightened attention given to poststructuralism at the expense of black aesthetics helps to make indistinct the fact that much of contemporary women's writing is still very much about racial uplift.

Dana A. Williams credits BAM for laying the foundation upon which a new tradition of African American literature was built: "[this new tradition] was one that took the horror and the beauty alike of black cultural traditions, one that explored the vastness of African American experiences, and the varied meanings of an African American self, and one that ushered *in the contemporary era of the novel as an agent of healing*" (*"In the Light of Likeness"* xiii–xiv, emphasis mine). Although Williams sees a black male author, Leon Forrest, as emblematic of this era, scholars like Darryl Dickson-Carr have convincingly argued that the reliance on satire in a great deal of canonized and contemporary male fiction often negates or at least challenges earlier novelist traditions of social uplift.[28] I also want to suggest that younger black male authors that have received recent notoriety do not often write with this imperative, while the trend continues for black women writers—both those who matured during the 1960s and those that grew up post–civil rights. But it is not my desire to discredit Williams's work; on the contrary, her text has persuaded me to take a closer look at male writers like Leon Forrest who have a similar agenda.[29] Rather, I base my own understanding of the contemporary literary era on the premise that the academic and popular publishing markets are currently dominated by black women writers, and so when one talks about this contemporary era's tendency to produce novels that facilitate healing among reading constituencies, such a claim must be read in this context of production.

It is not a coincidence to me that bell hooks also uses the term "healing" to describe writing of contemporary black women:

> Progressive black women artists have shown on-going concern about healing our wounds. Much of the celebrated fiction by black women writers is concerned with identifying our pain and imaginatively constructing maps for healing. *Sassafrass, Cypress, and Indigo; The Bluest Eye; The Color Purple; Praisesong for the Widow; Maru; The Salt Eaters;* and many others address the deep, often unnamed psychic wounding that takes place in the daily lives of black folks in this society. (*Sisters of the Yam* 11)

To this list I would add Gayl Jones's *Corregidora* (1975), Alice Walker's *Meridian* (1976), Sherley Anne Williams's *Dessa Rose* (1986), Toni Morrison's *Beloved* (1987), Gloria Naylor's *Mama Day* (1988), Octavia Butler's *Kindred* (1979) and *Parable of the Sower* (1993), Sapphire's *Push* (1996), A. J. Verdelle's *The Good Negress* (1996), Sister Souljah's *The Coldest Winter Ever* (1999), Nalo Hopkinson's *Midnight Robber* (2000), and Sofia Quintero's *Picture Me Rollin'* (2005). When Williams talks about the novel as a healing agent or when hooks speaks of the woman writer's desire to "heal our wounds," I interpret references to "healing" as a metaphoric way of talking about a decolonizing imperative that contemporary women writers share. Therefore, in slight contrast to Williams, I label the contemporary era of African American writing "the era of the revolutionary diva" because the women who spearhead this movement share in common with black aesthetics the desire to decolonize their black readership.

BAM was largely successful in changing the way we view ourselves as African Americans, but even Amiri Baraka conceded that what was missing from the program of black aesthetics were models that served as alternatives to those of whites. Baraka writes, "'The Destruction of America' was the Black Poet's role . . . to contribute as much as possible to that. But now, I realize that the Black Poet ought also try to provide a 'post-american form,' even as simple vision, for his people" ("Statement" 257). Even though the movement provided many models of revolutionary action, no "post-american forms," or decolonizing texts that reflected the espoused new world order, were created. I assert that creating decolonized texts, or literary representations of "post-american form[s]," has largely been the task of contemporary African American women who have continued where the black aestheticians ended. I am inclined to believe, as C. W. E. Bigsby maintains, that the black aesthetic movement is not actually over but has changed instead.

While contemporary African American women writers continue to pursue the objective of social uplift in their works, they do so by asserting what Bigsby recognizes as a "literary and personal identity outside the axial lines of passivity and revolt" (*The Second Black Renaissance* 7). Contemporary black women construct spaces outside the parameters of "identity politics" and create revolutionary writing that provides alternate visions for our society. Julia Sudbury quotes June Jordan as stating that "black women's visions are not limited to narrow and essentialist identity politics. . . . Black women have 'other kinds of dreams' which are broader and far more revolutionary" (*"Other Kinds of Dreams"* 2). In this quotation, both the politics of black aesthetics and traditional white feminism are implicated. Paraphrasing the sentiments of Audre Lorde, Filomina Steady, Angela Davis, and bell hooks, Patricia Collins asserts instead that African American women present humanistic models of decolonization that promote self-actualization, self-definition, and self-determination instead of embracing theories of empowerment based on domination. The rhetoric of manhood that abounded in the 1960s overshadowed the more inclusive potential humanistic models of decolonization that I list above. Like the example of black John's sister in Du Bois's Reconstruction tale "Of the Coming of John," the presence of women both during and after the black aesthetic movement demonstrates that women also embraced discourses that promoted black self-sufficiency while they additionally addressed how sexism, racism, and classism acted as further hindrances to processes of identity formation for black women.

However, given what Charles Johnson says about contemporary African American women writers in *Being and Race* (1988), it would appear that he would take issue with the statement that their writing is broader. Writing specifically about contemporary prominent black women writers and their quests for identity, Johnson states:

> Analysis of the novels under review shows this search [for identity], far from being finished, has only just begun. It is more at the stage of criticism of social crimes than of presenting a coherent, consistent, complete "identity" for black women, one that distinguishes its essential elements from Cultural Nationalism or Negritude. . . . The conjoining of race and sex, we

see, thematizes the black experience in hitherto unexplored ways, but it *triples* the number of philosophical and political dilemmas to be resolved in the pursuit of selfhood. Du Bois might have said of black women writers of the 1980s [and here I would add the 1970s as well since many of the women Johnson is critiquing began their writing careers during that decade] that they ever feel their "threeness; an American, a Negro, a woman; three souls, three thoughts, three warring ideals in one dark body." (117)

While Johnson is eager to suggest that black female oppression is manifold, his critique is suspect because he ultimately believes that these contemporary women writers never transcend the need to give voice to their oppression, or rather that they fail to evolve beyond their urge to testify to the multiple oppressions of black women. And by extension, Johnson further suggests that the characters that African American female writers create merely lament their social condition, and therefore offer no constructive solutions.[30] Looking specifically at Toni Cade Bambara's *The Salt Eaters* (1980), Johnson asserts that, like most African American writing (and American writing in general), the novel lacks what he calls "presentedness," meaning that it lacks a "masterful sense of dramatic scene, that special moment in fiction when the opposing aims of characters force them into a collision that changes them before our eyes, leading them toward self-discovery or a moment of recognition" (103). Johnson fails to see that contemporary black women writers do more than outline the social problems faced by black women; through their characters' quest for self-discovery, black women writers offer solutions and healing paradigms for their readership. Not only does their process of self-discovery change the protagonist, but it also is designed to change the audience.

Johnson also tends to essentialize black women writers with his expectation that they construct "a coherent, consistent, complete 'identity' for black women." Not only is this task impossible and dangerous for anyone, it also suggests that there is only one identity for African American women to ascribe.[31] Additionally, Johnson's comments assume that once one establishes an identity it becomes fixed instead of something that is constantly in flux.[32] For the purposes of this study, I have chosen to use the term "subjectivity" because it speaks to the shifting consciousness of a subject. Amina Mama states that she regards subjectivity "as being continuously constituted and changing, as being locked in a recursive relationship of mutually advancing production and change" (*Beyond the Mask* 1). Therefore, to speak of a "coherent, consistent, and complete 'identity' for black women" is problematic because a person's subjectivity is not just about how one defines herself, but how she defines herself in relation to her audience, or her perceived community (and its outsiders).

Additionally, Johnson's statements are problematic because when he calls for black women to differentiate themselves from discourses of cultural nationalism and negritude, he sees race and sex as mutually exclusive. By calling for such a dichotomy, he is inherently labeling each movement as not just male-dominated (which would be reasonable), but as inherently male movements in which women played no part and would not be specifically implicated. The authors of "The Combahee River Collective Statement" state, "Black feminist politics also have an obvious connection to movements for Black liberation, particularly those of the 1960s and 1970s. Many of us were active in those movements (Civil Rights, Black Nationalism, the Black Panthers), and all of our lives were greatly affected and changed by their ideologies, their goals" (*Home Girls* 273). Likewise, Madhu Dubey sees black nationalism as the "pre-text" of black novelist conventions in black women's writings of the 1970s (*Black Women Novelists* 11). She reminds her audience that "[b]lack women's fiction in the 1970s was written, published, and received in a cultural context powerfully shaped by black nationalist ideology" (14). Many major black women writers like Bambara, Jones, Morrison, Shange, and Walker came into political consciousness during the 1960s. It is therefore logical to assume that one would find, in varying degrees, more than just remnants of cultural nationalism and negritude.[33]

Aside from his statements' being highly questionable because of the aforementioned reasons, most of Johnson's negative critiques stem from a rigid definition of what makes for good fiction. By drawing strict parameters concerning what constitutes "literature," Johnson neglects to accept texts that fall outside of these parameters on their own merits. Such a decision becomes highly problematic when examining a text like *The Salt Eaters,* which can be considered, in both content and structure, a decolonizing novel that has at its very core the desire to debunk traditional notions of what can be considered literature (in terms of its "high art" connotations).

For example, in her book *Immigrant Acts,* Lisa Lowe analyzes what she terms the "decolonizing novels" of immigrant Asian and Asian American writers and defines such novels as participating in a continuous disturbance of "colonial mode(s) of production." Because these authors are writing in response to "material pressures," she asserts that the texts they produce "resist the formal abstraction of aestheticization that is a legacy of European modernism and a continuing feature of European postmodernism" (108).

It is important for me to once again highlight that my use of the phrase "decolonizing texts" is not meant to imply that such writing is the sole propriety of African American women writers; my understanding of a decolonizing text derives from the larger context of postcolonial and feminist discourses. For example, Diana Brydon and Helen Tiffin use the phrase "decolonising fictions" to describe novels that "question the values once taken for granted by a powerful Anglocentric discourse" and "write back against imperial fictions and texts that incorporate alternative ways of seeing and living in the world" (*Decolonising Fictions* 11). Using the essays and fiction of Caribbean author George Lamming as an exemplar, A. J. Simoes da Silva employs a similar definition when discussing Lamming's "decolonizing project" as "a consciously formulated literary and ideological engagement with the legacy of four hundred years of imposed colonial occupation" (*The Luxury of Nationalist Despair* 3). More specifically, Simoes da Silva explains that Lamming acts as spokesperson for the colonized subject and on behalf of that subject he develops a "theoretical framework" through which colonized subject (the author and his intended audience) can critique "colonial representations of Otherness" (12–13).

Although my definition shares much in common with those above, I prefer to use the phrase "decolonizing *texts*" rather than "fictions" or "novels" because I see this imperative as one that transcends genre specificities; I want to explore how this revolutionary impulse is reflected in other literary genres such as the autobiography, essays, and poetry, as well as demonstrate how black bodies in the public sphere can also be read as decolonizing texts. Additionally, I purposefully steer away from the term "fiction" to avoid the assumption that the works I discuss are somehow "untrue" rather than that they use fiction as a device to uncover a particular "truth."

As stated in the introduction to this project, a decolonizing text can be defined as one in which the author places black subjects and their theoretical/social/political preoccupations in the center of the creative endeavor. A decolonizing text is also one that positions blacks, either locally or globally, as its intended audience. These texts are not concerned with speaking to whites either to appeal to their sense of morality or in protest. In terms of African American women, decolonization involves not just removing whiteness from a centralized position within the psyche, but also removing the phallus. Decolonization for African American women further entails envisioning black women as the intended audience. hooks states that once she made the decision to place African American women in the center of her audience, she too "was transformed into a consciousness of being" (*Talking Back* 15). Another aspect of a decolonizing text is a re-evaluation of a national rhetoric that positions blacks as marginal figures, rather than central agents in American culture and history. As a contrast to hooks's use of the margins as a site of power, Toni Morrison's *Playing in the Dark* seeks to empower African Americans by placing them as central rather than marginal figures to American literary traditions and history. In addition to re-evaluating national rhetoric in order to reposition blacks as central to U.S. self-definition, decolonizing texts also do not subscribe to the notion of victimization as a fixed concept. These texts suggest ways to avoid internalizing the rhetoric of victimization that blames the victim for her or his own oppression. Contemporary African American female writing is a product of choice, of agency, rather than solely a reaction to victimization. Toni Morrison writes, "We are the subjects of our own experience, and in no way coincidentally, in the experience of those with whom we have come in contact. We are not, in fact, 'other.' We are choices. And to read imaginative literature by and about us is to choose to examine centers of self and to have the opportunity to compare these centers with the 'raceless' one with which we are, all of us most familiar" ("Unspeakable Things Unspoken" 208). Above all else, decolonizing texts provide models for achieving balance, wholeness, or self-actualization.

It is the current convention for black women writers to experiment with literary forms to create a structure that correlates with the theme of decolonization.[34] For example, Alice Walker likens the structure of *Meridian* to the female folk art of quilting; she weaves together a narrative that necessitates that one must make connections between each supposedly individual and seemingly insignificant story within the text in order to understand the novel in its entirety. In *Beloved*, Morrison uses a circular plot to demonstrate how each character's past will always come back to haunt her or him until the cycle is broken.

Contemporary African American women writers also provide models of decolonized subjectivity through the examples of their female characters. In *Dessa Rose*, Sherley Anne Williams's title character demonstrates that decolonization at times means violent self-defense and at others times it is dependent upon feminist alliances with white women. Sapphire's portrayal of Precious Jones as a young woman sexually victimized by both her parents and essentially shunned by mainstream society in *Push* is one that rivals Morrison's depiction of Pecola as the quintessential victim of contemporary African American literature. But even though Precious's situation seems bleaker, unlike Pecola she finds salvation by participating in a literacy program, thus evoking the trope of literacy equaling freedom that finds its earliest utterance in Douglass's first narrative. Barbara Christian writes that Avey Johnson, of Paule Marshall's *Praisesong for the Widow* (1983),

> must discard her American value of obsessive materialism . . . [she] must remember the ancient wisdom of African culture—that the body and spirit are one, that harmony cannot be achieved unless there is a reciprocal relationship between the individual and the community—if she is to define herself as a black woman. . . . So too with Audre Lorde's *Zami* (1982) in that she probes the cosmology of her black maternal ancestors in order to place herself. ("Trajectories of Self-Definition" 243)

Often, however, the characters' experiences do not only serve as models for their black readership, but for the larger society as well. For example, Helene Moglen writes, "Morrison's project is to explore the ways those who have been systematically deprived of psychic and social identities can in fact sustain and reinvent themselves, while she wishes also to reveal how those positioned as oppressors might not be doomed endlessly to repeat the fearful process of their own de-subjectification" ("Redeeming History" 207). According to Moglen, Morrison is therefore concerned for the wellness of the entire nation, offering remedies for both black and white subjects in America's racialized script. Andrea Stuart's critique of Morrison's work suggests that the multiple oppressions that African American women face uniquely enable black women writers to critique the nation. Stuart summarizes Morrison's perspectives concerning this position as follows:

> I think you [Morrison] summed up the appeal of black women writers when you said that white men, quite naturally, wrote about themselves and their world; white women tended to write about white men because they were so close to them as husbands, lovers and sons; and black men wrote about white men as the oppressor or the yardstick against which they measured themselves. Only black women were not interested in writing about white men and therefore freed literature to take on other concerns. (Quoted in Henderson's "Speaking in Tongues" 37)

Here Stuart contends that contemporary black women writers, more so than either white women or black men, have freed themselves from white patriarchy by resisting the communicative paradox that sees white men as its focus. So, what makes these texts "post-american," to bring Baraka's terminology back into play, is the authors' desires to effect real revolutionary change through the act of writing. Believing in the infeasibility of building on a corrupt foundation, these authors push readers to re-evaluate American ideals and values as they call for a total restructuring of our most fundamental beliefs. These women see an inherent connection between the world, the text, and use of the fictional space of the novel, and other literary genres, to critique material structures and institutions existing in the real space of the nation.

Two

"WHO IS THE BLACK WOMAN?"

Repositioning the Gaze and Reconstructing Images in
The Black Woman: An Anthology *and* Essence *Magazine*

> This time, as I listened to her talk over the stretch of one long night, she
> made vivid without knowing it what is perhaps the most critical fact of my
> existence—that definition of me, of her and millions like us, formulated
> by others to serve out their fantasies, a definition we have to combat at an
> unconscionable cost to the self and even use, at times, in order to survive;
> the cause of so much shame and rage as well as, oddly enough, a source of
> pride: simply, what it has meant, what it means, to be a Black woman in
> America. —PAULE MARSHALL, "REENA"

Often lauded as one of the first stories featuring black women who
were college-educated and politically active, Paule Marshall's widely
anthologized short story "Reena" centers around the reunion of two middle-class women—one Bajan (the narrator), the other African American
(Reena)—who had once been childhood friends. Functioning under the
guise of two women "catching up," the story confronts issues that have
existed as consuming vexations of black women during the 1960s and
1970s, as well as to those of us born in the post–civil rights era: white
standards of ideal beauty, interracial dating, the disparity between professional black women and working class black men, combating negative
stereotypes of black women, and, most importantly, defining "the black
female experience" in America.

The work of black female scholars such as Hazel Carby, Barbara
Christian, Ann duCille, Patricia Hill Collins, Cheryl Gilkes, Trudier
Harris, Mae G. Henderson, bell hooks, Deborah K. King, Valerie Smith,
Hortense Spillers, Michelle Wallace, and a host of others I have regret-
tably overlooked has collectively provided a thorough investigation of

the myriad ways the black female body has been Othered, functioning simultaneously as an anathema and an enigma within U.S. society. Their research has shed a spotlight on how African American women have been consistently misnamed, misconstrued, and rendered as scapegoats in society's attempt to unravel "the mystery of the black woman."

Hortense J. Spillers's essay "Mama's Baby, Papa's Maybe: An American Grammar Book" (1987) is one of the many examples of how African American female scholars challenge and critique the rampant mislabeling of black women. Offering her now legendary roll call of monikers[1] as proof that being an African American woman is synonymous with being a "marked woman," Spillers describes the figure of the black woman as "a locus of confounded identities, a meeting ground of investments and privations in the national treasury of rhetorical wealth." She concludes, "My country needs me, and if I were not here, I would have been invented" (65). In many respects, the black woman *was* invented: exploited for labor under the label "mammy," objectified as a lascivious beast in the figure of "Jezebel," vilified as a sycophant if she was a welfare recipient, and labeled a manly, castrating bitch if she was a professional woman. Identifying the stereotypes I list above as primary "controlling images" with which African American women have historically had to contend, Patricia Hill Collins argues that these prevailing images of black womanhood not only help society to clarify its boundaries, but they also show how black female subordination benefits the status quo and serves in the interest of furthering capitalistic enterprise.

Although Du Bois originally conceived of double-consciousness as a gender-neutral term that he appropriated to explain the African American experience of being Othered, the texts of many African American women function as both testimony and reactive responses to the condition of being objectified as racial *and* sexual Other. *The Black Woman: An Anthology* (1970) is fundamental in any discussion involving the ways black women are treated as Other in part because of the inclusion of Frances Beale's groundbreaking essay "Double Jeopardy: To Be Black and Female." In this essay she distinguishes herself as one of the first contemporary scholars to dilate Du Bois's concept to include the plight of black women and how we are in "double jeopardy," having been subjugated by mainstream society and by black men. Deborah K. King would later add the modifier "multiple" to define the black female experience in her 1988 article "Multiple Jeopardy, Multiple Consciousness: The Context of Black Feminist Ideology." Expanding the metaphor of doubleness used by Du Bois and Beale, King sought to highlight the classist oppression suffered by African American women, asserting that the "modifier 'multiple' refers not only to several simultaneous oppressions but to the multiplicative relationships among them as well. In other words, the equivalent formation is racism multiplied by sexism multiplied by classism" (297).

Taking my cue from King and the other female scholars mentioned earlier, this chapter shifts my project's attention from double-consciousness to the multiple consciousnesses of African American women, the psychological battle to come to terms with the interrelated pressures of sexism, racism, and oftentimes classism. Like Beale, Collins, and King, my preoccupation with the overlapping "isms" and prevailing images of black womanhood has less to do with a curiosity concerning mainstream society's perception of black women than with my desire to analyze the extent to which contemporary blacks have internalized these images and have also been culpable in perpetuating them. Additionally, I am intrigued by the multifarious ways that black feminists who came of age during the 1960s and 1970s have negotiated their own identities in the face of these prevailing stereotypes often by repositioning the gaze—or rather establishing blacks as their primary focal group—and by reconstructing black womanhood in an image that is more conducive to black female self-actualization, while still aligning themselves with the basic tenets of black aesthetics and black nationalism. In short, I am interested in conversations like the one exhibited in the epigraph to this chapter—conversations in which black women discuss among themselves who they really are.

In her essay "The Making of a Writer: From the Poets in the Kitchen," Paule Marshall confesses that her early literary influences were the black female friends of her mother that would often congregate for lively conversations in her mother's kitchen:

> I grew up among poets. Nothing about them suggested that poetry was their calling. They were just a group of ordinary housewives, my mother included—the basement kitchen of the brownstone house where my family lived was the usual gathering place. Once inside the warm safety of its walls the women threw off the drab coats and hats, seated themselves at the large center table, drank their cups of tea or cocoa, and talked while my sister and I sat at a smaller table over in a corner doing our homework, they talked endlessly, passionately, poetically and with impressive range. No subject was beyond them.[2]

When examining the body of Marshall's work, it is apparent that her experiences listening to these women instilled in her a profound respect for the female intellect and illustrated the necessity of creating spaces in which black women could dialogue with and disseminate information

to each other. The image of Marshall and her sister doing their home-
work while the debates of these spirited women raged on in the background is symbolic. Marshall and her sister were developing what Verta
Mae Smart-Grosvenor would call a "kitchen consciousness," or rather an
understanding that domestic spaces could also be a site for radical trans-
formation.³ I would also add that they were learning that it is important
for black women to bequeath not only their knowledge to future generations, but the unfaltering belief that black women have the right to speak
on any topic they see fit.

It is no wonder that Toni Cade Bambara,⁴ the editor of *The Black
Woman,* made the decision to reprint the story in an anthology she dedicated to "the uptown mammas who nudged me to 'just set it down in
print so it gets to be a habit to write letters to each other, so maybe that
way we don't keep treadmilling the same ole ground'" (12). Implicit in
both the quotation from "Reena" that I use in the epigraph and in Bambara's dedication is the expressed desire of African American women
to, as Bambara puts it, "get basic with each other"—or to discuss among
themselves issues pertinent to black women so that they might develop
strategies to improve their predicament in the United States.

At the end of the first chapter of this project, I speculate that the wan-
ing of the black aesthetic as a dominant ideology in African American
writing was solidified in part by Ntozake Shange's successful off-Broad-
way run of *For Colored Girls* in 1976 at the Anspacher Public Theatre.
But it is 1970 that first ushered in the current trend in African American
writing that I label "the era of the revolutionary diva." This epoch of black
female writing was first evidenced by "the growing visibility of Afro-
American women and the significant impact that they were having on
contemporary Black culture" (Christian, "But What Do We Think We're
Doing Anyway," 58). In her article "Conflict and Chorus: Reconsidering Toni Cade's *The Black Woman: An Anthology,*" Farah Jasmine Griffin reminds her readers that 1970 commemorated the beginning of Toni
Morrison's literary career, with the publication of *The Bluest Eye,* and the
year that Angela Davis became the first black woman to appear on the
FBI's ten most wanted list ("Conflict and Chorus" 116). In addition to
these events, Maya Angelou published *I Know Why the Caged Bird Sings*
and Cheryl A. Brown (Miss Iowa) became the first black woman to compete in the Miss America pageant. As emblems of this era, 1970 is also
pivotal because it marks the year that *The Black Woman* was published
and the year that *Essence* magazine made its public debut.

Griffin writes that "*The Black Woman: An Anthology* is one of the first
major texts to lay out the terrain of black women's thought that emerged

from the civil rights, Black Power, and women's liberation movements" (116). She argues that to decipher the mission of the current moment of black feminist thought and "its relationship to black feminist politics, black women's lives, and related struggles for black liberation," black feminists need to "reconsider" the legacy that *The Black Woman* has wrought (116). In addition to proving that black females were viable consumers, and further demonstrating the marketability of black female subject matter to mainstream society, the publication of *The Black Woman* was a major milestone in black feminist history because it was the first mass-marketed anthology written by and for black women and their concerns, and thus positioned black women as functioning subjects rather than as objectified Others. Not only is *The Black Woman* credited as the quintessential text of black feminist thought of the second wave, its inclusion of poetry and short stories alongside essays effectively blurred the lines between theory and fiction, thus situating both as essential to any program of revolution. In so doing, *The Black Woman* further valorized creative writing as an effective political tool. Furthermore, its structure has served as a model for black and women of color anthologies that have followed since its publication.

Although I am in agreement with Griffin about the necessity of re-evaluating *The Black Woman*'s legacy, I further argue that a more thorough analysis of *Essence* magazine should be included in any attempt to decode the current moment in black feminist history for both second- and third-wave feminists. More in-depth analyses of both publications would also broaden and complicate contemporary discourses of black female empowerment and its relationship to black nationalism. As the first black female lifestyle magazine to reflect the attitudes of the black aesthetic and black power movements, *Essence* functioned in its first year as an emblematic site for and a galvanizing force of crucial discourses on black womanhood. By the time this book goes to print, *Essence* will have been in circulation for approximately forty years. Born in the same year of *Essence*'s inauguration, I have literally grown up on *Essence*. Not only did *Essence* reflect for me a myriad of ways that black was beautiful, for years *Essence* has met my needs as a consumer and has served as a vital source of information on professions, healthcare issues, and political topics that are germane to the African American community in general. Even black celebrities like Queen Latifah and Star Jones have commented on the importance of *Essence* to their self-worth. Jones states, "As a young person, you really don't know who you are or where you fit into this world—*Essence* was my entree—so I grew up with a tremendous amount of confidence by its being there."[5] It is, therefore, not an exaggeration to state that *Essence* has played a crucial role in the constitution of contemporary black female identity.

Although many African American scholars pay homage to *The Black Woman* in their works, only Farah Jasmine Griffin has attempted to do a more rigorous textual analysis of *The Black Woman* thus far. Additionally, aside from Jennifer Bailey Woodard and Teresa Mastin's "Black Womanhood: 'Essence' and its Treatment of Stereotypical Images of Black Woman" (2005) and the cursory analyses in *Propaganda and Aesthetics: The Literary Politics of Afro-American Magazines in the Twentieth Century* (1979), and *Ladies' Pages: African American Women's Magazines and the Culture That Made Them* (2004), there has been no significant exploration of *Essence* magazine in the area of literary criticism. As a corrective to the paucity of scholarship analyzing the specific content of these texts, not only will I provide a critique of *The Black Woman*, I will also furnish an in-depth analysis of *Essence*'s first year in existence.

While Woodard and Mastin examine *Essence* over a span of three decades in order to validate it as a feminist text and to determine the extent to which the magazine challenges stereotypical portrayals of black women as mammies, matriarchs, sexual sirens, and welfare mothers or queens, I take its feminist leanings as a given—even though I complicate its labeling as such by explaining how the magazine merges its feminist impulses with its black nationalist ones. Therefore, I focus primarily on *Essence*'s first year in order to accentuate its expressed commitment to black nationalist struggle, especially since *Essence* germinated in part from the revolutionary fervor of the black power movement. Centering on *Essence*'s first year of publication also enables me to highlight Ida Lewis's role as the magazine's first editor-in-chief (she resigned in 1971).[6] Lewis functioned as the public face of and initially outlined the parameters for "The *Essence* Woman."

This chapter is divided into four additional sections. In the first section, I pay particular attention to how *The Black Woman* and *Essence* offer public forums for presenting alternatives that rivaled the pre-eminent position of white beauty in mainstream society. In the second section, I argue that *The Black Woman* and *Essence* can be seen as responses to the 1965 publication of the Moynihan Report in that both discuss the issue of the rampant stereotyping of black women as "matriarchs" and "welfare mothers" during the late 1960s and early 1970s. While both publications sought to recoup black female images and actively debated the extent to which black women themselves were culpable in their own vilification, I demonstrate that their contributors were more divided on the topic than one might imagine. The third section provides an opportunity for me to reflect upon the ways *The Black Woman* and *Essence* function as examples of black nationalist feminism. I explain how this hybrid (the conflation of nationalist and feminist discourses) resulted from awareness, on the part of the contributors, of the intersectionality between gender, race, and class. In the final section, I delve more deeply into the ways both texts cultivated a black nationalist readership. Not only do I explore who the intended audiences were for both, I discuss the extent to which this goal was augmented or complicated by expectations that both texts serve as feminist venues.

"YOU MAKE ME FEEL LIKE A NATURAL WOMAN": MARKETING BLACK BEAUTY

Black women the world over fall victim to a hierarchical system of beauty that venerates white women while defaming black women in comparison. Speaking specifically of how the beauty hierarchy functions in the United States, Deborah Grayson writes:

> Within the context of American beauty culture the visibility of body textures that are defined as "Black" have frequently served as the very antithesis of attributes of (white) feminine beauty. We need only look a the apparent preferences for light as opposed to dark skin and straight as opposed to curly or coiling hair found in electronic and print media to see examples of how these attributes are hierarchized within beauty culture. Though this hierarchical system changes somewhat over time, often it does so only on a superficial and ephemeral level as different looks go in and out of style. For the most part American beauty culture continues to be dependent upon a hierarchical system that devalues Black looks. ("Is It Fake?" 14)

Given Grayson's comments, I contend that for black women the process of decolonization very often entails a re-evaluation of Western notions of beauty and femininity.

Farah Jasmine Griffin remembers being transformed by her first glimpse of the cover photo for *The Black Woman* while on an outing with her father to their favorite Philadelphia bookstore, Robins, when she was seven or eight years old. The cover art that appeared on both publications when *The Black Woman* and *Essence* premiered in 1970 offered a counter to mainstream magazines as well as to the Hollywood film industry, which had virtually ignored the existence of black women; both featured attractive young black women wearing Afros. Therefore, one could argue that both texts served as a corrective to mainstream media images that either disregarded or denigrated the beauty of black women.

Griffin's recollection of *The Black Woman* cover demonstrates how beauty images can positively affect the psyche of darker-complexioned black children who have never seen images in the mainstream media to which they can relate.[7] In the preface to the reprint edition of the anthology, Eleanor W. Traylor calls Griffin's initial encounter with *The Black Woman* one of "self-discovery" ("Recalling the Black Woman" x). Griffin recalls:

> I had to have that book. At home, huge pictures of Kathleen Cleaver—perfect Afro, light glistening eyes, beauty mark in the middle of her forehead—and of Angela Davis—huge Afro and round granny glasses—graced my bedroom wall. I loved these women, they were my idols. . . . Those photographic images of Angela and Kathleen were my iconography for what it meant to be a revolutionary black woman.
>
> However, one crucial thing stood between me and the golden beauties who graced my wall. In the still color-conscious black world of McDaniel Elementary School in South Philadelphia, I was constantly reminded that I was "black" (which always seemed to be qualified by phrases such as "and ugly," "and shiny," "and crispy"), not at all like Angela or Kathleen who were light-skinned. So, you see, I was in desperate need of a browner, Afroed revolutionary image. ("Conflict and Chorus" 114)

Ironically, Griffin's desire to possess the book eerily mirrors Morrison's depiction of Pecola's literal consumption of Mary Jane candy and her figurative consumption of Mary Jane's image that appears on the wrapper: "To eat the candy is somehow to eat the eyes, eat Mary Jane. Love Mary Jane. Be Mary Jane" (*The Bluest Eye* 50). The important deviation in Griffin's tale of possession is that it is affirming because it represents her desire to possess herself, while Pecola's tale invalidates the possibility of black beauty; Pecola wants to be a white girl so that she will be loved. For Griffin, wanting *The Black Woman* is affirming because she can project her own aspirations onto the image, and thereby widen the possibilities for her future—one that seemed limited before because of the lack of an appropriate role model:

> I needed a rapping sister, a poet or a journalist or writer. And this anonymous sister on the Cade anthology was going to be the one. Lacking name, or voice, she could become what I was going to make her, of us—revolutionary, writer, lawyer, and world traveler. By possessing the book, I could possess the woman, I could become the woman—or so I reasoned. (114)

Leslie W. Rabine argues that "from its inception" even *Essence*'s fashion spreads "have acted as political critique of the enforced norm embodied by the slender, light-skinned, thin-lipped models in the ads" ("A Woman's Two Bodies" 68). In contrast to Rabine, and Woodard and Mastin, I would argue that the ways tropes of beauty and femininity function in both *Essence* and *The Black Woman* are more complicated than a discussion of whether or not either includes positive or negative images of black women. For example, Rabine's argument becomes a bit suspect when one considers reactions by *Essence* readers concerning the context of the magazine. In the July 1970 issue of *Essence,* in the column "Write On!" in which readers express their opinions of earlier published articles and editorials, Eugene Richardson of Washington, D.C., complains that the fashion models featured in *Essence* conformed too closely to those found in mainstream magazines. He writes, "The basic content far overshadowed the photography and the photographer's models. The female models were mere replicas of their flat-chested white contemporaries." Here he alludes to the widespread belief that black men prefer fuller-figured women, as well as implying that images of women displayed in the magazine do not correspond with the content, which calls for a break from European aesthetics. As a corrective, Mr. Richardson suggests, "Give our buxom, black beauties a forum from which to do their thing. Those with the gaunt, hungry look may be held in awe on the continent, but not in Washington, New York, Cleveland, Buffalo or Frisco" (6).

Additionally, in contrast to the brown-skinned model on *The Black Woman*'s cover, a lighter-complexioned African American woman with a curly Afro graced the first cover of *Essence.* In light of Griffin's comments, perhaps the editorial staff of *Essence* decided to use a cover model that more closely resembled the female revolutionary icons of the day, with whom the audience would be more familiar, like the women Griffin mentions, such as Kathleen Cleaver, Angela Davis, and even blaxploitation star Pam Grier—all of whom have light complexions. It could be, though, that the editors were trying to have it both ways by playing up to the fashion and mood of the times by highlighting the Afro while still privileging light skin.[8]

Also consider that the signifier of both revolutionary action and black beauty that links the lighter-skinned women like Cleaver and Davis to the unnamed woman on the cover of *The Black Woman* is the Afro. Grayson reminds us that black women's hair has always been political:

When thinking about the visual, cultural, and political re/presentation of Black women's hair it is important to consider the relations of power working obscurely and not so obscurely upon Black women's hair and hair styles. Black women are constantly engaged in a battle of recreating and re-interpreting cultural signs in regard to our hair. We cannot easily dismiss, as is so often done, either the very real consequences of making certain choices about hair style and how these choices can limit mobility or the position of authority others attempt to take over our hair in their assumptions that they can read it "correctly." ("Is It Fake" 25)

If we consider that often job advancement, or employment in general, has been predicated on the extent to which an African American could physically conform to white standards of beauty, the emphasis on black hair further shows the historical inscription of politics on the African American body.

In a transcript of a 1969 women's workshop published in *The Black Woman,* the participants talk about the how the Afro has affected white mainstream ideas of beauty as well. Not only do these women recount instances where whites, particularly white men, wanted to touch their hair (and were often surprised at its softness), but they also talk about the fact that some whites try to make their own hair into Afros. One woman complains, "Like white people have nothing of their own. Can't identify with the American culture. Can't sing old country tunes. So they latch onto ours. Take from everybody else, these young white kids. See them wearing Indian clothes, buffalo boots. Try to get an afro. Start wearing a dashiki. Everything from everywhere but nothing of their own" (181). Citing H. Rap Brown and using an *Ebony* magazine cartoon as evidence of the Afro's declining significance, Maxine Leeds Craig notes, "By the turn of the decade the Afro was dismissed by many as merely a style" (*"Ain't I a beauty queen?"* 107).

While I am interested in how images of Afrocentric beauty can raise self-esteem in black women, I am also concerned about the problematic discourse of black authenticity in the face of black nationalist consumerism. Maxine Leeds Craig explains that in 1961 black mainstream presses like *Ebony* and *Jet* "first noted the appearance of black women in the jazz world [such as Abbey Lincoln, Odetta and Melba Liston] wearing unstraightened hair" often described as "au naturel" or "au naturelle" (*"Ain't I a beauty queen?"* 87). With this thought in mind, I make playful use of Aretha Franklin's lyrics in this section's heading; for both *The Black Woman* and *Essence* being a "natural woman" was a black nationalist stance rather than a biological imperative. For example, the choice of fashion photography for *Essence* was often not so much about finding a new way to represent black female bodies, since one can easily recognize many poses as imitative of other mainstream women's magazines, but about selling black nationalism as a style. In many ways the concept of revolutionary style would fall right in line with the aim of many consumer magazines whose goal is to make the consumer believe that she or he is cultivating an individual style; in the instance of *Essence*, the magazine offered the consumer a way to privatize revolutionary struggle.

Besides containing "black" versions of feminist product placement advertisements by companies like Virginia Slims, *Essence* featured advertisements for makeup and gave makeup tips designed especially for black women. Flori Roberts, for example, advertised "Melanin Make-Up" with the slogan "the look is Natural, the style is yours, and these shades won't change color." Asarté cosmetic ads featured a striking bald model with high cheekbones. Asarté's slogan began, "For the first time in cosmetic history, someone has truly met a need, your need, the woman of color." In the June 1970 issue, one spread dealt with makeup application in conjunction with the natural hairstyle: "With all the current interest in the natural look, that sensitive area around the eyes is in the spotlight." The editorial stylist goes on to advise readers that to accentuate the eyes, one must be subtle in the application of eyeshadow.

While *Essence* unconsciously toyed with the idea of the *natural* as a statement of authentic blackness, oftentimes there was nothing natural about the hairstyle in question, Ayana D. Byrd and Lori L. Tharps comment on the irony that some Afros were not really natural, but chemically processed styles as well: "While it may seem to go against the very ideas behind a style called Natural to chemically kink your hair into an Afro, for many *not* having a 'fro was akin to being a race traitor" (*Hair Story* 59). Because black hair comes in several different textures, there are some textures of hair that do not lend themselves to the Afro style without chemical manipulation. In her essay "Black Pride? Some Contradictions," Ann Cook explains that companies routinely make money by promoting hairstyles or products that are supposed to be "natural" (i.e., chemical free). She writes, "We do not mind wearing an afro if we have the 'kind' of hair that can make a bush or if our straightening comb can help us out. So again, it is 'good hair' afros. That is really what Afro-Sheen, Raveen, and all the other complex kits of sprays are all about— getting the kinks out" (*The Black Woman* 151).

Through its fashion spreads and commercial advertisements, *Essence* demonstrated to its readers that a direct correlation could exist between one's politics and one's sense of fashion. Perhaps due to the historical denigration of black women's looks and sexuality, the attention to fashion should not be taken as a trivial concern. For example, in *Autobiography*

as Activism, Margo V. Perkins interestingly comments that Huey Newton had a proclivity for bourgeois attire that made women, in his opinion, look more "feminine." Considering the long-standing stereotypes of
black women as distinctly masculine, or at least unfeminine, Newton's
predilections most assuredly would have made the women he encountered in the party insecure. Perkins explains that the Black Panther
women then faced a dilemma: how to look both revolutionary *and* be
sexually appealing. Ironically, these women might have found an answer
in the pages of *Essence;* in its earlier years, *Essence* strove to make revolution a fashion statement. One's attire could communicate one's political
agenda.

Newton's comments are interesting in light of *Essence's* heteronor-
mativity. Much of the discourse regarding Afrocentric beauty aesthetics revolved around black women competing with white women for the
affection and attention of black men. For example, in the June 1970 issue,
Essence ran an article called "Cornell in Crisis," which dealt with the April
19, 1969, armed black student takeover of Willard Straight Hall; the students were rallying to have Black Studies instituted on campus. Interestingly, a large portion of the article claimed that interracial dating, black
men with white women, was a key component in the takeover. Expected
to adhere to a Victorian ethic of chastity to squelch the stereotyping of
black women as inherently promiscuous, the black female college student at Cornell found herself virtually dateless and in competition with
white women for black male attention. According to the article, she also
sought out light-complexioned mates—again conforming to bourgeois
ideals of the previous generation. With the ensuing black power movement, however, both black men and women were forced to re-evaluate
their connection to each other. Therefore, what this article demonstrates
is that black male/female relationships and their relation to American
beauty standards played a large part in the decision of Cornell students
to advocate for re-education.

While "Cornell at Crisis" provided an interesting and thought-pro-
voking insight into the student dynamics as a microcosm of what was
happening in the larger country, more often than not, *Essence* ran articles that hyped up such controversies rather than show the underlying
causes. Rather than just relying on black women's voices throughout the
magazine, *Essence* employed a seemingly more democratic approach by
offering its readers viewpoints from whites and black men. While the
inclusion of multiple viewpoints might, on the surface, make *Essence*
seem more objective on subjects such as miscegenation, for example,
and which race possessed the most alluring (i.e., feminine) women, a

closer analysis of the material reveals that *Essence* either exploited the anxieties of many of its black female readers concerning white women, or it merely reversed traditional beauty hierarchies by essentializing black women as the ideal. Such exploitation sometimes ran counter to its expressed goals to aid in black self-awareness and offer women a way to "talk back" to patriarchy.

BATTLE DELINEATIONS: BLACK WOMEN "TALKING BACK" TO PATRIARCHY

The Black Woman and *Essence* emerged in 1970 as a response to tensions that many African American women faced in organizations run by black men or white women, but both also could be said to have surfaced as a reaction to the publication of the Moynihan Report. *The Black Woman* and *Essence* furnished venues for women to "talk back," or rather to challenge mainstream constructions of black female identity. To bell hooks, talking back is "a political gesture that challenges politics of domination that would render [black women] nameless and voiceless" (*Talking Back* 8). Talking back also requires a paradigm shift— whether the audience she addresses is black or white, the audience must become accustomed to listening to a black woman and to viewing her as an authority figure. Additionally, "talking back" enables black women to be central rather than marginal to discourses surrounding definitions of black womanhood.

As I explain in chapter 1, it is roughly in 1965 that the public face of black activism radically shifted from the platforms of civil rights and integration to that of black power and black nationalism. In *Ain't I a Woman: Black Women and Feminism,* hooks argues that the adoption of black power as a mode of discourse really meant that black men failed to envision a power dynamic that did not rely on male dominance and female subservience as its primary ingredients. She writes:

> While the 60s black power movement was a reaction against racism, it was also a movement that allowed black men to overtly announce their support of patriarchy. Militant black men were publicly attacking the white male patriarchs for their racism but they were also establishing a bond of solidarity with them based on their shared acceptance of and commitment to patriarchy. The strongest bonding element between militant black men and white men was their shared sexism—they both believed in the inherent inferiority of women and supported male dominance. (98–99)

This adherence to patriarchy was evident in many ways, such as Ron (Maulana) Karenga's US organization,[9] which promulgated the subservience of women to men, Stokely Carmichael's infamous comment that the only place for black women in the movement was prone,[10] and in the common complaint that many black men rarely endorsed black female leadership. In agreement with this latter point, Toni Cade Bambara reminisces, "It would seem that every organization has had to struggle at one time or another with seemingly mutinous cadres of women getting salty about having to man the telephones or fix the coffee while the men wrote the position papers and decided on policy" (*The Black Woman* 107).[11]

As the creative arm of the black power movement, so labeled by various scholars, it is not unusual that the black aesthetic movement also comprised of male writers that mimicked the misogynist behavior and discourse mentioned above. Perhaps the most extreme examples lie in advocating the abuse of women, such as in LeRoi Jones's (Amiri Baraka's) play *Madheart: A Morality Play* (1967) and Eldridge Cleaver's "rape-on-principle" theory outlined in *Soul on Ice* (1968).[12] While the 1970s are known for their rhetoric of black male castration and the 1980s can be credited with spearheading the conception of the black man as an endangered species, the multiple attacks against black feminism and black womanhood, as well as the resulting backlash from black women, is ascribable to the period in which black nationalistic rhetoric gained predominance in the realm of black liberationist politics.

The flagellation of African American womanhood reached an apex, however, with the November 1965 publication of Daniel P. Moynihan's *The Negro Family: The Case for National Action,* a report commissioned by President Lyndon Johnson as part of his "War on Poverty" program. It is significant that Moynihan's report "had been 'approved' by the civil rights establishment, including King, Roy Wilkins, and Whitney Young, head of the National Urban League . . . [and] Moynihan had borrowed heavily from established Black sociologists [including] E. Franklin Frazier" (Giddings, *When and Where I Enter,* 327–328). Their endorsement essentially sanctioned an attack on black womanhood by blaming black women for their own economic victimization. Patricia Hill Collins credits the Moynihan Report for introducing and widely circulating the stereotype of the black matriarch, characterized as follows: "As overly aggressive, unfeminine women, Black matriarchs allegedly emasculated their lovers and husbands. Their men, understandably, either deserted their partners or refused to marry the mothers of their children" (*Black Feminist Thought* 75). Collins contends that matriarchs are punished because they fail to adhere to approved "gender behavior" and that by labeling these women as unfeminine, and therefore unlovable, the assertiveness of African American women is effectively curtailed. When the publication was released, Moynihan found himself under widespread attack for stating that the black family structure was pathological because it was generally headed by single women and that this matrifocal structure was attributable to the slave era, in which black women supposedly welded a great deal of power within the slave community.[13] As a remedy to this "disorganized and matrifocal family life," he suggested that black male youth join the army to escape from "a world away from women" to a "world run by strong men of unquestioned authority" (Rainwater and Yancey, *The Moynihan Report and the Politics of Controversy*, 42).

In this section I argue that the publication of the Moynihan Report polarized the black community and subsequently mobilized politically conscious black women and men to attack the rampant use of black women as scapegoats for the economic oppression of blacks. Additionally, I argue that the Moynihan Report sparked widespread discussion concerning how patriarchy inadvertently seeks to police black female bodies by insisting that black women conform to an antiquated Victorian ethic and by vilifying women whose lifestyles seemed to conflict with this ethic. I label this section "Battle Delineations: Black Women 'Talking Back' to Patriarchy" to emphasize the struggle that radical black women waged to gain a voice in the male-dominated black power movement. I further explain the rhetorical strategies employed in *The Black Woman* and *Essence* to recoup the black female image in the wake of demoralizing stereotypes.

I interpret LeRoi Jones's (Amiri Baraka's) call for blacks to unify under the principles of patriarchy in the July 1970 issue of *Black World* as being in accordance with Moynihan's assessment of the black family as pathological and with the perception that black male/female relationships are problematic because of a perceived imbalance of power in favor of black women. Rather than offer military service as a corrective to the supposed influence of the black matriarch, Jones takes a culturally nationalistic stance by urging black men and women to pay a stricter adherence to traditional "African" models of gender behavior:

But we must erase the separateness [between black women and men] by providing ourselves with healthy African identities. By embracing a value system that knows of no separation but only of the divine complement the black woman is for her man. For instance, we do not believe in the "equality" of men and women. . . . We could never be equals . . . nature has not provided thus. The brother says, "Let a woman be a wo-man . . . and let a man be a ma-an. (Quoted in hooks, *Ain't I a Woman*, 95)

By hailing back to so called "healthy African identities," Jones contends that the natural role for the black woman is to be a "complement" to her man. He intimates that for a black woman to be self-actualized in her own right, she would be acting under European rather than African dictates; therefore, he codes feminism as "white" and, by extension, counterrevolutionary. Consequently, for a man to be a "ma-an," he must serve in a hierarchical position over the black woman; his manhood, as well as her identity as an "African" woman (i.e., the quintessential black woman), is predicated on her subservience to her male counterpart. Oddly enough, it would appear that Jones envisions a "healthy" black female identity as one that embraces constricting gender roles that place her as a necessary *accessory* to revolutionary black manhood. Although embedded in black nationalist rhetoric, Jones's image of the natural African woman, like the vilification of the black matriarch, serves to thwart the assertiveness of black women.

In "Is the Black Male Castrated?" Jean Carey Bond and Patricia Peery argue that the most puzzling and detrimental outcome of the Moynihan Report was how many blacks "swallowed his assumptions and conclusions hook, line, and sinker" (*The Black Woman* 114). Bond and Peery reveal the irony prevalent in the fact that while blacks were hell-bent on rejecting the constrictions of white definitions of black life, "many members of the avant-garde [were] still capable of being mesmerized by racist social scientific thought, which has utterly failed to produce in depth studies of that Afro-American social structure" (114). In a jocular attempt to perhaps answer the question raised in the title of Bond and Peery's article, Toni Cade Bambara critiques men and women who participate in the charade of male superiority and taunts any man who feels this way for being "obsessive about his balls" and therefore not sufficiently secure in his manhood (unmanly?) if he must resort to subjugating his mate. She retorts, "Of course there are any number of women around willing to walk ten paces back to give [the black man] the illusion of walking ten paces ahead. I happen to love my ole man and I would be loathe to patronize him in that way. But perhaps that is because I don't have to, for he is not obsessive about his balls" (*The Black Woman* 108).[14] Sister contributor Gwen Patton further laments that as a reaction to the rampant charges that they were emasculators, some black women allowed themselves to be subjugated by black men in order to promote "harmony" (143).

By demonstrating that blacks were being duped by people like Moyni-han because their behavior more aptly mimicked the white ideals they deplored rather than exemplified an African ideal, contributors to *The Black Woman* sought to decolonize the minds of their male readers and women of a similar mindset. The essays and poetry of Toni Cade Bam-bara, Frances Beale, Jean Carey Bond, Joanna Clark, Kay Lindsey, Gwen Patton, Patricia Peery, and Fran Sanders are not only blatant critiques of black men's acceptance of patriarchy, they offer clever rhetorical strategies and instructive models for combating sexist discourse and challenging depictions of black women as castrating matriarchs.

The first strategy used was to challenge the notion that feminism was counterrevolutionary by demonstrating that sexism was actually an anti–nation-building stance. In "Double Jeopardy," Beale writes:

> Those who are exerting their "manhood" by telling Black women to step back into a domestic, submissive role are assuming a counter-revolution-ary position. Black women likewise have been abused by the system and we must begin talking about the elimination of all kinds of oppression. If we are talking about building a strong nation, capable of throwing off the yoke of capitalist oppression, then we are talking about the total involve-ment of every man, woman, child, each with a highly developed political consciousness. (*The Black Woman* 93)

Here she offers a more inclusive vision of black nationalism than the one provided by Jones. Beale explains to black men that constructions of black masculinity that are predicated on black female subordination are counterrevolutionary because not only do they deplete the number of able-bodied warriors, they also prevent the possibility of creating a stronger black nation, one in which everyone is politically conscious.

The second method these women employ to challenge black men to curb misogynistic behavior is juxtaposing sexism as a complementary oppres-sion to racism. For instance, obliquely referencing the adage that a woman's role in revolutionary struggle is to birth more sons for the revolution, Kay Lindsey equates sexism with racism in a piece simply titled "Poem":

. . .

But now that the revolution needs numbers
Motherhood got a new position
Five steps behind manhood.
And I thought sittin' in the back of the bus went out with Martin Luther
    King. (*The Black Woman* 17)

On par with Lindsey, in "On the Issue of Roles" Bambara castigates black men who have experienced dehumanization "both personal and historical" and yet still "ignore the danger of having one half of our population regard the other with such condescension and perhaps fear that half finds it necessary to 'reclaim his manhood' by denying her her peoplehood" (*The Black Woman* 103). Bambara's suggestion that black men who think in such an archaic manner "fear" black women is analogous to charges that the subjugation of blacks is the direct manifestation of white fear. In this essay, Bambara uses this method of inversion more overtly when she recalls editing a black male student's paper titled "Reflections on Black Women" by replacing all markers of sex with racial signifiers so that when she read the paper aloud, all the sexist language was interpreted as racist language by her unsuspecting students. Although she reports that the author of the essay was outraged that his piece had been taken out of context and that the attendance in class dwindled after this experiment, Bambara mentions feeling vindicated: "But at least the point had been made: racism and chauvinism are anti-people. And a man cannot be politically correct and a chauvinist too" (*The Black Woman* 107).

Yet another tactic used by contributors to *The Black Woman* is to dispute pandemic claims that active female participation in the "Movement" is divisive because sexism is "a lot of honkey horseshit" (*The Black Woman* 102). Because the fear of black female activism mirrored black males' societal anxieties of female domination and the fear of being figuratively castrated, contributors to *The Black Woman* had to aggressively critique black male angst regarding the figure of the black matriarch as the archetype of female empowerment. For example, Frances Beale counters the stereotype of the black matriarch by explaining how capitalism not only exploits black people economically but also defines both manhood and femininity in ways that serve its own interest, often resulting in warped and spiritually debilitating perceptions of what makes someone a *real* man, such as monetary success, or a *real* woman, such as dependency and docility.

Of the feminine ideal presented to black women, Beale contends that "[t]hough we have been browbeaten with this white image, the reality of the degrading and dehumanizing jobs that were relegated to us quickly dissipated this mirage of womanhood" (*The Black Woman* 91). Yet even though several black men bore firsthand witness to the discrepancy between this ideal perception of womanhood and the actual realities of black female lives lived by their mothers and grandmothers, Beale laments that several men in the "Movement" were seduced by this conception: "[The black man] sees the system for what it really is for the most part, but where he rejects its values and mores on many issues, when it comes to women, he seems to take his guidelines from the pages of the *Ladies' Home Journal*" (92). Gwen Patton, in her article "Black People and the Victorian Ethos," concurs with Beale and contends that black male investment in patriarchy is synonymous with embracing the Victorian ethic. In so doing, Patton strategically equates the misogyny practiced by black men to an impulse stemming from a white cultural tradition. To cast misogyny as a *white* value, then, was astute on Patton's part because the fundamental rhetoric of the black aesthetic and black power movements revolved around deconstructing whiteness and reassessing its cultural import.

In "On the Issue of Roles," Bambara offers three alternatives to the Victorian ethic. The first alternative is to look at how masculinity and femininity are being redefined by black public figures. Bambara relates that she thought of manhood in terms of the figures of the pimp and the athlete until she was presented with masculine figures like Malcolm X and Muhammad Ali, who refused to be either a hustler or a "white man's pawn." Conversely, she remembers a time when women were thought of in terms of actresses—pretty and glamorous—until beauty was redefined and measured by the black woman's commitment to the "Struggle" in the example of Nina Simone, Abbey Lincoln, and Kathleen Cleaver.

In this essay, Bambara discusses the topic of "the black woman's role in revolution." As a way of answering the implied question, her second option calls for the creation of "androgynous" selves that would see commitment to black liberation as its primary mission: "Perhaps we need to let go of all notions of manhood and femininity and concentrate on Blackhood" (*The Black Woman* 103). Here Bambara insists that she is not asking that one deny one's sex, but that one "shifts" one's priority to developing a self that is not predicated on proscribed gender roles, but on one's dedication to the "Struggle." Like Beale, she argues for a more inclusive definition of the black revolutionary that lies in the rejection of rigid notions of femininity and masculinity that not only tend to be a barrier to achieving political consciousness, but a hindrance to "self-autonomy" or self-actualization. Bambara maintains that there is a symbiotic relationship between the "revolution of the self" and inciting revolutionary change: "you find your Self in destroying illusions, smashing myths . . . being responsible to some truth, to the struggle. That entails . . . cracking through the veneer of this sick society's definition of 'masculine' and 'feminine'" as well as the roles that such terms connote (108).

The last alternative, according to Bambara, is to utilize examples found in "pre-capitalist, non-white societies." Bambara's examples include

Iroquois women ("who had mobility, privileges, a voice in the governing of communities") and the Vietnamese men and women who were bonding together in the "common struggle to liberate their nation" (104). Her most potent example, however, is that of African women. Bambara writes:

> There is nothing to indicate that the African woman who ran the marketplace, who built dams, who engaged in international commerce and diplomacy, who sat on thrones, who donned armor to wage battle against the European invaders and the corrupt chieftains who engaged in the slave trade, who were consulted as equals in the affairs of state—nothing to indicate that they were turning their men into faggots, were victims of penis envy, or any such nonsense. (103)[15]

This example is important because it is a direct contradiction of Jones's and others' use of Africa as a model of correct (i.e., submissive) feminine behavior. Rather than African traditions that promote female subservience, Bambara offers examples of female enterprise, female leadership, and female participation in liberation struggles as African models of female empowerment that did not result in the subjugation of men in favor of women.

The final maneuver that contributors of *The Black Woman* employed against misogyny was aimed specifically at deconstructing the ever-present stereotype of the black matriarch, which later spiraled into the vilification of the so-called welfare mother. They provided testimonials (both by real and fictional women) of what life was really like for a woman running a household under the welfare system. For example, Joanna Clark's autobiographical essay "Motherhood" deals candidly with the problems she faced as a mother of two children and the wife of a man who was unable or unwilling to support his family. Clark's story demystifies the supposed glamour of the welfare queen. She states, "Anyone who can live on welfare should be courted by Wall Street. He is a financial genius. I paid $40 dollars a month in rent and received $69 every 15 days" (*The Black Woman* 65). Her experience dramatizes the institutionalized racism that black women face in the health care and welfare institutions. She reports that her wishes to breastfeed and not to circumcise her son were vehemently challenged by the hospital. When she wanted daycare assistance for her children, she was told to go on welfare. When poverty forced her to finally go on welfare, she was not able to obtain assistance to finish her college education. Once on welfare, she was also at the mercy of her husband's ego when he reported to her welfare counselor that he could support his family. But when she appealed to the court to force her husband to pay child support, she was only granted $15 dollars a week.

Patricia Hill Collins argues that the construction of the welfare mother is a counterpart to the mammy and the black matriarch in that all of these labels demonstrate a white patriarchal desire to control black women's fertility. The welfare mother is portrayed as "being content to sit around and collect welfare, shunning work and passing on her bad values to her offspring" (*Black Feminist Thought* 79). According to Collins, unlike the matriarch, the welfare mother is vilified for not being aggressive enough, and unlike the mammy she is castigated because she refuses to nurture white families and raise white children. Collins concludes that:

> Creating the controlling image of the welfare mother and stigmatizing her as the cause of her own poverty and that of African American communities shifts the angle of vision away from structural sources of poverty and blames the victims themselves. The image of the welfare mother thus provides ideological justification for the dominant group's interest in limiting the fertility of Black mothers who are seen as producing too many economically unproductive children. (80)

Sherley Anne Williams's "Tell Martha Not to Moan," published in *The Black Woman,* challenges the negative coding of black women on welfare as unfit mothers because of their laziness and unwillingness to instill the proper work ethic in their children. "Tell Martha Not to Moan" is told in the first person by Martha, a seventeen-year-old rural girl who is on welfare, is a high school dropout, and has one child while she is pregnant with another. Standing in stark contrast to the college-educated women found in Paule Marshall's "Reena," in many respects Martha is what white America both fears and expects from black womanhood. Originally written in 1968 in the wake of the black power movement, "Tell Martha Not to Moan" is a poignant tale about a woman who learns to embrace the adage that "black is beautiful," as well as one about gender politics in black male/female relationships. Most importantly, however, this story usurps traditional expectations of welfare mothers as lazy dependents of the state.

On the very first page the reader discovers that Time, Martha's lover and the father of her unborn child, has left her, presumably to return to the North. At first glance, this scenario reads like a cautionary tale warning young women to beware of smooth-talking musicians. Therefore, like Martha's mother, the reader is skeptical when Martha insists that Time will return. Through Martha's description of their relationship, it becomes evident that she loves Time because he is the first person to tell her that she is beautiful *because* she has a dark complexion. As a product of the changing times, he subjects her to a redefinition of beauty that places dark-complexioned women as the ideal. Moreover, by questioning Martha about her plans for the future Time subtly pushes Martha to become a more self-actualized person.

Though Time, her mother, and possibly even society believe that Martha lacks ambition, she is not unintelligent nor devoid of a political consciousness. She relays to Time and their friends how she "got over" on "the man." Martha tells them about an incident where she took money from a white man in exchange for sex, but then got out of the car in a black neighborhood without consummating the deed. The white man, given the location, was too fearful to make a scene. In this example, Martha demonstrates that she knows how to use prevailing assumptions about black female lasciviousness against white men without having to sexually compromise herself. It is more significant, however, that Martha also sees through the revolutionary persona that Time dons; he thinks of himself as better than the "squares" of Martha's hometown and as more evolved than Martha herself. Frustrated that Time and his friends continuously talk about "the man" and about leaving town for New York, Martha confronts him: "You ain't gon no damn New York City and it ain't the white man what gon keep you. You just using him for a scuse cause you scared. Maybe you just can't play" (54). Here Martha is suggesting that Time and his friends use their hatred (which can also be read as fear) of whites as a crutch that prevents them from accomplishing their stated goals.

Martha's accusations wound Time's ego so much that he slaps her. Although I don't believe that Williams wants us to read Time as an abusive man, she does, however, want us to see him as weak-willed. Time himself readily admits that "he is not what he is," that he has yet to reach his full potential. Williams also lets the ambiguity of how to interpret the slap reside in the reader's own level of consciousness. On the one hand, if one buys into the rhetoric that women should not talk back to men in this manner, that she deserved to be slapped, then Martha becomes the infamous emasculator described in the Moynihan Report. On the other hand, it is clear that there is truth in what Martha has charged. If Time is able to rise to the level to which he strives, then Martha is the type of woman he needs by his side.

I contend that Time is momentarily overwhelmed both by the realization that he is more vested in whiteness than he originally thought and that Martha is more astute than he originally imagined. The significance of the title, "Tell Martha Not to Moan," is twofold. One either interprets it as directing Martha to be strong—perhaps cautioning her not to become a blues song cliché, wasting her time pining away for a man. Or one can surmise that if Time is to become what "he is"—perhaps the fully conscious "androgynous" or "autonomous" self that *The Black Woman* editor, Toni Bambara, envisions—he must relinquish his investment in patriarchy. By the end of the story, like Martha, I have learned to have faith in Time.

As for *Essence* magazine's contributions to the debate surrounding the Moynihan Report, what is disheartening about *Essence*'s discussions of the black matriarch is that many of its contributors displayed tendencies like those described by Bond and Peery. For example, a poignant instance of a black woman's acquiescence to being labeled an emasculator can be found in *Essence*'s premiere issue. In an article titled "Black Man, Do You Love Me?" novelist Louise Meriwether at first appears to chastise men who are not able to deal with intelligent black women when she writes, "Brainy and logical, with a thirst for knowledge, I found myself a threat to your shaky manhood" (15). She quickly castigates herself, however, and other black women by extension, for her own emasculating tendencies:

> And how many times did I, in my insecurity, reject and flagellate you, Black brother? Your image was inferior to that of the white conqueror, whose looks and accomplishments were the standards by which all others were judged. I magnified your weakness, minimized your strength, stunted your growth. There are those who say I added to your psychological castration, my husband, my son. I will not dispute them, I stand accused. (15)

While on the surface Meriwether seems to be suggesting that both parties are at fault in black male/female relationships, it is significant that black women are not only assigned greater blame, but can obviously offer very little argument in their defense.

Manet Fowler's article "Heritage: The Sande Rituals," published in *Essence*'s premiere issue, is yet another example of how black women can sometimes perpetuate myths of black womanhood and thus become culpable in defaming more assertive black women. Credited as being the first black woman to receive a PhD in anthropology, Fowler uses her article to dispute charges of black female lasciviousness as stemming from African ancestral traditions:

> Of all the unhappy stereotypes that surround Black women, the first one that should be demolished is that we have received from our African

ancestors a tradition of unrestrained sexual passion. Quite the contrary, in Liberia, Nigeria and Sierra Leone on Africa's west coast for example, secret societies for both men *(Poro)* and women *(Sande)* have for centuries exercised more controls over the sexual customs of adolescents beyond those existing in our Protestant/Catholic/Jewish/Muslim cultures. (82)

What is highly problematic about this article is that Fowler casts the control of black female sexuality in these African cultures as being a positive thing. In her zest to exhibit that these traditions are more puritanical than the Protestant, Catholic, and other religious traditions she mentions, Fowler offers the examples of the Mende tradition of the dowry, the "Sande" rituals in Sierra Leone and Liberia (where, in three years time, a girl is to be "fully instructed in how to please her future husband sexually, and how to raise and bear children"), and the process of the clitoridectomy. She concludes by stating that in the tribes of Liberia and Sierra Leone where this operation is performed, "As a female citizen, she is also expected to be able to match her intelligence, ability, understanding and wisdom with that of her husband" (82). A pseudo-feminist statement at best, this comment stands alone in an article that offers an uncritical look at these African traditions. Fowler never reports that these traditions can be just as disabling, if not more so, to black women as stereotypes that code black women as oversexed.

It is also significant that Ida Lewis, the editor-in-chief, did not directly tackle the issue of black male misogyny more forcefully herself. For example, when Lewis had the opportunity to interview LeRoi Jones (Amiri Baraka) for the September 1970 issue of *Essence*, while she was more than capable of questioning his one-time marriage to a white woman, she neglected to challenge his views on women's liberation, although it seems abundantly clear that throughout her term as editor-in-chief Lewis was a staunch proponent of women's rights. Given that Jones had already divorced his Jewish wife, Hettie Cohen, and had publicly denounced their marriage, Lewis won a hollow victory. Lewis asked Jones, "With all this talk about Women's Liberation, how do you interpret the role of the black woman today?" Jones gave a watered-down version of what he had written earlier in the July 1970 issue of *Black World:*

Black women should be concerned with inspiring their men, educating their children, contributing to the social development of the black nation. The mother brings consciousness to the child in her body. The baby begins to learn there. The body does teach. Emotions teach before words. As black men and women, we have to work out how we can live in harmony and achieve this new nation that we have been talking about. But we should not confuse the roles. We have both suffered from slavery, oppression, and frustration at being unable to develop on our own capabilities. (25)

Once again the woman is relegated to the position of breeder and helpmate. It is also obvious that Jones does not see the contradictions implicit in his own words. While he stresses that both sexes, because of the stigma of being black, have known "frustration at being unable to develop on [their] own capabilities," he does not consider that the "roles" he relegates to women might also induce frustration. While Lewis briefly focuses on Jones's interracial marriage, perhaps to sensationalize a topic that *Essence*'s readers would be sensitive to, she does not challenge Jones on any of these points and instead moves on to another question.

It is actually a man who emerges as the most prominent voice when looking for complementary instances of someone "talking back" against negative stereotyping of black women as castrating matriarchs in *Essence* magazine. In his column "The Psychiatric Dimension," Alvin Poussaint, MD, should be granted the accolade of being a *black male feminist* predecessor to men like Michael Awkward and Mark Anthony Neal for his segment titled, "Black Women Are Doubly Subjugated." He writes, "Amidst the booming, anguished shouts for 'Black manhood,' the cries heard on behalf of 'Black womanhood' are often barely audible. Even during this period of the Black revolution, we are often so preoccupied with society's racist castration of the Black male that we all but forget the long-standing dehumanizing rape of the Black woman in America" (75). According to Poussaint, the dehumanization of black women on the part of both white America and black men has created "sociopsychological difficulties" that black women must constantly strive to overcome. Poussaint is not interested in deciphering whether or not these difficulties cause black women to live up to their negative stereotypes, but is instead concerned with how the perpetuation of these stereotypes and how not being of the "fair sex" (i.e., not being a white woman) is to the further detriment of black female psyches.

In 1965, Poussaint became the southern field director of the Medical Committee for Human Rights in Mississippi, where he helped to desegregate health care facilities across the South.[16] At the time of his column's publication, he was also an associate professor of psychiatry at Harvard Medical School. These credentials more than qualified Poussaint to contradict Moynihan's findings, which he construed as being instrumental in promulgating the myth that the black woman was responsible for her own bad press:

> What is important today is the attempt of the dominant society to persist
> in viewing Black women negatively. For example, the slave masters dis-
> rupted Black family life and forbade Black marriages. Now under the guise
> of 'social science,' whites attack Black women for being matriarchs, poor
> mothers, and unfeminine emasculators of their Black sons' manhood.
> You seldom hear praise of the Black woman's heroic role in the survival of
> Black people or the positive aspects of her adaptation to a racist society.
> Is it any wonder, then, that white men, white women, *and Black men* fre-
> quently tend to look down upon Black women and oppress them? (75)

Additionally, by arguing that sexism is just as dehumanizing as racism,
Poussaint employs a strategy similar the one applied by writers in *The
Black Women* to force men to examine their chauvinistic behavior. He
writes, "Black men often have a great sensitivity to 'castration' because
of their own insecurity as men. In very much the same twisted manner
of racists, it is necessary for the women to be 'inferior' in order for some
Black men to feel 'superior' or 'adequate.' It's hard to admit, but when you
hear a Black man call a Black woman an 'evil bitch' he sounds like a white
man calling a Black person a 'nigger'" (75).

Because Poussaint was an MD, his condemnation of the Moynihan
Report legitimated the perception of many black women that the report
was inherently racist and sexist. The decision to feature Poussaint in
Essence was an astute move on the part of the editors because it demonstrated that there were black men who would be willing to stand with
black women to combat sexist oppression. When Poussaint equates black
male sexism with white racism, as he does in the quotation above, he is
not only revealing that sexism is a function of an inferiority complex on
the part of black men, he is also insinuating that an antisexist approach
is crucial to black nationalist programs. In the section that follows, I provide a closer look at the attempts made by *The Black Woman* and *Essence*
to merge black nationalist impulses with feminist agendas.

BLACK NATIONALIST FEMINISM: AN OXYMORON OR
AN EMBLEM OF BLACK REVOLUTIONARY WOMANHOOD?

Far from finding feminism always liberating, many black women
wrote about their experiences in white feminist organizations in ways that
mirror the complaints black women had about serving in black nationalist organizations. Common to both organizations was the charge of
tokenism, the refusal to let black women operate in leadership positions.
Feeling stifled in their dialogues with their black male counterparts,

coupled with the racism they often encountered working within white feminist groups, and further multiplied by the fact that black womanhood was being publicly defined as "pathological" by perceived aficionados on the topic, several black women activists responded by creating their own organizations. Their frustration resulted in the 1973 founding of the National Black Feminist Organization in New York and of Black Women Organized for Action in San Francisco, as well as the 1974 founding of the Combahee River Collective in Boston. Black female activists also responded by writing books such as *Black Women's Liberation* by Maxine Williams and Pamela Newman, *The Black Woman: An Anthology* (both in 1970), and Angela Davis's autobiography, published in 1974. Additionally, anticipating that these tensions would create a yearning for commercial publications that centered around topics of interest to black women, the Hollingsworth Group founded the Essence Corporation in 1968 and launched *Essence* magazine in 1970.

According to the authors of "The Combahee River Collective Statement," the lack of specific attention given to black women also resulted in the creation of revolutionary ideologies that were more inclusive than those represented in either organization: "It was our experience and disillusionment within [black male and white female] liberation movements, as well as experience on the periphery of the white male left, that led to the need to develop a politics that was anti-racist, unlike those of white women, and anti-sexist, unlike those of Black and white men" (*Home Girls* 273). Madhu Dubey also argues that both the black nationalist and the women's liberation movements "at once catalyzed and constrained the formation of a feminist politics centering around the black woman" (*Black Women Novelists and the Nationalist Aesthetic* 15). Dubey explains that more black women were involved in activism during the 1970s than at any other time in U.S. history and that this involvement provided women with invaluable experience in political organization. Additionally, Dubey writes that

> although black nationalism was clearly dominant in the ideological mapping of black womanhood, it was by no means a tightly closed, self-sufficient system that precluded alternative ideological mappings. The internal gaps and contradictions of black nationalist discourse, especially visible in its construction of black womanhood, opened the space for an alternative black feminist definition of womanhood. (15)

Because black nationalist rhetoric has historically been interpreted as misogynist, the adherence to black nationalistic ideology by *The Black*

Woman and *Essence,* both women-centered publications, exhibits the complex rather than the monolithic character generally associated with the black aesthetic and black power movements. Furthermore, the adoption of black nationalism by both texts also widens our contemporary understanding of how feminism functions in the lives of black women.

While both *The Black Woman* and *Essence* offered a challenge to black chauvinistic nationalism, they also challenged white feminism by embracing the nationalistic rhetoric of the movement and its attentiveness to the plight of the black masses. Issues such as welfare and the related themes of motherhood and black health care were topics showcased in both publications as germane to lower-income women. Therefore, *The Black Woman* and the first year of *Essence* magazine serve as two examples of oppositional stances that placed black female issues in the center of their venues and offered black women another option—one that I loosely term "black nationalist feminism."

The definition of black nationalism I am using is best articulated by Wahneema Lubiano in her essay "Standing In for the State: Black Nationalism and 'Writing' the Black Subject." She writes:

> Black nationalism in its broadest sense is a sign, an analytic, describing a range of historically manifested ideas about black American possibilities that include any or all of the following: racial solidarity, cultural specificity, religious, economic, and political separatism (this last has been articulated both as a possibility within and outside of U.S. territorial boundaries). Black nationalism has most consistently registered opposition to the historical and ongoing racism of the U.S. state and its various institutions and apparatuses, and has been deployed to articulate strategies of resistance. (157)

According to Lubiano, a frequent complaint by black feminists concerning black nationalist ideology is that it "insufficiently breaks with patriarchal modes of economic, political, cultural (especially familial), and social circulations of power that mimic Euro-American modes and circulations" (157). Indeed, one finds some of the most vociferous critiques of black nationalist ideology in *The Black Woman,* and therefore it seems almost oxymoronic to coin the phrase "black nationalist feminism" to describe the ideologies of *The Black Woman,* or *Essence* magazine for that matter.

Farah Jasmine Griffin explains that in Toni Cade Bambara's introduction to *The Black Woman* she "situates the anthology at the nexus of two oppositional discourses—black nationalism and feminism—both of which were profoundly limited by their failure to acknowledge sexism and racism respectively" ("Conflict and Chorus" 117). *Essence* magazine, as would any other black female journal during the late 1960s and 1970s, had to negotiate these two discourses. Griffin reports that while *The Black Woman* does not fit with our contemporary understanding of black feminism, it nevertheless "paved the way for an emerging black feminism that came to flower in the late seventies and early eighties" (118). What Griffin sees missing in contemporary black feminism is the type of dialogue between black nationalist women and leftist black feminists that was possible in the pages of *The Black Woman* (of course, I see this also occurring in *Essence*). And although Griffin admits that scholars like Deborah Grey White and Paula Giddings have "argued convincingly that black nationalism and black feminism have historically been 'like oil and water,'" she believes that as a consequence of the belief in the incompatibility of these two discourses, black women scholars have forfeited the ability to impact the lives of a large number of black women who reside outside the academy (123).

I envision both publications, as black nationalist texts, as serving in the same capacity as the proverbial "Speaker's Corner" found in black communities nationwide, but with the revolutionary diva acting as the street-corner proselytizer. Toni Cade Bambara posits Speaker's Corners as permeable sites in which blacks are able to dialogue with each other about both local and international issues and determine the relevancy of those issues to the black community, thereby creating a decolonized space where blacks feel central and not marginal to the larger world. Bambara further states, "I do not think a community is viable without a Speaker's Corner. If we can't hear Black people speak, we become captive to the media, and we disacknowledge [*sic*] Blackspeak. Our ears are no longer attuned to any kind of sensible talk" (*Deep Sightings* 214). A Speaker's Corner, then, serves as a sort of filter through which news of the nation and abroad gets sifted for truth and relevance, and disseminated to the black community. Without this filter, "Blackspeak," folk wisdom, porch or armchair philosophizing, street knowledge, not to mention African-based philosophies or other philosophies that are deemed pertinent to black people, are not considered credible. Without Speaker's Corners, black people would be perpetually subject to the definitions and whims of the dominant culture.

Both *The Black Woman* and *Essence* can be considered to be black nationalist feminist (or, as some might prefer, womanist) renditions of the "Speaker's Corner" in that both actively strive to demonstrate the relevancy of world affairs to the lives of all black women. For example, in *The Black Woman*, in a partial review of the film *The Battle of Algiers,*

Francee Covington speculates on the feasibility of using strategies from the film to organize people in Harlem, and in "Poor Black Women's Study Papers by Poor Black Women of Mount Vernon, New York," Pat Robinson includes as an antiwar statement a letter written by a black woman in 1968 to a North Vietnamese "sister" in which she sympathizes with North Vietnam. I envision *Essence* as a black nationalistic vehicle because in their attempt to cultivate a black audience, the editors and publishers of *Essence* fundamentally sought to "saturate" its audience in "blackness."[17] For example, in addition to articles relevant to black women, the bulk of the advertising for the first issue depicts black women or advertises products designed for black women's uses. Even the horoscope segment depicts cartoon renditions of black women with natural hairstyles heading each of the twelve signs of the zodiac, and the travel section featured the Bahamas as an ideal vacation spot for its African American readers. Sparing no expense, the first issue also included well-known black writers Clarence Major, Nikki Giovanni, and Toni Cade Bambara to write book reviews, and it commissioned Roy Ayers[18] to write a music review.

Of *Essence,* Noliwe M. Rooks explains that

> The magazine positioned African American female readers within a 1970s Black nationalist rhetoric and discourse that drew upon varying aspects of their identity. *They rejected feminism.* They were warriors, at the forefront of political struggles for racial advancement. They were strong women who stood by their men. They were queens unable to understand why their kings slept with and married white women. They were women who were Black, and race mattered greatly to them. *They did not wish to embrace dominant constructions of femininity."* (*Ladies' Pages* 144, emphasis mine)

But whereas *The Black Woman* was fairly clear in its desire to galvanize women and men around a less patriarchal brand of black nationalism than what was currently in vogue, *Essence*'s aspirations for politicizing its audience were a bit more opaque. With this thought in mind, and given Griffin's thorough analysis of how black nationalism functions within *The Black Woman,* in this section I deal more specifically with *Essence*'s approach to feminism.

Given the plethora of black women's (and men's) voices that found their way into *Essence* in the first year alone, Rooks's essentialist characterization of its contributors as "strong women" and "queens" and her generalization that they "rejected feminism" warrants questioning. In *Essence*'s first year in circulation, the relevancy of the feminist movement to black women was actually a highly debated topic. That Ida Lewis, *Essence*'s first editor-in-chief, questioned both LeRoi Jones (Amiri Baraka) and Myrlie B. Evers[19] about their views on feminism attests to her interest in the topic. While I discussed Jones's remarks in detail earlier, Evers expresses ambivalence and a bit of disdain toward the feminist movement. She indirectly codes "women's lib" as individualistic and selfish, while "the black woman has always been busy working for equality for her people, not just for herself" (November 1970, 27). For Evers, and perhaps for many other black women, racist oppression trumps sexist oppression, and even though the things she lists make white feminist concerns seem trivial to the plight of black women, they show the intersectionality of class, race, and sex that the majority of black women face: "[The black woman] must be able to get a job before she worries about whether or not she has pay equal to a man's. My main concern is trying to provide food, clothing, and a decent education for my children rather than worry about whether there are going to be lenient abortion laws" (27). Lewis counters in favor of feminism: "Of course, being a woman in this society can be a handicap, just like being black." Evers replies, "Yes, you are right. But it is only recently that I have really begun to think about sex discrimination" (27). Ironically, she gives an example of being excluded from a New York restaurant because she was a woman, rather than reflecting on how being a woman affected her experiences in the political arena.

The inclusion of articles like "Five Shades of Militancy," by Gilbert Moore (May 1970), "Do Black Women Need the Women's Lib?" by Madelyn Conley (August 1970) and "Birth Control and the Black Woman," by Kay Lindsey (October 1970) serve to further contradict Rooks's statement. "Five Shades of Militancy," written by Gilbert Moore and photographed by Gordon Parks and Gordon Parks, Jr., is an excellent example of what I see as the magazine's attempt to illustrate black nationalist feminism. In this article, Moore attempts to rescue the term "militancy" from its rampant misuse. According to Moore, "the word is supposed to mean 'aggressively active,' and engaged in warfare" (16). The article featured Rosa Parks, Kathleen Cleaver, Barbara Ann Teer, Shirley Chisholm, and women of the Nation of Islam. Moore explains that while the women are all different, "they are bound together—by race, by sex, by impatience, by the simple/complex proposition that Black people shall have dignity in America, in the world" (16). Rather than buy into the usual divisiveness that would pit Martin Luther King against Malcolm X, Moore gets Rosa Parks to admit that she can understand why black youths were moving away from nonviolence. He also explains that while Kathleen Cleaver might not approve of Shirley Chisholm, Moore concedes that blacks might need someone "operating from within." And although he graciously classifies Parks as a "southern lady," Moore does not seem to believe that femininity should be considered antithetical to militancy. At the same moment that he takes note of Teer's blunt way of speaking, he does not castigate her for speaking in a manner unbefitting a lady, but instead he insists that she epitomizes the tone and tenor of "militancy"— although Teer herself expresses disdain for the term.

While she is clear to point out the general aversion many black women have to feminism, the writing strategies that Madelyn Conley employs throughout her article "Do Black Women Need the Women's Lib?" demonstrate her desire to persuade black women of feminism's relevancy to their experiences. For example, she gives a brief history of the women's movement and "draws parallels between Women's Liberation and black civil rights" (30). Conley chooses Nikki Giovanni, Florynce Kennedy, Novella Nelson, Eleanor Norton, and Barbara Ann Teer[20] as representational voices to answer the several questions the article poses about black women and their connection to the women's liberation movement: "Is the Women's Lib Movement relevant to the black female? Do black and white women have common personal and social problems? Have we the same priorities? What benefits might we gain from their program? (30).

While Kennedy begins the discussion by declaring that women's liberation is for everyone and by suggesting that women unite to effect change and "break down . . . institutionalized oppression" in the consumer industry, Conley is careful to outline the different priorities of and approaches to feminism that black women have when contrasted to white women (31). She relates six points that highlight the intersectionality of race, gender, and class for black women that differentiates their experiences from that of middle-class white women. First, Conley makes a case for Alice Walker's later formulation of womanism. She writes, "Our priorities and differences are shaped by our relationship to this society as well as to our men and families" (31). Second, Conley explains that given slavery's legacy of rape, black women mean something different by "sexual exploitation" than do white women. Third, the history of black women in the workplace differs from that of white women; black women have always worked outside of the home while white women were just beginning to seek economic equality in the workplace. Fourth, she argues that black women's relationships to their male counterparts are also different; black women seek "reconciliation with Black men, while White women are seeking equalization and isolation" (33). Fifth, in that reconciliation is also the desire to fight for black liberation beside black men, rather than walking behind them. Finally, Conley explains that black and white women differ in their ideas of child rearing: "we seek to strengthen the black family. White women seek the demolition of family" (33). Furthermore, she advocates "tribal living"—or the collective responsibility of all blacks for black children—rather than an adoption of white American values.

Nevertheless, Conley insists upon black women learning valuable lessons from the women's liberation movement. Rather than admiring rich and middle-class white women and their leisurely lifestyles, she insists that the emergence of women's lib signals that "life in suburbia perched on a pedestal is not utopia" (33). According the Conley, black women should also understand that the political gains afforded to white women will also be afforded to black women. For Conley, the movement should also reveal to black women that they are not as active as they should be in fighting for interests and concerns relevant to their lives. Conley ends the article by explaining how ordinary black women—women not engaged in political activism—can get involved with both the black and women's liberation movements by doing volunteer work or even donating money to an organization that they would otherwise spend on a revolutionary hairstyle, for example.

The inclusion of Kay Lindsey's article on birth control in the October 1970 issue should be seen as yet another attempt by *Essence*'s editors to interest black women in feminist issues. The central question on which the article was based ("Is [The Pill] Self-Preservation or Genocide?") accurately summed up the dilemma black women faced regarding family planning. From 1966 to 1969, black Pittsburghers Dr. Charles Greenlee and William "Bouie" Haden joined forces with Charles Owen Rice (a white Catholic priest) to lead a campaign against birth control.[21] In 1967 the Pittsburgh branch of the NAACP issued a public statement that Planned Parenthood used birth control to contain birth rates in low-income rural and urban communities.[22] Lindsey opens her articles by referencing the incident in which the aforementioned black Pittsburgh men closed a family planning center on the grounds of black genocide, "only to have it reopened by the women in the community which it served." She quotes one black woman as saying, "they're men, they can't speak for women . . . birth control is none of their business" (56).

Lindsey explains that the issue of birth control has become a divisive issue within the black community, not only because black women are assuming more control over when and if they should become pregnant, but because "black men have become hypersensitive to the political implications of an ever-growing black population" (56). When she gives a history of forced sterilization of U.S. minority and Third World populations, the fear that has prompted the alleged "hypersensitivity" among black men seems more than warranted. It is significant that Lindsey, who also was a contributor to *The Black Woman,* was chosen to write this article. The choice to have Lindsey, a black woman who advocated for the use of the pill, write the article signals *Essence*'s attempt to separate the issue of forced sterilization from a woman's right to choose.[23] Lindsey also offers scathing critiques of Dr. Jerome S. Holland, "former president of Hampton Institute . . . and now U.S. Ambassador to Sweden," who was elected chairman of Planned Parenthood–World Population (PPWP) in 1968. Lindsey finds fault with Holland's appointment because PPWP had recently "approved a policy recognizing abortion and sterilization as proper medical procedures" (70). Another black man to come under her fire was Dr. John L. S. Hollomon, who had been recently elected to the board of the Association for Voluntary Sterilization. Lindsey ends her article by urging blacks not to let these issues divide them.

Ida Lewis's own editorial column, "Perspective," introduced in the premiere issue, offers the most pertinent example of *Essence*'s employment of black nationalist discourse—particularly given her position as the public face of *Essence* magazine. Lewis offered readers a program for decolonization that utilized black power (economic and social independence and equality) and the elevation of black self-esteem as the preferred method of social uplift. With her first editorial, "Black Is the Pursuit of Excellence," Lewis not only seeks to define "*The Essence* Woman," but to explain the extent to which *Essence* is relevant to the "Black struggle." Lewis understood that a lifestyle magazine for black women in the 1970s had to be concerned with more than just fashion and entertainment—it essentially meant adopting a revolutionary stance in order to assist black women with the issues that they potentially would face on a daily basis. Lewis explains that blacks should have learned the value of action over "loud emotional rhetoric" as one of the principal lessons of the 1960s. She writes, "It is not always those with the loudest voices who can get the job done. It is not always those who must shout Black is Beautiful who believe it or live it" (June 1970, 13). Lewis insists that, in lieu of grandiose slogans, blacks work to pursue real power by way of achieving social and economic equality. She also cautions that "opportunity brings with it the burdens and responsibilities of competition" (13).

In conjunction with her belief that blacks must prepare to be adept business competitors, Lewis also insists that blacks eschew the notion of complete victimization by the white power structure. In the August 1970 editorial, Lewis uses her column to launch a three-part series on drug abuse in the black community. Rather than believe blacks to be defenseless prey to the drug epidemic, she asks her readers, "Can it be that we are as helpless as we appear to be in dealing effectively with the drug problem?" (19). By way of an answer, Lewis suggests the use of black power (read in this instance as community activism) to make neighborhoods "unsafe" for drug pushers. Additionally, she urges parents to take a more aggressive stance against drug abuse by watching their children more closely and involving them in after-school or community programs.

In the September 1970 installment of "Perspective," Lewis uses her column to celebrate the June 1970 election of Kenneth Gibson[24] as mayor of Newark, New Jersey. For Lewis, Gibson's election serves as a concrete example of black nationalist politics at work. She asks her readers to reflect on what his election means in terms of black power. Lewis writes that "we must delight in the death of political inertia [in Newark]. The emergence of what LeRoi Jones calls the people's movement heralds the discovery of new springs of life in the black community"(19).[25] Lewis sees Gibson's victory as an example of what black people can do when they unite to back a political candidate. Although she does not mention black nationalism directly, given her comment about Jones and her own undisguised elation at Gibson's appointment, she is definitely in favor of it.

While this section has dealt with the intersections of feminism and nationalism in these publications, what most piques my interest about the escalation of black feminist or women-centered organizations and publications during the 1970s is who they saw as their intended audience. Given their ties to both the black power and feminist movements, with whom did they hold a greater allegiance? Were black men welcomed as audience members? What about white women, or white men for that matter? Was their primary goal to speak to like-minded women who would be more open to black nationalist and feminist ideologies, or to convince ordinary women that raising their racial and feminist consciousness would greatly improve the quality of their lives as black women? If we assume that their aim was to solicit both types of women for inclusion, how were they able to indoctrinate the less politically savvy constituents without boring the converted? In the next section, not only do I attempt to answer these questions, I begin by arguing that *The Black Woman* and *Essence* evaded the latter problem by delineating outright the characteristics that their readers should embody. In the case of *The Black Woman*, in order to demonstrate that the politically minded black woman was potentially every black woman, its editor sought to be as inclusive as possible in its audience selection. Conversely, *Essence* laid out a certain standard for its readership; by setting in place an ideal that was both provocative and in accordance with more customary moral rhetoric on black womanhood, *Essence* encouraged its potential readers to aspire to be the ideal that the magazine described.

THE UNVEILING OF THE MYSTERY WOMAN: AUDIENCE CULTIVATION IN *THE BLACK WOMAN* AND *ESSENCE*

Who Is The Black Woman?
    She is a college graduate. A drop-out. A student. A *wife*. A divorcée. A *mother*. A lover. A *child of the ghetto*. A product of the bourgeoisie. A *professional writer*. A person who never dreamed of publication. A *solitary individual*. A member of the Movement. A *gentle humanist*. A violent revolutionary. *She is angry and tender, loving and hating. She is all these things—and more. And she is represented in a collection that for the first time truly lets her bare her soul and speak her mind.*
                        —EPIGRAPH TO *THE BLACK WOMAN*[26]

The ESSENCE woman? Who is she? I imagine her as an unpolished diamond, virtually unaware of her beauty; a possessor of hidden talents and smothered desires. She is a knowledge-seeker, the inheritor of the 300-year quest which is yet to result in acceptance and self-realization. We at ESSENCE hope to provide the proper setting in which she can blossom and come into her own.
            —IDA LEWIS, "BLACK IS THE PURSUIT OF EXCELLENCE"[27]

The two epigraphs that open this section seek not only to define black womanhood at the historical juncture of the 1970s, but to delineate each publication's desired constituency. The epigraph from *The Black Woman* attempts to unveil the identity of the mysterious black woman. Alternating between regular typeface and italics, the first epigraph strives to encompass all black women by systematically demolishing the binaries that routinely divide women along class lines, educational status, and ideologies, divisions that often block any opportunity for intraracial solidarity.[28] In terms of class, the anthology includes stories about college-educated black women ("Reena") and poor black women ("Tell Martha Not to Moan"). Within the text, regional differences between black women are also assuaged; this inclusiveness incorporates rural blacks as well as women from the cities.[29] This maneuver is of particular importance because it broadens the parameters of "the black masses" typically conceived of by many black aestheticians as pertaining only to blacks living in northern cities. *The Black Woman* also widens its arc of concern to include women in Africa and its Diaspora, as well as other people of color.[30]

The last line of the first epigraph demonstrates that *The Black Woman* saw itself as not only giving voice to black women who had heretofore been repressed, but it also envisioned itself as the voice of black women. It is significant that the three short stories included in the anthology are told in the first person, which further exhibits Bambara's desire to let black women speak for themselves. Additionally, Bambara saw *The Black Woman* as a space for showcasing the voices of radical and "Movement" women. In the preface to *The Black Woman*, Bambara confesses that the anthology grew out of a sense of impatience:

> an impatience with the all too few and too soon defunct Afro-American women's magazines that were rarely seen outside of the immediate circle of staff's and contributor's friends. It grew out of an impatience with the half-hearted go-along attempts of Black women caught up in the white women's liberation groups around the country. Especially out of an impatience with all the "experts" zealously hustling us folks for their doctoral theses or government appointments. And out of an impatience with the fact that in the whole bibliography of feminist literature, literature immediately and directly relevant to us wouldn't fill a page. (10–11)

Later in her posthumously published collection of fiction and essays, *Deep Sightings and Rescue Missions* (1996), Bambara explains that she decided to launch the anthology because she knew that black women's voices were not being heard and because she wanted to prove that there was a place for black women in the publishing arena. Frances S. Foster contends that Toni Cade Bambara's anthology was not just about black women's self-definition; that Penguin Books decided to publish the text attested to the increasing influence of black women in U.S. society ("Changing Concepts of the Black Woman" 435). *The Black Woman* was so popular that it went into a new edition in its second month (*Deep Sightings* 230).

In slight contrast, *Essence* magazine was spawned as a reaction to the dearth of positive black female images found in mainstream media publications. That the circulation of the magazine rose to over 100,000 by its anniversary issue in May 1971 was a testament to the magazine's popularity.[31] The original publishers, Jonathan Blount, Cecil Hollingsworth, Edward Lewis, and Clarence Smith (the Hollingsworth Group), saw 1970 as a pivotal moment in which the identity of African American women was in flux, having been influenced by both black power and feminist discourses. Exposed to a redefinition of both blackness and femininity, the group understood that black women were looking for publications that more directly spoke to their specific concerns.

Traci Spencer reports that the Hollingsworth Group sought to create a bond with their black female readers with its first issue. In their publisher's statement, the Hollingsworth Group addresses head-on the black female audience that they seek to cultivate. The voice the editors affect in this statement can be likened to that of a concerned friend, and it exhibits their desire to act as a mouthpiece and forum through which black women could air their vexations:

> With the swelling wave of Black consciousness around the world, you, the Black woman, are at long last coming into your own. The impassioned cry "Black is Beautiful" lifts you up for the first time onto a pedestal and into the spotlight of ESSENCE magazine—the magazine that will speak in your name and in your voice.
>
> You, the Black woman in America, are wrestling with your own identity and undergoing a process of change. No matter where you are in this process of change, you have expressed a need for information, inspiration, understanding, and guidance. Answering this need, ESSENCE will include the most significant developments in public affairs, education, entertainment, and the arts as they relate to our Black community, as well as fiction, poetry, and features on Black heritage, travel and careers. It will talk to you about your personal problems with your men, your children, your emotional and physical well-being. It will help you toward fulfillment in every aspect of your life. (*Essence,* May 1970, 13)

As evidenced by the letters to the editor, many black women did in fact feel that *Essence* positively represented them as black women and filled a gap that mainstream women's magazines had yet to fulfill. For example, Esther J. Carter of Philadelphia writes, "Thank you for bringing me, 'the unknown black woman' alive. For years, I subscribed to all the so-called women's magazines. . . . Then it finally dawned on me that they didn't have me in mind. . . . The one or two black models every two or three months were thrown in as palliatives" (July 1970, 6). However, the controversy that ensued prior to the publication of the first issue debated whether the relationship between *Essence* and its female readers was symbiotic or just another way to exploit black women desperate to see themselves reflected in mainstream media.

Abby Arthur Johnson and Ronald Maberry Johnson report that *Essence* magazine initially came under fire because of three main points: (1) the ownership was suspect, for while the Hollingsworth

Group consisted of four black businessmen, they also had white financial backing,[32] (2) Gordon Parks, editorial director of *Essence* from 1970 to 1973, was labeled a "cultural renegade" by Askia Muhammad Touré, who charged, "Mister Gordon Parks is alleged to have remarked that 'Black people have no culture.' . . . There is no 'Black point of view.' . . . There are no good Black illustrators or photographers . . . We're not interested in 'color'; we're interested in quality"[33] and (3) the magazine had an integrated staff (*Propaganda and Aesthetics* 168). The fears about *Essence* seemed to come to a head in 1971 when partial ownership of *Essence* was granted to *Playboy*. This partnership caused Jonathan Blount to resign from the Hollingsworth Group and Ida Lewis to quit her position as editor-in-chief. To answer charges that *Playboy* had "seized control of ESSENCE" and that its acquisition signaled a "new philosophy of chauvinism" within *Essence*'s pages, the group published "ESSENCE, The Real Story" in its August 1971 edition. In this piece the group declared, "As for those of our readers who await the appearance in these pages of ESSENCE Playmates and black women in cottontails—you wait in vain" (31).

Noliwe M. Rooks writes that early African American women's periodicals, like African American presses in general, were "tightly tied to a tradition of political protest and political organization" (*Ladies' Pages* 8). But the mode of protest in African American women's periodicals revolved around recouping the image of black women as "ladies": "For African American women, slavery, sexual abuse, and the defense of their character and morals in the face of dominant, as well as African American, male sentiments formed the nineteenth- and early-twentieth-century political basis for the magazines they published" (*Ladies' Pages* 8). It is no wonder, then, that readers were leery of *Essence*'s association with *Playboy*. Like earlier lifestyle magazines for black women, *Essence* set upon the task of presenting an exemplar model of black womanhood during an overtly political and volatile era—one in which the image of the black woman still found itself under siege in much the same way as that of her maternal ancestors. *Essence*'s method of social uplift, though, would be predicated on the tenets of black nationalism rather than on demonstrating the morality of black women in order to gain acceptance into the white mainstream. Initially, *Essence* straddled the fence between bourgeois materialism and various concepts of black militancy—all of which called for a divestment of material wealth for individual gain. By embracing black nationalist discourse, the editors were able to have it both ways by sending the underlying message that blacks acquiring wealth was indeed revolutionary.

Although couched in black bourgeois language reminiscent of earlier rhetoric concerning social uplift for black women, as I demonstrated in the previous section, Ida Lewis's model for ideal black womanhood was founded on black nationalist and black power principles. Using the second epigraph as an example, Lewis began the premiere issue of *Essence* by asking the identity of "The *Essence* Woman." While her question seems similar to the one posed in the first epigraph, the moniker "The *Essence* Woman" rather than "The Black Woman" suggests that *Essence* seeks a more selective demographic for its audience. When Lewis writes that she visualizes the *Essence* Woman as an "unpolished diamond" (language that echoes that of historically black female colleges), she sought to mold the *Essence* reader, fashioning her in the image of the *Essence* Woman. Rooks explains that "[i]n the twentieth century, fashion itself came to represent a dividing line between groups of African American women: northern versus southern, rural versus urban, educated versus illiterate, homeowners versus renters, migrants versus long-term residents" (23). Recognizing that a fashion magazine by definition is predicated on such divisions and that black nationalist rhetoric of the 1960s and 1970s focused on the working class, Lewis employed the rhetoric of social uplift used by historically black women's colleges that focused on shaping female students into the ideal embodiments of the colleges' values. Readers of the early *Essence,* then, were diamonds in the rough that, with the magazine providing "the proper setting," Lewis intended to shape into the ideal models of black womanhood. She sought women who desired to be affluent while maintaining a sense of social responsibility. Lewis envisioned her newly acquired readers as real go-getters on a "quest" for either "acceptance" or "self-realization," although she never proposed which might be the better path.[34]

While Lewis set up the parameters of the ideal *Essence* Woman, readers were also encouraged to critique her choice of topics. In the August 1971 issue, the publishers declared, "The principal teachers have been you, our readers. You have taught us with your letters, your telegrams, and telephone calls—telling us when we 'did it right,' telling us when we messed up. Out of this exchange has come a product which we trust reflects your interests" (30). This reciprocal relationship between the editorial staff and the audience not only demonstrates *Essence*'s sense of social responsibility, but it also alludes to the debates that ensued between black women around various topics that the magazine addressed.

Essence's sense of democracy also extended itself at times to white women, white men, and black men. While the inclusion of multiple and seemingly contradictory voices might make *Essence* appear objective, a closer analysis of the articles that dealt with miscegenation or which race (black or white) possessed the most alluring (i.e., feminine) women reveals that *Essence* sometimes exploited the anxieties of its black female constituency by merely reversing the traditional beauty hierarchy and essentializing black women as the ideal.

For example, novelist Rosemary Santini serves as a native informant when she reveals to *Essence* readers the innermost thoughts of white women on the subject of dating black men in her article "Black Man: White Woman." Perhaps given the tenor of the article "Black Man, Do You Love Me?" that Louise Meriwether published in the premiere issue, it is not surprising that Santini begins with the conclusion that interracial relationships between black men and white women *do not work*. Santini explains that all but one of the more than twenty-four women she interviewed had ended their relationships with black men they had dated either casually or seriously. But of the women interviewed, only five are actually represented in the article itself. As if to answer the question about the type of white woman who would date black men, or perhaps to destroy the negative stereotypes associated with such women, Santini details their level of attractiveness and describes each of their upbringings, which vary between bohemian to WASP. The commonality shared between the women, according to Santini, is their disillusionment with mainstream white society. Additionally, she explains that "in their several ways, [the white women interviewed] may have been using black men to resolve their emotional crises" (July 1970, 64). Although Santini obviously views herself as objective, both the white women and the black men they have dated are characterized in extremely neurotic terms. And while Santini acknowledges that there are probably interracial relationships between black men and white women that are based on love and mutual respect, these relationships are conspicuously absent from the article.

Santini's alleged objectivity comes into further question when dealing with Sally, a model who has chosen to marry a black man. She admits she is puzzled by Sally's decision and she questions Sally's motives:

This essentially superficial girl—she notices your clothes, your handbag, your hair, your life-style—is nonetheless willing to commit herself to a man who does not make things easy for her. Her security comes from the things that money and position can buy, yet she plans a marriage that she knows society will condemn. Is she showing off a beautiful black man as she would a beautiful black jewel? (64)

While Sally admits that the sex with her fiancé, Jack, is wonderful (I am sure black readers would have bristled at this well-worn cliché about black men's sexuality) and confesses that they argue a great deal about racial issues, Santini's attempt to cast Sally as purely materialistic falls short. Sally says she's willing to weather the storm with Jack because "[h]e wants me to be a complete person. He is now in the theater and is constantly pushing me into different kinds of things that I never would have thought of doing. . . . [He even] convinced [my family] that I should be an actress. I don't know how he did it. He is the only person who has successfully moved them in any way" (13 and 64). Based on her observations of Penny, another interviewee (that she has not dated a black man since she learned to think of herself as "an entire person rather an accessory"), it is possible that Santini either ignores or rejects the fact that Jack seems supportive of Sally. When one considers Santini's possibly tainted observations and the prevalence of what she calls "black is beautiful" rhetoric, it is not surprising that she predicts that relationships between black men and white women are on the decline.

Given that in 2005 it was reported that at least 29 percent of *Essence*'s subscribers were men, it is not surprising that black men both served as contributors to the magazine and were considered part of *Essence*'s audience from the beginning. But it might surprise many to know that white men—those who valued black women—were also welcomed as a part of *Essence*'s constituency. In the September 1970 issue of *Essence,* in the column "Men on Women," Walter D. Glaser explains why he likes black women. Reminiscent of the type of white authority found in slave narratives, no credentials are offered from Glaser; he is allowed to publish his editorial because of the very fact of his whiteness. Glaser, however, gives his own rationale for why he should be granted an audience with *Essence* readers:

> I have made love to several dozen black women, after having made love
> to several dozen white women; I was married to a black woman for eight
> good years, after two shorter marriages to white women; I have raised
> white children and black children; I have come all the way from a white
> childhood in Nazi Germany to now, wearing with pride my red-black-
> and-green button wherever I go—having turned from a mere nigger lover
> into a nigger somewhere along the road; I have seen black women from a
> white perspective and from a black perspective, and with these credentials
> I say: There is nothing on earth like a black woman. (72)

We are left to wonder whether Glaser should be considered white at all; having slept with black women and having raised black children, by osmosis he has, by his own admission, "turned from mere nigger lover into a nigger somewhere along the road."

It is clear that the editors chose to ignore the romantic racialism implicit in Glaser's words because his essentialist veneration of black women fit with many of the prevailing essentialist notions that black women held of themselves or wanted to hear about themselves: that black women know "more about life," are more "sensual" than white women, and "the darker the more beautiful." Glaser, however, makes an unconvincing distinction between his then current views of black women and his exoticism of black women from his "white days": "my main fascination with black women was of course their being different: exotic, mysterious. (And I admit that occasionally I still get an extra sexual thrill from seeing my light skin against dark skin)" (72). Glaser ends his editorial by professing his love of black people and his commitment to black liberation—thus subtly reinforcing *Essence*'s insistence on black nationalist discourse, even if it is delivered by a white man.

Throughout its existence, *Essence* has either overtly or covertly embraced black nationalism. I say "covertly" because even Susan Taylor's contemporary espousal of spiritual uplift has more than faint traces of nationalism. The question for today's readers is if, as many believe, we are currently living in a postracial nation, what is to become of magazines like *Essence* and anthologies like *The Black Woman*? Have both passed their usefulness? Traci Spencer speculates on the future trajectory of *Essence* in a Spring 2002 online article titled "Midlife Crisis: Is *Essence* Losing its Essence?"[35] Her article features an illustration of a fictitious *Essence* magazine cover which depicts an attractive but serious-looking black woman of undeterminable age, wearing coiffured dreadlocks—the updated natural replacing the Afro that donned most of the cover models in *Essence*'s first year. The face of the woman gracing the cover is literally being erased by a white hand. Such an image not only symbolizes the erasing of the black essence of the magazine, but also calls into question the magazine's necessity, given that 49 percent of Essence Communications Partners was acquired by Time Inc. in 2000.[36] Time Inc. acquired the remaining 51 percent in January 2005.

The crucial question that Spencer raises is whether or not *Essence* continues to be relevant to black female audiences. According to Spencer, *Essence* has been criticized for not offering enough articles pertinent to younger women and is consequently facing competition from other magazines such as *Heart and Soul, Honey,* and *O* (Oprah Winfrey's magazine).[37] To the ever growing list of magazines marketed to black female consumers, I would add *Jolie, Today's Black Woman,* and *Vibe Vixen*.[38] Because of the Essence Communications Partners' decision to sell its remaining shares to Time Inc.,[39] Noliwe M. Rooks casts doubts about *Essence*'s long-standing reign as an African American women's magazine. This later point should, therefore, be added to Spencer's list of components that make *Essence*'s relevancy questionable because such a move effectively ends *Essence*'s existence as a black-owned magazine.

As I am sure several feminist scholars would attest, *The Black Woman* was the predecessor to several black feminist and women of color anthologies, such as *But Some of Us Are Brave* and *This Bridge Called My Back*. The new millennium, however, has yet to produce a similar wave of anthologies that feature the writings of postsegregationist women of color or black feminists. Notable exceptions would be *When Chickenheads Come Home to Roost: My Life as a Hip Hop Feminist* (1999), *Colonize This!: Young Women of Color on Today's Feminism* (2002), and *Black and Brown Waves: The Cultural Politics of Young Women of Color and Feminism* (2009). Joan Morgan's book *When Chickenheads Come Home to Roost* situates hip-hop as the defining cultural marker of contemporary black feminism. Not surprisingly, anthologized essays concerning black women follow her lead and rarely place the feminist practices of black women in Generations X or Y outside the context of hip-hop. Additionally, the discussions of female participation in hip-hop culture are similar to those that occurred in the 1960s regarding female participation in black liberation movements: what is a woman's place in hip-hop? More specifically, it seems that what is at stake in both instances is that black women want access to (or recognition of female participation in) movements that seek to empower or politicize blacks. What is missing from discussions between postsegregationist black women, however, is any rigorous discussion of the interconnectedness between gender, race, and class as it pertains to black women; in this regard, *The Black Woman* has yet to find its equal in more contemporary literary marketplaces.

While I ultimately believe that an updated version of *The Black Woman* should be published with the aim of raising the political and racial consciousness of this younger generation, I am equally convinced that all facets of black art should have some sort of accountability and responsibility to black audiences. The endurance of *Essence*, a magazine that it now faced with the task of addressing the concerns of two and possibly three generations of black women, is a prime example of the twin demands of consumerism and social responsibility. For forty years *Essence* has been precariously dangling between its expressed commitment to the black community, as it has envisioned it, and the pressures of a capitalistic market that seemingly values making a profit over any expressions of racial pride or solidarity. In fact, *Essence* has attempted, with varying degrees of success, to merge these two apparently competing goals.

Reading *Essence* is like talking to your best girlfriend, who might not always be down for the struggle but keeps you abreast of current events and is always there to lend you a shoulder, a sympathetic ear. In a commercial market that often denies my existence as a black woman, over the years I have come to believe in the magazine's mantra, "When you miss *Essence*, you miss you."

Three

CONSTRUCTING DIVA CITIZENSHIP

The Enigmatic Angela Davis as Case Study

> We should call . . . things by their name. When people start saying that
> we are subversive, we should say, Hell yes, we are subversive. Hell yes,
> and we're going to continue to be subversive until we have subverted this
> whole goddamned system of oppression.   —ANGELA DAVIS

On July 21, 2008, *The New Yorker* hit newsstands brandishing a satirical cover that featured the Obamas in the Oval Office enacting what has
come to be known as their signature move, the fist-to-fist "bump." Many
saw the caricature as offensive because Barack Obama is attired in traditional African or Muslim garb, complete with a kufi cap, while Michelle
Obama sports army fatigues with a row of bullets and a machine gun
slung over her body. In the periphery of the image, the American flag is
burning in the fireplace over which hangs a picture of Osama bin Laden.
The fist-to-fist bump, Michelle's smirk and sidelong glance to Barack,
as well as Barack's own smirk and cryptic look at the viewer serve to
indicate that if Barack Obama were to win the presidency, the Obamas
would have essentially "gotten over," or succeeded in hiding their anti-
American and terrorist leanings from mainstream America. Once in
the White House, however, their true intentions would be sure to surface and they would free themselves of their bourgeois facades and don
themselves in outfits more befitting their insidious plot to replace our
free-market economy with their socialist regime. Whether one reads
the cover as incendiary or as a satirical attack on right-wing trepidation over Obama's possible election, this image speaks volumes about
how much notions of ideal U.S. citizenship is predicated on race, culture,
and religion. For the purposes of this project, what interests me is the

striking similarity between the caricature of Michelle Obama and the 1960s image that one generally associates with Angela Davis.[1]

It is impossible to find a picture of Davis during the height of her popularity that does not highlight her Afro.[2] Looking at picture after picture of Angela Davis gracing the cover of old magazines, in newspapers, and scratchy microfilms and microfiches, it is impossible to ignore the powerful image her Afro produced. In many cover stories, Davis's Afro takes up much of the page, a dark wooly mass, a black halo that ends in an austere brown face. Her Afro became almost an entity unto itself, one with a peculiar presence that at once spoke to the political nature of black American life and the lingering effects of cultural images. Although it would be erroneous to credit Davis for the Afro, it is important to think about what it meant when, in 1969, a lecturer, a public intellectual, elected to embrace such an image of blackness that could be coded by the dominant society as an act of militancy. Davis's Afro marked her as not just African-identified, but also as a radical being belonging to a group of countless others set upon rejecting European images of beauty that had been historically imposed on the black body or, in this instance, on the scalp.

In the September 7, 2009, issue of *Time,* Jenee Desmond-Harris explains that Michelle Obama's "hair is the catalyst for a conversation that begins with style but quickly transcends outward appearances and ultimately transcends Michelle herself—a symbol for African-American women's status in terms of beauty, acceptance and power." Desmond-Harris further argues that *The New Yorker*'s satirical rendering of Michelle Obama with an Afro communicated the fear of black radicalism that culminates in a rejection of Afrocentric coiffures. She muses that the United States is not ready for a "First Lady with kinky hair." What makes Desmond-Harris's discussion of Michelle Obama's choice of hairstyle so poignant is that it is ultimately irrelevant that Michelle Obama made a deliberate choice to don a more acceptable hairdo. She undoubtedly will find her hairstyle and dress under similar media scrutiny, as Davis did in the late 1960s and 1970s.

In "Afro Images," Davis's recollection of how the mainstream press first used her photographic image may shed some light on what Michelle Obama will have to contend with beyond Barack Obama's term as president. She writes:

With the first public circulation of my photographs, I was intensely aware of the invasive and transformative power of the camera and of the ideological contextualization of my images that left me with little or no agency.

On the one hand I was portrayed as a conspiratorial and monstrous communist, i.e. anti-American, whose unruly natural hairdo symbolized Black militancy, i.e. anti-whiteness. Some of the first hate mail I received tended to collapse "Russia" and "Africa." I was told to "go back to Russia" and often in the same sentence (in connection with a reference to my hair) to "go back to Africa." On the other hand, sympathetic portrayals tended to interpret the image—almost inevitably one with my mouth wide open—as that of a charismatic and raucous revolutionary ready to lead the masses into battle. Since I considered myself neither monstrous nor charismatic, I felt fundamentally betrayed on both accounts, violated on the first account and deficient on the second. (88)

In the process of reporting on Davis, then, the press made her into an icon, a symbol. Once Davis was relegated to the level of the symbolic, she felt robbed of any agency to create herself. By making her image synonymous with anti-American communist rhetoric, the mainstream media thwarted Davis's earlier efforts to express the stake she and other blacks had in the future of America. Similarly, *The New Yorker*'s ad communicates the fear of the right that the Obamas' ideologies are anti-American. An additional result of Davis's fame was that sympathetic presses forced her into a leadership position, almost against her will, by casting her as essentially a folk hero.

Much like Adolph Reed explains of Malcolm X, Davis argues that people active in the black power movement are reduced to personalities because of the "fragility and mutability of historical images" of those in African American history ("Afro Images" 87). The fragile and mutable nature of Davis's own image serves as an apt example, especially when she is confronted with people who solely connect her with her Afro hairstyle. For example, the *New York Times Magazine* listed her as "one of the 50 most influential fashion [read hairstyle] trendsetters over the last century" ("Afro Images" 87). By extension, as a "trendsetter," how she was coiffed and dressed is read not only as revolutionary style, but as the outfit of an outlaw.

In *Angela Davis: A Political Biography*, the members of the New York Committee to Free Angela Davis use quotations by Davis to state:

In these times, when the fight to uphold one's humanity is a revolutionary act, the false difference between "personality" and "politics" can no longer be maintained. It is in this light that we must understand the life of Angela Davis, for, as she said, the struggle of a true revolutionary is "to merge the personal with the political to the point where they can no longer be separated." In the profoundest ways, it is only when "you don't see your life, your individual life, as being important that it begins to become important," politically, for others in the common fight for freedom. (171)

Unfortunately, with figures like Angela Davis and Malcolm X what is actually remembered is the personality. Davis, however, has consistently opposed such a reading and instead has publicly explained that her decision to wear an Afro was just one way she strove to make her life "inseparable from struggle."

Referring to how young black women respond to Davis, bell hooks correctly charges that:

> Though young black women adore Davis, they do not often read her work, nor seek to follow her example. Yet learning about those black women who have dared to assert radical subjectivity is a necessary part of black female self-actualization. Coming to power, to selfhood, to radical subjectivity cannot happen in isolation. Black women need to study the writings, both critical and autobiographical, of those women who had developed their potential and chosen to be radical subjects. (*Black Looks* 56)

A re-evaluation of Davis's words and of her historical image can serve as a corrective to the exclusion of Davis from her rightful place in everyday remembrances and academic research concerning the civil rights era. Such a re-evaluation also widens our understanding of how African Americans have used their public visibility to demonstrate more radical models of black subjectivity to others who would follow in their path.

In the anthology *Call and Response,* the editors state:

> Few African American authors and scholars have had more influence on spheres of political and social power in the United States than Angela Davis. . . . Davis's continual interaction with very liberal and left-wing organizations put her in the vanguard of forces determined to bring about major social change. As one of the important figures of the Civil Rights Movement of the 1960s, she was one of the key instruments in making that change possible. (1433)

Davis's rise to fame (or infamy) in the late 1960s and early 1970s marks a reconfiguration of the image of the African American revolutionary to include women. In chapter 2 I noted that according to Toni Cade

Bambara, one of the ways to challenge Victorian notions of masculinity and femininity is to examine how black public figures reconfigure these ideals. Davis's presence as cultural icon marks yet another example of a redefinition of black womanhood, one that is determined first and foremost by one's commitment to the black masses. Davis's public presence as a revolutionary committed to the plight of oppressed blacks recalls the efforts of earlier American women such as Shirley Chisholm, Fannie Lou Hamer, Sojourner Truth, Harriet Tubman, Ida B. Wells, and others. These women were also subversive and knew how to shoot a gun or wield a pen in protest against unjust laws. Angela Davis's presence, then, further highlights an established tradition of black women leading others in the "warrior direction," to use Davis's own words, a tradition often muted in our contemporary recountings of the civil rights movement.

In her essay, "'The Darkened Eye Restored': Notes Toward a Literary History of Black Women," Mary Helen Washington asks, "How does the heroic voice and heroic image of the black woman get suppressed in a culture that depended on her heroism for its survival?" (32). It is perhaps a combination of the United States' distaste for powerful women and its propensity to romanticize martyrdom that Davis's words do not roll off the tongue like those of Martin Luther King or Malcolm X when we speak of leaders who fought in the struggle for black liberation during the 1960s. Davis is perhaps also forgotten because she is more difficult to categorize given her connection to the Communist Party, the Black Panthers, and "black folk," unlike King and Malcolm X, who represented the public faces of the supposed extremes of the black liberation movement.

In her book *Autobiography as Activism: Three Black Women of the Sixties,* Margo V. Perkins deals with the various ways in which Elaine Brown, Angela Davis, and Assata Shakur construct revolutionary personas in their autobiographies. While I briefly deal with Davis's autobiography later on in this chapter, I am more concerned with how Davis wrestles with the media to maintain control over her image. In other words, I want to read Davis's public appearances as texts much in the same way I dealt with the implications of *Essence* and *The Black Woman* as instructive venues through which black women learn how to be radical subjects. Through an investigation of her classroom lectures, interviews, trial, and her autobiography, I evoke the figure of the diva to demonstrate how Davis enacts a revolutionary performance for both U.S. and international audiences.

DIVA CITIZENSHIP: MAKING ONE'S LIFE
"INSEPARABLE FROM STRUGGLE"

To take our first step towards freedom, we, too, must pick up the sword.
Only a fighting woman can guide her son in the warrior direction. Only
when our lives, our total lives, become inseparable from struggle can we,
Black women, do what we have to do for our sons and daughters. . . . For
the Black female, the solution is not to become less aggressive, not to lay
down the gun, but to learn how to set the sights correctly, aim accurately,
squeeze rather than jerk and not be overcome by the damage.

—ANGELA DAVIS[3]

I begin this section with an excerpt from a letter in which Davis is
explaining to George Jackson her views on the necessity of female participation in liberation struggles. Davis makes advantageous use of the
then common belief that black women's participation in the black liberation struggle was only valuable as a body to birth male warriors. Rather
than encourage black women to be little more than breeders, a role sadly
reminiscent of black women's experiences in chattel slavery, Davis argues
that black mothers can better serve their progeny as role models who
perform revolutionary duties. Instead of urging black women to be more
docile or servile, Davis wants black women to stoke the embers burning
within. To "lay down the gun" would indeed be more lady-like behavior, but Davis encourages black women to be responsible for their own
defense, even if such a responsibility means that women bear arms. Further, that defense should be conscious, not reflexive ("squeeze rather than
jerk") and once the shot is fired, female revolutionaries should be prepared for the consequences and not flinch or, like stereotypical women,
be "overcome by the [resulting] damage."

To reach black women, Angela Davis must have grappled in some
manner with the question bell hooks poses: "how do we create an oppositional worldview, a consciousness, an identity, a standpoint that exists
not only as that struggle which also opposes dehumanization but as that
movement which enables creative, expansive self-actualization?" (*Yearning* 11). I argue that Davis enacts Diva Citizenship to achieve "expansive
self-actualization" or a radical subjectivity. Ultimately, I am interested
in the ways Davis conceives of her public persona as a performative
stance—one in which she not only models revolutionary behavior for
women who might want to follow in her footsteps, but actively attempts
to counter media portrayals that highlight her "enigmatic" nature rather

than show the connection between her personal life and her politics or depict all facets of her life as "inseparable from struggle."

In this chapter, by juxtaposing an analysis of media-constructed images of Davis as an enigmatic figure with how she counters such portrayals at every turn and consciously reconstructs herself as a homegrown revolutionary, I demonstrate how Angela Davis presents herself as model of Diva Citizenship. I borrow the term "Diva Citizenship" from Lauren Berlant's book *The Queen of America Goes to Washington City*, in which she argues that the "Reagan Years" ushered in a new national discourse of ideal citizenship that has transformed the public sphere into a more intimate space predicated on family values and other private concerns rather than on civil politics. Berlant further argues that the Reaganite right offered a mythical or "cartoon" version of a nation in crisis peopled by "victim citizens" or "iconic citizens" (read as white, male, and heterosexual) who have lost "access to the American Dream" or privileges that have formally allowed them to remain "unmarked." In short, contemporary society has saddled white males with the burden of identity. Berlant asserts that this version of a crisis of citizenship is a deliberate attempt on the part of the conservative right to "dilute the oppositional discourses of the historically stereotyped citizens—people of color, women, gays, and lesbians" (2).

Further, Berlant rejects the notion of the public sphere because she sees "no context of communication and debate that makes ordinary citizens [i.e., white working and middle-class citizens] feel that they have a common public culture, or influence on a state that holds itself accountable to their opinions, critical or otherwise" (3). I submit that mainstream media—post–Kennedy assassination and pre-9/11—has often been mistaken for the voice of the American public and as such has served as a stand-in for the public sphere. The benefits, however, of recasting or exposing the public sphere as a "pseudo public sphere," as Berlant does, allows for the possibility of multiple public spheres. Such a classification disempowers/decenters iconic citizenship, thereby enabling us to envision citizenship and "Otherness" as both contested and shifting categories.

Given that Davis first caught the public eye as the result of her clash with Ronald Reagan, then the governor of California, it seems more than appropriate to use Berlant's discussion of the "Reagan Years" as a springboard for my treatment of Davis's assertion of her citizenship rights. Berlant's phrase "Diva Citizenship" aptly describes Davis's confrontation with Reagan and the Board of Regents, as well as her manipulation of the media. What proved to be problematic for the Board of Regents at UCLA was when Davis, as an Afro-wearing black radical, openly admitted to being a communist at a time when communism and the fear and hate it evoked had had a particularly tainted history in California. Regina Nadelson writes:

> The Right Wing and much of the local California population hated [Davis]. They were about as keen to have a Communist in their schools as, say, a rapist. Communism still provokes shudders of fear and hatred in much of America, and at that point California's school system was in a state of shock from the furor over black "radicals." Nathan Hare had been dismissed as chairman of the School of Ethnic Studies at San Francisco State College; Eldridge Cleaver had been refused permission to lecture at Berkeley. The appointment of Sydney Walton as principal of Sausalito's Martin Luther King Elementary School had produced a confrontation that made headlines; books by Eldridge Cleaver and LeRoi Jones were removed from the reading lists at San Francisco high schools. A lot of fear got mixed up in the smog that hangs low over California. (*Who Is Angela Davis?* 5–6)

So it was the combination of Davis's perceived radicalness and the fear of communism that compelled the Board of Regents to side with then California governor Ronald Reagan to terminate Davis's contract with UCLA. Davis's persecution in 1969 for her communist affiliation was thought by many not only to be an infringement on her constitutional rights, but a step backward.[4]

Angela Davis troubled many of her white liberal supporters, however, when she equated her dismissal from her privileged position as a lecturer at UCLA because of her membership in the Communist Party with the plight of the prison inmates known as the "Soledad Brothers." The Soledad Brothers were George Jackson,[5] Fleeta Drumgo, and John Clutchette, three black inmates at Soledad Prison. They were accused of killing a white prison guard in retaliation for his alleged murder of three jailed black activists, a charge for which the guard was subsequently acquitted. Although they maintained their innocence, the Soledad Brothers feared they would be murdered because of their political views; they had formed a Marxist collective within the prison. Davis is quoted as stating, "What happened to me . . . is only a tiny minute example of what can happen to them. I suppose I just lost my job because of my political beliefs. The Soledad Brothers can lose their lives" (Gillespie and Van Downing, "Angela Davis," 66).

I want to briefly compare Davis's statement with Berlant's definition of "Diva Citizenship." Berlant explains:

Diva Citizenship occurs when a person stages a dramatic coup in a public sphere in which she does not have privilege. Flashing up and startling the public, she puts the dominant story into suspended animation; as though recording an estranging voice-over film we have already seen, she renarrates the dominant history as one that the objected people have once lived sotto voce, but no more; and she challenges her audience to identify with the enormity of the suffering she has narrated and the courage she has had to produce, calling on people to change the social and institutional practices of citizenship to which they currently consent. (*The Queen of America Goes to Washington City* 223)

I see Davis as an example of Diva Citizenship because she refused to let the dominant society place her experience into a more socially accepted role for African American women on America's racial stage. Once she became involved with the Soledad Brothers, she was at times portrayed as a modern-day gun-toting Sapphire—Sambo's highly sexualized counterpart. Davis, however, rejected constructions of herself as a sexualized being and any other image that sought to overshadow her revolutionary zeal. Refusing to read the script the media wrote, Davis used the public spotlight to not only define her own political agenda but to highlight the political struggles of others.

Part of Davis's role as a public intellectual meant relinquishing her own personal notion of self. Davis considered the alignment of herself with the plight of the Soledad Brothers as a test of her revolutionary ideals. It was not enough for her to talk about freedom and liberation in the abstract; to consider herself a true revolutionary she had to act on her beliefs. It is, however, at Davis's first public lecture that she begins her cyclical dance with the press, where the press interprets her as an oddity and she must then demonstrate how her experiences are connected to the larger black population and its history. To claim the right to be intelligent, Davis must bruise (and I use this term because I do not foresee their destruction in either her lifetime or mine) the mechanisms at work that would portray a black female intellectual as an oddity.

Davis's first lecture in her Philosophy 199 course, titled "Recurring Philosophical Themes in Black Literature," was attended by more than 1,500 students and faculty members. Such an enormous turnout creates an overwhelming impulse to read Davis's act of lecturing as yet another performative act as a revolutionary subject. Although the act of teaching in general can be seen as performative, Davis's lecture was even more so given the direct correlation between the crowd size and the media attention that surrounded her then pending dismissal. I would imagine that many in the crowd were curious to hear what a communist/black radical/black woman would teach, while others were either waiting for her to live up to her growing reputation or to fail, and I am sure that there were still others who were swayed by the sensationalism and came merely to be entertained.

Not only does Davis use her lecture to explain the importance of Black Studies programs and African American history, she constructs a revolutionary pedagogy that challenges people to resist passive readings of history and literature. She wants her audience to study the past to salvage its useful lessons concerning liberation. Davis also wants to inject theoretical lessons and lessons learned from the past into present-day practices. She writes:

> History, literature should not be pieces in a museum of antiquity, especially when they reveal to us problems which continue to exist today. The reasons underlying the demands for Black Studies Programs are many, but the most important one is the necessity to establish a continuum from the past to the present, to discover the genesis of problems which continue to exist today, to discover how our ancestors dealt with them. We can learn from the philosophical as well as the concrete experience of the slave. We can learn what methods of coming to grips with oppression were historically successful and what methods were failures. The failures are crucial, because we do not want to be responsible for the repetition of history in its brutality. We learn what the mistakes were in order not to duplicate them. (*Lectures on Liberation* 13)

Using Hegel to read *The Life and Times of Frederick Douglass* (1881), Davis encourages her students to use both theory and history as guides for modern-day resistance. Davis begins her lecture by critiquing Greek society, the supposed birthplace of democracy and the foundation of what is now known as the United States, where "Thomas Jefferson and the other so called Founding Fathers formulat[ed] the noble concepts of the Constitution of the United States" (3). Davis argues that the hypocrisy that both societies exhibit lies in the fact that while each society espoused such "noble concepts," the concrete reality was that many were not allowed to participate in democracy. Davis notes that in Greece, "[w]omen were not citizens and slavery was an accepted institution," and in the United States people held in bondage were "persons who do not merit the guarantees and rights of the Constitution" (*Lectures on Liberation* 3).

Because the focus of her lecture is on "the nature of freedom," Davis elects to use black literature to explore this theme; she believes literature to be a vehicle through which black people worldwide have projected their consciousness. Davis continues by explaining Hegel's concept of the reciprocal relationship between the master and the slave, in which the master's freedom is dependent upon keeping others enslaved. Given that his freedom is conditional, Davis shows that it is questionable whether or not the master's position can actually be considered freedom. Davis further uses Hegel to contend that the "authentic consciousness" of the oppressed lies in the realization that the master's definition of freedom is a false one, made false by the very fact of the enslaved's existence as such. Davis states, "The first phase of liberation is the decision to reject the conditions which the slave-owner has created, to reject his own existence, to reject himself as a slave" (7). According to Davis, understanding the necessity of negating the master's conception of herself or himself as a slave is the realization of authentic consciousness. Davis uses Hegel to read Frederick Douglass's narrative to prove that liberation occurs when the oppressed black replaces the double-consciousness imposed on her or his psyche with her or his own definition of self.[6]

Once the slave achieves her or his authentic consciousness, not only does she or he mentally cease to be a slave—subject to the "whims of another"—she or he must then move to free the physical self. Here Davis advocates the use of violence. She states, "The first condition of freedom is the open act of resistance—physical resistance, violent resistance" (7). She uses the scene in Douglass's narrative in which he has a violent confrontation with the "nigger-breaker" Covey to explicate the necessity of physical resistance as the primary condition of freedom. Astutely, Davis shows that there is a direct correlation between Douglass's manhood and his act of physically defending himself against Covey. In his redefinition of himself, Douglass also redefines the meaning behind Covey's title of nigger-breaker. Covey has broken the "nigger" out of Douglass. Douglass's act of resistance, then, marks the shattering of the master's image of himself and also marks the pivotal point when he becomes self-actualized. The subtext of Angela Davis's lectures, of course, is not missed by her audience. Her audience is supposed to mentally substitute the plight of the blacks of the slavery era with those of Davis's own era. The lesson she outlines using Douglass's text mirrors what had already begun to happen with the rise of the black power movement; contemporary blacks were being urged by Davis to continue rejecting images of themselves imposed by white society.

The established media's response to Davis's lecture was to downplay the obvious depth of her analysis and to ignore the level of respect her university position would have commanded had she been white and male. In her biography on Davis, Regina Nadelson includes a brief transcript of an interview that Davis did with a reporter.[7] Although the reporter came to interview Davis about her teaching, he became side-tracked by her skirt and instead asked her questions regarding its length and material. He also asked whether or not her sexuality was a disruption to the classroom. Not only was she sexualized, but her intellectual prowess was also called into question. J. A. Parker states that on October 7, 1969, the Associated Press wrote, "Miss Davis sprinkled her lecture with quotations from Karl Marx, existentialist Jean Paul Sartre and philosopher Herbert Marcuse" (*Angela Davis* 111). Here, the writer trivializes her lecture by making her seem nothing more than a name-dropper who "sprinkles" lectures with quotations from famous leftists.

It should be noted, however, that at this juncture the bulk of publicity was favorable toward Davis, even if it was often sexist. Nadelson states that prior to Davis's taking up the cause of the Soledad Brothers:

> It would be unfair to say that Angela was let down by the "established press"—that blanket under which huddle, among others, those "liberal" publications that are slightly to the left of the middle. The press, in fact, took her up very much indeed. Angela stories, especially in the more liberal publications, were as popular as a Black Panther at a party in those days. And those who could not unreservedly praise her used her as a peg for editorials in favor of academic freedom. (*Who Is Angela Davis?* 4–5)

Once Davis turned her support to the Soledad Brothers, however, the attitude of the press also turned. The press shifted from defining Davis as an object of sexual desire to defining her as a criminal. Davis states that many people advised her not to link herself to the Soledad Brothers because they were afraid she would lose support. She was counseled that "restricting my utterances to a defense of the right of any qualified individual to teach, unhampered by tests of political nature, I would surely win ample support to counter [California governor Ronald] Reagan's plans to fire me. Even reactionary academicians would be compelled to concede, however reluctantly, the formal principal of academic freedom" (*Who Is Angela Davis?* 5). In "The Radicalization of Angela Davis," published in *Ebony* (which would latter prove to be an avid supporter of Davis), Davis explains the reasons she was drawn to the Soledad Brothers:

> My job was in jeopardy because I had attempted in my small way and as a member of the Communist Party to defend the rights, interests and visions of my people. But in Soledad Prison, there were three Black men,

one an avowed Marxist-Leninist, all three vehement exponents of Black liberation, whose very lives were in jeopardy as a consequence of their principled political stand. Had I continued to wage my own struggle without exposing the threads which tied it to the fight which had to be conducted around political repression in the prisons, I could have been correctly accused of the utmost hypocrisy. (Sanders, "Dear Black Man," 117)

When Davis later states that "I elected to assume, or at least to approximate, the posture which I felt *most closely befitted a revolutionary*," she admits to losing the support of some, but she was more concerned with offering black people, and those aligned with the cause of black liberation, a model of revolutionary agency they could respect (117, emphasis added). By and large, African Americans were able to see how Davis was connecting the two situations—her dismissal from UCLA and the Soledad Brothers' unfair treatment in prison—and were simultaneously able to rally for both causes.

During Davis's work on the campaign to free the Soledad Brothers from prison, she began a romantic relationship with George Jackson, one of the prison inmates. She also developed a close friendship with his younger brother Jonathan. It would be her connection to these two men that would forever change her life and her relationship with the media, which would label her as one of "America's Most Wanted."

NO PLACE TO BE A BLACK GIRL: "PLACING" THE ENIGMATIC DAVIS

If, as I argue in chapter 2, *Essence* magazine saw itself as a vehicle through which African American women expostulated and received information relevant to their experiences, it seems fitting to offer a brief look at how *Essence* dealt with Angela Davis's image. Given that Davis's fame reached an apex at twenty-six, making her one of the few young black women in the public eye during the late 1960s and early 1970s, *Essence*'s readers would have had a particular interest in her story. In the November 1970 issue of *Essence,* Marcia Gillespie and Ronald Van Downing published an exposé titled "Angela Davis: Black Woman on the Run." At the time of the issue's release, Davis was a fugitive from "justice"; while her name was already synonymous with subversion, the actions that prompted Gillespie and Van Downing to write about Davis were quickly causing her name to become equated with criminality.

The subsequent charges filed against Davis stemmed from what her chief counsel, Howard Moore, Jr., terms the "Slave Insurrection of August

7, 1970" in which Jonathan Jackson, the younger sibling of George Jackson, held a courtroom at gunpoint and freed, and armed, three convicts waiting to testify in a trial in which one was accused of assaulting a guard. J. A. Parker writes:

> Wiring a shotgun to the neck of Judge [Harold J.] Haley, they took him, Assistant District Attorney Gary W. Thomas, and three women jurors as hostages, intent on escaping in a rental van waiting outside the courthouse. Officers opened fire. All the kidnapers but [one] died. Haley's head was half blown off by the shotgun. Thomas was shot in the spine and permanently paralyzed. One of the women jurors was shot but survived. (*Angela Davis* 169)

Although she maintained her innocence, Davis was implicated because she purchased the guns used in the courthouse shooting. Once her involvement in the courthouse incident was made public, Davis became a fugitive. Charged with first-degree murder, first-degree kidnapping, and conspiracy, on August 15, 1970, Davis became notorious.

Although a series of events led to the myth making of Davis as a revolutionary icon, it was the FBI manhunt, her subsequent prison time stemming from her involvement with the Soledad Brothers, and her release that solidified her image as a hard-core black revolutionary in the minds of blacks and whites alike. Davis's chief counsel, Howard Moore, Jr., wrote:

> The use of Angela Davis as a symbol—a sort of latter day Harriet Tubman leading her people through the ideological thicket of decadent bourgeois democracy—is a manifestation of the long struggle in the United States between Black led progressive forces and white [*sic*]-led forces of reaction. If Angela is a symbol to those forces which would willingly destroy her, she is equally a symbol to Black people and all oppressed people inside the United States. (*Angela Davis* 200)

Thus, Davis became both communist villain and black folk hero.

As a black folk hero, Davis was usually protected by black and leftist presses. For example, well aware of the negative publicity Davis had been receiving, the writers of the *Essence* article "Angela Davis: Woman on the Run?" decided to tackle the issue of her alleged criminal involvement head-on. In the article the writers repeatedly ask, "Who Is Angela Davis?" By way of an answer, Gillespie and Van Downing begin by listing the facts of her biography that have led her to infamy: "She is the third woman and the first black woman to be placed on the FBI's most-wanted list. Her name in bold type, two photographs, and her vital statistics now appear on posters displayed in police departments and post offices across the country. She is also being sought in Canada, Mexico and parts of Europe" ("Angela Davis" 50). By beginning their investigation into the "truth" behind Davis's criminal image with a description of the FBI poster, Gillespie and Van Downing offer their audience the "official" narrative of Davis's most recent past. The writers then counter this narrative with one that challenges the government's label of Davis as a criminal and enables *Essence*'s readers to identify with Davis as another persecuted member of the black community who has possibly been mislabeled by the FBI:

> She is an attractive, tall, intelligent, Afro-coiffed, bronze-skinned woman, 26 years old, Alabama-born. She is polite, direct, soft-spoken and self-possessed. She is someone's daughter, a sister, and perhaps, one man's woman. She is young enough to think of middle age as her parents' generation; old enough to vote and face the gas chamber if apprehended and found guilty as charged. She is bright enough to teach philosophy on the college level. Proud of her blackness, she seeks answers to its meaning. She is a shy girl who would rather avoid the limelight than seek it; and yet a fighter for things that she believes in. (50)

In a 1975 article for *Black World*, historian Paula Giddings also reminisces about the particular familial feelings of many blacks following the media coverage of Davis while she was a fugitive:

> Of all the activities in the sixties and early seventies, it was Angela Davis who seemed to kindle a more personal concern. She was thought of as a sister, granddaughter or daughter. During her flight many secretly wished that she would knock on *their* door seeking protection, so that they could defy the authorities with a moral indignation not unlike those who harbored runaway slaves. Angela seemed vulnerable, almost fragile, though her actions betrayed that image. Her anger at the System somehow seemed less self-serving than the others, perhaps because she was a woman, and had a comparatively privileged background. And it was probably because of that very image, in addition to her political leanings, that the authorities showed themselves at their brutish best; and those in the White House and the [California] Governor's mansion revealed a crudeness and hysteria to the nation unmatched in recent times. (*When and Where I Enter* 93)

Giddings's comments suggest that the packaging of Davis, her upbringing, and her educational background was potentially threatening to white patriarchal power. Here was a black woman from a relatively privileged background who still felt the sting of racist oppression. From this vantage point, Davis was willing to speak out against class and racial subjugation, and she succinctly articulated how the oppression of underprivileged groups served in the interest of the status quo.

Perhaps in response to her multiple subject positioning (black, female, communist, intellectual), the mainstream media sought to construct Davis as an enigma; she defied easy stereotypes of black womanhood and made blacks and whites alike question assumptions both groups might have had concerning black authenticity. While black presses claimed her, it was perhaps easier for the mainstream media to see Davis as an oddity rather than concede that her decision to become a revolutionary and a public figure was a direct result of life experiences common to many blacks raised in the South. Giddings's comments on the black response to Davis's fugitive status, however, seem to suggest that many blacks were also puzzled by Davis and sought to rewrite her actions to fit a script of black femininity that called for protection and succor. Even though it was common knowledge that Davis was well-versed in the use of firearms and other weaponry, one can infer from Giddings's comments on Davis's supposed fragility and vulnerability that many blacks saw her to be more of a victim because she was a woman fighting the establishment. More egregious accusations along this line characterize Davis as a pawn; because she was a woman, she was often thought to be incapable of making her own decisions. For example, Eldridge Cleaver once suggested that Davis might be being manipulated by the Communist Party. Also, during her trial, the prosecutor, Albert Harris, coded Davis as a victim of love, implying that George Jackson had co-opted Davis into participating in the courtroom takeover.

Davis baffled popular media, both leftist and mainstream, of the late 1960s and early 1970s because of what many felt were her conflicting and problematic alliances, given her middle-class background. Reflecting on her publicity, Davis explained, "*Life* Magazine came out with a provocative issue featuring a cover story on me. Illustrated by photographs from my childhood years through the UCLA firing, the article probed the reasons for my supposedly abandoning a sure trajectory toward fulfillment of the middle-class American dream in order to lead the unpredictable life of a "Black revolutionary" ("Afro Images" 89). Nadelson offers a comprehensive analysis of the problems the media faced in the myth making of Davis: "What disturbed the press . . . was that despite the neat set of labels (black, brilliant, beautiful, red, etc., etc.), it wasn't actually all that easy to shove her into categories. Stereotypes did not suit her" (*Who Is Angela Davis?* 4). Unable to unravel the mystery her presence signified, the press felt comfortable labeling her an enigma, a puzzle or riddle they were determined to solve. They attempted to do this by questioning why she ran in the first place if she was innocent.

Life magazine, specifically, wrote a number of articles dedicated to deciphering Davis's persona and her motives. Davis, in turn, interpreted *Life* magazine. Davis believed the *Life* magazine spread to be a vehicle that FBI director J. Edgar Hoover used to help make her life on the run that more perilous; she charged that it was *Life*'s photo spread, more than the post office and police wanted posters, that endangered her the most:

> The life-sized headshot on the cover of the magazine would be seen by as many people, if not more, than the much smaller portraits on the F.B.I. poster. Having confronted my own image in the news store where I purchased the magazine, I was convinced that F.B.I. Chief J. Edgar Hoover had conspired in the appearance of that cover story. More than anything else, it seemed to me to be a magnification and elaboration of the wanted poster. ("Afro Images" 89)

Davis went to great lengths to combat images of her criminality both while she was imprisoned and even after she was released. In *Ramparts* magazine, she stated:

> The media did not confine their misrepresentations to continual allegations of my culpability. They misconstrued my present condition as the personal tragedy of a black woman who has simply misused all the traditional American opportunities presented to her throughout her life. Much journalistic labor was expended to forge an enigmatic image geared to create the impression that my revolutionary commitment is simply the product of a confused mind. Of course the press consistently fails to discuss the nature of my political beliefs and activities. (Myerson, "Angela Davis in Prison," 23)

After her clear articulation of the subtext behind the articles, Davis's commitments to communism and black people definitely do not seem to be a "product of a confused mind."

As a leading black popular magazine, *Ebony* would come to call Davis its own. In Rita J. Simon and Norma Pecora's article "Coverage of the Davis, Harris, and Hearst Trials by Major American Magazines," the authors write:

Among the general interest magazines, *Ebony* gave Angela Davis the most coverage. Right or wrong, Davis belonged to *Ebony* and it was happy to claim her. . . . About her politics, about the Communist Party, about terrorism, they said little. Much of the attention was on her childhood, on her education, and on the fact that she is black and beautiful. (126–127)

Although I agree that *Ebony* foregrounded its articles on Davis by focusing on her external beauty, I would not agree that *Ebony* ignored her politics as the above quotation implies. In the *Ebony* article "A New Look at Angela Davis," the editors allowed Davis to use *Ebony* as a vehicle through which to explain to the black population her reasons for believing in communism and other philosophies, and although they too wrote about her childhood and education, it was only to explain how Davis rose to her present title as "revolutionary." By chronologically following the events in Davis's life, the reader interprets her desire to become a revolutionary as something that seems predictable and almost inevitable given the events of her life. In a sense, her image as a revolutionary icon is demystified; she is not enigmatic after all—anyone could put themselves in her place.[8] While white mainstream presses like *Life* and other general interest magazines used the same sort of format as *Ebony*, these presses steered readers to position Davis as a confused criminal by negating the positives of choosing a life based on revolutionary struggle. Instead, such publications made light of Davis's politics and sought to make the term "revolutionary" synonymous with criminal.

Davis's criticism of the "bourgeois press" in *Black Panther Newspaper*, published during the height of her celebrity, demonstrates that Davis was aware early on of how the media attempted to avoid dealing with her as a political figure. Davis states:

Focusing the bulk of its articles on my personality and background, the press has clearly attempted to camouflage the political issue involved in my case. . . . While newspapers and magazines wasted pages upon pages, attempting to resurrect my past, they should have instead been cognizant of hundreds upon hundreds of American revolutionaries who have been confronted with a fate no different than mine. (Heath, *Off the Pigs*, 254)

Davis's decision to use the *Black Panther Newspaper* as a forum for voicing her ideas was strategic. Not only was she able to tap into an audience that was sympathetic, black, and overtly political, she was able to counter the influence mainstream media might have had on this audience. Davis was able to lessen the power of the established press to an extent by exposing its underlying agenda of distracting readers from her politics and constructing her as merely a "personality," devoid of serious political commitment.

On October 26, 1970, *Time* ran a story about Davis's capture by the FBI that called into question Davis's continued appeal to blacks and leftists. The article proclaimed, "Angela in handcuffs remained no less enigmatic than Angela on the lam" ("Radicals: Enigmatic Angela" 28). The article goes on to say:

> In Manhattan, gray-haired Communists, Afroed young blacks and a scattering of long-haired whites demonstrated in Angela's support, but some of her sympathizers found their heroine a puzzling and tarnished figure. As one white radical with close ties to the Panthers put it: "Maybe she just wasn't what we thought she was." (28)

It is interesting to decipher the messages behind these statements. The author lists a set of diverse peoples that reflect the multiple alliances Davis had. Yet amidst this show of wide support, the journalist decides to pull out a person who comments negatively about Davis. It is almost as if the author is implying that with her capture she became somehow less dynamic (although no less of an enigma). The article also includes a statement from William Kunstler, a defense attorney in the Chicago conspiracy trial, who says, "She now seems to be torn between the old-line theory and her friendship with black people. Remember, her education is all white-oriented—Brandeis, the Sorbonne, Marcuse. . . . The differences between the party and the movement are irreconcilable. The Communist Party is against the young and their revolutionary activity. She must make a choice." The writer's comments suggest to the reader that Davis is somehow less *black* because of her "white-oriented" education. *Time*'s use of the "white radical with close ties to the Panthers" and also of Kunstler further implies that with her capture her supporters are beginning to turn on her.

To imply that her support had lessened, however, was a definite inaccuracy on the part of *Time*. Once incarcerated, not only did Davis obtain the support of black magazines like *Ebony* and *Jet,* but also of leftist publications like *Ramparts* and *Political Affairs* and feminist publications like *Ms.* Angela Davis's plight also gained the attention of writer James Baldwin. In the book *If They Come in the Morning,* co-authored by Davis and other political prisoners, Baldwin writes an open letter to Davis that ends up producing the book's title. He states:

The enormous revolution in Black consciousness which has occurred in your generation, my dear sister, means the beginning or the end of America. Some of us, white and black, know how great a price has already been paid to bring into existence a new consciousness, a new people, an unprecedented nation. If we know, and do nothing, we are worse than the murderers hired in our name.

If we know, then we must fight for your life as though it were our own—which it is—and render impassable with our bodies the corridor to the gas chamber. For, if they take you in the morning, they will be coming for us that night. (18)

Baldwin's quotation once again points to the reciprocal nature of the relationship between the black masses and their appointed revolutionary leaders. While Davis's plight points to a rising new consciousness because of her affinity to the masses, the masses in turn are challenged to save her, as exhibited by massive "Free Angela" campaigns.

Once imprisoned, Davis granted several interviews to talk radio programs and began to label herself a "political prisoner." In a broadcast interview titled "Angela Davis Speaks: The Controversial Marxist Leader in the Black Movement," Davis states, "More and more black people are being incarcerated not because they committed a crime, but because of their political beliefs and the activities they undertake to bring our people together in the struggle for freedom." She goes on to explain that political prisoners are the result of using "criminal charges in order to stifle leadership, in order to isolate leaders and activists from the community." By calling herself a "political prisoner," Davis attempts to move beyond media constructions of herself as an enigmatic personality by shifting the focus from her individual predicament; instead she highlights an established pattern the government has demonstrated in its dealings with so-called subversives.

"IF LOVING YOU IS WRONG, I DON'T WANT TO BE RIGHT": ANGELA ON TRIAL

Angela Davis's trial began in the spring of 1972. She acted as her own co-counsel to directly challenge prosecuting attorney Albert Harris's depiction of her as a confused woman who had fallen under the manipulative influence of her lover, George Jackson. Barbara Harlow writes, "Throughout her much publicized trial, the main effort of the prosecution was to nullify Angela Davis's political offense by rendering it instead as a 'crime of passion,' the action of an emotional female on behalf of

George Jackson, who was incarcerated in Soledad Prison and alleged by the prosecuting to be her lover" (*Barred* 67).

One of the crucial tactics Harris used in presenting Davis as a manipulated and lovesick woman was to critique personal letters Davis had written to Jackson. Harris wanted to advance the theory that Davis had deployed Jonathan Jackson, George's brother, to take the courtroom hostage out of her love for George Jackson and her desire to see him free. In one of the more interesting letters, Davis discusses the role of black women in the black liberation movement, possibly to get Jackson to rethink the sexist assumptions he made concerning black women in his autobiography, *Soledad Brothers* (1970).

Dated June 2, 1970, the letter states, "We [black women] cannot be dismissed as counter-revolutionaries. . . . Nor can it be said that we ought to blot out our natural instincts for survival. Why, why is our condition so wrought with contradictions? We, who have been forced into performing the most degrading kind of labor—a sex machine for the white slave master" (Aptheker, *The Morning Breaks,* 209). Davis contends that if we consider that the roots of black rebellion in this country began in slavery and that the exploitation of the black female slave woman was twofold—she was exploited both for her labor and her reproductive organs—it seems natural that contemporary black women, who were deeply affected by persisting racist and sexist ideas, should participate in their own liberation.

Predating Patricia Hill Collins's analysis of how stereotypes of black women further the capitalistic enterprise in the United States, and like many of the contributors to *The Black Woman* argue, Davis writes:

> The reign of barbarous capitalist society could not have been secure without the continued subjugation of Black people (and they would use any means necessary). "Divide and Conquer." It never fails. Rape the Black woman and make the survival of the race dependent on that vicious rape. No recourse to the Black male except death. After raping the Black woman, give her a piece of the pie. Make the survival of the Black family dependent on a chasm within. Pound into the mind of the Black male that his superiority, his manhood, has been diminished, has been irreparably damaged by the female of his race. Give him no room, no work with which to objectify his potentialities. Convince the female that he is a lazy son-of-a-bitch. The chasm within. (Aptheker, *The Morning Breaks,* 209)

Here Davis explains that it is to the benefit of capitalist America to pit black men and women against each other, to have them blame each other for oppression rather than the system itself.

Davis then proceeds to give Jackson examples of women who have participated in liberation movements outside the United States. For example, she mentions that the success of the Algerian revolution would have been in doubt had it not included the participation of women. Davis also shares with him her positive impressions of the Cuban and Vietnamese women warriors she met while visiting Cuba. Davis ends the letter by making her final point: "Liberation is a dialectical movement—the Black man cannot free himself as a Black man unless the Black woman can liberate herself from all the muck—and it works the other way around. And this is only the beginning . . . Women's liberation in the revolution is inseparable from the liberation of the male" (Aptheker, *The Morning Breaks,* 211, ellipses in original). Revolution, then, is not a "male thing" nor is it a "female thing"—it is a "black thing."

Interestingly, Harris used this same letter in court to exhibit what he saw as Davis's obsession with Jackson. Harris's reading of this letter in the courtroom brings a private correspondence between Davis and Jackson to the level of spectacle. As Barbara Harlow states, because this letter was used by both the prosecution and the defense, the jury was left to determine how to interpret the letter as text: "The courtroom and the ongoing trial are turned into sites of critical combat over the significance of the gender narrative as 'personal' or 'political'" (*Barred* 68). Davis and Harris were both left with the task of convincing the jury that each one's perception of Davis's character was the correct one. Harris could be said to have had an advantage given that he was a white man. As a black woman, it would be difficult for Davis to be heard; she would be forced to ask jurors to wade through their own projected assumptions of the black female intellect as an inferior one. But what the letter itself makes clear is what Davis had been saying all along in the media. Harris reads this letter as personal, but the letter makes no clear distinction between the personal and the political. Their correspondence demonstrates a relationship in which Davis functions on an equal level with Jackson; she communicates with him as one revolutionary to another. It is the politics that have informed both their lives that draws Davis and Jackson to form a personal relationship with each other.

Harris's tactics, of course, failed miserably. From the very beginning of the trial, Davis anticipated Harris's court strategy. In her opening statement Davis states:

Now he [the prosecutor] will have you believe that I am a person who would commit the crimes of murder, kidnapping and conspiracy, having been motivated by pure passion. He would have you believe that lurking behind my external appearance are sinister and selfish emotions and passions which, in his words, know no bounds.

Members of the jury, this is utterly fantastic. It is utterly absurd. Yet it is understandable that Mr. Harris would like to take advantage of the fact that I am a woman, for in this society women are supposed to act only in accordance with the dictates of their emotions and passions. I might say that this is clearly a symptom of the male chauvinism which prevails in our society. (Harlow, *Barred*, 68)

By labeling Harris a male chauvinist, Davis is at once linking her individual struggle to the larger struggle against sexism, while simultaneously vilifying Harris. In juror Mary Timothy's book *Jury Woman*, she shows that Davis's act of naming Harris's tactics did a lot to sway the jury: "Male chauvinism? I would never have thought of that! But once said, it became obvious. Of course the prosecution would find it far more reasonable that a woman, a *black* woman, would act from sexual passion rather than political motivation. They would also assume that the jury would accept that motive more easily" (88, emphasis mine).

Here we see that in her act of "reading" Harris, Davis simultaneously shattered the stereotypical image of the black woman as libido-driven. Davis's act of self-representation also softened the already preconceived notions the jurors might have concerning irrational militants. As Mary Timothy states, "She [Davis] established her identity with us. Instead of looking across the room at an enigmatic figure representing black militant communism, we were given a chance to discover her as a fellow human being" (*Jury Woman* 95). It is important that Timothy does not vilify Davis; we see that revolutionaries are people too. It was perhaps appropriate that Davis was forced to confront the image of herself as Jackson's pawn in a courtroom setting; what was also on trial was whether or not America was willing to accept women as revolutionary agents in their own right.

GOING IN THE WARRIOR DIRECTION: CONSTRUCTING THE POLITICAL AUTOBIOGRAPHY

What I have demonstrated thus far is Davis's struggle with both her adversaries and mainstream media for control over her public image. It is with her autobiography, however, that Davis best enacts a Diva Citizenship unencumbered by external interference in the construction of her radical self. Published in 1974, Davis's autobiography is one of the few female autobiographies by an activist written virtually in the moment—written when people were still vested in the "movement" and when the 1960s' call for black liberation had overflowed into the next decade.

At this juncture, Davis is so famous that her name alone is enough to attract readers. Written in large part as a response to media-constructed images of Davis as a criminal, her text is what Sidonie Smith would label "self-consciously political." Because of the vast media coverage surrounding her once she became a wanted fugitive, Davis's act of writing an autobiography can be read as her final attempt, during this time period, to challenge and/or reconstruct her public image from an enigmatic personality to revolutionary person.

In her article "The Autobiographical Manifesto: Identities, Temporalities, Politics," Sidonie Smith states:

> Autobiographical practices become occasions for the staging of identity, and autobiographical strategies occasions for staging agency. Thus . . . the autobiographer can lay out an agenda for a changed relationship to identity. . . . Purposeful, bold, contentious, the autobiographical manifesto contests the old inscriptions, the old histories, the old politics, the ancient regime, by working to dislodge the consolidations of the Eurocentric, phallogocentric "I" through an expressly political collocation of a new "I." In service to a new "social reality," . . . the manifesto offers an arena in which the revolutionary can insist on an identity in service to an emancipatory politics, even if, as Robert K. Martin argues, that identity is "assumed." (189)

Using Angela Davis's autobiography as an example, I see a definite connection between Smith's definition of the autobiographical manifesto and Lauren Berlant's "Diva Citizenship." Davis's decision to write an autobiography demonstrates the strategic way in which she capitalizes on her fame. Publishing her autobiography is yet another way for her to seize the spotlight in the public domain. Additionally, like an "autobiographical manifesto," Davis's act of writing resists the urge to individualize her oppression as a black woman. Davis instead writes an autobiography that speaks to the collective nature of oppression, an action that Smith calls "an expressly political collocation of a new 'I.'"

Although the term "autobiographical manifesto" seems appropriate, Davis labels her text a "political autobiography." In her preface to the autobiography, Davis outlines her intentions for the narrative: "When I decided to write the book after all, it was because I had come to envision it as a political autobiography that emphasized the people, the events and forces in my life that propelled me to my present commitment" (xvi). In

Davis's updated introduction, found in her 1988 reprinted edition, she elaborates on her writing philosophy: "So I did not really write about myself. That is to say, I did not measure the events of my own life according to their possible personal importance. Rather I attempted to utilize the autobiographical genre to evaluate my life in accordance with what I considered to be the political significance of my experiences" (viii). Davis's act of muting her individual self in her autobiography mimics the various ways she strives to present her life as "inseparable from struggle" and to assert a collective self when dealing with the media. Davis also challenges Western autobiographical traditions that privilege the individual "I" over notions of a collective "I."

Whether we term Davis's autobiography an "autobiographical manifesto" or a "political autobiography," her act of writing autobiography can be considered a scarification ritual. By constructing a text that seeks to merge the personal with the political, Davis not only marks herself as one of the "folk," she also initiates her readers as potential warriors for the revolution. By privileging the collective "I," Davis uses her autobiography as a road map for others interested in becoming radical subjects.

Reviewers like Irene Williams, however, were put off by Davis's attempt to politicize her life story. In "Women in Dark Times: Three Views of the Angela Davis Trial,"[9] Williams states, "as an ideological attitude, the refusal to individualize one's predicament seems to me to be as false to reality as its opposite—the insistence on personalizing everything that happens (which we recognize as pathological)" (41). Williams's comments suggest that there is a truth to be had in the first place, and they exhibit a belief in the myth that autobiographies are actual representations of reality rather than carefully constructed narratives that are as selective in their characterizations of the autobiographical self and other characters as they are in the remembrance of events. More importantly, her comments signify a fundamental difference between the expectations of American autobiographies written by whites versus those written by blacks. Additionally, Williams's insinuation that Davis might be "pathological" in her desire to write a narrative in which her individuality is second to her political commitment further points to a lack of awareness of traditional representations of the self in black autobiographies.[10]

The slave narrators' mediation between the individual and the representative for a white readership and the political mission that spawned the slave narratives initiated a tradition on the part of both races of linking the black author with the black "masses." Frances Smith Foster explains, however, that the mediation between the individual and the community self is not solely indicative of autobiographical writings by blacks, but that what differs is that African American authors have historically had to defend their humanity and citizenship to others. She writes:

> For the slave narrator, the question [of writing autobiography] is complicated by his status as a black man in the United States. When white writers realize a dichotomy between their individual perceptions and the expectations of society, they must weigh one legitimate role against another. Egoism confronts socialization. The tension is internalized because the white writer is a member of the same society that he is addressing. Slave narrators were not recognized as members of the same society as their audience. The slave narrator was an alien whose assertions of common humanity and civil rights conflicted with some basic beliefs of that society that he was addressing. (*Witnessing Slavery* 5–6)

To make assertions of a "common humanity and civil rights," slave narrators were prompted to participate in an intertextual debate with the master texts of our nation—the Declaration of Independence and the Constitution—over who is to be included in the autobiographical utterances of "We the People." In *Altered Egos*, G. Thomas Couser points to the "autobiographical dimensions" of the Declaration of Independence and the Constitution. Of the Declaration of Independence, Couser echoes Edwin Gittleman's claim that the Declaration is a "variant of the slave narrative, in which the American people as a whole assume the role of the enslaved." Couser goes on to state that:

> Because Congress suppressed what John Adams referred to as Jefferson's "vehement philippic against negro slavery," the official document commits a serious hypocrisy that later (black) slave narratives would endeavor to expose and correct. This collective American autobiography called forth a subgenre that would amend the original document by, in effect, restoring the missing philippic. Slave narrative was in this sense evoked—or provoked—by a master text whose comprehensiveness and moral authority it questioned. (29)

Spurred on by the continuing hypocrisy between American ideals and American sociopolitical practices, blacks who were frustrated over not being counted as one of the "people" shifted away from integration in the mid-1960s. Like her autobiographical antecedents, Davis and her contemporaries were still striving to highlight the discrepancy that existed between America's most sacred documents and its institutional practices that promoted unequal treatment among its citizens on the basis of race and class.

In *If They Come in the Morning,* Davis offers a counterhistory to that of the discourse of blacks as marginal figures in U.S. society—one that challenges the "master text." Davis privileges the fact of black human bondage as the basis of American capitalism. In so doing, Davis's words suggest that we should not conflate who bears the mark of privileged citizenship (superior education, superior housing, superior representation in the courts, and greater mobility; i.e., class status, employment, and even literal mobility within the United States) with the nature of true citizenship as determined by birthright. In a prison interview, printed in *If They Come in the Morning,* Davis states:

> for the essence of a successful revolution in this country will not be the
> destruction of the country, but rather the destructions of institutions
> which deter the [black] people from having access to their own creations.
> And no one can deny that the genesis of U.S. capitalism was inextrica-
> bly bound up with the exploitation of slave labor. Black people created
> the basis for all the wealth and riches accumulated in the hands of a few,
> powerful families in this country today. We therefore have a right to this
> wealth. (181)

Additionally, Davis, like the slave narrators, also recognized the political necessity of using the autobiographical genre to claim one's citizenry. In examining the similarities between the missions of slave narratives and autobiographies like Davis's written in the 1960s and 1970s, one must not overlook the historical and social positioning of African Americans that informs both types of narratives, a positioning in which the narrators are seen as both representative of a larger community and yet somehow unique. Using *Incidents in the Life of a Slave Girl* as a comparison to Davis's text, both *Incidents* and Davis's autobiography have a sense of urgency, the former in its desire to help abolish slavery, the latter in its desire for the racial, social, political, and economic equality of blacks who, having overcome the sting of the whip, were now feeling the sting of the fire hose. The difference, however, between Davis and slave narrators like Jacobs lies in the perception of audience. While slave narrators were forced to engage a white audience in order to persuade them that slavery should be abolished, Davis—like the black aesthetic movement in its entirety—attempts to write an autobiography in opposition to white constructions of black identity. By aligning herself with an aesthetic movement that thrives on its incongruity with "the Man," Davis's first concern is for her black audience. While the slave narrator must make herself or himself representative of the larger black population for the benefit of a white audience that had power over her or his situation, Davis must make herself representative of her black audience to further situate herself as "one of the folk" and to empower other African Americans to be radical subjects with control over their own destiny.

What becomes problematic, however, is that even in her attempts to speak to the black masses and their sympathizers, Davis, because of her position as a public intellectual, is still subject to interpretation by a white audience. In her preface it seems clear that Davis realizes she is still under the scrutiny of a white audience: "I was not anxious to write this book. . . . I felt that to write about my life, what I did, what I thought and what happened to me would require a posture of difference, an assumption that I was unlike other women—other Black women—and therefore needed to explain myself" (xv). Although her autobiography seeks to further thwart the image of herself as an enigma and as the "isolated maverick" that Valerie Smith associates with traditional white autobiographers, many reviewers of Davis's text made compelling arguments that it was impossible to see Davis as anything but unique. For example, in her review "First Person Impersonal," Karen Durbin states, "Any other sister or brother might have become the cause célèbre that Angela Davis was, but I wonder if, had Davis been fat, ugly and inarticulate, we would be reading her story now, selling for $8.95 and dust-jacketed with a glossy photographic portrait of Davis's handsome, pensive face, dramatically silhouetted against a backdrop of dark red" (38).

Durbin, a white critic, challenges Davis's claim that any "sister or brother" could have been in her place. Davis writes, "The one extraordinary event of my life had nothing to do with me as an individual— with a little twist of history, another sister or brother could have easily become the political prisoner whom millions of people from throughout the world rescued from persecution and death" (*Angela Davis* xv). It is most probable that if Davis had not possessed the qualities Durbin outlined she would not have caused such a stir with the popular media or the black masses, nor would I be devoting a chapter to an analysis of her image and her texts. However, what ultimately makes Davis seem unique to Durbin is that her very existence seems improbable to both Durbin and the mainstream media as a whole. Durbin herself admits that she is unable to see Davis as one woman. She states, "Angela Davis's autobiography is a fascinating, if peculiarly schizophrenic book. There are really three Angela Davises. One is a black woman, one is a middle-class intellectual, and one is a revolutionary activist, an almost entirely political creature who speaks with careful, even impersonal passion and whose narrative is flecked with prim political clichés" ("First Person Impersonal" 38). It seems that Durbin creates three Davises because somehow being a middle-class, black female, intellectual and revolutionary seem to be incompatible with each other. To be all these things at once, to Durbin, seems crazy or "schizophrenic." Durbin's desire to fragment Davis seems odd and covertly bigoted given that we are all racialized, gendered, and belong to a particular class group and have specific political affiliations or tendencies.

Durbin's reading of Davis's autobiography also seems to be a misreading of the era. If we concede that Davis's position is unique, we would be failing to situate her plight with that of other revolutionary leaders who also captured the nation's attention. We would also be remiss in looking at the examples of various urban riots and the dissatisfaction of youth, both black and white, with the American government, which prompted student and grassroots activism en masse. Such a reading would also ignore the fact that public support for Davis aided in her release. Durbin's reading of Davis's autobiography is reminiscent of how some white readers and reviewers of slave narratives were skeptical that the writers had ever been slaves. To these white readers, it seemed impossible that one so eloquent could have actually been a slave in the first place and therefore representative of the black masses.

There are many places in Davis's narration that mimic the structural format of the slave narratives; her autobiography supports the notion, developed in my introduction, that racial oppression and resistance to it in the United States repeat themselves: (1) in her preface Davis states a political agenda (which I have already addressed); (2) her text contains silences about political allies and the whereabouts of wanted fugitives as well as silences concerning her sexual life; (3) she uses the tropes of masking and passing in her narration; (4) she details her incarceration by couching her own plight and that of other sister inmates in terms of the complications of class and racial oppression; and (5) she plots out the awkward and disjointed kinship relationships that develop as a result of imprisonment. The remainder of this chapter provides a reading of Davis's text and an analysis of how Davis both constructs herself as a revolutionary within the narrative and represents the plight of other oppressed blacks.

Davis begins her narrative by placing her readers in the heat of the FBI chase when she was in hiding as a wanted fugitive. On a purely sensational level, Davis is perhaps attempting to capitalize on residual media hype concerning her trial. One could, however, read Davis's autobiography as a literary road map toward revolutionary action for a black readership. As such, from a stylistic perspective, Davis begins her narrative *in medias res* to create a sense of urgency and to demystify the glamour associated with being a fugitive from "justice" by recounting for her audience the fear and paranoia she felt. Davis states:

> Living as a fugitive means resisting hysteria, distinguishing between the creations of a frightened imagination and the real signs that the enemy is near. I had to learn how to elude him, outsmart him. It would be difficult, but not impossible.
>
> Thousands of my ancestors had waited, as I had done, for nightfall to cover their steps, had leaned on one true friend to help them, had felt, as I did, the very teeth of the dogs at their heels.
>
> It was simple. I had to be worthy of them. (5–6)

By likening her situation to that of fugitive slaves, Davis places herself in a tradition of resistance to the unjust laws of this country. Drawing strength by evoking her ancestors, Davis expresses her commitment to carrying on their legacy to fight for freedom.

Like the fugitive slave who had to develop several strategies to avoid capture, Davis literally employs the trope of masking by wearing a disguise. It is interesting that the "mask" Davis wears necessitates hiding the most important vestige of revolution Davis possesses, her Afro. By wearing a wig and the other costumes she selects, Davis chooses to play the role of the oversexed black woman—a familiar stereotype of black women—for her survival as a fugitive. Davis states that the "wig was straight and stiff, with long bangs and elaborate spitcurls. She [a woman helping Davis] pulled out half of my eyebrows, glued false eyelashes to my lids, covered my face with all sorts of creams and powders and put a little black dot just about the corner of my lip. I felt awkward and overpainted, but doubted my own mother could have recognized me" (10). What is curious and poignant about her decision to "mask" in this manner is that Davis has separated out the political revolutionary from the sexualized woman. She seems to be made up almost like a harlot—Davis's evocation of her mother implies that her mother would have disapproved of her attire. By donning a mask that exaggerates her sexuality, Davis has chosen an effective guise, one that would not be considered befitting of a revolutionary, and therefore one that the authorities would be likely to overlook.

Once Davis is captured, the narrative begins to read more and more like a modern slave narrative. The prison replaces the plantation as a "peculiar institution" that profits from the prisoner's labor, and the prisoner functions as the slave who is dehumanized or belittled; Davis notes that female prisoners are called "girls" no matter how old they are. If we read the prison as a modern plantation, Davis's goal, much like that of the slave narrators, is to describe to each audience (black/white, leftist) the conditions that exist within each institution. Davis's desire, however, is to push her audience toward prison reform. She first describes the infrastructure of the prison by setting up a comparison between her treatment by white guards and then by blacks. Davis then discusses how a "robust white matron" snatches her wanted poster off the wall in a gesture of triumph. In contrast, Davis talks about a young black female guard who wore her hair in a natural style and who did not approach her with hostility. Regarding this encounter, Davis writes that meeting the black guard "was a disarming experience. Yet it was not the fact that she was Black that threw me. I had encountered Black matrons before—in jails in San Diego and Los Angeles—but it was her manner: unaggressive and apparently sympathetic . . . she told me, 'A lot of officers here—the Black officers—have been pulling for you. We've been hoping all along that you would get to someplace that was safe'" (20). Throughout the narration of her prison experiences, Davis talks about black women guards who are sympathetic to her plight and explains that their sympathy causes problems for them with their white co-workers. She also evokes a strategy of the slave narratives in not naming these guards specifically. Davis writes:

> Unfortunately, I cannot describe the sympathetic officers or refer to them by name. My words might mean the loss of their jobs. They were an interesting conglomeration of Black women, both young and old, whose political sentiments ranged from "liberal" to straight-out sympathy with the most militant wings of the Black Liberation Movement. . . . In a way, these officers were prisoners themselves, and some of them were keenly aware that they were treading ambiguous waters. Like their predecessors, the Black overseers, they were guarding their sisters in exchange for a few bits of bread. And like the overseers, they too would discover that part of the payment for their work was their own oppression. (43)

Like the slave narrators, she conceals the identity of those not already implicated or under investigation by the FBI to shield them from persecution or embarrassment. What is also interesting about the above quotation is that though Davis seems sympathetic to the position the black women guards are in, she also offers a chilling critique of their participation in their own oppression. But she is not suggesting that black women should not work as prison guards, and in fact states that they are very helpful to the prisoners, risking their positions to deliver books or a pick for natural hairstyles.

While prison officials might not have known about the solidarity that was developing between Davis and black female prison guards, they were very suspicious of the unity forming between Davis and other prison inmates. It was clear that many inmates (particularly black and Hispanic women) felt an affinity toward Davis. At "lights out" they included her in their ritual of shouting good night to their friends. Prison officials were so leery of Davis's interactions with other prisoners that they sought to remove her from the general prison population to stave off potential riots. Davis was segregated from the general population, first in a psychiatric ward and then in solitary confinement. In addition to talking about how the black female guards react to her, Davis is also careful to show the overall conditions of the prison, as well as to tell the stories of prison inmates.

Returning to the similarities between Davis and the slave narrators, Davis's candor about her personal experiences in jail and her testifying for others, as well as the stories of specific women, can be likened to the format of the slave narrative in which narrators include a "chapter of horrors" that accumulate the horrors of slavery (substituted here by prison life) as well as stories of other slaves whose lot was often worse. The purpose of including the stories of others is identical in both cases: it exhibits the desire to be representative. In many subtle ways, Davis uses the method of remembering the plight of earlier slaves in her text. For instance, she uses slave terminology—she talks about an "underground railroad" for revolutionaries trying to leave the country and she calls the police "overseers." It is also interesting that as this chapter unfolds, the I/them binary seems to disappear and Davis begins to use "we" in talking about her experiences in prison. In explaining what goes on in prison and by telling the stories of others, all the while reminding the reader that she too is a prisoner, Davis is not just being representative, she is also demystifying prison for the reader by humanizing the prisoners and challenging the stigma and stereotypes surrounding the term "felon." Her theory is that if the reader is privy to a prisoner's story and if the reader remembers that dehumanizing felons also means dehumanizing Davis, the reader is more likely to sympathize with their stories.

Davis's sympathies toward her sister inmates move her to go on a hunger strike to protest attempts by prison officials to separate her from the general population. As a result, an actual uprising does occur in the prison, and when officers try to subdue her, Davis physically fights back. This scene is reminiscent of slave narratives like those by Frederick Douglass when he fights Covey or Harriet Jacobs's *Incidents in the Life of a Slave Girl* when she verbally stands up to Dr. Flint—all are moments of active resistance. Davis's hunger strike is important because it demonstrates that she is prepared to physically defend herself in a violent confrontation—and acts of violent self-defense during Davis's era were a definite mark of a "true" revolutionary. The chapter ends with her being transported to California. What is interesting is the way she describes being moved from New York to California: "New York removed its handcuffs. California produced theirs and locked them around my wrist" (70). She uses the technique of personifying these states to demonstrate to the reader how each state, and by extension America, functions as the oppressor.

While the opening chapter I have just described catapults the reader into the throes of Davis's story, the chapter titled "Rocks" shows the reader the path that leads Davis to her present predicament. It is titled "Rocks" because we are to read this chapter, dedicated to her early years, as the foundation of her radicalness. Although the media highlighted her middle-class background as cause to wonder why she would choose a life of radical activism, we learn that living in Birmingham, Alabama, when houses and churches were being bombed on such a regular basis that her neighborhood was called "Dynamite Hill," which is enough to clear up any speculations on why she would choose a radical path. We also learn in this chapter that both of her parents were educators and active in the community. Davis specifically highlights her mother's activism and also talks about her grandmother's sharing with her stories of her own mother's enslavement. With all of these ingredients combined, Angela Davis comes to activism not just from her own experiences, but from the experiences of her immediate ancestors.

Being brought up amidst such violence caused Davis to be angry at white people, a tendency her parents actively fought against. She states, "The more steeped in violence our environment became, the more determined my father and mother were that I, the first-born, learn that the battle of white against Black was not written into the nature of things. On the contrary, my mother always said, love had been ordained by God. White people's hatred of us was neither natural nor eternal" (79). However, this was a lesson that took a long time for Davis to accept.

By writing about her anger during her childhood, Davis validates it—why shouldn't one be angry at such horrible treatment? The ways in which speaking about her anger plays out in her narrative, however, is quite different from her slave narrator ancestors. Gone are the days of mediating anger for a white audience's consumption. What we see in Davis's autobiography is that there is now a shift in the black writer's perceived audience that brings about a change in the tone of the work. No longer is anger masked as it was, by necessity, in the slave narrative. In "The Structuring of Emotion in Black American Fiction," Raymond Hedin discusses how at the same time the black writer was trying to change the attitudes of the white readers, she or he became increasingly angry at the treatment whites have given blacks over the years. This anger had to then be negotiated so that the writer would not fall victim to the stereotypical view of the angry black male. Hedin states that it is in the slave narrative that black writers first responded to attacks on the black man's humanity by developing narrative strategies to convey intense emotions without sacrificing the impression of rational control. The masks Davis dons in her autobiography, however, in no way represent repressed anger. Instead, the anger and bitterness she feels against racial injustice become unmasked even in the act of using the trope of masking.

Recounting a childhood fantasy about wearing a white face mask, Davis states, "After thoroughly enjoying the activity [participating in white-only activities in the South], I would make a dramatic, grandstand appearance before the white racists and with a sweeping gesture, rip off the white face and laugh wildly and call them all fools" (85). Later on in her text, Davis describes acting out a variation of this by going into a clothing store with her sister and pretending to be an exotic black by speaking French while her sister plays the role of interpreter. While the white sales clerks fall all over themselves to wait on the two, Davis steps out of her role and says, "All Black people have to do is pretend they come from another country, and you treat us like dignitaries" (87). Here Davis profoundly alters the significance of the tropes of masking and passing. "Wearing the mask" is not so much a defense mechanism or survival tool to protect her true emotions from white folk, but rather what she fantasizes wearing in order to "pass" as white because her skin color alone won't allow it. In the real-life scenario, the use of French becomes the mask she uses, and one she uses subversively. Davis attempts to pass not to better her own individual lot but to expose the hypocrisy of how U.S.-born blacks are treated. Even as a young girl, her profound and indignant words to the clerk show her developing sense of unity with other blacks.

Davis's earlier wisdom is widened once she goes to New York to attend high school and stays with a white family, the Melishes. Here is where she first comes into contact with *The Communist Manifesto*. Reading the manifesto allows her to begin to make connections between her plight as a black woman and communist doctrine. Davis states:

What struck me so emphatically was the idea that once the emancipation of the proletariat became a reality, the foundation was laid for the emancipation of all oppressed groups in the society. Images surged up in my mind of Black workers in Birmingham trekking every morning to the steel mills or descending into the mines. Like an expert surgeon, this document cut away cataracts from my eyes. The eyes heavy with hatred on Dynamite Hill; the roar of explosives, the fear, the hidden guns, the weeping Black woman at our door, the children without lunches, the schoolyard bloodshed, the social games of the Black middle class . . . the back of the bus, police searches—it all fell into place. What had seemed a personal hatred of me, an inexplicable refusal of Southern whites to confront their own emotions, and a stubborn willingness of Blacks to acquiesce, became the inevitable consequence of a ruthless system which kept itself alive and well by encouraging spite, competition and the oppression of one group by another. (110)

While the slave narratives attempted to engage the Constitution and the Declaration of Independence in a discussion about freedom, Davis does not see either document as a path toward liberation and opts instead to embrace communist doctrine as a liberating ideology.

In ending her autobiography with her trial, Davis takes democracy to task. The final chapter begins with the quotation "Walls turned sideways are bridges." This chapter is aptly titled "Bridges" not just because it follows a chapter called "Walls," but "turning a wall sideways" is an awesome metaphor for revolution. This chapter also serves to link the readers back to the present-day narration Davis began with her first chapter. In this chapter, we receive not only detailed information about the trial covered by other sources, but we are finally privy to firsthand accounts of Davis's actual thoughts and feelings. This section is significant because while other texts show how Davis is being constructed by the prosecutor and interpreted by the jurors, here we see Davis's interpretations of others. One example can be seen in the way she discusses the only potential juror that was a black woman—"Mrs. Janie Hemphill." That Davis remembers her name so distinctly and with such respect is of the utmost significance and points to the affinity and actual "family feeling" Davis felt toward Hemphill. Davis states that Hemphill reminds her of her mother. Having found a potential ally in Hemphill, Davis is not surprised when she is eliminated and makes a special note to the reader that Hemphill is the only juror asked to answer questions from the witness stand. We are therefore left to read Hemphill's treatment as black womanhood itself being on trial.

This chapter is of further importance because it shows how the prosecutor also put Davis on trial for her politics. Margo V. Perkins argues that "[a]ctivists' *texts* give voice to oppositional or counterhegemonic ways of knowing that repeatedly invite readers to challenge their own assumptions and level of comfort with the status quo" (*Autobiography as Activism* xii, emphasis mine). While I agree with Perkins's statement, examining the actions of Angela Davis at the height of her fame also challenges people to gauge their "level of comfort with the status quo" while it enables young scholars to see themselves in Davis rather than to conceptualize her as an icon and her radicalism as an anomaly.

The ultimate significance of this chapter and my reason for ending my analysis of Davis's autobiography with the trial scene is to highlight that it was Davis's entire belief system that was on trial. Therefore, her attempts at Diva Citizenship seem finally vindicated when she emerges triumphant from the struggle over her image. But such a reading is too simplistic given that Davis still had to contend (and is battling even to this day) for control over her image.

In his book *Stirrings in the Jug: Black Politics in the Post-Segregationist Era,* Adolph Reed contends that contemporary interpretations of Malcolm X's image have become little more than "black power consumerism."[11] Reed argues that Malcolm X has become a "decontextualized icon" of an abstracted "greatness" to be commodified on buttons and T-shirts rather than someone from whom youths can actively learn. Unlike those who had access to a *live* Malcolm, Reed laments that those born after segregation, or those too young to have experienced it firsthand, only have access to a *dead* Malcolm—dead in the sense that he no longer has a "dynamic connection to the lived reality of the youth who invoke him" (201). In contrast, he argues that for earlier generations:

> the Malcolm X who engaged us was moving inside the history that we were
> living. He responded to it, tried to understand it, describe it, and shape
> its course.... In fact, Malcolm's appeal grew largely from the way that he
> counter-punched in very concrete terms against the changing elements
> of that reality—for example, in his responses to the Birmingham church
> bombing, the sanctimony surrounding the Kennedys, the civil rights move-
> ment's strategic reliance on the stereotype of the patient-suffering-slow-
> to-anger Negro. Malcolm emboldened us, or those of us whom he did,
> because he was an interlocutor with current orthodoxy, expressing forbid-
> den thoughts hidden in the black silences of our time; he energized us by
> playing the dozens (a black narrative form of exposé, with humor) on the
> official narratives of race and power under which we strained. (200)

Because she was spared martyrdom, even today Angela Yvonne Davis battles black power consumerism regarding the use of her image on commodities. Davis offers an interesting example of how images of revolution are co-opted when she does a critical reading of the fashion section of the March 1994 issue of *Vibe* magazine, titled "Free Angela Davis: Actress Cynda Williams as Angela Davis":

> The photographs I find most unsettling . . . are the two small headshots of Williams wearing a huge Afro wig on a reproduction of the FBI wanted poster that is otherwise unaltered except for the words "FREE ANGELA" in bold red print across the bottom of the document. . . . This is the most blatant example of the way the particular history of my legal case is emptied of all content so that it can serve as a commodified backdrop for advertising. . . . What is also lost in this nostalgic surrogate for historical memory . . . is the activist involvement of vast numbers of Black women in movements that are represented with even greater masculinist contours than they actually exhibited at the time. ("Afro Images" 90)

Although I can recognize this fashion spread as an (albeit misguided) effort to pay tribute to Davis and an attempt to possibly speak to a desire among many young people to get back the revolutionary zest of that era, not only does it reduce revolution to a fashion statement, it makes a caricature of the participation of women in these movements. What is interesting to me about Davis's objections to the spread is not that it relegates black women's involvement in revolutionary organizations to the realm of what might be considered trivial concerns (i.e., fashion, glamour, and beauty), but that the pictures actually strip Davis of her femininity and therefore reinforce the notion that if revolution is not just the pursuit of men, then it is also the pursuit of masculine women.

Davis's critique of the *Vibe* article is reminiscent of the "counter-punching" or active engagement for which Reed fondly remembers Malcolm X. Like the live Malcolm X that Reed describes, Davis also encouraged blacks and subversive groups by publicly providing a running critique of then current events. In addition to critiquing U.S. public policies, Davis also continuously waged war against the mainstream media for control over her own image. Given the similarities between the living Malcolm and the dynamic model of radicalness that Davis exudes, I argue that if Malcolm X represents our black manhood, then Angela Davis epitomizes the revolutionary potential of black womanhood.

What is important about studying Davis is that her constant willingness to do battle for her image is a rejection of outside constructions and a consistent push to see her existence, and that of other American blacks, as being central, and not marginal, to American culture and history as a whole. By continuing to demand the right to create herself, Davis achieves self-actualization as a revolutionary subject. And though Davis's critics use her victory in an arena—the American criminal justice system—that she had vehemently critiqued as proof that the court system in this country actually does work and is fair, what she has actually shown is the tenacity and unmitigated gall of herself and her supporters to make the system work in her favor.

Davis's model shows that it is not up to others to define for us what our place should be as blacks in a country we built. Angela Davis is a revolutionary diva who carved out a space for herself, and consequently paved the way for others, in a country that tried to make a myth out of her image and strove to label her existence as a black revolutionary female intellectual as improbable. Specifically for me as a black woman scholar, Davis's example demonstrates that my place is wherever I am standing.

Four

RETURN TO THE FLESH

The Revolutionary Ideology behind the Poetry of Jayne Cortez

The poet can chronicle where we as a people have been and where we'd like to go. But unlike the politician, the poet can give vision and the space. The politician gives a vision that says, "If you follow me all your problems will be over," while the poet says, "If you understand where I'm coming from you will gain the tools to solve your own problems."

—NIKKI GIOVANNI, "FOREWORD" TO *BLACKSPIRITS: A FESTIVAL OF NEW BLACK POETS IN AMERICA*

I want to influence people to understand what is happening, what *should* happen to us. To raise consciousness, to overcome our limitations, our position in the United States. I want to create images and messages that linger. I want my poetry to inspire others to write, to see that you have to take full responsibility for your life, that things can be changed.

—JAYNE CORTEZ

Throughout *Writing the Black Revolutionary Diva,* I lament the ways discourses surrounding double-consciousness and the multifariously damaged African American subject obscure the decolonizing impulses found in many contemporary African American texts. Given that poetry emerges as a dominant genre in the black aesthetic movement, it is imperative that I examine how a female poet uses her work to encourage the internal decolonization of her audience. Because Giovanni is herself a product of the black aesthetic movement, it is easy to view the poet she renders in the first epigraph as one modeled after the black aesthetician, particularly since she endows her poet with an ethical imperative to use her vision to essentially help African Americans to help themselves.

Although there are several female poets that would aptly correspond to Giovanni's composite, Giovanni included, I have chosen to examine the earlier work of the black aesthetic movement protégée Jayne Cortez.

The quest to free BAM from its association with essentialism has often resulted in less than rigorous analyses of the subversive potential of poetry like Cortez's.[1] Furthermore, the bulk of the scholarship written about Cortez tends to focus on her jazz poetry and various praise poems. While I hardly find this choice negligible, I am more interested in the ideological implications of her earlier works that demonstrate her affinity with the profane, her use of the grotesque, and her coinage of "supersurrealism" as an apt label for her creative aesthetic.

In the second epigraph, Cortez explains that she wants to "create images and messages that linger." Her earlier poetry is renowned for its use of profanity and its dissection of black flesh. In terms of creating lingering images, Cortez cracks open black flesh and digs into its innards as a consciousness-raising exercise. As a poet, Cortez functions as my exemplar of a "revolutionary diva" because of how she strategically uses imagery and language in a cooperative rather than in a divisive fashion to unite blacks throughout the Diaspora and to foster better relations between black women and men. My interest in Cortez as a revolutionary diva is threefold. First, she consistently depicts black flesh as dissected or disemboweled so that her audience might have a more visceral representation of how First World nations exploit people of color and Third World nations. I further contend that Cortez uses the flesh as a pedagogical tool, one that challenges our traditional understanding of theory. Her use of black flesh necessitates a re-evaluation of experiential knowledge as another valid means of theorizing. Second, I argue that Cortez positions herself as a "Third World poet" or one of "the folk." From this vantage point, she functions as an insider both in the realm of black Diasporic and black nationalistic spheres. Cortez also uses this dual subject positioning to promote global unity among blacks. Therefore, Cortez insists on a holistic understanding of blackness, and within that understanding women's issues are central rather than marginal concerns. Third, I explore the womanist implications of Cortez's work, particularly Cortez's use of the profane as a method of unshackling women from traditional societal norms of what constitutes lady-like behavior and speech.

Although she was born in Arizona in 1936, Jayne Cortez came of age in the infamous California ghetto of Watts. In an interview with Alexis DeVeaux, Cortez states, "Los Angeles was very different from Arizona. In Arizona I could be in and out of my fantasy world, but moving to the Watts community in Los Angeles, I was faced with other realities, the reality of living in a big-city ghetto" ("A Poet's World" 77). Cortez's "fantasy world" consisted of watching Lena Horne, her idol, at the movies and fantasizing that she was her daughter. The connection she felt to Horne and also to Billie Holiday was fueled by her own desire to be an actress.[2] Cortez's fantasy world, one built on Hollywood films, was destroyed once she was forced to negotiate life in Los Angeles. When she moved to Watts, not only was she confronted by urban poverty, Cortez also had to deal with the negatives that came with attending an integrated junior high school; previously she had gone to a segregated black school in Arizona. In an interview with D. H. Melhem, Cortez states:

> We had integration and segregation and domination at the same time. And it was like, very miserable. Miserable simply because of the attitudes of both the white students and the white teachers. Almost every book we read was about their lives, their history, their values, their culture. Things would really get tense when we got to the slave era. It was repulsive. They taught such lies about Africa. I tell you I had to fight every day. I mean when a white kid called me "nigger," I had to jump up and beat the hell out of him or her. And I did that constantly. My mother was always at the school. . . . I learned very early about what's ugly, and racism is very ugly. (198)

Cortez complicates the positive connotations associated with "integration." Rather than being synonymous with equality, the type of integration at work in Cortez's junior high school meant little more than black attendance. It did not include social interaction between black and white students, nor did it entail the dismantling of a hierarchy of education that placed white cultures above black cultures. Not only did Cortez learn the ugly face of racism prevalent in the U.S. educational system, she also apparently discovered her own outrage at receiving an education that did not recognize blacks as viable contributors to history. Because of the skewed historical perspective that students received in her school, Cortez had to physically defend herself against the verbal assaults of white students who thought themselves superior to blacks.

Cortez's life experiences inform her aesthetic principles and align her with that of other black aestheticians and black nationalist poets. In *Drumvoices* (1976), Eugene Redmond uses Cortez's poem "Festivals and Funerals" (also the title of Cortez's fourth book of poetry) as an epigraph to and title of his sixth chapter. This phrase encapsulates the pace of the lifestyles many black poets led during the 1960s and 1970s—they were either attending festivals or funerals. He writes:

Assassinations, high-level political corruption, upheaval, violence, change, clash of ideologies, flaming rhetoric—all describe the contemporary period. Revolutions (of all kinds) mock and mold the world. From Cuba or Vietnam, Harlem to Chile, Pakistan to Watts, Nigeria to Indonesia, Kenya to Berkeley, Jackson State to Kent State—the facts and symbols of change have been dramatic and violent. (296)

The political climate of the times influenced Cortez and enabled her to see the similarities between social upheavals in the United States and liberation movements in other countries.

While more extensive biographical information can be obtained from Melhem's *Heroism in the New Black Poetry* and various other sources, there are two other experiences I would like to highlight from Cortez's life. First, Cortez joined Fannie Lou Hamer in Mississippi to participate in the voter registration drives of 1963 and 1964. Second, in 1964, Cortez cofounded the Watts Repertory Theatre Company, "where she directed plays, acted, and read her poetry, supporting herself meanwhile by factory and office work" (*Heroism in the New Black Poetry* 182). Both of these experiences helped her make connections between her plight as a laborer and her mission as a poet. As a product of the Watts Repertory Theatre, one of the several black arts schools set up during the 1960s, she and her fellow (sister) poets were able to "take [their] poetry to the taverns and parks, to city squares and parking lots. Instead of taking the poems to the academic level, they took them back to the people" (Troupe and Schulte, *Giant Talk*, xxxix). The Watts school's desire to speak to the masses mirrors that of other writers of the black aesthetic who wanted to dismantle the hierarchical notions of art imposed by traditional white artists. For example, in "Black Cultural Nationalism," Ron (Maulana) Karenga writes that for black aestheticians, "[o]ur contention is that if art is from the people and for the people, there is no question of raising people to art or lowering art to the people, for they are one and the same thing" (35).

Referring to Cortez's second book of poetry, Barbara Christian cautions that "[t]he poems from *Scarifications* are not for the fainthearted. Insisting that we experience our present, where we are, and what is happening to us, they abound with images of New York City where Cortez now lives. . . . Poems from *Scarifications* are just that—scarifications" ("There It Is" 235–236). In other words, Cortez's poems are both poetic explorations and expressions of the myriad manifestations of oppression that blacks have faced on U.S. soil and abroad. These poems not only address the wounds of racism, but they force us to participate in our own struggle for decolonization. Like the black aesthetic movement did for the collective consciousness of the 1960s generation, her poems jolt our "racial memory."[3] Cortez's earlier poems are often angry, graphic, profane, and ugly, and as such they are intended to unnerve her audience. These poems mark us.

THEORIES OF THE FLESH: ANATOMY AS METAPHOR

In his book *Freedom Dreams,* Robin D. G. Kelley gives a cursory historical analysis of the ways surrealism has featured in the lives and creative production of blacks throughout the Diaspora, using Jayne Cortez as one of his exemplars. Franklin Rosemont defines surrealism as follows: "Surrealism, a unitary project of total revolution, is above all a method of knowledge and a way of life; it is lived far more than it is written or written about, or drawn. Surrealism is the most exhilarating adventure of the mind, an unparalleled means of pursuing the fervent quest for freedom and true life beyond the veil of ideological appearances" (quoted in Kelley, *Freedom Dreams,* 158). Although there are several definitions of surrealism that I might use, I was drawn to the one that Rosemont provides because of his assertion that surrealism is a revolutionary process, his equation of surrealism with the search for freedom, and his use of the veil as a metaphoric separation between truth and appearances, all of which have particular resonances in African American cultural history.

However, as Kelley is quick to point out, if one is to consider black life in general as a surreal state, in such an instance its manifestation becomes far less felicitous than Rosemont defines. Of Cortez, Kelley writes, "Jayne Cortez dreams anti-imperialist dreams. It is not enough to imagine what kind of world we would like; we have to do the work to make it happen. Today, in an era when many young people believe that surrealism is merely an aesthetic or a hip style, Cortez exemplifies the revolutionary commitment that has always been at the heart of the black radical imagination" (187). What is lacking from Kelley's assertion is the precise manner in which young people can make use of Cortez. Additionally, what is problematic about Kelley's use of Cortez is his failure to acknowledge Cortez's coinage of the term "supersurrealism" that stands in slight contrast to the surrealists mentioned in his text that Cortez herself would have also studied.

While many authors use surrealism in their works, Cortez surpasses the aims of most. D. H. Melhem writes, "The intense vision of reality in Cortez moves beyond the intellectual and unconscious aspects of Surrealism, itself a revolutionary movement, into a divine and infernal realism"

(*Heroism in the New Black Poetry* 181). In an interview with Melhem, Cortez challenges the assertion that her work is a reflection of an "infernal realism" and instead she labels her poetic style as "supersurrealism." Cortez not only uses the dreams and the subconscious in her work, but also black flesh in its entirety, from its vital organs to its waste. In many ways, her dreams amount to nightmarish glimpses of how imperialism and racism affect blacks. Cortez explains supersurrealism as follows:

> I use dreams, the subconsciousness, and the real objects, and I open up the body and use organs, and I sink then into words, I ritualize them and fuse them into events. I guess the poetry is like a festival. Everything can be transformed. The street becomes something else, the subway is something else. Everything changes: the look of a person changes, their intentions change, the attitudes are different, experiences become fiercer. Voices become other voices. So that's what I do in my poetry. I keep making connections. (*Heroism in the New Black Poetry* 205–206)

As a purveyor of black heritage, Cortez envisions her poems as "festivals" or "rituals" of transformation in which she celebrates blackness or indoctrinates her audience into radical activism. For Cortez, both events are rituals of transformation, and therefore part of the revolutionary process.

Akin to the carnivalesque, as articulated by Mikhail Bakhtin, Cortez sees her poems as vehicles of transformation through which she seeks to symbolically invert social hierarchies. Randal Johnson explains, "In the carnivalesque, a material bodily principle, especially of the body's 'lower stratum' (including eating, drinking, copulation, defecation, and other bodily functions), prevails as a positive force" ("Carnivalesque Celebration" 218). While Cortez does use some of the same "material bodily principle[s]" as the carnivalesque, it is not necessarily her intent to evoke these principles as positives, but rather to demonstrate, like the hierarchical inversions found in the carnivalesque, how these bodily principles can be used as tools for revolution. Through a fusion of the metaphysical with the "real" and by laying the innards of both the poem and the symbolic black flesh bare, Cortez not only wants to transform words into something unifying and revolutionary—she also seeks to transform her audience, awakening individuals to their decolonized selves as well as to their connection with both their local and global black communities. By focusing on anatomy as an integral part of the poetic process, Cortez also eschews the traditional separation of the body from the mind. Indeed, Cortez seems to want her readers to be conscious of their bodies as marked sites by reinforcing the notion of the African and African Diasporic body as simultaneous sites of colonial domination *and* decolonization. As poetic rituals of transformation, Cortez's poetry works on her reader like an initiation rite.

In *Beloved,* Toni Morrison offers a compelling look at the lingering psychological effects of slavery. The newly freed slaves depicted in the present-day textual narration also must undergo a transformation, or an initiation rite, in order to be truly free. Not only must they come to terms with the marks that slavery has left, but with what it means to be a *marked* person. To be marked as Other, according to Morrison, means "that anybody white could take your whole self for anything that came to mind. Not just work, kill or maim you, but dirty you. Dirty you so bad you couldn't like yourself anymore. Dirty you so bad you forgot who you were and couldn't think it up" (*Beloved* 251). In many ways, the psychological dirtying to which Morrison alludes is comparable to what Frantz Fanon defines in *Black Skin, White Masks* (1967) as the "racial epidermal schema." Fanon's "racial epidermal schema" is yet another way of talking about what it means to be racialized as Other, to simultaneously exist under the white gaze as both "transparent" and highly visible in that one's body serves as the physical locus for all the negative stereotypes associated with blackness: "I was battered down by tom-toms, cannibalism, intellectual deficiency, fetishism, racial defects, slave-ships, and above all else, above all, 'Sho' good eatin'" (*Black Skin, White Masks* 112).

Located somewhere on the outskirts of Cincinnati in a secluded part of the woods aptly named "the clearing," Baby Suggs, the seemingly self-appointed lay preacher of Morrison's *Beloved,* encourages blacks to purge themselves of definitions that seek to mechanize black bodies. She preaches the glorification of black flesh as a counter to the psychological trauma of slavery and the subsequent postslavery condition of second-class citizenship. In her sermon, Baby Suggs offers her congregants a racial epidermal schema that stands as an antithesis to the schema that Fanon outlines: Here . . . in this here place, we flesh; flesh that weeps, laughs; flesh that dances on bare feet in grass. Love it. Love it hard. Yonder they do not love your flesh. They despise it. (*Beloved* 88)

It is important to note that Baby Suggs's focus is on the *flesh* and not the *body*. In her groundbreaking essay "Mama's Baby, Papa's Maybe: An American Grammar Book," Hortense J. Spillers makes the distinction between "body" as a captive subject-position and "flesh" as a liberated subject-position. She explains:

Even though the European hegemonies stole bodies—some of them female—out of West African communities in concert with the African "middleman," we regard this human and social irreparability as high crimes against the *flesh*, as the person of African females and African males registered the wounding. If we think of the "flesh" as a primary narrative, then we mean its seared, divided, ripped-apartness, riveted to the ship's hold, fallen, or "escaped" overboard. (457)

If the flesh is the primary narrative, internal decolonization necessitates a *return to the flesh* or at the very least a recognition of what it might mean to exist outside of a racial epidermal schema.

Baby Suggs seeks to highlight the visceral realities of black life both during and after slavery; the sensual veneration of black flesh is a revolutionary act that is as much an act of defiance as it is a ritual of internal decolonization. Although she still centralizes black skin as the racial sign of difference, this difference is mitigated by her use of oppositional rhetoric to challenge racist notions of blackness. This difference is further tempered by Baby Suggs's reconfiguration of audience. Shifting the emphasis from the white gaze to that of the black, Baby Suggs methodically breaks the black body into parts—eyes, hands, mouth, neck, liver, and especially the heart. Baby Suggs invites her congregants to participate in what can be considered a cleansing ritual in which they must "claim ownership" of their freed selves because "yonder"—beyond the veil, whites habitually abuse, maim, and generally mistreat black flesh.

Although their methods differ, both Fanon and Morrison provide us with what Cherríe Moraga and Gloria Anzaldúa would term theories "in the flesh"—defined as a theory in which "the physical realities of our lives—our skin color, the land or concrete we grew up on, our sexual longings—all fuse to create a politic born out of necessity. Here, we attempt to bridge the contradictions in our experience" (*This Bridge Called My Back* 23). These theories of the flesh, then, can be interpreted as strategies through which people of color make sense of and sometimes rectify their marginal existence within the confines of white majority cultures. Unlike Fanon, however, Morrison and Cortez participate in the dissection of black flesh to instruct their respective audiences about its value beyond the body's usefulness to whites.

D. H. Melhem writes, "Anatomy as metaphor informs [Cortez's] dominant themes: identification with the working class and underclass, with Black pride and vitality, with heroic figures, and with Black music" (*Heroism in the New Black Poetry* 184). For Cortez, lurid renderings of black flesh, due to racist persecution and economic exploitation in the United States and the Diaspora, depict "the martyred flesh with its living testimony toward solidarity" (185). Compare, for example, Cortez's "They Came Again in 1970 and 1980" with sections of Baby Suggs's sermon that I quoted earlier. In both cases each speaker instructs a black audience about the misuse of black flesh.

"They Came Again in 1970 and 1980" is a poem about the effect missionaries and scientists have had on developing countries in Africa. Cortez writes:

> And in the name of god and progress
> and stuffed pockets after so much torture
> and so many invasions in the blood
> your veins are
> air strips for
> multi-national corporations
> Your native sweat is
> aviation fuel for
> drilling rig (*Coagulations* 82)

In contrast to Morrison, Cortez presents an ideology of black flesh under duress that is markedly different. While Morrison uses Baby Suggs's scrutiny of individual body parts as a way to be specific about the reasons for glorifying black flesh, Cortez eviscerates flesh as a testament to the global exploitation of blacks. Here Cortez links the abuse of Third World people with the abuse of so-called Third World countries, a comparison she frequently makes in her poetry. The bodies of Third World people are depicted as sites for exploitation—"after so much torture / and so many invasions in the blood / your veins are / air strips for / multi-national corporations." That land is personified in the visage of black flesh and fluids demonstrates the direct connection between African nations and African peoples, because it alludes to the fact that black nations were depleted of both their riches and their peoples.

It is significant that Cortez, like Baby Suggs, uses the brutality of racist oppression as a common denominator of blackness. If the martyred flesh serves as a testament to black solidarity, as Melhem also argues, then the employment of this rhetorical strategy predates that of contemporary writers. Frederick Douglass employed a similar strategy in 1847 when he expressed in "To Our Oppressed Countrymen" the *North Star*'s commitment to blacks who remained in bondage. He stated:

> Remember that we are one, that our cause is one, and that we must help each other, if we would succeed. We have drunk to the dregs the bitter

cup of slavery; we have worn the heavy yoke, we have sighed beneath
our bonds, and writhed beneath the blood lash;—cruel mementoes of
our oneness are indelibly marked in our living flesh. We are one with you
under the ban of prejudice and oppression—one with you under the slan-
der of inferiority—one with you in social and political disfranchisement.
What you suffer, we suffer; what you endure, we endure. We are indissolu-
bly united, and must fall or flourish together. (*Life* 283)

Here Douglass employs what I call a theory of scarification as a rhetorical strategy; he evokes the image of abused flesh to unite blacks. Given
Douglass's example, scarification can be interpreted in two ways: (1) in
terms of the scars left by oppression (slavery, colonialism, imperialism)—
mental scars as well as physical, and (2) as ritualistic tribal markings that
not only define the people to whom you belong, but the place.[4]

In a strictly African American context, however, one must join these
two definitions so that "scarification" means that as African Americans
we all belong to the same tribe and bear the markings of oppression to
prove it. In 1855, ex-slave William Grimes would employ the same technique in his autobiography. He writes, "If it were not for the stripes on my
back which were made while I was a slave, I would in my will leave my
skin as a legacy to the government, desiring that it might be taken off and
made into parchment, and then bind the constitution of glorious, happy
and *free* America. Let the skin of an American slave bind the charter of
American liberty!" (*Life of William Grimes* 83–84).[5] The place that defines
us (notice I did not say the place that accepts us or the place that we can
always call home) is also the place where we received our markings—the
United States. The use of scarification as a theoretical tool, however, does
not mean that one should ultimately define oneself by the oppression one
faces. Instead, it attempts to validate the need to express how it feels to be
degraded and the mental scarring that can also occur.

THEORIZING FROM THE POSITION OF THE "FOLK": CORTEZ AS A THIRD WORLD POET

In an interview with Alexis DeVeaux, Cortez explains that "[i]t's
necessary, and it's part of the heritage itself in being a poet, an African
poet, a Black poet, to keep those memories, the Black poetic spirit, alive
because they are valuable both in my life and to the spiritual life of the
Black community" ("A Poet's World" 78). As the second epigraph to this
chapter also exhibits, Cortez wants to use her position as a poet to help
blacks think critically about our lives so we might be able to better our

condition in the United States and abroad. For Cortez, however, the reference to the black community extends beyond the U.S. border. Because of the reciprocity she sees between Africans and blacks in the Diaspora, Cortez should also be considered a "Third World poet." Quincy Troupe and Rainer Schulte define the "Third World" as "the world of the politically and economically oppressed and exploited. . . . Third World writers may be African farmers or Latin American academicians. They are those writers who identify with the historically exploited segment of mankind, and who confront the establishment on their behalf" (*Giant Talk* xxiii).

Cortez explains the ways Africa has affected her writing:

> I visit there often and I'd love to live there, but I couldn't make a living. And I'm tied to my people here. But I can produce the most work there because it's peaceful and it's Black. I can think more clearly in countries used to ceremonies, rituals, work, where I'm exposed to festivals and funerals. I see us all as one people in different locations, our commonality—culturally, politically Africa is the kind of world I'd like to be in all the time (DeVeaux, "A Poet's World," 106).

It is Cortez's affinity to Africa and its cultures' predisposition to ritualizing life events that has deeply affected her writing style. To say that she can "think more clearly" in countries that emphasize rituals also demonstrates Cortez's need to disassociate herself from Westernized ideologies. In her poetry, Cortez often makes connections between blacks in Africa and its Diaspora. As Jon Woodson points out, "In 'For the Brave Young Students in Soweto,' Cortez details the similar fates of blacks in New York and in South Africa: 'When I look at this ugliness / and see once again how we're divided and / forced into fighting each other / over funky jobs in the sewers of Johannesburg / divided into labor camps / fighting over damaged meat and stale bread in Harlem.'" (72).

In an African American context, Cortez functions as a revolutionary diva by speaking on behalf of "Third World" people from the simultaneous vantage points of both spokesperson and sister worker. Solidly a product of a working-class upbringing, Cortez, like other black aestheticians, sees herself as one of the people. Given this supposition, much of Cortez's poetry is geared toward the black proletariat. In an interview with Cortez, Melhem questions Cortez about the affinity she feels toward black nationalism, countering that her work instead seems more "worker oriented and more general, class oriented." But Cortez responds that her work is "Black worker oriented. I am a Black person in a Black family in the Black nation, so nationalism is a natural fact" (*Heroism in the New*

Black Poetry 203). In other words, Cortez not so much privileges race over class, but sees that class is generally a function of race. Her words also negate attempts to separate her race from some sort of individual essence—therefore, she affirms that her experiences are predicated by her race.

Melhem also argues that Cortez's poetry relating to working-class populations is not so much about an individual's struggle with poverty, but rather the struggle of impoverished communities and the tendencies to blame these communities for their own predicament. In an interview with Cortez, Melhem queries, "Rather than personal sadness, you were really talking about sadness in the environment" (201). Cortez replies, "Being unemployed and without food can make you very sad. But you weren't the problem. The problem existed before you knew there was a problem. The problem is the system, and you can organize, unify, and do something about the system. That's what I learned [working on the voter registration drive in 1964–1965]" (201). In this quotation, Cortez turns the phrase "Negro problem" on its head. The problem is not with the so-called Negro population as it is with institutions that create second-class citizenship for its African American population.

Cortez's poem "I'm a Worker" (*Festivals* 14–15) is partially autobiographical and is dedicated to "all my sisters in the garment industry." The blue-collar speaker believes that all of her problems would be solved by getting some "survival money"—money that will be just enough to get by: "If I had some honey / If I had some gunnie / I think I'd have that thing called survival money." The speaker believes her life would improve if she had either a man who could supply her with money or a gun so she could get money on her own. Here she demonstrates the connection between survival and materiality. Cortez suggests that possession of material goods serves as an access to power—making the converse also true.

The speaker's willingness to resort to soft-core prostitution or theft demonstrates the actual violence that poetry does; it strips people of their moral fortitude. The speaker realizes that living paycheck to paycheck on dirt wages can create a heavy sense of desperation and justifiable anger. The poem suggests two methods of obtaining "survival money"—one reactionary, the other revolutionary. She can either subjugate herself to a man or she can commit a violent act of what can be described as self-defense. At the end of this poem, the speaker states:

> I got the landlord gas lights
> the union telephone department store

subways buses & 4 human beings
to feed
so tell me tell me tell me
do you think a revolution is what I need. (*Festivals* 15)

It is interesting to note that the last sentence does not have a question mark, which suggests that the question is a rhetorical one. What Cortez means by "revolution," however, is less obvious. She could mean both overturning the system and destroying the way it treats working-class citizens, or a personal revolution—the speaker needs to undergo a transformation so that her life is not preoccupied by the come and go of the dollar. But for the latter to happen, the first must occur, because when bills must be paid. even union dues, it is very hard to devalue the importance of money. Indeed, I suspect Cortez would say that devaluing the importance of material goods is a luxury afforded only to the rich.

As a Third World poet who consciously identifies as such, and given her tutelage under the black aesthetic schools, Cortez's proletarian tendencies compel her not only to blur the lines between so-called high and low art, but to dismantle European ontology. If one considers the autobiographical tenor of a poem like "I'm a Worker," then it is easy to see how Cortez makes use of lived experience to develop theories that work better to explain the lives of marginalized populations. Cortez reminds us: "The intellect and the intuition—that's all one thing. Can't be one without the other" (quoted in Melhem, *Heroism in the New Black Poetry*, 206). When she equates the intellect with intuition, she is acknowledging a long-standing practice of disassociating the two. Cortez also demonstrates an awareness that blacks have historically been thought to intuit rather than express intellectual faculties. Rather than eradicate this stereotype, Cortez seeks to validate other ways of approaching life.

Cortez's statement also seems to recognize that to code the types of analyses performed in the academic arena as "theoretical" and work from lived/learned experience as merely anecdotal, rather than also instructive, creates a hierarchical binary in which lived experience is forever on the bottom.[6] Cortez undercuts the hierarchical position of academic theory in her poem "There It Is," which serves as a perfect example of how she uses poetry as a space through which to filter notions of upheaval.

Cortez writes:

My friend
they don't care if you're an individualist

a leftist
a rightist
a shithead or a snake
They will try to exploit you
absorb you
confine you
disconnect you
isolate you
or kill you. (*Coagulations* 68)

In this stanza of the poem, I envision Cortez explaining Fanon's racial epidermal schema; as a black person, no matter what type of political agenda you adopt, no matter what your ideological stance, your politics will not save you from being victimized and manipulated by the power structure. Exploitation, like death, knows no ideologies. For Cortez, then, the idea of race as a construct becomes irrelevant when faced with the reality of racism.

Because Cortez, like other revolutionary divas I examine in this project, wants her readers to move past the idea of victimization as a permanent condition, she offers a resolution. Revolution through organization and unification, Cortez concludes, is the only means of combating the ruling class and saving ourselves from the perils of victimization:

And if we don't fight
if we don't resist
if we don't organize and unify and
get the power to control our own lives
Then we will wear
the exaggerated look of captivity
the stylized look of submission
the bizarre look of suicide
the dehumanized look of fear
and the decomposed look of repression
forever, and ever and ever
And there it is. (*Coagulations* 70)

Cortez not only itemizes the various ways one can be a victim, but she shows what the face of each mode of victimization looks like. Though the "looks" might change, Cortez warns that the cycle of abuse will continue unless we strive to break it—and that is Cortez's bottom line.

Cortez's poem "To the Artist Who Just Happens to be Black" (*Festivals* 8) serves as an appeal to the artist who rejects the scarification process or denies her or his markings (i.e., denies that racism is a very real factor in the life of blacks). In light of her connection to the black aesthetic movement, in her poetry Cortez demonstrates a rejection of nonpoliticalized art. In "Black Cultural Nationalism," Ron Karenga explains this sentiment when he states:

> in fact, there is no such thing as "art for art's sake." All art reflects the value system from which it comes. For if the artist created only for himself and not for others, he would lock himself up somewhere and paint or write or play just for himself. But he does not do that. On the contrary, he invites us over, even insists that we come to hear him or to see his work; in a word, he expresses a need for our evaluation and/or our appreciation and our evaluation cannot be a favorable one if the work of art is not first functional, that is useful. (33–34)

In "To the Artist Who Just Happens to be Black," Cortez entreats the artist who believes that art should be divorced from politics and who views "blackness" as an accident of birth and would rather look past the color of her or his skin toward a contemplation of seemingly more productive issues. In this poem, Cortez is echoing Langston Hughes in his landmark essay "The Negro Artist and the Racial Mountain," where he writes:

> One of the most promising of the young Negro poets said to me once, "I want to be a poet—not a Negro poet, " meaning, I believe, "I want to write like a white poet"; meaning subconsciously, "I would like to be a white poet"; meaning behind that, "I would like to be white." And I was sorry the young man said that, for no great poet has ever been afraid of being himself. (*Festivals* 88)[7]

While Cortez piggybacks on Hughes's notion of the role of the black artist by critiquing the same type of "art for art's sake" philosophy that negates lived-through oppression, it is important to note the differences between Cortez's subject positioning and Hughes's. Hughes appropriates a folk culture that is not his own, fancying himself as a vanguard of the people, unlike Cortez, who is decidedly *one of the people.* She asks:

> Listen
> why is your grandaddy's chopped up penis the
> magic mallets of truth you hide from

your grandmamma's vagina torn by mangy dogs
her hemorrhaging womb the blood mouth of
the blues you deny
Listen to us our own. (*Festivals* 8)

Cortez transforms the notion of oppression into a concrete, physically brutal manifestation, an experience that moves the poet from the level of mere contemplation (art for art's sake) to a poetry that is actively engaged with African American heritage. The overall message, then, is that black writers who would rather write without acknowledging their cultural heritage are not only indirectly denying oppression, but also denying the emasculation of their grandfathers, the rape of their grandmothers, and the whole ideology behind the blues. To deny this legacy of oppression, then, is to devalue the experience of millions of African Americans who lived, loved, and died under the lash. To deny oppression is to try to efface the scars lashed into the very matrix of U.S. society. To deny oppression is to deafen your ears to a song that not only sings of pain, but of the victory found not only in surviving, but in fighting back.

It is significant that Cortez applies the use of direct address in this poem. Phillip Brian Harper argues that it is indicative of the black arts project for writers to directly address their perceived black audiences with the second-person pronoun. He explains that "this aspect of the poetry is notable not only because it is the verbal indicator of the Black Arts poets' keen awareness of issues of audience and of their desire to appear to engage directly with their audience, . . . but because the *you* references also—and paradoxically, given the Black Aesthetic's nation-building agenda—represent the implication of intraracial division within its Black Arts strategy" ("Nationalism and Social Division" 248). Because she, as a revolutionary diva, is concerned with unifying blacks instead of attacking the wayward poet, Cortez attempts to enlist the artist into her own agenda. Cortez, as Harper contends is true of most black aestheticians, is vested in transforming this poet into a black nationalist subject. Therefore, while Cortez questions the poet's choice of audience, she refuses to call the artist a traitor or an "Uncle Tom," but rather labels the poet "our own." In the last stanza she asks, "Why are you forsaking us?" This question follows a plea—an invitation for the artist to join the struggle and to rise up and "kill" the oppressor:

and you my brother
my sister
my strength

my power
my god of vision
why do you reject us
twin of blackness oppressed by the same oppressor
whom in unity we must kill
why
oh why are you forsaking us. (*Festivals* 8)

Much in the same rhetorical fashion used by June Jordan in her poem "Okay, 'Negroes,'" according to Harper the "you" of both Jordan and Cortez's poems "is the African-American who has not yet developed an understanding of the raciopolitical forces that impinge on black subjectivity" ("Nationalism and Social Division" 250). But Cortez does not just reserve this type of rhetorical strategy for unenlightened blacks.

"So Many Feathers" (*Coagulations* 33–35) is another poem in which Cortez chides an artist for an affront to her fellow and sister blacks; in this instance, she calls Josephine Baker to task. Rather than criticize Baker for succumbing to the image of the primitive, exotic Other in her performances, Cortez acknowledges the erotic power she exudes in her dance. She labels Baker "feather-woman of terror" and thus connects her performance to the larger issue of black struggle. Scholars like Michael Borshuk concur with Cortez's portrayal of Baker when he argues that critics have ignored the "parodic agency" of Baker's performances that both poke fun at colonial fantasies and demonstrate a feminist intentionality to expose stereotypes of black female sexuality. In regards to the latter instance, Borshuk explains that "[b]oth of these contexts—white specularity of the black female body and 'moral panic' over the black women's sexuality—are germane to a rereading of Baker's early performances. Baker played with these constructions in the context of her jungle scenarios; time and again she appeared on-stage as a sexual beast that needed to be captured or contained" ("An Intelligence of the Body" 47).

What is ironic, however, about "So Many Feathers" is that many scholars have referred to it as solely a praise poem that celebrates Baker; they ignore that the initial praise she has for the starlet unfortunately turns to bewilderment at Baker's seemingly antiblack actions. Cortez writes:

Josephine you had every eyelash in the forest
every feather flying
why give your beaded snake-hips
to the death white boers in durban
Josephine didn't you know about the torture chambers

made of black flesh and feathers
made by the death white boers in durban
Josephine terror-woman of terrible beauty of such feathers
I want to understand why dance
the dance of the honorary white
for the death white boers in durban (34)

In this quotation, Cortez criticizes Baker's decision to perform in Durban and Johannesburg in 1974.

Initially, I equated "So Many Feathers" with Alice Walker's essay "In Search of Our Mother's Gardens," in which Walker tries to recoup Phillis Wheatley's image as a race traitor by explaining that Wheatley suffered from "contrary instincts"—the instinct to love her captors competing with the instinct to love her race. But Cortez does not try to explain Baker's actions to her readers and instead directly entreats Baker to rethink her actions. The direct appeal is symbolic of the respect Cortez has for Baker—a respect that she extends to other seemingly wayward blacks throughout her body of work. Cortez does not strip her of the title of "feather-woman of terror" for her transgression, and instead uses the poem to jog Baker's memory of why she became an expatriate in the first place. Cortez does not accept Baker's supposed contrary instincts (Walker's term for Wheatley's divided consciousness), given that her immigration to Paris was in part a deliberate attempt to flee the American South's version of apartheid.

One could argue, however, that Baker did not forget her earlier battles for civil rights. For example, her biographer, Ean Wood, explains that Baker attempted to desegregate the audiences during her performances in South Africa, much like she had in earlier times in the segregated South or in Argentina, but to no avail.[8] It would appear that she underestimated the strength of apartheid. Wood reports, "Angry and upset, she performed poorly, and the tour became a procession of disputes and hostile reviews" (*The Josephine Baker Story* 314). Baker also endured bomb threats and refused to leave the hotel in which she was housed as a form of protest. Wood reports that she told the *Radio Times* in London that "[t]hey are all sick here. The place reminds me of a stagnant pool, never changing, breeding malaria. But why should I run away? There are many people here who can see what is happening, but who are not running away from it. Then why should I?" (315). One could argue that Baker simply had more faith in the humanity of the whites in South Africa than was actually warranted, and in the end she came away from her South Africa tour disillusioned. Ultimately, I would argue that Baker's motives still qualify her for the feminist moniker of "revolutionary diva."

PUTTING HER "MOUTH ON PAPER":
LOCATING THE FEMINIST IMPERATIVE IN CORTEZ'S POETRY

Given Cortez's focus on icons like Josephine Baker throughout her body of poetry, this next section deliberates on the extent to which her poetry can be considered "feminist." This section addresses Cortez's acceptance within the purported masculinist black aesthetic movement, even though she often flouted the unwritten rules that dictated proper etiquette for women (e.g., the use of profanity). I argue that her strategic use of rhetorical appeals, which I deal with in a more rigorous fashion further into this section, is one reason Cortez avoids censure. Another reason may be that Cortez espoused the proverbial party line in instances where male homosexuality was deemed counterrevolutionary by many in BAM. For example, although Cortez challenges sexism throughout her work, the inclusiveness one has come to expect from feminist and womanist ideologies seems conspicuously absent in a poem like "Race."

Karen Ford notes that Cortez's homophobia and blunt sexual imagery "signal adherence to the program of the Black Arts movement" (*Gender and the Poetics of Excess* 219). The first line from her poem "Race" reads: "Men do not lay with men to claim god-hood." Cortez also demonstrates in this poem her belief that homosexuals cannot be revolutionaries and in fact are a detriment to the revolution that should be eliminated:

> Bleeding as we must slaughter these our sons to bring a revolution on /
> For what good will there be when time is here a non functioning product
> used openly against / We as he pleads his creative ability / Ability to create
> what? A Race called Faggot Oh black man quick please the laxative so our
> sons can shit the White Shit of Fear out and Live. (*Pissstained Stairs* 13)

In *Home Girls,* Cheryl Clarke, a black lesbian critic, discusses a printed flyer left on every seat at a conference on self-determination she attended in 1981. The contents of this flyer explain the ideology working behind Cortez's poem:

> Revolutionary nationalists and genuine communists cannot uphold
> homosexuality in the leadership of the Black Liberation Movement nor
> uphold it as a correct practice. Homosexuality is a genocidal practice.
> . . . Homosexuality does not produce children. . . . Homosexuality does
> not birth new warriors for liberation . . . homosexuality cannot be upheld
> as correct or revolutionary practice. . . . The practice of homosexuality is

an accelerating threat to our survival as a people and as a nation. ("The Failure to Transform" 197–198)

In a 1990 interview with D. H. Melhem, Cortez attempts to explain this poem by stating that "'Race' was written for a friend of mine. I don't think it indicts homosexuals. I think it talks about the contradictions of a particular person. The poem is about contradictions and inconsistencies. . . . I wrote the poem in 1968 at the request of a friend. He never rejected the tone of the piece" (*Heroism in the New Black Poetry* 207). This statement, however, scarcely absolves Cortez from the charge of homophobia.

It is because of her apparent homophobia that one must question the extent of the inclusiveness of Cortez's revolutionary agenda; she seems bound by black aesthetic convictions that homosexuality is counterrevolutionary. While quick to scorn those who scar heterosexual flesh, Cortez's words advocate what she would see as the necessary murder of homosexual men. Her words serve to rape the homosexual character of her poem of his dignity and humanity.[9] In 1970, however, Huey P. Newton published a rebuttal to this type of thinking in *The Black Panther*. Newton suggests that maybe the opposite is true, that "maybe a homosexual could be the most revolutionary" because of the various levels of oppression she or he has had to fight against (15). What is a bit sad and ironic is that had Cortez adopted Newton's position on homosexuals, she might have been able to see what Alexis DeVeaux sees, that society's fear of lesbians is an indictment against female independence.

Cortez's earlier poetry has not only offered a rallying cry for female independence, but has simultaneously implemented androgynous imagery—or at least imagery that obscures the distinction between oppression that is specifically masculine or feminine—to provide a space in which men and women can empathize with each other and thereby unite to fight racist oppression worldwide. At the same time, Cortez does not shun what can be considered distinctly "feminine" poetry, like the love poem, in order to put forth a revolutionary agenda. For example, in 1966 Amiri Baraka wrote "Black Art," in which he proclaimed, "Let there be no love poems written until love can exist freely and cleanly" (*Norton Anthology* 1943). Love poems tended to be frowned upon in the black aesthetic movement or even considered to be counterproductive in the face of revolutionary struggle. But in many ways having the courage to write a love poem, particularly as a woman, was in fact subversive.

Perhaps, however, Cortez evades censure for her love poems because she eschews romantic conceptions of love that derive from Western culture. In "Lonely Woman," for example, Cortez once again employs the use of anatomy as a metaphor; in this instance, her goal is to describe the pain of solitude. It is the blending of the profane or grotesque with the tenets of a love poem that possibly removes Cortez from the censure that many women poets felt when trying to express their feelings about heterosexual relationships.

In "Lonely Woman," her use of anatomy as a metaphor is more subtle as she equates a black woman's tears with warm sperm designed to "melt the calling—calling flesh." Here again, Cortez references the flesh, this time in connection with black female sexual desire. Additionally, to liken tears to sperm blurs the lines between the feminine and masculine. Given Cortez's tendency to eviscerate black flesh to demonstrate the ways it has been negatively impacted by imperialism or racial oppression, her use of flesh in this instance places heartbreak almost on par with other devastations of the flesh. In "Lonely Woman," Cortez also exposes a feminine vulnerability when she compares herself to a cricket, "small, weak, dark," while her presence tends to loom large, whether emanating from the page or during one of her performances. She exposes herself further, so to speak, by alluding to her failed marriage to jazz saxophonist Ornette Coleman.[10] Cortez writes that she is "Stripped—nude / from the trembling cadence of fire / Lit— / in Ornette's horn," lines that indicate the longing as much as the despair.

Jayne Cortez's third book of poetry is titled *Mouth On Paper*. One romantic interpretation evokes the image of red lipstick imprinted in the shape of a pucker on a tissue. The poems included in this volume, however, do not match this picture. Instead, the "mouth" referred to in the title more assuredly belongs to an audacious woman—a mouthy woman who says what is on her mind regardless of the consequences. Through poems that praise blues icons like Billie Holiday and Dinah Washington, for example, Cortez emphasizes her appreciation of sassiness (aka bitchiness). Cortez's "bitchiness" also surfaces in her depiction of heterosexual romantic relationships. In "Dinah's Back in Town," she writes, "I wanna be bitchy / I said I wanna be a bitch / cause when you nice / true love don't come into your life" (*Pissstained Stairs* no page number). In this line, Cortez demonstrates the ways "bitchiness" can manifest as a defense mechanism. She also seems to imply that "bitchiness" is a more honest emotion than any niceties a woman can exhibit.

In her poem, "Phraseology" (*Scarifications*), the term "bitch" asserts itself again. Cortez explains her use of language as follows: "I say things to myself / in a bitch of a syllable / an off tone wisp remarkable / in weight and size / completely savage to the passing of silence." The "bitchiness" of her words can be interpreted as Cortez's revolutionary voice, complaining about her Third World condition in a First World nation. Cortez eradicates the notion of female silence and uses her spoken words to viciously attack imperialism, racism, and sexism. As I state in this project's introduction, the revolutionary diva's voice can be interpreted as a political instrument for female empowerment, one that transforms the speaking subject into a radical agent.

I see Cortez as committed to reshaping society's perception of what it means to be feminine. Cortez, like Audre Lorde, challenges women to assert rather than repress our anger, to use anger as a revolutionary tool. Lorde explains, "My response to racism is anger. I have lived with that anger, ignoring it, feeding it up, learning to use it before it laid my visions to waste, for most of my life" ("Feminism" 38). In an interview with Alexis DeVeaux, Cortez seemingly concurs: "There is something within me, an intense feeling of outrage. I've always felt it. I don't know where it comes from. I just know it's there and I use it. It's the thing, the energy that makes you you, how you put it down, how you use it, how it comes out" ("A Poet's World" 106). By conceding that anger can be useful, both make a distinction between nihilistic rage and revolutionary rage. Nihilistic rage is anger that obliterates the self, while revolutionary rage defines anger as an act of self-defense/self-preservation, or as an act of protection.[11] Cortez and Lorde also inadvertently refute the stereotype that anger is a masculine trait.

Both Karen Ford and Peter Michelson comment on the fact that linguistic violence and profanity in general are hallmarks of the black aesthetic. Michelson writes:

> Obscenity and sexuality have . . . served an important tactical function in the development of black poetics, especially in its self-conscious formulation in the 1960s. The radical black analysis was that the first step toward racial liberation required blacks to define themselves and identify with their blackness. . . . For writers this entailed the use and validation of black language. The most identifiably black language was street argot with its frequent obscenity. . . . The obscenity, like idiolective grammar, spelling, and syntax, had the political purposes of dismissing white standards and validating black ones. (*Speaking the Unspeakable* 28–29)

What Michelson neglects to provide, however, is a gendered analysis of how the use of obscenities and sexuality in poetry might have had different consequences for women than for men. In her book *Ain't I a Woman: Black Women and Feminism*, bell hooks explains that the dismissal of white standards did not always necessitate a rejection of patriarchy; on the contrary, it often meant the embracing of patriarchal ideals predicated on African traditions. With hooks's comments in mind, male black aestheticians and even black audiences in general were sometimes averse to women poets who employed obscenity and sexuality in their works.

Speaking specifically of Carolyn Rodgers, Bettye J. Parker-Smith writes, "The use of obscenities and Black speech patterns was a very brave act indeed, especially for the female artists. But it represented a total rebellion against the restrictive English language as well as a defiance against their restrictive women modes" ("Running Wild in Her Soul" 405). According to Karen Ford, although women like Nikki Giovanni, Carolyn Rodgers, and Sonia Sanchez used profanity in their poetry, there came a point when they bowed to the external pressures and changed the tenor of their words. Ford argues that Jayne Cortez is one of the few female poets of this ilk that continues to use profanity as a revolutionary tool in her writing.

Of Carolyn Rodgers, Parker-Smith also explains that "[s]he struggles to affirm her womanliness. However, she is not strong enough to move beyond those obstacles that threaten the full development of Black womanhood" (395). Here, Parker-Smith is referring to her affirmation of her motherhood and Rodgers's fears that she would not be taken seriously by others if she chose topics that were women-centered. As confirmation of Rodgers's concerns, take for example Melhem's statements about Cortez's work. Referring to Cortez's poems "Rape" and "If the Drum is a Woman," Melhem writes, "Rather than as narrowly feminist statements, the poet intends the pieces as 'human rights poems'" (*Heroism in the New Black Poetry* 191–192). In addition to revealing a circumscribed interpretation of feminist polemics, Melhem's statements ignore the historical context in which the poems were written; "Rape," in particular, is based on two landmark court cases of the feminist movement involving working-class women of color. In these poems, Cortez links women's issues to political struggle. With the publication of "Rape" in 1982, Cortez entered into the discussions surrounding the controversial rape trials of Inez Garcia and Joanne Little.[12] For example, *Ms.* published an exposé on Inez Garcia in the May issue in 1975, while in June 1975, Angela Davis published "JoAnne Little: The Dialectics of Rape" in the forum section of *Ms.* magazine.[13]

Melhem's statement also negates the fact that both Inez Garcia and Joan Little eventually came to see their cases as emblematic of women's rights. In one interview Little is quoted as saying, "My case is important for all women . . . but it's more important for black women. It's for the future, so this won't happen to other black women" (W. King, "Focus of

Slaying Trial," no page number). Little's comments intimate an alternative to positioning feminism as antithetical to "human rights," as Melhem does; instead, poems such as "Rape" and "If the Drum is a Woman" reflect the *specificity* of black female oppression.

In "Rape, Racism and the Capitalist Setting," Angela Davis explains that in capitalist countries like the United States, from their inception rape laws were created to protect wealthy men at the expense of working-class women. Scholars such as Patricia Hill Collins and Deborah King have written extensively about the intersection of gender, race, and class oppressions, but as Davis notes in her article, in the late 1970s (when the above article was written), black women were largely absent from the antirape movement. She explains that this absence "is, in large part, [black women's] way of protesting the movement's posture of indifference toward the frame-up rape charge as an incitement to racist aggression. . . . Moreover, as rape victims themselves, they have found little if any sympathy from these men in uniforms and robes. And stories about police assaults on black rape victims are heard far too frequently to be dismissed as aberrations" (25).[14] The highly publicized murder trials of Inez Garcia and Joan Little, women who were tried for killing their rapists, had assuredly done much to shape Davis's conclusions. Though these trials eventually served as benchmarks of the antirape movement spearheaded by white women, they also illuminated how working-class women of color faced further persecution under the judicial system.

Of Cuban and Puerto Rican heritage, Inez Garcia was sexually assaulted by two Latino men (Louis Castillo and Miguel Jimenez) who were visiting her apartment to buy heroin from her roommate, Fred Medrano, who, as a white Texan, was considered an outsider in the Latino community in Soledad, California, where she resided. According to several newspaper accounts, Garcia's rape was both an act of retaliation (her attackers were jealous of Medrano's success as a drug dealer) and was initiated because they believed she was dating Medrano, a white man; therefore, Garcia was, in their eyes, a traitor to her race.

From the witness stand, Garcia described what was going through her mind during the rape:

> I was going through a whole lot of changes because I was thinking here I am, a person is using me, he hit me, he's raping me; I have a gun, I could be defending myself, but I can't even use it because they might use it on me.
>
> I couldn't do nothing; I felt helpless, and all I could do was go along with it so I could stay alive because I was scared and I didn't know what

to do and I was scared that if I might put up a fight that I might have been killed or stabbed or whatever because they were talking inside the house about stabbing before the whole thing started.

I let them use me.

He said, "They're all the same, when you get down to it, they're all the same." (Wood, *The Rape of Inez Garcia*, 103)

The emphasis Garcia places on being "used" by these men, coupled with the rapist's sentiment that all women are the same, suggests that the attempt to degrade and humiliate her was in some respects almost as damaging as the actual rape itself.

Jim Wood, the author of *The Rape of Inez Garcia*, argues that in many ways Garcia was subject to yet another rape at her trial. Tellingly, Wood explains that "[a]ccording to [Judge Stanley] Lawson, this was not a rape trial, 'whether the lady in question was actually raped is problematical, she didn't utter a cry, she voluntarily took her clothes off, later on we hear all about rape'" (210). Garcia's comments, however, reveal a belief in the viability of using violence as an act of self-defense in instances of rape—a belief that in 1974, when the rape occurred, was not supported by law.

On August 27 of the same year Garcia was raped, prisoner Joanne Little stabbed her white jailer, Clarence Alligood, eleven times with an ice pick that Alligood was reported to have brought into her cell to intimidate her. Little then fled from the cell, allegedly leaving Alligood alive and locked behind bars in her place. Little eluded North Carolina police for eleven days before surrendering herself, with her lawyer present, to the authorities. The sixty-two-year-old jailer was found in Little's cell naked from the waist down and holding an ice pick; the medical examiner would later testify that there was evidence of sexual activity. During her trial, the key issue up for debate was whether Little seduced Alligood into her cell to murder him so she could escape, or killed him in self-defense against imminent rape.

Although Inez Garcia and Joan Little both were working-class women, there was a marked difference in how they were portrayed in the media. Garcia was a devout Catholic mother and a woman of a lighter complexion than Little, and much was made of her beauty and sexual innocence. Even though she was living with a man who was not her husband, sympathetic magazines like *Ms.* were quick to point out that the relationship was both platonic and a matter of convenience—Garcia, who worked in the lettuce fields, simply could not afford to live on her own and support her son. Additionally, Garcia did not initially report her rape. In the article "The Pride of Inez Garcia," Maria Del Drago explained that, as a devout Catholic Latina, Garcia would have been ashamed to reveal the true nature and details of her assault lest she bring disgrace to her family—which was one way of explaining why she initially downplayed her assault to police.

In contrast, Joanne Little was treated less favorably by the mainstream media. Much was made of her juvenile delinquency as well as her several bouts with the law for petty crimes. One must keep in mind that Little's reputation was already suspect given that she was incarcerated at the time of the offense. On July 28, 1975, *Time* ran an article about Little's case, titled "A Case of Rape or Seduction?" In many ways, the writers attempted to present a balanced view of the case, writing:

> To them [Little's advocates], this is a classic example of the way rape victims can be railroaded by male-dominated legal systems, and of how black women prisoners are sexually abused by white guards, especially in the rural South. To the prosecutors, as well as the local white population, Joan is a burglar and a woman of loose morals who lured Alligood into making sexual advances in order to break out of jail.

In dealing with how Joanne might have been perceived by whites in North Carolina, the anonymous writers evoke long-standing stereotypes of the black Jezebel, which originated during slavery—the supposed inherent lasciviousness of black women caused their widespread rapes. In his book *The Innocence of Joan Little: A Southern Mystery,* James Reston, Jr., then a professor at the University of North Carolina, also explained the mindset of many white North Carolinians and their representatives in the state's judicial system; their belief in black inferiority cast a certain tenor on how Little was handled by the state and initially by white mainstream media. Ultimately, however, Little became cause célèbre for feminists and black activists alike, and even counted the Black Panther Party (especially Elaine Brown) among her supporters. *Time* reported that more than five hundred demonstrators could be heard chanting "One, two, three, Jo-an must be set free. Four, five, six, power to the ice pick."[15]

Not surprisingly, given the tenor of the times, Little resorted to writing poetry as a means of self-expression:

I grew up in the slums,
But I am somebody
I got in with "bad company"
Begging, stealing for what
   I thought was right,

That didn't make me any less—
I am still somebody (W. King, "Focus of Slaying Trial," no page number)

The poem's tone and Little's heart-wrenching assertion of her human-ity (a la Martin Luther King) demonstrates a sensitivity to her neg-ative portrayal in mainstream media because of her criminal record and low economic status. Little is using poetry as an act of self-defense against those who would strip her of her humanity because she is impoverished.

One of the main reasons Garcia's and Little's cases garnered so much attention, however, was because they did not *act* like stereotypical rape victims; instead of internalizing their anger, they externalized their rage in a very literal way—they killed their attackers. When describing how she killed the man that held her down while she was being raped by his friend, Inez Garcia proclaimed, "I took my gun, I loaded it, and I went after them . . . and another I want to say, I am not sorry that I did it and the only thing I am sorry is that I missed Louie" (Wood, *The Rape of Inez Garcia*, 184). Furthermore, as Garcia's comment shows, neither woman expressed remorse for her actions.

In "Making Female Bodies the Battlefield," Susan Brownmiller explains the significance of rape as a tool of war:

> Rape of a doubly dehumanized object—as women, as enemy—carries its
> own terrible logic. In one act of aggression, the collective spirit of women
> *and* of the nation is broken, leaving a reminder long after the troops
> depart. And if she survives the assault, what does the victim of wartime
> rape become to her people? Evidence of the enemy's bestiality. Symbol
> of her nation's defeat. A pariah. Damaged property. A pawn in the subtle
> wars of international propaganda. (172)

Although Brownmiller is speaking literally about rapes that occur dur-ing war, in her poem "Rape" Cortez uses sexual assault as a metaphor for war. She equates colonization (i.e., the rape of black nations) with the rape of Third World women. Cortez circumvents the stigma of rape (i.e., "damaged property") by turning the Third World rape victim into a revolutionary hero. The narrator empathetically asks the reader, "What was Inez supposed to do for the man who declared war on her body / the man who carved a combat zone between her breasts." It is significant here that Cortez once again omits the question mark and thus presents Inez's actions as logical given the circumstances in which she found her-self. Inez retaliated in war/rape time like a defending country bearing arms against an unwanted invasion. The woman's act of violence is redefined as self-defense, and her victory has her dancing over her dead rapist—celebrating his defeat by proclaiming it a holiday:

> She pumped lead into his three hundred pound of shaking flesh
> Sent it flying to the Virgin of Guadalupe
> then celebrated day of the dead rapist punk
> and just what the fuck else was she supposed to do. (*Coagulations* 63)

The bodies of the women, Inez and Joanne, are war zones. Man, specifically coded as white according to Cortez's agenda in this poem, is therefore depicted as the oppositional country, colonizing into submission through brutal penetration of the black female body/nation. Using poetic license in the rendition of Inez Garcia's story, Cortez envisions Garcia's retaliation as more immediate than it actually was. Perhaps for Cortez, immediate action is necessary to emphasize the need for imminent revolution. Additionally, that Cortez neglects to mention to the reader that Garcia's attackers were also Latino is strategic. Garcia's rape was a matter of class. Louis Castillo was a landowner; Garcia's circumstances made her more vulnerable to an attack. Furthermore, Cortez's poem is not just a castigation of the rapists' actions, but of the U.S. system that does not recognize violent self-defense as a valid response to rape, while that same system has historically been responsible for figuratively raping Third World nations of their natural resources.

In the section that deals with Joanne Little, Cortez presents Little as another female "country," this time besieged under a vicious police state (i.e., the United States). Cortez questions the godlike power of the police and their racist brutality. That the rapist is a white policeman and the victim is his black female prisoner shows how violence, rape, and racism are institutionalized. The fact that Joanne—written as country—kills the policeman can be read as an attempt to dismantle and overthrow such institutions on a level that surpasses individual revolution:

> This being wartime for Joanne
> she did what a defense department will do in times of war
> and when the piss drinking shit sniffing guard said I'm
>   gonna make you wish
> you were dead black bitch
> come here
> Joanne came down with an ice pick in
> the swat freak motherfucker's chest . . .

Joanne did the dance of the ice picks and once again from
   coast to coast
house to house
we celebrated day of the dead rapist punk
and just what the fuck else were we supposed to do.

In this poem it is just as important for the victim to voice her rage and retaliate; therefore, the poem advocates violence as a necessary means of self-defense. Simply identifying or naming the pain is not enough for Cortez when pain can reoccur and voices are routinely silenced. Cortez moves away from the language of victimization by not only valorizing the right to be angry over America's scarring of the black (in this case female) body with its systematic oppression, but by advocating violence as a means of preserving the self.

In "Rape" Cortez also uses aggressive obscenities to radically redefine what constitutes a woman's language, a vocabulary of rage and retribution—a language that has been claimed by many contemporary female poets like June Jordan, Audre Lorde, and Adrienne Rich. Of "Rape," Barbara Christian explains that "[h]er precise naming of rape as a declaration of war on a woman's body reminds us why we also talk about countries being raped: that rape of a woman is as evil an act as an attack on one's country. . . . It is clarity about what *is* really happening, the ability to name the truth beyond the muddle of propaganda, that characterizes Cortez's poetry" ("There It Is" 238). The excessive use of profanity and obscene imagery throughout the poem is necessary to emphasize the filthiness and ugliness of rape itself. Additionally, Cortez's use of the profane offers no protection or mediation for her readers. Since rape is generally considered a distinctly female trauma, perhaps we can see this language as also being feminine—and even therapeutic.

Since the first time I taught "Rape" as a graduate student, I have routinely been approached by female students who disclose that they have been rape victims. These women feel empowered by Cortez's poem because it validates their anger. Many of these women have expressed feeling frustration at the ways mainstream media offers a proscribed script of the rape victims' behavior that is predicated on the redefinition of the woman as an eternal victim. The poem, then, gives them an alternate mode of behavior (externalizing—i.e., blaming the victimizer) and justifies their anger.

Even though I have several unmarked copies of "Rape," I continue to teach a particular version to my students. I first discovered "Rape" in a library copy of Cortez's book *Coagulations* (1984). What struck me about this copy was that a person, whom I assume to be a woman, had written both in the margins and in the body of the poem; she had effectively changed the poem into a first-person narration by crossing out the names of Inez and Joanne and replacing them with "I" and "me." I could envision the woman's balled fist, tight around a scribbling ink pen, marking the margins with the memory of pain not forgotten—leaving her scars on paper. "Rape" obviously served as an outlet for the anonymous woman's rage, because when she arrived at the section where Joanne kills the policeman, she wrote, "I am at that step." Jayne Cortez, then, had inspired at least one person to revolt.

Karen Ford suggests that the impact of the poem might be lessened when one considers that Cortez reserves her strongest attack against white men who violate women of color rather than at black men who do the same. She writes, "Perhaps the reason Cortez escaped censure [for her use of profanity as a woman] . . . is that the men targeted by her excess were white. [In "Rape,"] Inez's rapist is compared to a 'giant hog,' suggesting pink skin, and Joanne's rapist is explicitly called a 'racist'" (*Gender and the Poetics of Excess* 220). Quite assuredly, Cortez associates whiteness with the capitalistic state, so while a giant hog could very well connote pink skin, I read it as more readily a reference to the derogatory moniker of "pig" that is often ascribed to police. Nevertheless, I believe there is some merit to Ford's insinuation, especially when one considers the difference in tone between Cortez's "Rape" and "If the Drum is a Woman."

Ntozake Shange exclaims, "I guess I've been in every black nationalist movement in the country, and I found that the flaw in the nationalists' dream was that they didn't treat women right" (quoted in Hogue, *Discourse and the Other,* 62). Such mistreatment, as I have explained in earlier chapters, caused women to expand the definition of black nationalism to fit feminine concerns. In chapter 2 of this book, I introduce "black nationalist feminism" as a precursor to Alice Walker's "womanism" to describe the feminist imperatives of those contributing to *The Black Woman* anthology. I submit that both of these terms, however, reflect the allegiance between black women and men. Such an allegiance, however, does not obscure discussions surrounding instances of misogyny or sexual abuse perpetrated by black men. Instead, as I argue in chapter 2, many women seek to decolonize rather than castigate sexist black men by employing several rhetorical strategies that elucidate the ways sexism is counterrevolutionary in both its divisive nature and its adherence to white patriarchal and capitalistic dictates. Cortez's poem, "If the Drum is a Woman," is one such example. Here Cortez moves out of the us/them binary language of the black aesthetic toward a space in which the white Other is marginalized—faded into the background.

In "If the Drum is a Woman," Cortez discusses violence against the black female body perpetrated by black men. The poem begins:

> If the drum is a woman
> why are you pounding your drum into an insane
> babble
> why are you pistol whipping your drum at dawn
> why are you shooting through the head of your drum
> and making a drum tragedy of drums
> if the drum is a woman
> don't abuse your drum don't abuse your drum
> don't abuse your drum (*Coagulations* 57)

The poem itself has a rhythmic quality akin to a drum. Melhem affirms that drums are "the symbol of cultural power, communication, and solidarity" (*Heroism in the New Black Poetry* 189).[16] Given the significance the drum is afforded in African cultures throughout the Diaspora, it serves as an apt metaphor to mirror Cortez's use of the appeal as a rhetorical device to both assuage and critique abusive black men. In personifying the drum as female, Cortez emphasizes the need to create a dialogue between black women and men.

In the next stanza, the speaker empathizes with the implied black male worker of the poem. She states, "I know the night is full of displaced persons . . . / I know the ugly disposition of underpaid clerks / they constantly menstruate through the eyes" (*Coagulations* 57). If we take the speaker to be Cortez, then we must remember that she was once a blue-collar worker herself. It is also significant to note that in this section Cortez chooses to use the word "menstruate" to describe the pain and frustration of the worker rather than "bleeding" or any other innocuous synonym. Cortez essentially *feminizes* the pain. She does more than just suggest female empathy with her wording; she implies that the racism that male blue-collar workers face is akin to a loss of manhood, or an act of castration. But if the female speaker empathizes with the male worker in question, Cortez also allows for the possibility of female castration.

Cortez then traces how these men, in their pain and bitterness at the system, translate their frustration into acts of violence against black women. Cortez makes it clear that the pain the underpaid male workers face is part and parcel of the American Way; this pain is a condition associated with the hypocrisy of American racist politics in the guise of white liberalism (hence the reference to Malcolm X's proclamation after Kennedy's assassination that "chickens are coming home to roost") and its imperialist impulses (symbolized in the figure of the "MX missile"). Cortez, though, underscores that this bitterness is a condition that black women must also face. Therefore, Cortez explains that it is counter-productive to substitute or compound one situation of oppression with another. Recognizing the scars they share, Cortez's methods seek to make black men aware of the widespread abuse of black women without making them defensive. Asking black men to take responsibility for their own actions, Cortez entreats black men to stop abusing black women. When Cortez insists that if the drum is as woman, she is not "docile," "invisible," or "inferior"; she insists that black men reject the stereotypes about women they have learned through their participation in patriarchy.

Although Cortez acknowledges how the exploited male worker, frustrated and scarred by racist oppression, can turn and then abuse his wife/mate/sister/daughter, she does not condone it. She seems to agree with Audre Lorde when Lorde states, "As Black people, we cannot begin our dialogue by denying the oppressive nature of *male privilege*. And if Black males choose to assume that privilege, for whatever reason, raping, brutalizing, and killing women, then we cannot ignore Black male oppression. One oppression does not justify another" ("Feminism" 19). Here the victimized male assumes the role of the oppressor and is in the position to produce further potential scar victims.

Cortez's use of the drum as a metaphor for the black woman can also be seen as a way for Cortez to place herself in intertexual dialogue with other male poets and musicians. For example, Aldon Lynn Nielsen astutely identifies Cortez's poem as an answer to Duke Ellington's song, "A Drum is a Woman."[17] I want to suggest, however, that Cortez's poem can also be read as a response to negritude poet Leopold Sédar Senghor's poem "Black Woman."

Senghor exclaims:

From the crest of a charred hilltop I discover you, Promised Land . . .
Naked woman, dark woman . . . Savanna of clear horizons, savanna quivering to the fervent caress
    Of the East Wind, sculpted tom-tom, stretched drumskin / Moaning under the hands of the conqueror. (*Collected Poetry* 8)

Cortez creates a dialogue between herself and Senghor, intertwining the notion of the drum as a beaten object with the notion of the woman as an abused object. While Senghor proclaims the black male speaker as "conqueror" of the female "Promised Land," Cortez thwarts and subverts the language of domination implied by both Ellington and Senghor by personifying the drum instead of objectifying the woman by giving her drum-like qualities.

Because of the way she successfully negotiates through layers of sexism without alienating men and while still holding a strong commitment to the concerns of black women, I see Cortez as a womanist. As a womanist, unlike much of Anglo-feminist writings and unlike Senghor and other black male writers of that ilk, Cortez defines a space for black women beside and in connection with—not in opposition or subordination to—their black male counterparts. For example, Amiri Baraka, who has been an ardent supporter of Cortez's work, presents an interesting contrast to Cortez. He includes Cortez's work in his 1983 anthology of African American women's writings, *Confirmation*.

In his introduction to this anthology, Baraka asks the following questions:

> What is it like here in the United States to be a black woman under the
> hammer of national oppression? What does this poison do to the woman
> herself, her life, her lovers, family? What does it take to survive? Can one
> "survive" and not survive at the same time? What does it take not only
> to survive but to triumph? How does one live under the rule and sway of
> national oppression, racism, and white supremacy? How does one keep
> one's sanity and balance in such a world, and how is this further compli-
> cated by being not just black, but a woman? (20)

The problem I have with the above series of questions is that Baraka implies that being a black male is synonymous with being black—"how is this further complicated by being not just black, but a woman?" That he could envision that someone could be "just black" is an excellent example of Baraka's attempt to work on his sexism. The attempt falls short, however, because although there are differences between types of oppression black women and men face, Baraka's questions leave little room for an intersection between the two experiences. Are we to assume that he does not know the answers to any of his questions? Unlike Baraka, in "If the Drum is a Woman," Cortez demonstrates an understanding of the plight of black men that Baraka—at least the Baraka of the 1960s to 1983—lacks. In "If the Drum is a Woman," the reader must remember the speaker's plea, "don't be forced into the position as an oppressor of drums and make a drum tragedy of drums," urging the oppressed male not to fall further prey to the evils of capitalism.

Throughout this chapter, I evoke the phrase "scarification" to explicate Cortez's revolutionary agenda. Through her graphic display of black flesh in turmoil and her implicit desire to employ scars (both figurative and literal, physical and psychological) as instruments of subversion, Cortez's poetry provides the most ocular and visceral representation of how to voice what Toni Morrison calls the "unspeakable things unspoken." By vocalizing the unspeakable as it pertains to the oppression of blacks and women of color, she offers her audience a way to free itself from the confines of racist and sexist domination. What an investigation of Cortez's poem "Race" demonstrates, however, is that if we are truly to heal the wounds of the past, we must learn to validate the various experiences of all marginalized people.

Scarification theory is born out of the black aesthetic movement's desire to acknowledge the materiality of African American existence and the poststructuralist notion that each person is a social construction—a blending of time, circumstance, environment, religion, ethnicity, and sexual preference. In this respect, testimonies of oppression or personal experiences in general become historicized. Scarification, then, recognizes that the nature of oppression and the marks that oppression leaves behind vary. When I speak of theorizing from the wound, however, I am also not exclusively referring to theorizing from the vantage point of a black female scholar. I am also thinking about theorizing from the gaping abscess racism has let fester within the very fabric of American society. Scarification then has implications for us all.

Whatever her flaws, there is no denying that the poetry of Jayne Cortez is about blood and revolution. Informed by the language of the black arts movement, Cortez stands as proof that all has not been said about the black aesthetic. Cortez proudly asserts her commitment to speak always through her scars to reach others who have perhaps yet to participate in the ritual. As Cortez's sixth book of poetry, *Coagulations,* reminds us, scarification is about blood, revolution, and most of all healing. Coagulation is the clotting of blood—the start of the healing process—and we can envision Cortez's poetry as a "clotting of blood poems." Blood poems could then be taken racially, to indicate that the commitment to the uplift of blacks is part of our heritage, passed down from "blood" to "blood" (either in the actual familial sense or metaphorically) through the bloodstream, through the blood that was shed by our ancestors, from generation to generation. Seen in this respect, the theorist/critic who theorizes through scars is not being naïve, but rather is fulfilling a long-standing legacy. And if we do not accept this responsibility as African American theorists, what will we do when "they" come cracking the whip again?

The revolutionary blood poems of Jayne Cortez epitomize the amalgamation of both the "intellect" and "intuition." Not only is Cortez committed to preserving our racial memory by recalling our tribal markings—our scarification—but she is also developing ways to use that memory, to use the scars, to fight oppression. Cortez writes to dismantle all oppressive institutions, to unpave all "hard roads" by all possible means. In the words of Jayne Cortez, "and just what the fuck else was she supposed to do?"

Five

SHE DREAMS A WORLD

The Decolonizing Text and the New World Order, Toni Cade Bambara's The Salt Eaters

Now, women forget all those things they don't want to remember, and remember everything they don't want to forget. The dream is the truth. Then they act and do things accordingly.

—ZORA NEALE HURSTON, *THEIR EYES WERE WATCHING GOD*

i used to dream militant dreams
of taking over america
to show these white folks how it should be done
i used to dream radical dreams
of blowing everyone away
with my perceptive powers of correct analysis
i even used to think
id be the one to stop the riot and negotiate the peace
then i awoke and dug
that if i dreamed natural dreams
of being a natural woman
doing what a woman does
when shes [*sic*] natural
i would have a revolution

—NIKKI GIOVANNI, "REVOLUTIONARY DREAMS"

all revolutions are rooted in dreams

—GRACE NICHOLS, "DAYS THAT FELL"

Zora Neale Hurston begins *Their Eyes Were Watching God* (1937) by reflecting on the ways women view the world differently than men. For men, "Ships at a distance have every man's wish on board. For some they come in with the tide. For others they sail forever on the horizon, never out of sight, never landing until the Watcher turns his eyes away in resignation, his dreams mocked to death by Time. That is the life of men" (1). Men, then, are governed by fate; destiny has ultimate control over wish fulfillment. According to Hurston, women function quite differently. At first glance, Hurston seems to negatively categorize female cognitive processes as selective, but she is actually suggesting that the ways women process memories can be interpreted as an act of survival; women discard memories that might prove damaging while they salvage memories that could be considered more life-affirming. Therefore, women shape their dreams, which they interpret as reality, to fit their own needs and agendas. Women not only have the power to make the dream the "truth," but privilege their vision of the world above all others—a power that has traditionally been ascribed to men.

I use Nikki Giovanni's poem "Revolutionary Dreams" as my second epigraph because it demonstrates more specifically the inherent revolutionary potential of black female subjectivity to which Hurston's quotation alludes. Giovanni's poem elucidates revolution as an evolutionary process by depicting the female speaker's metamorphosis from militant to radical to revolutionary. The transformation she undergoes is analogous to the process of decolonization that I put forth in the first chapter of this book. Her *militant* dreams are neither revolutionary nor decolonizing because they are grounded in the desire to "show these white folks how it should be done" and therefore do nothing to disrupt the double-consciousness paradox; her actions still demonstrate a prioritizing of a white audience and are motivated by her preoccupation with whiteness. Her *radical* dreams place the poem's speaker a step closer to decolonization, but ultimately she misses the mark because she is vested in self-exaltation, the individualistic and prideful desire to be viewed as savior. She finally concludes that her *natural* dreams are what will catapult her into a revolution. Here, the speaker looks inward for transformation and becomes decolonized when she is centered within herself as a "natural" black woman.

The third epigraph comes from Grace Nichols's first collection of poetry, *I Is a Long-Memoried Woman* (1983), which deals with black female subjectivity in the context of the historic oppression of Caribbean women. Using a Guyanan-born poet to conclude my rumination on the potency of black female dreaming allows me to make a Diasporic link between Caribbean and African American women and our twin struggles toward decolonization. Additionally, this poem articulates for me a fundamental truth that informs my thinking concerning this chapter: "all revolutions are rooted in dreams." One must first be able to envision a new world in order to call it into existence.

These three literary divas not only demonstrate the latent potential of black female dreaming, but they also continue the legacy of Diasporic African writings that have at the core of their traditions an inherent desire to spark a revolution that would remake the world into a more hospitable and humane place for all peoples. Their words place blacks as active agents in the making of history, but more specifically they call for women to shape our own individual futures and challenge us to remake the world in our own image. Their words ignore the historical tendency to render black female voices mute, our existence invisible.

Foreshadowing Dr. Martin Luther King, Jr., and Langston Hughes, to whom this chapter partially owes its title, "dreaming a world" means to manifest a vision of an integrated egalitarian society in which everyone would be capable of successfully pursuing the American dream. In his poem, "I Dream a World," Hughes writes, "I dream a world where all will know sweet freedom's way.... A world where black or white, whatever race you be, will share the bounties of the earth and every man is free" (*The Collected Poems of Langston Hughes* 311). In this poem, Hughes fathers a dream that has gestated in the creative wombs of many others, and although the dream has not been aborted, it has yet to reach maturity.

Black aestheticians of the 1960s called for a re-evaluation of the dream of integration and questioned its effects on the mental health and well-being of black people. Black aestheticians used the rhetoric of revolution to usurp the notion of the American dream and promoted the apocalyptic vision of a "new world order "—one that would be informed by African ontology and governed by black people. As I discuss in chapter 1, the black aesthetic movement was largely successful in changing the way we view ourselves as African Americans. But even in his essay "Statement," Amiri Baraka concedes that what was missing from the program of black aesthetics were "post-american forms," models that would arise in the aftermath of the revolution and serve as alternatives to those aesthetic models of whites.

Toni Cade Bambara's *The Salt Eaters* (1980) serves as the most explicit example of the "post-american form" for which Baraka calls. *The Salt Eaters* embodies what Hurston, Giovanni, and Nichols would view as the power of black female creativity. Bambara's text further demonstrates the possibility of envisioning black women as agents of change in U.S. society and the world at large. I argue that Bambara uses the theme of the apocalypse to signify the ultimate dream that will catapult both the characters and her readership into revolutionary action. I further argue that Bambara believes that revolutionary action *is* a decolonizing impulse. Bambara's use of the apocalypse as a metaphor for revolutionary change makes *The Salt Eaters* an exemplary model of a decolonizing text.

Throughout the body of the text and when she discusses how she conceived of the text, Bambara consistently uses the concepts of dreaming, spiritual/revolutionary mediums, and the apocalypse as interchangeable vehicles of revolutionary action. For Bambara, the act of dreaming is almost synonymous with writing in that both can precipitate paradigmatic shifts in thought for both the dreamer/writer and those that share the vision. She writes:

> I discovered, among other things, that writing is akin to dreaming. Writing, like dreams, confronts, pushes you up against the evasions, self-deceptions, investments in opinions and interpretations, the clutter that blinds, that disguises that underlying, all encompassing design within which the perceivable world in which society would have us stay put—operates. ("Salvation is the Issue" 42)

Bambara's mission, then, is to challenge not only the ease with which we take European and American ideologies and mythologies as a given, but the very process by which we become indoctrinated into a particular way of thinking or viewing the world that brands us as "Western."

In an interview with Zala Chandler, Bambara talks about how we have been taught as a society to believe that the world is governed by logical and rational principles rather than also being guided by a spiritual order; she labels this type of thinking as the "American disease" of "disconnectedness." Bambara traces the beginnings of this American disease and the Western bias against alternative ontologies to the Pilgrims' arrival in the New World:

> Those astringent Pilgrims who arrived in the New World with what they considered a more perfect way to worship, took one look at the "unruly" bunch that met them at the shore, the hospitality committee, and called them savages. (This was the beginning of the 'disconnectedness' as an American disease.) And they proceeded to ban the drum, ban smoke signals, and ban what they called fetish religions. In its place, they would impose a system of logic on the American psyche, the American sensibility, the American political reality, and, indeed, American life and literature that was aimed all the while at a total control of society by a few. ("Voices Beyond the Veil" 347)

According to Bambara, in addition to preventing Native Americans from practicing their religions, the Pilgrims prohibited them (and the enslaved Africans that would follow) from communicating with each other by forbidding the traditional tools used for that purpose—"the drum" and "smoke signals."[1] Prohibiting such communicative devices demonstrates that the Pilgrims wanted to disengage Native American populations from their heritage and ways of conveying their own philosophies to each other. Similarly, proponents of slavery sought to bring about the same type of cultural estrangement among African populations in the United States.

Throughout the novel, Bambara uses black cultural nationalism[2] as the theoretical and philosophical foundation of her novel in order to construct a text that thwarts the racist and imposed Western "system of logic" and better promotes her own revolutionary agenda—one that is committed to decolonizing her reading audience. Bambara's writing style usurps and unmasks the hierarchical position of Western traditions. Bambara centrally positions African and other Third World ideologies and philosophies. In the body of her text, alternative mythologies and philosophies are granted equal weight with biblical references and allusions to Greek mythology. Bambara writes as if U.S. readers will automatically understand a reference to the Vodoun god, Damballah, as readily as we would a reference to Jesus Christ—the Third World essentially is put on equal footing with the First World. *The Salt Eaters* serves as a complex example of an author using the basic tenets of cultural nationalism not just as a theme within the novel, but as the very constitution of the novel itself. *The Salt Eaters* is therefore a direct reflection of what Toni Morrison calls "Third World cosmology." Morrison writes:

> In the Third World cosmology as I perceive it, reality is not constituted by my literary predecessors in Western culture. If my work is to confront a reality unlike that received reality of the West, it must centralize and animate information discredited by the West—discredited not because it is not true or useful or even of some racial value, but because it is information held by a discredited people, information dismissed as "lore" or "gossip" or "magic" or "sentiment." ("Memory, Creation, Writing" 388)

With the creation of *The Salt Eaters*, Bambara prophesies a potential new world order that counters more popular uses of the term. In centralizing a "Third World cosmology," and therefore lending credibility to ways of knowing that have been constantly "discredited by the West," Bambara enables her audience to be active participants in the reading process.

Bambara offers an epistemological challenge to anyone brought up in the United States by insisting that the reader recognize alternative ways of thinking and of being in the world. To fully comprehend *The Salt Eaters,* the reader must undergo a mental revolution, a process of decolonization. Writing *The Salt Eaters,* then, is a corrective, a cure for both the American diseases of "disconnectedness" and double-consciousness.

Although de-centering Western cosmology is one way *The Salt Eaters* functions as a decolonizing text, the structure of the novel also reflects a decolonizing design. Like many writers before her (Audre Lorde comes to mind), Bambara wonders about the feasibility of creating a decolonized text when her basic mode of expression, writing, is essentially colonized, bound by language and the conventional expectations of the novelistic genre. Bambara circumvents this dilemma by conceding that African Americans are in fact Westerners and as such are entitled to use the language and myths they grew up with to their full advantage. In fact, she often selects Christian, Hindu, Greek, and West African allusions that demonstrate her "design of the world"—a world in which there are no coincidences, where "everything is everything," or rather where all things are connected. Bambara writes:

> The setup in *The Salt Eaters* is as close as I have come at this stage in my development to coaxing the "design" of the world I intuit and attempt to signify/communicate come through. Intimations that what I'm striving for—to work at the point of interface between the political/artistic/metaphysical, that meeting place where all seeming contradictions and polarities melt, that bicameral mind membrane . . . can be explored more senseably [*sic*] in some language other than what I've been using, prompts me of late to experiment more with new kinds of writing materials and writing forms. ("Salvation is the Issue" 43)

African American writers have traditionally merged the artistic with the political. But Bambara's revolutionary endeavor is to explore how the metaphysical functions in harmony with art and politics. It is no coincidence that Bambara calls her method of writing "dream work." Bambara believes that rather than viewing art, politics, and metaphysics as separate entities, a combined emphasis on all three would make readers more susceptible to the idea of revolutionary change; revolution would be seen as not just a political imperative, but a spiritual one as well.

In 1969, Mercer Cook and Stephen Henderson wrote that "Black writers . . . can save us, all of us, from this strange disease [racism], for the Movement is secular now. Our poets are now prophets. They have come to baptize us in blackness, to inform us with soul" (*The Militant Black Writer* 72). Not only does Toni Cade Bambara epitomize the writer/ prophet that Cook and Henderson visualize, she is also a revolutionary diva. I bestow this title upon Bambara because she uses writing as a vehicle to lead other blacks (through what Henderson would call a "baptism in blackness") to a decolonized subjectivity. As a revolutionary diva, Bambara has an affinity with her black audience that induces her to view herself as her audience's catalyst or spiritual/revolutionary medium.[3]

This connection Bambara has with her audience is mirrored by the communal element of the novel. In many ways, *The Salt Eaters* is not just Velma Henry's story, but also the story of the entire community of Claybourne. The novel opens with the public healing of Velma Henry after a failed suicide attempt. Through the example of her cathartic illness and her subsequent metamorphosis into a revolutionary subject, Bambara demonstrates the potential pathways to self-actualization for her readership. Velma Henry, like Bambara, acts as a medium through which the other characters in the novel become "whole,"[4] or rather become revolutionary agents, or at the very least accept the responsibility to become radical subjects. In *The Salt Eaters,* the theme of wholeness functions in triplicate, moving in a widening arc of concern for the wholeness of the individual woman (Velma Henry), to the wholeness of African Americans as collective people (represented by the citizens of Claybourne), to the wholeness of our nation.

To display the metaphysical dimension in the novel, Bambara experiments with alternative ways of presenting her narrative and demonstrating the intricate spiritual connection between the characters. Rather than use a traditional omniscient narrator, Bambara's "dream work" positions the narrator as *medium.* The narrator acts as a conduit, channeling Bambara's desire for revolutionary change to her readers. For the narrator to successfully fulfill the role of medium, Bambara eschews linear literary conventions by constructing a text that functions in multiple dimensions. For example, during her healing ritual that takes up the entire length of the book, Velma Henry has visions in which she travels to visit earlier times in her life, travels back in time to visit her "mud mothers" (her first, perhaps prehistoric, maternal ancestors), and is also visited by biblical and classical figures. Flashbacks and glimpses of alternative realms of reality occupy equal, if not more, space than the present moment of the novel. Gloria T. Hull contends that in *The Salt Eaters* "[t]ime (synonymous with timelessness) is not fixed or one-dimensional or solely horological; instead, it exists in fluid manifestations of its various dimensions. Past, present, and future are convenient, this-plane designations which can, in fact, take place simultaneously" ("'What It Is I Think She's Doing Anyhow'" 222). Time, or timelessness, described in this fashion has its own revolutionary potential. Using time in this manner enables Bambara to demonstrate how the past, present, and future are intrinsically bound.

The textual fluidity that Hull mentions has also been described as a sort of stream-of-consciousness writing. In the afterword to *Conjuring,* Hortense J. Spillers briefly discusses *The Salt Eaters* as "the tale of Velma Henry . . . articulated through a seamless web of a combined narration of central intelligence and stream-of-consciousness" (257). It is significant that Spillers does not solely rely on the phrase "stream-of-consciousness" to describe the narration of the text. M. H. Abrams defines a stream-of-consciousness as "the name for [a] special mode of narration that undertakes to reproduce, without a narrator's intervention, the full spectrum and the continuous flow of a character's mental process, in which sense perceptions mingle with conscious and half conscious thought, memories, expectations, feelings, and random associations" (*A Glossary of Literary Terms* 202). In many ways, Abrams's definition works as a description of the novel's structure. *The Salt Eaters'* mode of narration, however, widens the traditional meaning of stream-of-consciousness. The stream-of-consciousness exhibited in the text, while often functioning as "half-conscious thought," is *never* dependent on "random associations." It is Bambara's belief that what we perceive as randomness actually has a pattern; all things are connected, "everything is everything."

The novel also offers a less individualistic example of stream-of-consciousness at work because it relies on the interconnectedness of its characters; the narrative fluidly shifts from one character's consciousness to another's. For example, Velma's godmother, Sophie, abruptly leaves the healing circle because she is disgusted by Velma's decision to commit suicide. When Sophie crosses the door's threshold, she steps back into time and relives the day she discovered a canvas sack containing a "screwdriver, syringe, clockworks, [and] dynamite" in her son Smitty's room (14). We learn that during the civil rights movement, Smitty was severely beaten by the police for leading a student demonstration. We are told that Sophie was also arrested and beaten in her jail cell by the sheriff. By reliving these moments, Sophie's painful memories are likened to Velma's illness. Similarly, when Sophie leaves Velma, the click of the door has a mystical effect on many others in attendance: "Sophie Heywood closed the door of the treatment room. And there was something in the click of it that made many of the old-timers, veterans of the incessant war—Garveyites, Southern Tenant Associates, trade unionists, Party members, Pan-Africanists—remembering night riders and day traitors and the cocking of guns, shudder" (15). The click of the door awakens what Julian Mayfield would call their "racial memory" and makes the others in attendance remember when they received their warrior marks, when they were first initiated into revolutionary struggle. What clicks in the minds of the "old-timers" is the memory of earlier episodes of crises and times when they were active in movements to promote revolutionary change. That these moments intersect or overlap with each other suggests that although the community members are trying to effect change through differing methods, they all want equality for blacks. The fluidity of the text enables the old-timers collectively and spontaneously to recall their individual moments of activism in a time (the late 1970s) when political activism no longer appears to be needed. *The Salt Eaters* functions under the assumption that the civil rights era did not cure the nation of its other long-standing illness—racism. Therefore, Bambara continues where black aestheticians left off, by using her text to demonstrate how one might become a radical or revolutionary subject in the post–civil rights era—an era of apparent apathy.

Aaron David Gresson argues that the task of contemporary American society is for people to "recover ways of being related and connected to something and someone larger than 'I' and 'me'" (*The Recovery of Race in America* 3). Gresson labels this task "the recovery project." *The Salt Eaters* can be considered a "recovery project" of sorts because Bambara strives to provide models for individuals seeking to mature into or maintain their radical subjectivity in an era in which civil rights no longer dominates the national agenda and in which collective activism has become passé. Melissa Walker writes that *The Salt Eaters* is "about the far more difficult choices that characters must make in a social context that does not mandate decisions. In the mid and late 1970s, hardly anyone knew for certain what they might do that would make a difference" (*Down from the Mountaintop* 168–69). Walker suggests that the initial audience for *The Salt Eaters* longed to return to the 1960s and its revolutionary vigor. *The Salt Eaters* obliges by evoking the apocalyptic feel of the 1960s to emulate a pivotal "time and place in History that forced the trivial to fall away" (169).

To inject the sense of urgency needed to rally most people to action, Bambara also uses her text to foreshadow the apocalypse—the penultimate trope of revolution, the absolute new world order. The apocalypse has often been described in Christian doctrine as God's peremptory solution to a decadent world and therefore serves as a metaphor for all life-altering events: war, pestilence, holocaust, middle passage, flood, famine, fire. It is also a cataclysmic moment in which all dichotomies must be reconciled, the physical with the spiritual and the spiritual with the political. The apocalyptic moment demands individual transformation; one must choose to be revolutionary or perish. It is a time of reckoning that forces one to take responsibility for her or his actions—to commit to a belief system. The trope of the apocalypse epitomizes decolonization because it insists upon a re-evaluation of one's world views and a restructuring of one's identity based on new paradigms of thought and in the service of righteousness.

The Salt Eaters is set roughly in 1978, "the third year of the last quarter of the twentieth century. . . . A very crucial moment in human history" (*The Salt Eaters* 134). In an interview with Claudia Tate, Bambara comments on the then approaching 1980s as follows: "The eighties are now upon us—a period a devastating conflicts and chaos, a period that calls for organizing of the highest order and commitment of the most sticking kind, a period for which the sixties was a mere referral and the seventies a brief respite, a breathing space" ("Toni Cade Bambara"14). Therefore, *The Salt Eaters* posits the coming millennium as one fraught with apocalyptic possibilities: revolution/transformation, the promise of a new world order, damnation or redemption. As a decolonizing text, *The Salt Eaters* seeks to prepare a space for a new world order. Bambara believes that this new world order has to be dreamed into being, that a new world order is contingent upon revolutionary action or an apocalypse. Bambara, therefore, uses the theme of the apocalypse to replace the conventional American dream of integration and upward mobility for African Americans.

In the remainder of this chapter I will analyze the ways Bambara uses the urgency associated with the apocalypse to induce her readership into a psychic metamorphosis. As the ultimate vision or dream prophesied in the Bible, I use the trope of the apocalypse to illustrate the how *The Salt Eaters* functions as a decolonizing text on multiple yet interrelated levels: authorial intent, the novel's structure and plot, setting (both the time frame and the geographical location of the novel), and character development. To discuss these issues, the remainder of the chapter is organized around three textual manifestations of the apocalypse: (1) apocalypse as theme, (2) apocalyptic spatiality, and (3) the apocalyptic self.

A NEW WORLD ORDER: THE APOCALYPSE AS THEME

If we do not now dare everything, the fulfillment of that prophecy, re-created from the Bible in song by a slave, is upon us: God gave Noah the rainbow sign, No more water, the fire next time.

—JAMES BALDWIN, *THE FIRE NEXT TIME*

The theme of the apocalypse permeates African American historic and literary traditions, in which it has been used to describe the middle passage, slavery, emancipation, migration, and the general persecution of African Americans.[5] It is my contention that the trope of the apocalypse undergirds several of the key issues covered in this project. It evokes Du Bois's concept of the veil, the chasm existing between the black and white worlds; the duality of the African American psyche and text; the discrepancy between American ideals and practices, as exhibited by the many experiences of blacks and other minorities in this country; and finally the desire to reconcile these rifts and contradictions.

To write apocalyptically is a decolonizing endeavor in its own right. Maxine Lavon Montgomery states, "Writing an apocalyptic novel is a socially symbolic act with a meaning often hidden from the eyes of those outside the culture, because the novelist uses language in an effort to inscribe a future that challenges the beliefs present in the American mythos" (*The Apocalypse in African-American Fiction* 3). As I state in the introduction to this chapter, the content and design of *The Salt Eaters* undercuts the apocalyptic rhetoric of the West. First, Bambara's use of a multirealm narrative is indicative of traditional African American notions of the apocalypse because it opts for "an absolute, linear (chronometrical) time moving from the creation to the judgment day, which, [blacks] felt, would be the day of their liberation" (Baker, *Long Black Song*, 46). Viewing the past, present, and future on interrelated levels enables one to see a time in a more absolute continuum—"from the creation to the judgment day." By commingling the past, present, and future, and thereby thwarting linear conventions of the novel, *The Salt Eaters* is in sync with traditional African American conceptions of time. Second, Bambara's use of the mythical and metaphysical not only suggests alternate ways of perceiving the world, but also speaks to the fact that different modes of narration must be devised to discuss and present African American experiences in the New World. Third, and most importantly, the centrality of African American subjectivity in the novel disrupts mainstream white America's conception of itself as the "New World." Both Houston Baker and Susan Bowers discuss how the perception of America as the New World is based on the premise of a "White American apocalypse." In the white American version of apocalypse, America is envisioned as a "land of rebirth and new life, as opposed to Europe, the Old World of decadence, decay and death" (Bowers, "*Beloved* and the New Apocalypse," 211). Baker writes, "White Americans, as R. W. B. Lewis, Perry Miller, and Leo Marx have demonstrated, considered themselves new Adams in a new Garden of Eden; they believed that thrift and industry, a powerful technology, the dictates of social Darwinism, and a laissez-faire economy would assure the endurance and growth of their paradise" (*Long Black Song* 46). America, then, emerges as a geographic space of infinite apocalyptic possibilities to be realized through industry, i.e., the Industrial Revolution.

Both Baker and Bowers agree that the black American and white American perceptions of the New World are in disagreement with one another. For Africans, the forced move from their homeland to the New World was apocalyptic in itself; therefore the New World did not project promise but rather "a world of suffering, death, and alienation" (Bowers, "*Beloved* and the New Apocalypse," 211). However, historian Nathan Huggins suggests that the New World experiences of black and white Americans were more similar than not because both groups were "ruptured from tradition"—blacks from Africa and whites from Europe (*Revelations* 127). Huggins further argues that like their European counterparts, African Americans, because we have often found our own history of slavery and oppression too debilitating, have historically "desired to leap over the Afro-American experience altogether, to place ourselves in a tradition which is not immediately ours but certain to give us a sense of grandeur and legitimacy" (129). Here, Huggins seems to be referring to back-to-Africa movements that often lead to romanticizing an illustrious African past that stands in contrast to a history that begins in bondage. This romanticizing, however, can be read as an attempt by African Americans to see themselves as actors in history rather than as objects that are merely acted upon. For example, in *Long Black Song*, Baker suggests that enslaved Africans used the Bible to assume the past of the Israelites in order to associate themselves with a history that would render them as significant historical agents "rather than as objects in the white historian's perspective on Africa and America, where blacks often find themselves portrayed as bestial, passive, and unheroic" (44).

The desire to view oneself as an active subject rather than a passive object in history was highly prevalent during the 1960s. James Baldwin's *The Fire Next Time* (1962), particularly the letter he wrote to his nephew and namesake on the "one hundredth anniversary of the emancipation," is emblematic of the prevailing apocalyptic rhetoric of the 1960s that envisioned the apocalypse as a battle between the black and white races. Baldwin writes:

> the danger, in the minds of most white Americans, is the loss of their identity. Try to imagine how you would feel if you woke up one morning to find the sun shining and all the stars aflame. You would be frightened because it is out of the order of nature. Any upheaval in the universe is

terrifying because it so profoundly attacks one's sense of one's own reality. Well, the black man has functioned in the white man's world as a fixed star, as an immovable pillar and as he moves out of his place, heaven and earth are shaken to their foundations. (9)

In this passage, Baldwin alludes to the new consciousness stirring within the African American youth population ever since roughly 1954[6]—a population that had grown tired of serving as background for the "white man's world" and sought to struggle to make the world over in their own image. In the apocalyptic vision presented in the above passage, the mere threat of revolution upsets the hierarchical position of whiteness. In Baldwin's vision it is possible for white Americans to lose their superiority complex and for blacks to see themselves on their own terms rather than in a sycophantic coupling with whiteness. Myriam J. A. Chancy argues, though, that Western notions of the apocalypse rarely take into consideration how Third World populations function in the apocalyptic milieus as positive change agents in the global arena; instead they are stereotyped as the embodiment or perpetrators of "the cataclysmic evil fatalists brace themselves against" (*Searching for Safe Spaces* 137).

Part of Bambara's project in *The Salt Eaters* is to suggest that the African and subsequent African American presence in the United States has forever altered the country's destiny. For example, Doc Serge, resident healer and ex-pimp, ridicules the short-sighted vision of "manifest destiny" for its failure to consider how the black presence in the United States might undermine plans for domination and expansion. When he philosophizes about America's "latent destiny," Doc Serge turns the phrase "new world order" on its head:

The man thought the new age and the new order began with his arrival on these shores. Hah! They convinced us they knew about this country's Manifest destiny. Clearly they were totally ignorant about its latent destiny, its occult destiny. Understand? Now, its latent destiny is a Neptunian thing, a Black thing, an us thing. Following? And the new age has only just begun to be ushered in. (134)

This quotation demonstrates how Bambara makes connections between seemingly incongruous concepts: a new age, America's destiny, astrology, and blackness. Here we also see a more pointed example of how Bambara commingles the metaphysical with the political.

Doc Serge's ominous warning, in addition to the sense of urgency promulgated throughout the novel, warrants labeling *The Salt Eaters* a "new age" text. Thomas McLaughlin's definition of New Age writing is apocalyptic in itself: "New Age writings share a conviction that we are at a crossroads in history, a time when personal, social, spiritual, planetary, and cosmic transformation is at hand" (*Street Smarts* 79). For Bambara, astrology is not a pseudo-science, but rather a plausible way of explaining how the world works. She uses the astrological significance of Neptune to offer an alternative future than that purported by the ideology of manifest destiny, one that envisions African Americans as a chosen people. In the above quotation, "a Neptunian thing" refers to the Neptunian Age or the Age of Pisces.[7] Astrologically, Neptune, then, functions on multiple levels as a metaphor of the apocalypse. For example, Neptune's zodiacal manifestation, Pisces, is a symbol of duality, both beginnings and endings, and like the apocalypse, it is also a symbol of completion. Additionally, many astrologers believe that the millennium, which coincides with the end of the Neptunian Age, signals the transition between the Piscean Age (the years between the birth of Christ and the new millennium) and the Aquarian Age (the post-Christian era). Therefore, Doc Serge's statement demonstrates that Bambara is using yet another mode of timekeeping—astrological time.

The reference to the Neptunian Age is an example of how African American literature abounds with authorial desires to dissolve boundaries. Therefore, it is relevant that Bambara sees the "Neptunian thing" as synonymous with a "Black thing." That Doc Serge makes Neptune synonymous with blackness is significant given that both Christianity and Hinduism use the fish as the symbol of the savior. *The Salt Eaters* posits blacks as the chosen people of God who, in the face of the apocalypse, must choose the path of virtue—which means, in this instance, the responsibility that comes with becoming a revolutionary agent.

In an interview with Beverly Guy-Sheftall, Bambara states, "I would argue . . . that there is an aspect of black spirit, of inherent black nature, that we have not addressed: the tension, the power that is still latent, still colonized, still frozen and untapped, in some 27 million black people. We do not know how to unleash, we do not even know how to speak of it in a courageous manner, *yet*" ("Commitment" 237). In *The Salt Eaters,* Bambara does more than simply call blacks to action; she pulls from the militant traditions our African American ancestors developed in response to this treacherous New World to offer models of revolutionary action. To counter white apocalyptic constructions of the New World, Bambara creates the fictional space of Claybourne to claim the New World for black people. Claybourne represents a geographic manifestation of black nationalism. A proverbial "nation within a nation," Claybourne is a site where black people and other people of color can decide together which revolutionary path to take.

THE DUALITY OF CLAYBOURNE: APOCALYPTIC SPATIALITY

Elsewhere, I have talked about the fact that coming home to black neighborhoods that were not controlled by a visible white presence provided black people the necessary space to recoup and regain a measure of sanity. The power of these segregated communities was that they were places where black folks had oppositional world views that helped us to sustain our integrity, our very lives. There are many segregated communities still but they are not often constituted as communities of resistance.

—BELL HOOKS, *SISTERS OF THE YAM*

The town of Claybourne functions as a community of resistance for which hooks yearns in the above epigraph. Claybourne is the New World that Bambara dreams into existence. The town's name suggests the meaning "born of clay" and therefore alludes to the biblical account of Genesis, a creation story that signifies not only the beginning of the universe, but also the power of transformation. Additionally, in a conversation about firing ashtrays held between Ruby and Jan, Velma's friends, we learn the underlying significance of the word "clay"—"Fire. Bake. Harden. Cure" (*The Salt Eaters* 192). This procedure for making ashtrays seems synonymous with the apocalypse. "Fire" represents the apocalyptic moment, while "Bake" and "Harden" symbolize the fomented revolution sparked by the apocalypse. "Cure" is the final result of the apocalypse—it represents the healthier state of the world. The town of Claybourne, then, is actually a site of apocalyptic possibility and apocalyptic transformation.

Claybourne, Georgia, is described only once in the novel, through the eyes of an outsider, Dr. Meadows,[8] who confronts the "stark reality of the street" while exploring one of Claybourne's poorer neighborhoods at night:

There were broken-down stoops that looked like city and leaning porches that looked like country. Houses with falling-away shutters and brick walkways that wouldn't make up their minds. Claybourne hadn't settled on its identity yet, he decided. Its history put it neither on this nor that side of the Mason Dixon. And its present seemed to be a cross between a little Atlanta, a big Mount Bayou, and Trenton, N.J. in winter. (*The Salt Eaters* 181)

The town's name and its landscape (bearing a resemblance to cities and towns in both the South and the North) is an example of *apocalyptic spatiality*.[9] In my use of the phrase, apocalyptic spatiality signifies both the physical site in which the battle will take place as well as the metaphysical site of cataclysmic transformation.

We are told that "Claybourne hadn't settled on its identity yet." As a town whose landscape is an amalgamation of both the South and the North, yet is really neither, Claybourne is set somewhere in the margins. Marginality is actually a site of overlap; those existing within the margins are both a part of the nation and simultaneously existing at its fringes. In her book *Yearning: Race, Gender, and Cultural Politics,* bell hooks envisions the margins as "a site of radical openness." For hooks and other African Americans, marginality means we must make a decision about how we position ourselves in relation to the existing power structure:

> do we position ourselves on the side of colonizing mentality? Or do we continue to stand in political resistance with the oppressed, ready to offer our ways of seeing and theorizing, of making culture, towards that revolutionary effort which seeks to create space where there is an unlimited access to the pleasure and power of knowing, where transformation is possible? (145)

As a town that appears to be governed by the tenets of cultural nationalism, Claybourne's inhabitants seem to have already decided to "stand in political resistance with the oppressed." There are three major institutions existing in the town of Claybourne that embody cultural nationalism, the Academy of the Seven Arts, which is a martial arts collective; the Seven Sisters, a Third World feminist collective; and the Southwest Community Infirmary, a hospital that specializes in homeopathic remedies or non-Western medical treatments. Through these institutions, Bambara has created a black nationalistic space in which black people can discuss their place in the world and decide on their own path of revolutionary struggle without outside interference. Claybourne exists as a "space where there is an unlimited access to the pleasure and power of knowing, where transformation is possible." Functioning within an apocalyptic space, however, each institution is experiencing a moment of crisis and must decide on a method of revolutionary transformation in the face of the impending apocalypse.

Because of the crisis of identity exhibited by the town's physicality and the conflicts existing within the institutions, Claybourne can be perceived as a geographical representation of double-consciousness, the identity crisis of African Americans that is a by-product of marginal subjectivity. bell hooks writes, "I make a definite distinction between that marginality which is imposed by oppressive structures and that marginality one chooses as site of resistance—as location of radical openness and possibility. This site of resistance is continually formed in that segregated culture of opposition that is our critical response to domination" (*Yearning* 153). Claybourne is a marginal space chosen as a "site of resistance." Therefore, unlike Du Bois's interpretation of double-consciousness, which is an imposed subjectivity, the double-consciousness at work in Claybourne is an active choice. The conflict existing in Claybourne is not one between African and white values as Du Bois suggests. Instead, there is a chasm developing in the black-centered institutions that inform Claybourne.

As a high-tech and contemporary Eatonville,[10] Claybourne is a symbolic representation of the black community as a whole. Bambara is invested in unveiling the potential power within the pockets of predominantly black communities throughout the United States. Bambara is particularly interested in communities that have established themselves as sites for preserving black culture and are seen as hubs of black intellectual and political thought, such as Harlem and Beale Street. As I explain in chapter 2, Bambara's interest in the potential of places like Harlem and Beale Street as sites where radicalism can foment can be gleaned from the importance she ascribes to what she calls the "Speaker's Corner"—a phrase borrowed from the London locale. Here it refers to a corner in which a black speaker uses the street as a platform to vocalize issues pertinent to the black masses. The whole of Claybourne can be viewed as a larger manifestation of the Speaker's Corner, a town governed by blacks that relies on its own cultural wisdom.

Given the initial quotation that describes Claybourne, with its references to "broken-down stoops" and "falling-away shutters" that signify both urban decay and rural slums, and given the pre-apocalyptic moment of the text, the phrase "identity crisis" is apropos to describe Claybourne. Not only is Claybourne undecided about the type of town it wants to resemble geographically, its inhabitants cannot decide which method to take to remedy "snakebites" (i.e., racism). As a result of this indecision, the community, like its poorest neighborhood, is starting to decay. Although the institutions that inform Claybourne's community make a positive step toward decolonization, they have lost their direction and momentum, much like the civil rights and black liberation movements of the 1960s were charged with not ultimately reaching fulfillment. The dream of equality and black self-actualization has not yet been realized.

Claybourne's decay mirrors the sickness of the larger society and world. Ann Fowell Stanford writes, "*The Salt Eaters* rests on the assumption that the world is sick and that in order to survive, human beings must be about the business of healing it through social, political, cultural, and spiritual channels" ("Mechanisms of Disease" 32). The novel suggests that the world is diseased because people are more focused on the material than on nature and the spiritual components of life. The novel states, "Now there was a Babel of paths, of plans. 'There is a world to be redeemed,' [Sophie Heywood] warned. 'And it'll take the cooperation of all righteous folks'" (*The Salt Eaters* 92). Although the citizens of Claybourne qualify as "righteous folks," they are so far unable to make the necessary decisions because not only do opposing factions exist within each institution, the institutions fail to recognize their connections to each other.

Because of the approach of a new millennium, the problems that have not been solved throughout the departing age are coming to a head in the novel and demand to be reconciled before it is too late. Velma's husband, Obie, recognizes the resurfacing of old, unresolved problems: "It was starting up again, the factions, the intrigue. A replay of all the old ideological splits: the street youth as vanguard, the workers as vanguard; self-determination in the Black Belt, Black rule of the U.S.A.; strategic coalitions, independent political action" (*The Salt Eaters* 90). While the resurfacing of militant organizations signifies a general desire to promote massive change, it also highlights that no real progress has occurred.

In an interview with Kalamu ya Salaam, Bambara states that there are:

> three kinds of calls I'm making in *The Salt Eaters* through the three institutions in Claybourne that are governed by Black people. In the Academy of the Seven Arts, Obie is attempting to bridge the gap between our medicine people and our warriors, and that's a call. . . . The other kind of call through the seven sisters is that they are obviously bridging the . . . political worldview and the artistic worldview, which has always been a tradition in our community. They are obviously reaching also for Third World coalitions, which is the struggle we really haven't explored. When we talk about coalitions, it always seems to be about Black and white. I think that's a real waste. . . . And, three, is the Southwest Community Infirmary. Those workers are attempting to merge the best of so-called traditional medicine with the most humane of so-called modern medicine. ("Searching for the Mother Tongue" 50)

By issuing these "calls" within the novel, Bambara is attempting to break the pattern of resistance that has existed in this country. She is suggesting that rather than fighting for change in separate factions, these organizations should come together with the understanding that their missions are intertwined.

We learn from Obie's masseuse that a white New Age community in a neighboring town considers "Claybourne a major energy center, one of the chakras of this country" (*The Salt Eaters* 163).[11] "Chakra" is a term used in certain forms of yoga that refers to any of the seven body centers "that are considered sources of energy for psychic or spiritual power."[12] To use a term associated with the body to describe a town points to the interconnectedness between Claybourne and its citizens. If Claybourne as an apocalyptic space is charged with untapped energy and potential, the same can be said for the apocalyptic subjectivity of African Americans, the direct human by-products of the New World.

THE APOCALYPTIC SELF AND THE NEW WORLD WOMAN

The newest people on earth are Afro-Americans. Our genesis is the blending of the old with the new. And our task is to keep both ovens alight without either of them catching fire.

—NIKKI GIOVANNI, FOREWORD TO *BLACKSPIRITS*

In the above epigraph, Giovanni is essentially echoing Bambara's character Doc Serge when he defines African American subjectivity in biblical and apocalyptic terms. Because of miscegenation and the chasm existing between African American New World conditions and Africa's Old World traditions, African Americans can also be thought of as "new people" or a hybrid population. Additionally, Du Bois's concept of double-consciousness indirectly points to the hybrid nature of African American subjectivity. Writing in 1972, Giovanni labels blacks as a people who are in their "springtime"—a time of blossoming and rebirth. Seeing springtime as an apocalyptic moment, Giovanni writes, "That's what the world is about—being new. . . . One must prepare oneself for change, just as one must be prepared for love. It takes a full knowledge of options before one is ready to say, I Chose This" (*BlackSpirits* ix). Giovanni implies that, as "new people," African Americans must embrace both their potential to *be* changed and to *effect* change. The conflict Du Bois articulates between the "American" and the "Negro" components present in the African American psyche is exacerbated because of the marginal position African Americans hold in U.S. society. Instead of viewing African American subjectivity as forever fixed within the rubric of American racism, Giovanni suggests that African Americans must be made aware that they have options. I submit that Bambara's purpose in writing *The Salt Eaters* is to also make African Americans cognizant of those options.

The title of the novel refers to both the Claybourne residents and those drawn to the town as a site of political, medicinal, spiritual, and/or psychic power. To label black people as "salt eaters" is significant. Throughout the novel, Bambara uses salt as a metaphor for the need to establish balance, too little or too much can be dangerous.[13] "Too little salt" speaks to the necessity of developing strategies for combating oppression (developing an immunity) to prevent "dropping dead from scratches" (164). Ingesting too much salt is even more dangerous than ingesting too little. Digesting too much salt represents succumbing to the serpent, or rather the tendency to wallow in unhealthy situations or to accept the rhetoric of victimization as an unalterable given for black people. *The Salt Eaters* uses the recurring motif of salt to make a distinction between "eating salt as an antidote to snakebite and turning into salt, succumbing to the serpent" (8). According to Bambara, "[s]alt is a partial antidote for snakebite. . . . To struggle, to develop, one needs to master ways to neutralize poisons" ("What It Is I'm Doing Anyhow" 165). Bambara is implying that African Americans have historically developed resistive strategies that have ultimately proved detrimental to their health. Eating "too much salt" indirectly refers to the fact that blacks are more susceptible to and die from high blood pressure and hypertension more than anyone else in the United States. The remedy for both diseases includes a reduction of salt intake, which can metaphorically be read as the reduction of the general stress associated with being black in this country.

In several places in *The Salt Eaters,* Bambara suggests that, as African Americans, we are used to seeing ourselves as victims and that it is this impression that prevents us from progressing at a more rapid rate. In one section of the novel, Bambara uses a form of numerology to explain the condition of African Americans. Through the memory of bus driver Fred Holt, we learn that:

> [Jimmy Lyons, an organ player] had told him he was a four, and fours were builders, but lots of fours never got around to doing what they were put on the earth to do cause they was so busy feeling boxed in by them four sides of their nature that they didn't have sense to look up and appreciate all that space they could build into. And Jimmy Lyons had told him another thing, that the Negro people were fours and so long as they paid more attention

to folks trying to pen them in, hem them in, box them in on all four sides thinking they had them in prison than to the work at hand, why then they would never get a spare moment to look up at the sun and build. (77)

In this passage, Bambara connects a spatial metaphor to the idea of internal colonization. She suggests that although African Americans possess an innate aptitude for building, we often cannot see our own potential and we often dream ourselves into a psychological prison instead of dreaming a new world. The quotation charges that we devote too much of our energy focusing on the various ways we have been subjugated rather than focusing on how to build our way out of oppression.

Although Bambara is concerned with the plight of black people in general, the phrase "new people" specifically refers to those who came of age during the 1960s and after segregation. *The Salt Eaters* makes a generational distinction between African Americans in order to discuss how children of the 1960s have become divorced from old ways of knowledge learned in the segregated communities of the South. The novel states that these new people embrace sickness:

They wore their crippleness or blindness like a badge of honor, as though it meant they'd been singled out for some special punishment, were special. Or as though it meant they'd paid some heavy dues and knew, then, what there was to know, and therefore had a right to certain privileges, or were exempt from certain charges, or ought to be listened to at meetings. But way down under knowing "special" was a lie, knowing better all along and feeling the cost of the lie, of the self-betrayal in the joints, in the lungs, in the eyes. Knew, felt the cost, but were too proud and too scared to get downright familiar with the conniption fit getting downright familiar with their bodies, minds, spirits to just sing, "Blues, how do you do? Sit down, let's work it out." (108)

Here Bambara argues that many African Americans see victimization as a sort of birthright, or rather they have embraced the negative consequences of double-consciousness. Consequently, the "specialness" blacks bestow upon their position as victims places them at a point of authority in public discourses on oppression. Bambara suggests that to view victimization in such a light makes blacks feel that the world owes them something or that they are "exempt from certain charges," such as being seen as oppressors in their own right. Bambara submits that this brand of "specialness" is an artificial subjectivity, the embracing of which causes the same sort of psychological damage as oppression itself. Bambara suggests that we need to have a consultation with pain, to understand not only why we feel pain, but how we can overcome it.

The further fragmentation of African American New World subjectivity can also be read along gender lines. In keeping with apocalyptic rhetoric, black women writers such as Toni Morrison have narrowed the concept of "new people" to "New World woman." In a videotaped interview discussing the title character of her 1973 novel, Toni Morrison explains why she labels Sula a "New World woman." Morrison states that the New World woman is "experimental, she's outlaw. She's not going to take it anymore. She's available to her own imagination and other people's stories, other people's definitions are not hers."[14] Although Velma Henry is a vastly different character from Sula, the label of New World woman is applicable to her as well. In descriptions of her childhood, Velma is remembered as willful and ambitious, so much so that she once tried to dig a hole to China even though she was told it was impossible—Velma is indeed "available to her own imagination."

I find the phrase "New World woman" appealing because it addresses the experimental quality inherent within Velma. As a product of the 1960s, Velma epitomizes the promise of her oppressed literary and historical foremothers. Velma Henry, as an experimental woman, is what Mary Helen Washington would identify as an "emergent woman."[15] But she is a failed one. In 1978, the present-day moment of the text, Velma has already undergone her initiation into the position of emergence because of her political activism during the 1960s. But after attempting suicide by slitting her wrists and partially stuffing herself into a lit oven, Velma can be said to have spiraled back to the second cycle identified by Washington—"the assimilated woman." Washington writes, "The women in the second cycle are also victims, not of physical violence, but of a kind of psychic violence that alienates them from their roots and cuts them off from real contact with their own people and also from a part of themselves" ("Teaching Black-Eyed Susans" 213).

As an assimilated woman, Velma has become disconnected with her history and has lost faith in her future. Her crisis occurs when, while combing her hair one morning, she realizes that "[s]omething crucial had been missing from the political/economic/social/cultural/aesthetic/military/psychosocial/psychosexual mix. And what could that be?" (*The Salt Eaters* 259). At this moment, Velma experiences her own personal apocalypse. Prior to her "revelation," Velma "[t]hought she knew how to build resistance, make the journey to the center of the circle . . . stay centered in the best of her people's traditions and not be available to madness" (258). She also thought that the 1960s had fixed things for the better, only to realize that in the 1980s "amnesia had set in anyhow" (258).

Velma's illness is symptomatic of living a fragmented lifestyle. Each segment of her life (her marriage, her extramarital affair, her work, and her community activism) is disconnected from the others. Likewise, in each aspect of her life, Velma is asked to either create a "vacuum," shutting the rest of the world out, or deal with people who think or view life in terms of abstraction, prioritizing theory over lived experiences. Both instances, creating a vacuum or abstraction, require a disassociation of the private from the public sphere, i.e., the individual from her history, the individual or marital unit from the community or outside world, work from home, or community activism from work.

Velma's marriage to her husband James (aka Obie) is rapidly deteriorating because they have different opinions about how to deal with the residual effects of racism. At a dinner where James hopes to convince Velma to reconcile, he tells Velma,

It's got to be costing you something to hang on to old pains. Just look at you. Your eyes slit, the cords jump out of your neck, your voice trembles, I expect fire to come blasting out of your nostrils any minute. It takes something out of you, Velma, to keep all them dead moments alive. Why can't you just . . . forget . . . forgive . . . and always it's some situation that was over and done with ten, fifteen years ago. But here you are still all fired up about it, still plotting, up to your jaws in ancient shit. (22)

Obie's comments suggest that even though Velma is still "fighting the good fight," her inability to come to terms with negative past experiences is becoming increasingly unhealthy. Velma, of course, cannot forget and counters by stating, "We're different people, James. Obie. Somebody shit all over you, you forgive and forget. You start talking about how we're all damaged and colonialism and the underdeveloped blah blah. That's why everybody walks all over you" (23). Her statements demonstrate that James's "forgive and forget" approach is not working either. Velma implies that James's approach is unhealthy because it causes him to see "colonialism" or being "underdeveloped" as a fixed state. In Velma's opinion, taking oppression as a given prevents a person from continuing to struggle against the oppression that still plagues her or him.

To facilitate reconciliation, Obie asks, "Can't we, Vee? Push all the past aside, dump all of it. . . . Create a vacuum for good things to rush in. Good things" (25). During the convalescing ritual, though, healer Minnie Ransom reminds Velma that "nature abhors a vacuum" (16).[16] According to

Minnie, it is not natural nor is it healthy for one to disassociate oneself from the outside world in such a permanent manner. Additionally, creating a vacuum is antithetical to the purpose of apocalypse, which strives to make people connect with a higher power, which does not necessarily entail avoiding the unpleasantries of life.

Velma is also breaking her marriage vows by having an affair with Jamahl, who is ironically characterized as her "prayer partner." Her affair, however, is only a partial hindrance to her reconciliation to Obie. Jamahl is described as constantly looking for solutions to problems in everyone else's culture but his own: "Tai Chi, TM, Reichian therapy, yoga" (169). Not only is Jamahl decentered (disconnected from his own people's traditions in favor of other cultures), he ultimately betrays Velma by stealing secrets from her office at the nuclear power plant.

By working at a nuclear power plant, Velma has aligned herself with forces that are antithetical to the apocalypse, since a nuclear holocaust would result in the end of human civilization and therefore make either redemption or revolution impossible. To say that Velma's job causes her stress is an understatement. Through her friend Jan we learn that "[t]he mere mention of plutonium and [Velma] goes off with dire predictions about a police state coming to insure or at least minimize against unauthorized access to nuclear materials. She has so little faith" (242). Velma becomes ill because she has lost faith in humankind and its ability to keep a nuclear holocaust from occurring. Working at a nuclear power plant is also antithetical for all Velma stands. First, her occupation is ironic given her community activism and her underlying desire to save the planet. Second, we learn that the nuclear power plant is environmentally classist and racist because it participates in dumping toxic waste in poor neighborhoods.

Velma's community activism is another added burden. Even though women do most of the work, like Velma's reported experiences with organizations during the 1960s, the black women activists of her group get little respect from their male counterparts.[17] The sexism that exists in the organization, as well as the turmoil in Velma's marriage, demonstrates a chasm in relationships between black women and men. Bambara suggests that these rifts must also be repaired by acknowledging female participation in black liberation movements.

Although Velma must come to terms with her own individual problems, the novel presents her situation as indicative of the daughters of the yam.[18] Minnie Ransom puzzles over the condition of these New World women in a conversation with Old Wife, a spiritual ancestor who aids Minnie in her healing rituals. Minnie asks:

What's wrong with the women? If they ain't sticking their head in ovens and opening up their veins like this gal, or jumping off of roofs, drinking charcoal lighter, pumping rat poisons in their arms, and ramming cars into walls, they looking for some man to tear his head off. What is wrong, Old Wife? What is happening to the daughters of the yam? Seem like they just don't know how to draw up the powers from the deep like before. Not full sunned and sweet anymore. Tell me, how do I welcome this daughter home to the world? (43–44)

Because they have forgotten the powers passed down to them from their original maternal ancestors, "the mud mothers," the daughters of the yam, like Velma, can be seen as representations of the assimilated woman—they are not only out of sync with their true natures, but with the traditions that would keep them from getting ill in the first place.

Velma's predicament of having to relearn what she thought the 1960s had already taught her, as with all daughters of the yam, points to a new cycle of African American women's experiences to add alongside Washington's three—the revolutionary diva. While Bambara's act of writing *The Salt Eaters* entitles her to this label, she also uses Velma as a model of a revolutionary diva. The reader identifies with Velma as the protagonist, and through Velma the audience also becomes transformed. As a revolutionary diva, Velma must undergo a new initiation ritual before she can become a radical agent once again. Rather than the initiation rites Washington speaks of with the emergent woman, Velma's ritual is one of scarification, as I have outlined in chapter 4. Scarification takes into consideration her New World subjectivity in a way that initiation rites of the 1960s did not. Rather than be baptized in Afrocentric traditions, the healing ritual presented to us in *The Salt Eaters* can be considered an act of scarification because Velma must take what is useful from all traditions in order to continue her activism. Velma's scarification ritual enables her to also pull from her own cultural traditions as a product of the New World, which would necessarily include Western ideologies.

Given Velma's suicide attempt, the phrase "New World woman" further implies an apocalyptic selfhood, a subjectivity based on both the notion of crisis and the possibility of transformation. In this sense, then, the New World woman has the inherent potential to become a revolutionary diva. As a New World woman, she is already the personification of change and revolution and must only embrace revolutionary agency to become a diva.

When Velma ponders aloud what she should do once she realizes that the 1960s had not cured America of racism, "the answer had almost come tumbling out of the mirror naked and tattooed with serrated teeth and hair alive, birds and insects peeping out at her from the mud-heavy hanks of the ancient mothers' hair" (259). It is important to note that Velma's revelation occurs when looking through the mirror. The mirror simultaneously signifies Velma's affinity with the images in the mirror and the fact that she is responsible for her own transformation into a radical subject. The sight of her first ancestors, the allusion to Medusa, coupled with her inability to rise to the challenge they pose, causes Velma to attempt suicide. The underlying reason for her suicide attempt, however, is that Velma has become overwhelmed by the responsibility of becoming a revolutionary agent that this mystical vision embodies.

Through a conversation between Jan and Ruby, the reader discovers that Velma has been contemplating suicide as a way to hasten reincarnation. Ruby states, "Velma . . . I think she's lost her marbles. Know what she asked me the other night? Suicide. When is it appropriate to commit suicide. . . . And did suicides reincarnate right away or have to wait around till full term" (215). It is significant that Velma asks when it is *appropriate* to commit suicide. Such a question makes the act of suicide a practical issue rather than a question of right or wrong in the eyes of an unyielding God. By attempting suicide, Velma not only nearly breaks her sacred covenant with "God," however defined,[19] but she also betrays herself because the attempt is a reactionary impulse. Huey Newton defines "reactionary suicide" as "the reaction of a man who takes his own life in response to social conditions that overwhelm him and condemn him to helplessness" (*Revolutionary Suicide* 4).[20] What is reprehensible, then, is not the suicide attempt itself, but what it represents to Velma. Velma has essentially given up, thereby allowing the social conditions of her life to consume her. Velma's suicide attempt can be considered reactionary rather than revolutionary because the impulse stems in part from her lack of faith in herself, and in black people in general, to effect change rather than from an inherent conviction to die in the service of the oppressed masses.[21]

To achieve wellness/wholeness so that she may emerge as an agent of revolutionary change, Velma must embark on an apocalyptic journey to find herself. In the text, Velma's illness is discussed as the loss of her "essential self." Velma's essential self can be found in her brazen and "womanish"[22] childhood, before she lost her faith in the people and before she gave up the notion of revolution. Her essential self is the assertion of her radical agency. Dr. Julius Meadows observes during the healing that "the patient was elsewhere. . . . So like the catatonics he'd observed in psychiatric. The essential self gone off, the shell left behind" (*The Salt Eaters*

57). The disassociation of mind and body in this sense is one way Bambara demonstrates Velma's decentered subjectivity. In another instance where double-consciousness is discussed in terms of apocalyptic spatiality, Velma is described as being in two places at once; her body is at the hospital while her mind is at times off on a "telepathic visit with her former self" and at others with her ancestral "mud mothers," or her mind is off grappling with the symbolic meaning of allusions, the deciphering of which is the key to her emerging healthy and whole once again.

Velma's catatonic state is just one outward manifestation of her illness. During the healing, Buster, a black youth of the community, believes he sees two faces at once on Velma and later characterizes what he's seen as her "double-exposure face." The photography reference is apropos because it alludes to the fact that Velma is both out of focus and has lost focus. Although the notion of two-ness or double-exposure seems to be synonymous with Du Bois's theory of double-consciousness, to say that Velma is experiencing double-consciousness is inaccurate. If anything, Velma is experiencing the double-consciousness Du Bois defines as being caught between the personal realm and the public sphere, as well as an alternate double-consciousness as I define it in chapter 1—the conflict between being both an individual and part of a larger black collective.

During her healing process, Velma undergoes a series of revelations and must ultimately make a choice to be well and to reclaim her self or to succumb to the negative forces impacting her life. Minnie Ransom tells Old Wife that Velma "[a]lways got options. . . . Affirmation and denial" (44). Through Velma's healing ritual, Bambara supplies five steps to the path of revolutionary subjectivity: (1) the affirmation of one's essential self (which Bambara sees as being synonymous with recommitment to a higher spiritual power), (2) becoming "self-centered," (3) the process of "self-recovery," (4) understanding that decolonization is a choice, and (5) choosing a method of revolutionary action.

In Christian doctrine, the apocalypse is about making choices, the most significant being whether to affirm or to deny God. In Velma's case, she must also choose to affirm or deny her essential self. Bambara believes that the promises one makes to oneself and the covenants one makes with God are interdependent. For example, in contemplating the empty pleasure of casual sex, Velma's aunt Sophie concludes that "she would not break her discipline to comfort herself in a shallow way. Would no more break discipline with her Self than she would her covenant with God" (153). During the healing ritual, Velma remembers her grandmother, M'Dear, saying, "Back in the days when the Earth was steady and the ground reliable under foot, we made our covenant with our Maker and were given our instructions" (266). The first step to becoming well or decolonized is for Velma, and by extension her audience, to recommence her pledge to God—in whatever manner that higher spiritual power is perceived.

To discern what those covenants might be, Velma must decipher a series of allusions presented to her on her visits to alternate realities: "Medusa, Lot's Wife, Eurydice, Noah. . . . They are all stomping, agitating the ground, agitating an idea, calling up something or someone, and the idea clusters in the image centers and settles there" (257). Each allusion teaches the importance of respecting and keeping one's promises to a higher spiritual power. Additionally, each allusion demonstrates the repercussions (the sense of loss or fragmentation) that result from breaking one's covenants with one's god. Bambara seeks to offer contrasting examples of what happens when one accepts—and rejects—the changing order of the world. For example Medusa is punished for desecrating Athena's temple, while Noah is rewarded for adhering to God's command. (The references to Lot's wife and Noah are of particular significance because they refer to other apocalyptic moments in the Bible.)

Medusa was punished by Athena for having sex with Poseidon, the god of the sea, in Athena's temple. Some accounts say Medusa copulated with Poseidon willingly, while other accounts say she was raped. In either event, Athena interpreted Medusa's actions as sacrilegious and retaliated by changing Medusa's once beautiful hair into a mass of writhing snakes. Lot's wife, fleeing to Zoar from Sodom with her family, disobeyed God's instructions not to look back at the wicked city. When she looked upon Sodom one last time, she was turned to a pillar of salt. Eurydice was a nymph and wife of Orpheus, the son of Apollo. Eurydice was bitten by a poisonous snake and died. Orpheus, known for the enchanting way he played the lyre, used music to charm his way into the underworld to retrieve Eurydice. Persuaded by his wife, Persephone, Hades agreed to let Orpheus take Eurydice back to the upper world—his only stipulation was that Orpheus not turn back to look at Eurydice until after they were both out of the underworld. Although they were almost out of the underworld, Orpheus could not resist looking back to make sure Eurydice was there. She was, but she faded from his view because he had broken his promise to Hades.

Velma seems to read the character of Medusa as a black woman (i.e., snakes equal dreadlocks), which is not an uncommon interpretation. On page 257, Velma reflects, "She would not have cut Medusa's head off. . . . She would simply have told the sister to go and comb her hair. Or gotten a stick to drive the serpents out." Because Velma is more sympathetic to and perhaps has an affinity with Medusa, Medusa offers an alternate lesson. I read the writhing serpents in Medusa's hair as a metaphoric reference to oppression, or its internalization, because her lethal hairstyle does not just call to mind the danger of the gaze, but the danger of the serpent's bite. In being transformed into a Gorgon, Medusa has the power to change men to stone; therefore, while Medusa was once a victim, she now has the power to victimize others. Medusa, then, serves as a cautionary tale about the dangers of internalizing victimization and becoming a victimizer.

Like Medusa, the allusions to Eurydice and Lot's wife refer to the idea of taboo glances. Eurydice, and Orpheus because he loves her, is punished because Orpheus, in looking back to make sure Eurydice is there, demonstrates his lack of trust in Hades's word. Lot's wife is also punished for looking back. While the backward glances of Orpheus and Lot's wife demonstrate that they do not accept God's word, Lot's wife also looks back because she cannot move forward. Her sin is not just in distrusting God, but in having divided loyalties. She "looks back" with her heart as well as with her eyes; something in her is not ready to leave Sodom behind and truly embrace God. She is essentially ossified. In *The Salt Eaters,* we are told that the lesson of Lot's wife and "the changing order" was one of Sophie's favorite topics. In looking back, Lot's wife demonstrated a "loyalty to old things, a fear of the new, a fear to change, to look ahead" (152). Lot's wife is thus punished because she cannot accept the new world order. Such a lesson suggests to Bambara's readers that there are dire consequences when one resists revolutionary change.

The second step to achieving wellness/wholeness is to become "self-centered" in one's own traditions, as well as within oneself. In the novel, being "self-centered" is posited as a good thing rather than a reflection of one's selfish nature. Through a conversation between Jan and Ruby, we learn that "Velma's never been the center of her own life before, not really. . . . Velma has worked hard not to hollow out a safe corner . . . of home, family, marriage and then be less responsive, less engaged. Dodgy business trying to maintain the right balance there, the personal and the public" (240). Although Bambara desires that the individual seek to connect with something larger than herself, she also stresses the importance of creating individual and personal spaces where one can regroup. Similar to Virginia Woolf's exhortation to women to seek and maintain a "room of their own," Jan talks about safe spaces as places where one can retreat from "confusion" to a "confined space, [where] everything is under your sure control." Velma has never had a place in which to center herself.

Becoming self-centered, then, does not just mean becoming grounded in one's own cultural traditions, but becoming grounded in the things that make a person unique. In her essay "On the Issue of Roles," Bambara writes, "Revolution begins with the self, in the self. The individual, the basic revolutionary unit, must be purged of poison and lies that assault the ego and threaten the heart, that hazard the next larger unit—the couple or pair, that jeopardize the still larger unit—the family or cell that put the entire movement in peril" (*The Black Woman* 109). Revolution, therefore, can be seen as "revolving" around a fixed and complete centered self.

To become self-centered, Velma must engage in the third step of Bambara's decolonization process, the process of "self-recovery" or "hunting." We are told in the novel that Velma has gone in search of her essential self and that she's gone "soul gathering." Bambara explains the differences between the Afrocentric and Eurocentric notions of hunting:

> And hadn't she [Velma] observed the difference, watched the different brands of hunting? The pulling of the bow, the pulling of the truck alongside the prey and mowing it down, taking it over. The cars pulling up alongside a woman or a kid ready to sell the self for a Twinkie. Bringing down a bird or a woman or a man stalked at a dance. Taking over a life. That was not hunting as the sisters explained it, sang it, acted it out. To have dominion was not to knock out, downpress, bruise, but to understand, to love, make at home. The keeping in the sights the animal, or child, man or woman, tracking it in order to learn their way of being in the world. To be at home in the knowing. The hunt for balance and kinship was the thing. A mutual courtesy. She would run to the park and hunt for self. (267)

To Velma, the Eurocentric conception of hunting means to have total control over your prey, where the Afrocentric conception means to have a symbiotic relationship between the hunter and the hunted.

Fourth, Velma must understand that not only is wellness or opting for decolonization a choice, but it is also her right as well as an enormous amount of responsibility. Once again, Bambara is urging African Americans to move away from the language of eternal victimization and to see health as a "right" rather than a privilege conferred solely upon whiteness. And finally, Bambara tells us that Velma has to choose her own cure. Minnie Ransom tells her, "Choose your cure, sweetheart. Decide what you want to do with wholeness" (220).

Many critics have compared Velma's illness to that of Alice Walker's title character, Meridian. For example, Susan Willis writes, "*The Salt Eaters* is in many ways a sad sequel to *Meridian*, not because Bambara is any less gifted a writer than Walker, but because the reciprocal relationship between the community and its revolutionary leader and the implicit understanding that their combined struggle will bring a transformed future into being no longer exists for the novel's Meridian-like figure, Velma Henry" (*Specifying* 130). I, however, argue that there *is* a reciprocal relationship between Claybourne's residents and Velma, albeit more subtle. As I have stated earlier, Velma Henry serves as the medium or conduit through which we, as readers, begin our own transformation. It is therefore important that Velma's healing ritual is made public. Velma's wounds are self-inflicted, while Meridian's wounds appear like stigmata. The similarity between her "sickness" and Meridian's is that both women become ill due to the overwhelming pressures of political activism. For Meridian, however, healing is an individual thing. When she collapses, she is careful not to let people see her fall. Velma's public healing, however, suggests that Bambara views healing as a collective process. The book-long process of Velma's healing serves as the channel for other characters to come into consciousness as revolutionary subjects. Each character's individual journey toward enlightenment converges with Velma's, so that Velma's quest for health and wholeness serves as the reader's model of how to achieve radical subjectivity.

In *Specifying,* Susan Willis writes:

> I know of no other novel that so poignantly yearns for cataclysmic social upheaval and understands so clearly the roots of black people's oppression in post–Civil Rights American society. It seems, in reading [*The Salt Eaters*], that revolution is only pages away. But for all its yearning and insight, the novel fails to culminate in revolution, fails even to suggest how social change might be produced. (129)

Derek Alwes, however, argues that Willis has missed a fundamental point of the novel. According to Alwes, the appearance of the "mud mothers" during Velma's suicide attempt demonstrates that each generation must be "nurtured and educated, has to be taught the old stories all over again" so that social change will have lasting impact ("The Burden of Liberty" 115). Alwes contends that the desire to see the novel end with a revolution is predicated on a "naive belief in one single, radical revolutionary transformation after which everything is changed forever"; instead, Bambara offers a more realistic ending that recognizes that "change occurs over time in the hearts and minds of the individuals who create, participate in, and identify with a strong unified community" (115–16).

I am persuaded by Alwes's argument and further submit that Bambara's mission is not to just suggest how social change might be produced;

her goal is to make people *receptive* to the notion of revolution, to help people rise to the challenge of the apocalypse. Bambara pushes for a revolution of self as the initial step toward political revolution. Toward that aim, the revolutionary diva must be receptive not only to Western ideologies, but to ideologies that on the surface seem to stand in opposition. Bambara demonstrates that the revolutionary diva must become steeped in the best of her own cultural traditions and study the ancestral and historical methods of dealing with oppression in order to pick the one that might prove most helpful. Finally, Bambara suggests that once the revolutionary diva comes to accept that wellness is a choice, she must also accept the responsibility to show others how to choose to be healthy. Bambara wants to help the reader, like Velma, see holistically in order to pick her or his own cure.

That the novel does not culminate in revolution, to Willis's dismay, is deliberate. Bambara does not envision her novel to be a work of fiction, but a warning, calling the readers to action before their day of reckoning commences. The revolution does not occur in the pages because it has yet to occur in real life. In a sense, *The Salt Eaters* is a fusion of dream and reality. *The Salt Eaters* is both Bambara's vision of the New World and a prophecy of the apocalypse. Bambara wrote the novel in 1980 as a cautionary lesson, encouraging readers to heed the urgency stressed on each page. A seemingly insignificant character in the text, whose bow tie makes him reminiscent of members of the Nation of Islam and their sidewalk speeches, attempts to awaken his street audience to their latent potential as world leaders. He shouts:

> History is calling us to rule again and you lost dead souls are standing around doing the freakie dickie. Never recognizing the teachers come among you to prepare you for the transformation, never recognizing the synthesizers come to forge the new alliances, or the guides who throw open the new footpaths, or the messengers come to end all excuses. Dreamer? The dream is real, my friends. The failure to make it work is the unreality. (126)

With these words, Bambara's black readership is also called to task. Through this sidewalk orator, Bambara asks us if we intend to stand around "doing the freakie dickie" or get on to the business of dreaming a world.

THIS IS NOT JUST ABOUT "INWARD NAVEL-GAZING"

Decolonizing My Own Mind as a Critical Stance

> Ours is a tradition, a literary tradition, certainly grounded in the autobiography, the conversion narrative, the spiritual narrative, and the slave narrative. It has never been a notion of autobiography that was just about me, myself and I. It's always been a notion of autobiography that also sought to give voice to an experience of people who seemed voiceless to the majority of society. So it was never just about inward navel-gazing. Therefore, it is only natural that as our criticism developed some of it would take on that autobiographical voice as well—and especially from women.
>
> —FARAH JASMINE GRIFFIN

In 1972, acclaimed novelist Sherley Anne Williams published her only work of literary criticism, *Give Birth to Brightness: A Thematic Study of Neo-Black Literature.* Her afterword, "The Demands of Blackness on Contemporary Critics," provides an interesting glimpse of a type of double-consciousness Williams had apparently been battling throughout the writing process—the conflict between being a literary scholar *and* a black woman. She writes, "The part of the role [of a critic] which dictated that 'one' be substituted for 'I,' 'them' for 'us,' and 'Black people' for 'we,' was trying. But necessity seemed to dictate my assumption of the *critic's mask* because I wanted to separate, as much as possible, my own personality from the ideas I have presented" (231, emphasis mine).

Given that the trope of the mask has a particular valence in African American culture, Williams's use of the term in this circumstance is quite telling. Her opinion that a scholar should maintain a critical distance is nothing new in the context of the academy; the discussion of the tendency to conflate black subjects with black texts on which I embark in my prelude, however, gives an insight into the rationale behind Williams's trepidation. In her afterword, Williams explains that her fears of self-representation are founded on the ways this conflation functions to neutralize or "co-opt" the black artist. She explains that the mask is necessary because "[o]ne of the great pitfalls confronting Black writers—whether novelist, dramatist, essayist, poet or critic—is the tendency of others to deal with the self, the *I* presented, merely reading into the works rather than dealing with the works themselves" (231). When one considers that in the 1970s critical explorations of black texts, let alone the texts of emerging black writers, was a fairly recent occurrence, Williams's decision to wear the mask seems quite understandable. For Williams, the dearth of literary criticism on black writers made her leery that attempts to "invalidate a literary work through the destruction of the author's character may well become a wholesale slaughter." Therefore it was out of deference to the continuation of "black literary history" that she chose to don the mask (231).

Williams's lesser-known work predates Henry Louis Gates, Jr.'s, *Signifying Monkey: A Theory of African-American Literary Criticism* (1988) by about sixteen years; it was Gates's mission to canonize African American literature and to develop new critical methodologies by which to evaluate this material that became the hot topic in the academy in the mid-1980s. The debates that encapsulated these topics reached their apex in the 1987 winter issue of *New Literary History,* with its publications of fiery articles by Gates, Houston A. Baker, and Joyce A. Joyce. The main arguments revolved around Joyce's objection to the increased application of poststructuralist theory to the works of African American writers. In a review of more contemporary works[1] whose intertextual connections mimic the 1987 debate, Sharon A. Holland recalls, by way of comparison, the response to Joyce's criticism:

> As is expected, Gates and Baker are put on the defensive and respond with all guns loaded, citing factual errors, theoretical misreadings, and personal inadequacies in Joyce's critique. Gates reminds Joyce that "simply because I have attacked an error in logic in the work of certain Black Aestheticians does not mean that I am antiblack, or that I do not love black art or music, or that I feel alienated from black people, or that I am trying to pass like some poststructual ex-colored man." ("The Revolution, 'In Theory'" 327)

Williams also expresses skepticism about the so-called objective stances that scholars adopt. Rather than widening the appeal to their work, she argues that a black critic who writes from an objective viewpoint hazards alienation from black readers. Gates's proclamation that he is not "some poststructural ex-colored man" seems to prove Williams's claims about how "objective" black critics might be perceived as race traitors. She writes,

> "objective critics" have their limits. When objective critics begin to talk about any of the important issues which confront Black writers, they tend to sound very patronizing, very white. They run the risk of addressing themselves to an ill-defined and, I suspect, non-existent audience, of being called oreo or coconut or something worse. I do not play that stuff. (*Give Birth to Brightness* 232)

Well, I do not play that stuff either.

After reading Williams's afterword, I became cognizant of the pronoun slippages in my own manuscript; there are several instances when I say "we" and "our" when I know that academic protocol favors "they" and "their." Rather than correct these discrepancies, I decided to let the slippages stand as a testament to the affinity I feel with the authors and texts that I have chosen to examine in this project. While I suspect that Williams likewise felt such an affinity, my decision also reflects the type of black nationalist feminism I employ in my analyses of the texts included in this project—one that acknowledges my indebtedness to the black aesthetic, earlier black women writers and scholars, and black poststructuralist critics. This decision also marks the privileged position from which I write—much of the hard work has been done for me.

I entered high school at the start of multicultural education; when I entered college, African American literature was in vogue; and when I entered graduate school there was already a plethora of scholarship on black texts. In many ways, I am the by-product of the debate Henry Louis Gates, Jr., and Houston Baker publicly waged against Joyce A. Joyce. The impetus for writing this book is due in part to my disdain for the hegemony of poststructuralism within African American literary studies and, because I entered the academy as a graduate student during the start of its reign, my own complicity in this hegemony. I was torn between being appreciative of the black aesthetic movement because it paved the way for Black Studies programs and, particularly for me, African American literary studies, and my interest in poststructuralism as a useful approach to analyzing black fiction.

While I would never go so far as to question Gates's loyalty to the black "race," the 1987 debate solidified in me a growing ambivalence toward the hegemonic nature of "theory." In an earlier version of my fourth chapter, published in 1998 under the title "Of Poststructuralist Fallout,

Scarification, and Blood Poems: The Revolutionary Ideology behind the Poetry of Jayne Cortez," I challenged the method by which Gates devised his theory of signification. He defines signification by underscoring a decision, similar to that made by Williams, to distance himself from his subject matter: "Signification is a theory of reading that arises from Afro-American culture; learning how 'to signify' is often part of our adolescent education. I had to step outside my culture, had to defamiliarize the concept by translating it into a new mode of discourse, before I could see its potential in critical theory" ("'Blackness'" 685–86). Although I understood what he meant, I have always felt uneasy about Gates's statement that he had to "defamiliarize" himself from a cultural practice he had previously participated in order to see its critical value.

In contrast, I used my earlier essay to develop a theory I call "scarification," which can best be described as what Cherríe Moraga and Gloria Anzaldúa term a "theory in the flesh,"[2] as an alternative critical methodology to Gates's employment of signification. Scarification, then, is a theory based on racial allegiances and the use of racist oppression as a referential grounding. I defined scarification as

> a theory that "arises from Afro-American culture"; learning how to use "scars" is often a part of our early childhood education—when parents teach their children ways to cope with and react to oppression (e.g., what to do the first time she or he is called "nigger"). Unlike Gates, I had to step deeper within my culture. I had to look back and remember how I defined for myself what it meant to be a "marked" person in the United States—when I first realized that I had double-consciousness and what it would mean to overcome it. I had to step inside my anger, my humiliation, my pain, and ultimately, my pride and determination in order to see the greater potential for using scars to theorize critically. (68)

Speaking specifically of black critics, Valerie Smith explains that the "conditions of oppression provide the subtext of all Afro-Americanist literary criticism and theory. Whether a critic/theorist explores representations of the experience of oppression or strategies by which that experience is transformed, he/she assumes the existence of an 'other' against whom/which blacks struggle" ("Gender and Afro-Americanist Literary Theory" 57). So while the critical apparatuses that I am most interested in are those that provide an epistemological shift as a method by which to combat racism and the processes by which it is internalized, I am equally aware that this book is as much of a personal exploration as it is a critical endeavor.

In accordance with Griffin's statements found in the epigraph to this section, I would like to indulge in a bit of "inward navel-gazing." Odd as it may seem, this project's genesis dates as far back as my undergraduate days at the University of Pittsburgh. It was there that I first learned not only what double-consciousness meant as a theoretical concept, but also saw it manifest itself several times in practice. Once when I was going to the post office to pick up a care package from my mother, I heard a male voice yell out "nigger" from an undetermined location. Not that it would have mattered much, but I was the only black person on the street—I determined this as I looked wildly about for the culprit. The white people who bustled around me refused to make eye contact, but I knew they had heard. I imagined two nondescript white men somewhere in one of the apartments above laughing at my expense. I envisioned one saying to the other, "See, I told you she'd know her name."

While seething in my anger and humiliation, I realized I had a choice to make. I could see myself through the eyes of those who would make negative assumptions about me based solely on the color of my skin, or I could switch audiences and see myself through the eyes of people like the one who had sent the care package—my mother—people who had an investment in me, who cared for my well-being, and who let me be myself. The choice was easy and I went inside the post office to retrieve my care package filled with items to make me feel at home when I was so far away.

On the surface, my autobiographical story might seem to reflect a rudimentary understanding of white supremacy and its global impact on black agency. However, this tale functions as a guiding metanarrative that underscores, in a concrete and personal way, key preoccupations that have permeated this text, such as the historical battle to wrest control of the black image from mainstream machinations, the recurring rhetoric of the black psyche in crisis, and the continuous struggle on the behalf of African Americans to rectify Du Bois's double-consciousness.

In an interview, Farah Jasmine Griffin describes her "academic project" as one that is preoccupied with African American "political, social and creative agency" (Rowell, "An Interview," 872). She writes:

> I've been very much interested in the effects of white supremacy and the ways that black people have tried to counter that, particularly in our art, in our music, and in our literature. . . . I think that our artists especially have been at the forefront of trying to give *us* a different picture of ourselves.
> . . . I think that has been the driving force behind a lot of critical work that

I've done, the critical question that has shaped what direction I would go in. How have we as a people managed not only to survive but to thrive in the face of this massive onslaught of physical and discursive violence against us? (872–73, emphasis mine)

My project shares much in common with Griffin's. At several points throughout the project, I have interpreted double-consciousness as an internal battle to resolve a crisis of identity brought about by a New World subjectivity that has placed African Americans at both our nation's periphery and center. One of the fundamental questions I have attempted to address is whether or not it is possible, in the racially polarized climate of the United States, to envision an autonomous black subjectivity informed by the dictates of a perceived black community rather than the way we typically conceive of blackness as indelibly linked to whiteness. Another concern of mine has been determining if it is possible to talk about black subjectivity in terms of duality or multiplicity without reading such segmentation as pathological.

Highlighting the cultural production by and for black women, I have suggested that African American cultural and literary traditions have consistently provided examples of decolonized subjectivities as models for their black readership. More specifically, my goal throughout this project has been to unearth the decolonizing properties inherent in the texts of contemporary African American women who seek to assist their audience in obtaining a healthy black consciousness—meaning one that insists upon the centrality of blackness, venerates (and sometimes critiques) black culture(s), values black unity, and is committed to racial uplift.

In her essay "The Occult of True Black Womanhood: Critical Demeanor and Black Feminist Studies," Ann du Cille explains, "the question I want to explore in this essay is what it means for black women academics to stand in the midst of the 'dramatically charged field'—the traffic jam—that black feminist studies has become" (393). This book is my own diva stance; it is my way of negotiating the traffic jam and dealing with the frustrations I have felt, first as a graduate student and then as a professor, in a profession that routinely devalues black bodies, black texts, and black ways of knowing.[3] Writing this book is my way of giving thanks to black women writers who have presented me hope when much of what I read about myself made me feel hopeless. It is not a little thing, then, to say that Toni Cade Bambara's *The Salt Eaters* once saved my life.

NOTES

PRELUDE

1. Maya Angelou appeared via satellite.

2. See "Tony Brown's Comments: *The Color Purple* is White." *The Herald,* January 1, 1986, 2, and Charles Johnson's *Being and Race: Black Writing Since 1970* (1988).

3. Founded in 1937, the College Language Association is a significant venue for Reed's speech given that its constituency is mainly African American scholars. As with any predominantly black audience Reed addressed concerning his animosity against feminists, Reed is voicing his concerns, for the most part, to insiders in "the black community." These insiders fit into two distinct groups: those who are either sympathetic to black feminist issues and might bristle at his pronouncements, or those who fit the typical perception of African Americans as being ambivalent toward feminism and fiercely protective of black men. Generally, Reed approaches primarily black audiences as though everyone fits into the latter category and as if an allegiance to feminism is antiblack and, more specifically, anti–black male.

4. Particular mention should be given to the special collections department of the University of Delaware's library. There, in the Media 1966–1995 portion of the Ishmael Reed Papers (collection number 398), I gained access to Reed's appearances on the *Today* show and *Tony Brown's Journal.*

5. In *Reckless Eyeballing* Tremonisha states that she's just going to "get fat, have babies, and write write write" (130). Her new play seeks to revise her earlier anti-male antics: "It's about a woman who leaves her husband for another woman only to discover that she's a batterer" (131). Tremonisha comes to the realization that the real "epidemic" that feminists are averse to reveal is that "women's shelters are full of women who are fleeing from [the abuse] of other women" (131).

6. With the 2005 Broadway release of the musical production of *The Color Purple,* produced in part by Quincy Jones and Oprah Winfrey, it is clear that the past criticism Walker endured still haunts her. For example, on Tuesday, November 1, 2005, when Walker was interviewed by Tavis Smiley, she became offended when Smiley compared her to Condoleezza Rice. Smiley attempted to make a connection

between the negative reaction Rice received when she attended the memorial service of Rosa Parks in Los Angeles to the negative response to Walker's project. She responded, "I really don't appreciate that comparison, actually. I find it very objectionable, because she is someone who has helped the President actually bomb people . . . kill people, starve people . . . enforced sanctions against Cuba, for instance, to hurt many of the people that I deeply love. So this is very different from just writing a novel that is made into a film that people say they've never watched, and they've never read the book. So the people have been . . . very untruthful, about how they actually perceive the work" (See PBS archives for a copy of the transcript; see http://www.pbs.org/kcet/tavissmiley/archive/200511/ 20051101_ transcript.html). I quote Walker at length not to condemn Smiley for the comparison (in the interview he apologizes profusely and it is clear that he admires Walker and her work), but because I see a similarity between this scenario and the fictional one Reed creates in *Reckless Eyeballing*. Because Reed equates Tremonisha's play with Nazi collaboration, it quite possible that he would see the comparison of Walker and Rice as appropriate.

7. For the purposes of this study, I have decided to use the term "black aesthetic" instead of "black arts." The word "aesthetic," coupled with the adjective "black," implies an inherent political agenda in determining a criterion for black art. With the term "aesthetic," one can also talk about perception and psychological responses to art. This is a significant distinction given that my project deals with the shifting of perceptions or world views from those that are determined by the mainstream population to those determined by African Americans.

8. Here I am trying to make a distinction between an author's intended audience, the audience the author images for her text, and a mainstream or public audience, which could comprise anyone able to read the text in English or a translation.

9. The phrase "dirty laundry," in the way I'm using it, comes from Reed's book of essays, *Airing Dirty Laundry* (1993). He explains the title's denotation as follows: "[t] he profitable literary scam nowadays is to pose as someone who airs unpleasant and frank facts about the black community, only to be condemned by the black community for doing so." According to Reed, "This is the sure way to grants, awards, prizes, fellowships, and academic positions" (3).

10. This quotation can be found in Bradley's foreword to William Melvin Kelley's novel *A Different Drummer*, xvi.

11. Here I am referring specifically to the attention given to works like Rigoberta Menchú's *I Rigoberta Menchú: An Indian Woman in Guatemala* (1983) and the late 1980s to early 1990s debates concerning postcolonial testimonial narratives. See Georg Guggelberger, *The Real Thing: Testimonial Discourse and Latin America* (1996), and John Beverly, *Against Literature* (1993), for definitions and debates concerning testimonial narratives.

12. Henry Louis Gates, Jr., *Colored People: A Memoir* (1994); bell hooks, *Bone Black: Memories of Girlhood* (1996); Deborah McDowell, *Leaving Pipe Shop: Memories of Kin* (1996); and Alice Walker, *Anything We Love Can Be Saved: A Writer's Activism* (1997).

13. Information on Frederick Douglass was obtained from the 1997 preface of the Norton Critical Edition of the *Narrative of the Life and Times of Frederick Douglass, An American Slave, Written By Himself*, viii.

14. See *Witnessing Slavery: The Development of Ante-bellum Slave Narratives*.

15. As I will discuss in further detail in chapter 2, in Frances Beale's "Double Jeopardy: To Be Black and Female" and Deborah K. King's "Multiple Jeopardy, Multiple Consciousness: The Context of Black Feminist Ideology," both women expand Du Bois's concept of double-consciousness to include the overlapping psychological effects of racism, sexism, and classism on African American female subjectivity.

16. The exception to this rule would be Madhu Dubey's *Black Women Novelists and the Nationalist Aesthetic* (1994) and Cheryl Clarke's *"After Mecca": Women Poets and the Black Arts Movement* (2005).

17. Found in Monifa Young, "High on the Hill," *Essence*, June 1998, 160.

18. This phrase derives from Paul Laurence Dunbar's 1895 poem "We Wear the Mask."

19. Lorde states, "When I speak of the erotic . . . I speak of it as an assertion of the lifeforce of women; of that creative energy empowered, the knowledge and use of which we are now reclaiming in our language, our history, our dancing, our loving, our work, our lives" ("Feminism and Black Liberation" 55). The "erotic," then, as Lorde interprets it, is an intense desire toward excellence and ultimate fulfillment.

1. FROM SOUL CLEAVAGE TO SOUL SURVIVAL

The epigraph is from the preface to the 1953 Jubilee Edition of *The Souls of Black Folk* published by Blue Heron Press.

1. See Distributed Arts Publishers, Inc.'s web address, www.artbook.com/0936 080922.html.

2. Here I would like to refer readers to recent work on color-blind racism and/ or the subtlety of racism in the post–civil rights era. See Michael K. Brown, Martin Carnoy, Elliott Currie, Troy Duster, David B. Oppenheimer, Marjorie M. Shultz, and David Wellman, *Whitewashing Race: The Myth of a Color-Blind Society* (2003); Patricia Hill Collins, *Black Sexual Politics: African Americans, Gender, and the New Racism* (2004); Eduardo Bonilla-Silva, *Racism without Racists: Color-Blind Racism and the Persistence of Racial Inequality in the United States* (2003); Ashley W. Doane and Eduardo Bonilla-Silva, eds., *White Out: The Continuing Significance of Racism* (2003); and Elaine Brown, *The Condemnation of Little B.* (2002).

3. Du Bois obtained an undergraduate degree from Fisk University in 1888.

4. Amina Mama's book *Beyond the Masks: Race Gender and Subjectivity* (1995) offers an excellent example of how the African "other" was constructed by eighteenth- and nineteenth-century whites.

5. In contemporary literature, authors like Toni Morrison have shown that viewing oneself through the "revelations of the other world" can prove to be highly detrimental to the black subject. In her novel *Beloved* (1987), Morrison uses the character of schoolteacher to show the severe and overarching impact of white racist definitions of black

subjectivity on enslaved blacks. Schoolteacher methodically divides black subjectivity into human and animal characteristics. *Beloved,* then, demonstrates the power of definitions. Through schoolteacher, Sethe and the other slaves of Sweet Home learn that "definitions belonged to the definers—not the defined" (*Beloved* 190).

6. From "An American Dilemma: A Review" (1944).

7. Toni Morrison's *Playing in the Dark: Whiteness in the Literary Imagination* (1992) is an exception to this rule. *Playing in the Dark* is crucial to reconfiguring the place of African Americans in U.S. society. Morrison contends that the African American presence shaped "the body politic, the Constitution, and the entire history of the culture" in the United States. She suggests that this presence is also "central to any understanding of our national literature and should not be permitted to hover at the margins of literary imagination" (5). Paraphrasing from Nahum Chandler's 1996 dissertation (University of Chicago), Tiffany Ruby Patterson and Robin D. G. Kelley also contemplate what a hybridized white identity might look like: "we might think of early New World Euro-Americans as possessing Du Bois's notion of 'double-consciousness': say, English and American, with whiteness as a means of negotiating this double-consciousness" ("Unfinished Migrations" 65).

8. According to Mama, what made the racial identity development theorists unique was that they "developed models for black identity as a dynamic and developmental aspect of selfhood which emerged within the black community rather than being defined by the external forces of racism. In other words, while they do not question but in fact reaffirm the preexisting idea of black self-hatred, this is now taken to be the starting point of black identity formation rather than a permanent psychological accompaniment to blackness" (*Beyond the Mask* 58).

9. See chapter 5 for a brief example of how I use hooks's notion of "self recovery" to analyze *The Salt Eaters.*

10. In an earlier version of chapter 4, published as "Of Poststructuralist Fallout, Scarification, and Blood Poems: The Revolutionary Ideology behind the Poetry of Jayne Cortez," in *Other Sisterhoods: Literary Theory and U.S. Women of Color,* I deliver a more lengthy discussion of Gates and what I see as the reign of poststructuralist theory in contemporary African American literary criticism.

11. Paul Gilroy's *The Black Atlantic: Modernity and Double-Consciousness* (1993) and David Krasner's *Resistance, Parody and Double Consciousness in African American Theatre, 1895–1919* (1998) should also be included in this list. Although I do discuss Gilroy in this project, I omit a closer discussion of his work because his interpretation of double-consciousness does not fall in line with that of the works discussed here. Krasner's use of double-consciousness seems appropriate given the time period he is researching. The texts by Adell, Boan, and Heinz more forcefully demonstrate methodologies that privilege dual texts or employ double-consciousness as a praxis through which to read African American texts.

12. See Kevin Quashie's *Black Women, Identity and Cultural Theory: (Un)Becoming the Subject.*

13. The theme of violence as a natural and valid means of self-defense is highly prevalent in African American literary traditions. Nineteenth-century examples

include Victor Séjour's short story "The Mulatto" (1837), which depicts a mulatto slave, Georges, poisoning his master's wife and chopping his master's head off with an axe. According to the *Norton Anthology of African American Literature*, "The Mulatto" (Le Mulâtre) is "the earliest known work of African American fiction. It first appeared in 1837 in a journal published in Paris, *La Revue des Colonies*, sponsored by a society of men of color. This [the version published in the anthology] is the first English translation of Séjour's pioneering story of racial exploitation and violent revenge" (286). In his novella "The Heroic Slave," Frederick Douglass offers a fictional account of the 1841 rebellion led by Madison Washington aboard the slave ship *Creole* (1852). The theme of violent self-defense is also evident in the title of the slave narrative *Silvia Dubois, A Biografy of the Slav Who Whipt Her Mistres and Gand Her Fredom* (1883).

14. See the prelude for a definition of Johnson's dual audience. On page 11 of *Souls*, Du Bois also concedes that to write for one audience or the other would still prove traumatic.

15. Frantz Fanon writes, "At the level of individuals, violence is a cleansing force. It frees the native from his inferiority complex and from his despair and inaction; it makes him fearless and restores his self-respect" (*Wretched of the Earth* 94).

16. Wright explains the influences that created Bigger in his essay "How Bigger Was Born."

17. For example, John Oliver Killens's novel *Youngblood* (1954) opens with eleven-year-old Laurie Lee Barksdale kicking, kneeing in the groin, biting, and fiercely (and bloodily) clawing the face of a white would-be molester as he tries to attack her on the street. Laurie Lee later marries Joe Youngblood and, with their son Robby, they stand as a family prepared to defend themselves against southern racism. Sherley Anne Williams begins her 1980 short story "Meditations on History" with a quotation from Angela Davis's essay "Reflections on the Black Woman's Role in the Community of Slaves." By writing a fictional account of Dessa, a pregnant black woman who leads a slave revolt, Williams answers Davis's call to resurrect "the black woman in her true historical contours" (126). Dessa becomes self-actualized once she realizes the meaning behind her murdered lover's dying words, "a nigga can do." What a "nigga can do" is act, retaliate, fight back. In one of the closing scenes in Morrison's *Beloved*, Sethe mistakes her daughter's new employer, who has come to retrieve Denver for work, for her former master and tormentor, schoolteacher. This scene can be read as a revision of Sethe's earlier decision to kill her children to protect them from slavery. What Sethe has learned is that slaying the oppressor as both the cure and the preventive medicine against victimization is better than killing her own progeny.

18. Although my primary focus is the black aesthetic movement, I want to point to 1954 as a particularly significant year for African Americans. *Brown v. Board of Education of Topeka, Kansas* was decided and the separate but equal doctrine was unveiled as a fallacy and ruled unconstitutional. This court decision marked the first phase of the black liberation struggle—one that saw the possibility of making progress by working within the existing system and by challenging that system through

nonviolent protest. This year was also significant in literary history. It marked the publication of Richard Wright's *Black Power* and John Oliver Killens's *Youngblood*. The publication of both books marked the second phase of the black liberation struggle, the shift away from strategies of nonviolence. While *Black Power* laid the foundation for the black nationalism that re-emerged during the 1960s, *Youngblood* spoke to this shifting consciousness with its depiction of a militant black family surviving and demanding respect in the South. With the court victory and literary representations of black power, 1954 actually begins the revolutionary fervor associated with the 1960s.

19. *Microsoft: Encarta Africana*, "Black Arts Movement."

20. See Houston Baker's article "Generational Shifts and the Recent Criticism of Afro-American Literature" for a more thorough explanation of the shift from the "poetics of integration" to black aesthetics.

21. Because of the link between militant blacks and Third World populations, the black aesthetic movement has been compared to the negritude movement. Negritude is defined as a "'black is beauty' doctrine originated by black intellectuals in pre-World War II Paris to assert the unique contributions, values, and characteristics of black men and black civilization" (Markovitz, *Léopold Sédar and the Politics of Negritude* 4). Léopold Sédar Senghor (Senegal), Aimé Césaire (Martinique), and León Damas (French Guiana) were the three main poets who had the strongest impact on black poetry in Paris during the 1930s and after World War II. Césaire claimed negritude for those of Africa and its Diaspora on the basis of the unifying experience of the middle passage and the New World plantation system, while Senghor called for African peoples to unite in a search for a "collective soul."

22. Although the Harlem Renaissance and perhaps even the negritude movement might seem similar to the black aesthetic movement, there are two significant reasons why both fall short of being movements responsible for the type of decolonized subjectivity prevalent in texts written by African Americans today. First, the Harlem Renaissance was fueled in a large degree by white patrons, some of whom took a very active part in the creative process. Because many writers were funded by whites, this also meant that many, in varying degrees, still deferred to the wishes of a white audience. Second, the Harlem Renaissance is typically considered a middle-class movement and therefore was seen as a movement that did not speak to the larger black population. David Levering Lewis calls the Harlem Renaissance "cultural nationalism of the parlor," while for Richard Wright "the chief failure of black writing had been its unconcern with bridging the gulf between the writer and the black masses" (Bigsby, *The Second Black Renaissance*, 18).

In comparison, the negritude movement was also often criticized for being elitist. Additionally, Irving Leonard Markovitz writes, "The African and West Indian prophets of Negritude may have claimed something more than France, but they never denied their 'Frenchness'" (*Léopold Sédar and the Politics of Negritude* 45). For this reason, Markovitz sees negritude as a rebellion but not a revolution because it was still designed to convince French colonial powers that blacks had attained a level of cultural equality with French civilization. He states that "Negritude argued only for a synthesis with French institutions. The administration could tolerate Negritude because it was not a program for change" (45). Nevertheless, the black aesthetic movement owes a debt to cultural nationalistic movements in other countries, as well as to African American traditions of resistance that arise in other literary eras like the Harlem Renaissance.

23. Douglass's first narrative offers more than one example of the consequences of failing to mask. In one instance Douglass tells the story of a slave who unknowingly meets his master on the road. His master owns so many slaves that he rarely has direct contact with them. When the master asks the slave who his master is and asks how he treats him, the slave answers truthfully and tells the man that his master treats him horribly. The slave is severely punished for his honesty.

24. See chapter 3 for an example of how Angela Davis strategically masks and unmasks throughout her autobiography. For a more detailed discussion of the depiction of anger in African American texts, also refer to Raymond Hedin's article "The Structuring of Emotion in Black American Fiction," *Novel: A Forum on Fiction* 16, no. 1 (Fall 1982): 35–54.

25. His threat further demonstrates how the politics of race and sexuality are played out on the body of the white female.

26. The term "counter-stereotyping" was coined by Robert Bone to describe an essential component of protest literature. See *The Negro Novel in America* (1958).

27. This notion of difference derives from W. Lawrence Hogue's book *Discourse and the Other: The Production of the Afro-American Text*.

28. See Dickson-Carr's *African American Satire: The Sacredly Profane Novel* (2001).

29. For example, I consider Ernest Gaines to be a prime example of a male writer whose agenda is to promote "healing" among his black readers. A work like *A Lesson Before Dying* (1994) not only serves to counter representations of black men as bestial and criminal, according to Keith Clark manhood is represented as antithetical to hypermasculine "ethos and performance" (i.e., violence, power, sexual domination). In *Black Manhood in James Baldwin, Ernest Gaines, and August Wilson,* Clark also maintains that in Gaines's work black manhood is also antithetical to "white patriarchy and privilege as the touchstones for selfhood"; Gaines's idea of manhood encompasses emotional, psychological, and spiritual growth. For the reasons listed above, *A Lesson Before Dying* can be labeled womanist; his approach to writing is reliant upon social responsibility, and the black male is read as communal rather than as an isolated maverick. And while *A Lesson Before Dying* is ostensibly a story concerned with black male victimization, men (and women) *do* possess agency and are not depicted as perpetual victims. Clark's assessment that Gaines's novels function as a rite of passage in which black men must "undergo a ritualistic process in which they must confront their deformation" and in which their perception of themselves is ultimately dismantled, bears a striking resemblance to my own description of decolonizing texts.

30. In *Introduction to Black Studies* (3rd ed. 2002), Maulana Karenga makes a similar claim; after foregrounding the 1970s as Alice Walker's emerging era, he makes an

arguable statement that writings of the 1970s "do not have the self-conscious urgency and fire of the sixties" (417).

31. bell hooks addresses this idea of a monolithic identity for African American poets in general when she writes, "The insistence on finding one voice, one definitive style of writing and reading one's poetry, fit all too neatly with a static notion of self and identity . . . our sense of self, and by definition, our voice, was not unilateral, monologist, or static but rather multi-dimensional" (*Talking Back* 11–12).

32. I can, however, concede that Johnson is taking black feminist critics to task in their desire to define what constitutes a feminist text or rather what characteristics make a text innately female.

33. For example, Madhu Dubey, in her book *Black Women Novelists and the Nationalist Aesthetic,* discusses the connection many contemporary black women writers have with black nationalist discourse, asserting that many of these women were writing in response to the marginalization they felt in black nationalist discourse and the black aesthetic movement in general.

34. I do not mean to suggest, however, that African American male writers, as well as men throughout the Diaspora, are incapable of creating decolonized texts in the manner in which I define them. As I mentioned earlier, Ernest Gaines's *A Lesson Before Dying* is one example.

2. "WHO IS THE BLACK WOMAN?"

The epigraph is from "Reena," originally published in *Harpers* in 1962.

1. The stereotypical names Spillers mentions are "Peaches," "Brown Sugar," "Sapphire," "Earth Mother," "Aunty," "Granny," "God's Fool," "Miss Ebony First," and "Black Woman at the Podium."

2. "The Making of a Writer: From the Poets in the Kitchen" is found in the preface to Marshall's collection of short stories titled *Reena and Other Stories* (1983).

3. From Smart-Grosvenor's essay "The Kitchen Crisis," in *The Black Woman: An Anthology,* 119–123. In her essay "Standing In for the State," Wahneema Lubiano explains that while Smart-Grosvenor's essay recounted "black cultural nationalist criticism of the dominant racial groups' domestic and social mores," it also "refigured our notions of 'appropriate' oppositional sites" such as the kitchen and other so-called female realms (*Is It Nation Time?* 163).

4. At the time of publication, the editor used the name Toni Cade. She later borrowed her surname from the Bambara people in Mali. Out of deference to memory and her decision to take "Bambara" as her surname, I will refer to her as Toni Cade Bambara throughout this chapter and the rest of this manuscript.

5. See "Consider This . . . Personal Impact of *Essence* Magazine," by Mikki Taylor, published in *Essence*'s May 2000 issue.

6. Lewis was the financial writer for the *New York Amsterdam News* from 1957 to 1960 and the financial editor for *The New York Age* from 1959 to 1961. After directing research at the Small Investor's Real Estate Plan for two years, she moved to France and, from 1964 to 1969, wrote for *Life, Le Figaro Litteraire, L'Express,* the *Washington*

Post, the *New York Times,* and other newspapers. Before returning to the United States as a news correspondent for *Jeune Afrique,* Lewis also interviewed African dignitaries for the BBC's African Service. She became *Essence* magazine's first editor-in-chief in 1970. After resigning from *Essence* in 1971, Lewis founded *Encore: American & Worldwide News* and served as its editor-in-chief and publisher for ten years. Lewis has also served on Columbia University's faculty as a journalism professor, has worked as a literary agent, and became the first editor-in-chief of the NAACP's magazine, *The New Crisis,* in 1999. This information on Lewis comes from http://www.media-alliance.org.

7. For some the use of an actual photograph of a woman, rather than an abstract image that would somehow symbolize the complexity of black women, might be construed as problematic since the model becomes both the embodiment of ideal black beauty and the epitome of revolutionary womanhood. The choice of a dark cover model might also be considered contradictory to the anthology's rhetoric of inclusiveness; within its pages, *The Black Woman* challenges notions of authentic blackness, confronts intraracial prejudice, and insists that black beauty comes in many hues. And yet when one considers that darker-complexioned women have historically been at the bottom of the beauty hierarchy, the choice to feature a darker model *is* a revolutionary choice.

8. Such a theory could explain why *Essence* debuted its second year (1971) with a cover model with a chemically permed hairstyle; throughout the first year the cover models were depicted either sporting Afros or other natural hairstyles. Coincidentally, Ayana D. Byrd and Lori L. Tharps mark 1971 as marking the decline of the Afro. Therefore, *Essence* might have been responding to the changing fashion trend rather than, as the then new editor-in-chief Marcia Gillespie suggested, "What we [at *Essence*] tried to do was to show the rainbow. And readers really wanted to see themselves and the range of black beauty" (*Hair Story* 66).

9. Founded in Southern California in 1965 in the wake of Malcolm X's assassination and the infamous Watts riot, US established itself as a cultural nationalist organization that was sometimes notorious for espousing the subservience of women on the grounds that such roles were a part of customary African cultural traditions. For more detailed information and a more positive spin on the organization, see Scot Brown's *Fighting for Us: Maulana Karenga, the US Organization, and Black Cultural Nationalism* (New York: New York University Press, 2003).

10. Stokely Carmichael made this comment at a SNCC conference held in Waveland, Mississippi, in 1964.

11. Such charges are rampant in the autobiographies of Angela Davis, Elaine Brown, Assata Shakur, and Anne Moody and in fictional accounts of "movement" women, such as in Alice Walker's *Meridian* (1976) and Toni Cade Bambara's *The Salt Eaters* (1980).

12. Billed as a "morality play," in *Madheart,* Baraka creates two characters, Black Man and Black Woman, who are obviously meant to represent black manhood and womanhood respectively. The dialogue between these two characters implies that relationships between black men and women have been all but severed. After Black

Man vows to "get [her] back" if he needs to, Black Woman cheekily responds, "You better get me back, if you know what's good for you" (98). In reaction to her uppity behavior, Black Man "wheels and suddenly slaps her crosswise, back and forth across the face" all while demanding that she act like a woman and submit to love and to a man (99). The irony of this scene is that although Black Man claims that the days when white men rape black women with impunity are gone because "the world is [his]," he fails to see his abuse as parallel to that of white slave masters; he sees nothing wrong with demanding submission as a condition of their relationship. In *Soul on Ice,* Cleaver discusses how he "practiced" raping black women so that he would be able to rape white women to strike a supposed revolutionary blow against their white fathers. For a more in depth analysis of *Soul on Ice,* see chapter 4.

13. The most compelling critique of the Moynihan Report can be found in Angela Davis's essay "Reflections on the Black Woman's Role in the Community of Slaves," published in 1972. In this essay, Davis countered Moynihan's charges that the matrifocal structure he identified as the most prevalent pattern in African American households derived from slavery, where African American women were typically perceived as dominant. Davis used her essay to demonstrate that rather than being empowered by their slave status, as Moynihan suggests, black women were sexual victims as well as exploited for their labor. Furthermore, Davis reappropriated the image of the slave woman as domineering and emasculating; instead she explained that black women often served as the "backbones" of the slave community as well as being active participants in slave revolts. More than offering a critique of Moynihan's sexism, and by extension the prevalently sexist character of U.S. society, Davis also used her essay to highlight a tradition of black women's participation in liberation struggles—suggesting to her contemporaries that black women did in fact have a place in contemporary struggles for black liberation. As evident from Davis's example, contemporary black feminism can be said to have partially developed to correct historical inaccuracies and to counter negative stereotypes of black women. For further discussion of Davis's assessment of Moynihan, see chapter 3.

14. Although I am enamored of Bambara's language in this quotation, I question her motives for using a personal anecdote in this instance. It is as if Bambara feels that being involved in a serious romantic relationship with a man somehow better qualifies her to talk about black male/female relationships. Or perhaps she seeks to ward off speculations that her feminist affiliations and ideals make her an unfit mate, or worse, an emasculator or lesbian.

15. I want to make it clear here that Bambara's use of language is an attempt to mirror the prevailing rhetoric of the era. Earlier in the article, she berates those who think that sensitivity equals homosexual behavior, and therefore her challenge that we adopt androgynous selves is a call to cast off constricting gender labels.

16. This information comes from the following website: http://www.thehistory makers.com/biography/biography.asp?bioindex'83&category'medicalMakers.

17. Stephen Henderson defines "saturation" as "(a) the communication of Blackness in a given situation, and (b) a sense of fidelity to the observed and intuited truth of the Black Experience" (*Understanding the New Black Poetry* 62).

18. During the 1960s Roy Ayers was one of the most prominent figures in the jazz industry. In the 1970s Ayers led the way for the movement called jazz-funk. Following in Gordon Parks's footsteps (Parks did the score for *Shaft* in 1971), Ayers would later produce the score for a blaxploitation hit *Coffy* (1973).

19. Myrlie B. Evers is most famous for being married to slain civil rights activist Medgar Evers. At the time of her interview with Ida Lewis, Evers was running on the Democratic ticket for Congress in the 24th Congressional District. Although she did not win, Evers received 38 percent of the vote.

20. At the time of the article's publication, Nikki Giovanni had already published several of her poems and was a well-known figure in the black aesthetic movement, while Florynce Kennedy was a black activist and an attorney. Novella Nelson had distinguished herself as a jazz singer, while Barbara Ann Teer was the director of the National Black Theatre. Madelyn Conley was a labor affairs representative for the National Urban League.

21. This information comes from Simone M. Caron's article "Birth Control and the Black Community in the 1960s: Genocide or Power Politics?" *Social History* 31, no. 3 (1999): 545–69.

22. For more detailed information on the history of birth control debates in the 1960s, see Samuel F. Yette's *The Choice: The Issue of Black Survival in America* (1971); Robert G. Weisbord's *Genocide?: Birth Control and the Black American* (1975); and Bobby Wright's *The Psychopathic Racial Personality* (1975).

23. It is interesting to note that in his 1969 autobiography *Die Nigger Die!: A Political Autobiography*, H. Rap Brown also makes a distinction between government-controlled sterilization of black and other poor minority populations and women's rights: "Birth control, as it's practiced by governmental programs dealing with the masses of poor, can't be called anything but an attempt at genocide. Birth control should be an individual decision. It should not be forced by the government" (138).

24. Elected in 1970, Kenneth Gibson was not only the first black mayor of Newark, New Jersey, but the first African American to be elected mayor in a northeastern city. Gibson served four terms and was defeated for a fifth term in 1986 by Sharpe James, also an African American. Many sources speculate that after the 1967 riots in the city, Newark was ripe for reform and Gibson's subsequent election resulted from the city's attempts to heal.

25. Jones was very vocal in his support of Gibson as a mayoral candidate. See Komozi Woodard's *A Nation within a Nation: Amiri Baraka (LeRoi Jones) and Black Power Politics* (1999) for more information on Jones's involvement in Gibson's campaign.

26. This quotation derives from an inserted page in *The Black Woman* that precedes the preface. Although no author is given, this quotation served as a marketing device designed to both secure the book's appeal to a wide range of black female readers while simultaneously demonstrating the diversity of black womanhood to mainstream readers.

27. From the very first installment of Lewis's column "Perspective"—a vehicle through which Lewis, as editor-in-chief, provided editorial commentary on various topics of interest to *Essence* readers.

28. Although the cover of *The Black Woman* depicts a dark-complected woman, Bambara's inclusion of Carole Brown's essay "From the Family Notebook" indicates an urge to thwart essentialist notions of "true" blackness as characterized as phenotypically brown or dark-skinned. As the title suggests, Brown is one of the "family"; she identifies herself as a light-skinned African American woman who, though both her parents would legally be classified as black, is light enough to pass as white. Brown not only discusses the pain of not being identified as black by both blacks and whites, but her intense love of black people.

29. For example, John Oliver Killens criticized the black aesthetic movement for its myopic focus on northern writers and its tendency to confine notions of "the black experience" to urban environs. He writes, "Even during the 1960s black writers themselves seemed to relegate the Southern experience to a state of unimportance and irrelevance, seemed to have thought that the only happenings worth writing about were those occurring in such Northern urban areas as Harlem, Chicago's South Side, and Detroit" (*Black Southern Voices* 2).

30. Proof that *The Black Woman* was also interested in Africa and its Diaspora is exhibited in the short story "Reena," which features U.S. black women of West Indian descent, and its inclusion of Alice Walker's "The Diary of an African Nun"—a story about a Ugandan woman who subtly critiques colonialism, particularly concerning what it means for an African woman to embrace a white religion.

31. This information comes from "ESSENCE, The Real Story," found in the August 1971 issue, p. 30.

32. What is interesting, or seems suspect to me, is the lack of public skepticism on the part of black women that four black men could best represent black female interests and create a magazine that professed to be the "essence" of black womanhood. If the reverse had occurred and four black women had created a magazine for black men, I cannot imagine that there would not have been a large public outcry on the part of black men. My own skepticism is, however, predicated on the fact that the Hollingsworth Group originally wanted to name the magazine *Sapphire*—which would only have furthered the widespread perception of black women as emasculating shrews.

33. Askia Muhammad Touré (Rolland Snellings) was one of the early prominent figures in the black arts/black aesthetic movement. Touré was also a member of the renowned Umbra Group (a black aesthetic poetry collective). Additionally, Touré was one of the main authors of SNCC's black power position paper. Gordon Parks was a freelance fashion photographer for *Vogue* and *Glamour* who became famous in the late 1960s for his photo essays on leaders of the black revolution. Also a composer, musician, and filmmaker, he wrote, produced, and directed the film *The Learning Tree* (1969—based on his 1963 novel of the same title), and he directed *Shaft* (1971). Parks was the editorial director of *Essence* from 1970 to 1973.

34. Concurrently, in a 2002 interview with Traci Spencer, partial owner Ed Lewis states that "unlike *O* and *Honey* [*Essence*'s current competition], *Essence* does not aim for a specific age group but rather a certain type of woman, a 'striver.'" Here Lewis is harking back to Ida Lewis's original declaration of the attributes of the *Essence* Woman.

35. No page number given. See "Midlife Crisis" www.jrn.columbia.edu/student work/nymagreview2002/midlifecrisis.asp.

36. This suspicion that many voice concerning *Time's* partial acquisition of *Essence* is similar to the controversy in 1971 when Playboy became affiliated with *Essence*. This situation has also been likened to BET (Black Entertainment Television), which was black-owned for twenty years, being bought out by Viacom on November 3, 2001.

37. According to their magazine profiles, *Honey* was aimed at urban women between the ages of eighteen and thirty-four, while *Heart and Soul* was marketed to health-conscious black women in general. In *Ladies' Pages,* Noliwe Rooks explains that Oprah Winfrey's magazine has a more multicultural demographic in mind. Both *Honey* and *Heart and Soul* became defunct when Vanguarde Media filed for bankruptcy in November 2003. *Heart and Soul* was relaunched in the summer of 2006.

38. *Jolie* magazine debuted on September 20, 2005, and was founded by Alicia M. Rivers, Rachel Breton, Michelle A. Pascal, and the actress Vivica A. Fox, who also serves as the editor-at-large. *Jolie,* which means "pretty" in French, is geared to black women specifically and women of color in general. See www.mommytoo.com/September5_2005. htm for more information on the magazine's founders. The official website for *Jolie* is www.jolielivepretty.com. *Today's Black Woman's* targeted audience is obvious; it is a lifestyle magazine written for a wide variety of African American women from eighteen to forty-nine. *Vibe Vixen* premiered in February 2005 and was created to be the female counterpart to *Vibe,* as well as to compete with *Suede.* Like *Suede, Vibe Vixen* was geared toward African American and other women of color who consider themselves a part of the hip-hop generation and seek venues that support their love of hip-hop rather than cast them as being complicit in their own exploitation, given hip-hop's widely publicized misogynist tendencies. The magazine folded in 2007.

39. Rooks ultimately concedes that *Essence* is still an African American women's magazine given that it has consistently been edited by black women and the majority of its audience is black women.

3. CONSTRUCTING DIVA CITIZENSHIP

The quotation in the epigraph derives from a public speech that Davis gave in the midst of the controversy with the California Board of Regents. Found in J. A. Parker's *Angela Davis: The Making of a Revolutionary.*

1. When the cover was released, many bloggers also saw a correlation between *The New Yorker's* depiction of Michelle Obama and media representations of Davis, as well as that of Kathleen Cleaver.

2. The only exceptions would be photographs published of her childhood and college years and photographs that were taken at Davis's capture by the FBI, while she was in disguise.

3. Excerpts from a June 2, 1970, letter to George Jackson reproduced in Bettina Aptheker's *The Morning Breaks: The Trial of Angela Davis,* 209 and 211.

4. Many academics sided with Davis in the name of academic freedom. Additionally, there was a general feeling that blacks were advancing in the academic arena.

For example, in "The Crisis of the Negro Intellectual: A Post-Date," Hortense Spillers writes, "The period 1968–1970 meant, at last, the fruition of a radical and pluralistic democracy, or so *it seemed,* with, for example, comparatively larger numbers of African American students admitted to the mainstream academy and agitation for the movements in black studies and women's studies, and their far-reaching implications for a radically altered curriculum, especially in the humanities" (68).

5. George Jackson is the "Soledad Brother" prison inmate to whom Davis was at that time romantically linked. He is most famous for writing a collection of letters published under the title *Soledad Brother* (1970), which went on to become a bestseller. On August 21, 1971, Jackson was shot to death in San Quentin's prison yard when he allegedly attempted to escape by using a gun, presumed to be smuggled into the prison by his lawyer Stephen Bingham, to take over the tier in which he was housed.

6. As I state in the first chapter, I agree that true liberation occurs when one begins to develop one's own subjectivity because what is problematic about the concept of double-consciousness is not that one is aware of the dominant culture's perception of oneself, but that negative outside perceptions are internalized and become the measuring stick of one's own self-worth.

7. Interestingly, in 1972 Toni Morrison delivered a scathing critique of Nadelson's work. To the question the title poses, "Who Is Angela Davis?" Morrison curtly riffs, "On the other hand, who is Regina Nadelson and why is she behaving like Harriet Beecher Stowe, another simpatico white girl who felt she was privy to the secret of how black revolutionaries got that way?" Morrison labels Nadelson a modern-day racist, arguing that Nadelson, like nineteenth-century whites who would credit the rebellious spirit of blacks to their white blood, erroneously credits white academics for Davis's activist desires.

8. I would also submit that Davis's flight and the black public support she received set the stage for Assata Shakur. As late as 1981, almost three years after her escape from prison, in areas like Harlem and Bedford-Stuyvesant, posters proclaiming that "ASSATA IS WELCOMED HERE" were plastered everywhere (Evelyn Williams, *Inadmissible Evidence,* 179).

9. "Women in Dark Times" is a review essay on Angela Davis's autobiography, Bettina Aptheker's book *The Morning Breaks: The Trial of Angela Davis,* and *Jury Woman,* by Mary Timothy.

10. Valerie Smith argues that there is a difference between slave narratives and autobiographies written by black Americans and those written by white Americans: "One basic difference between the two forms of autobiographies is that whereas black autobiographies do not confine themselves merely to personal reminiscence and move on to the treatment of the community as a whole, the white autobiographer confines his experience to the development of the self, in some cases unrelated to the community—an isolated maverick" (*Self-Discovery and Authority* 31). Here Smith is stating that black autobiographers view themselves as a part of a community rather than as individuals. Sudhi Rajiv concurs with Smith when he states, "In the black autobiography, the 'self' is always inseparable from group reality and the future of the race" (*Forms of Black Consciousness* 152). As I state in the introduction to

this project, from the slave narratives to contemporary black autobiographies, black autobiographers in this country have recognized their dual position as individuals and part of the collective. The authors of slave narratives understood that they were acting in the role of "native" informant for their predominantly white audience, bearing witness to the injustices of an oppressed people while simultaneously offering testimony to their own abuses.

11. Reed makes a distinction between "black power consumerism" and "black power ideology." He defines black power consumerism as a derivative of political activism in that it parasitically uses the "rhetoric of black assertiveness" as a vehicle through which to peddle radical black identity as a commodity (*Stirrings* 202–203).

4. RETURN TO THE FLESH

A version of this chapter appeared as "Of Poststructuralist Fallout, Scarification, and Blood Poems: The Revolutionary Ideology behind the Poetry of Jayne Cortez," in *Other Sisterhoods: Literary Theory and U.S. Women of Color,* ed. Sandra Kumamoto Stanley (Urbana and Chicago: University of Illinois Press, 1998), pp. 63–85. The epigraph is from the interview "A Poet's World: Jayne Cortez Discusses Her Life and Her Work," conducted by sister poet and playwright Alexis DeVeaux.

1. The black aesthetic and black power movements, and consequently the ideologies therein, have been defined as essentialist, monolithic, sexist, homophobic, and ahistorical. Theodore Mason, in *The Johns Hopkins Guide to Literary Criticism* (1994), uses all the adjectives to define the criticism, fiction, poetry, and prose of the black arts movement. Critics such as Elliot Butler-Evans and Henry Louis Gates follow suit by labeling the black arts movement as "nationalist essentialism" (Butler-Evans, "Beyond Essentialism," 123) and as a movement that did not "think deeply enough" and was bounded by naïve idealization of an imaginary black essence (Gates, *Black Literature*, 7).

2. Of Billie Holiday, Cortez exclaims, "When she sings, I hear the forced migrations of the Black world in her voice" (DeVeaux, "A Poet's World," 77).

3. In his essay, "You Touch My Black Aesthetic and I'll Touch Yours," Julian Mayfield states, "[The] Black Aesthetic . . . is our racial memory, and the unshakable knowledge of who we are, where we have been, and, springing from this, where are we going. Where have we been? Up a hell of a long, hard road" (26).

4. For African Americans, I see this method of scarification as both a way to reclaim U.S. territory as our birthright, as well as a way to embrace Africa as our mythical motherland.

5. I was introduced to this text by Professor William L. Andrews when he presented an analysis of it at the "Speculating on the South: Reimagining the Historical South through Scholarship and Art" conference, sponsored by University of North Carolina–Chapel Hill, November 6–8, 2007.

6. In *Teaching to Transgress,* bell hooks demonstrates how notions of "experience" and "commitment" can have a place in poststructuralist teaching. In her article "Essentialism and Experience," hooks finds useful ways to include and validate "experience"—both her own and her students—without letting either academic

theory or the theory derived from lived experience stand as the only legitimate authority. Instead of inverting the hierarchy, therefore placing lived/learned experience on the top, both "experiential" theory and "hypothetical" theory are given equal time and are seen in conjunction with each other.

7. This recollection shows that even during the Harlem Renaissance, Hughes is deconstructing the notion of "whiteness."

8. For more information on Baker's activism, please refer to Ean Wood's *The Josephine Baker Story* or Mary L. Dudziak's article, "Josephine Baker, Racial Protest and The Cold War" (1994).

9. Nonetheless, I submit that homophobia during the black liberation movement was not a notion that Jayne Cortez created. Indeed, what makes the poem "Race" even more interesting as a study of homophobia during this time period is that she labels homosexuality as a by-product of racist oppression. Homosexuality, then, is coded as white; therefore, if you are a black homosexual then not only are you anti-revolutionary, but you are emulating your oppressors.

10. Cortez's marriage to Coleman lasted from 1954 until 1964.

11. See Huey Newton's *Revolutionary Suicide* for a more complete definition of both "revolutionary" and "reactionary" suicide.

12. The correct spelling of Little's first name is up for debate; it has been written as Joan, Joanne, and even Jo Anne, depending on the reporter's inclination. Journalist Wayne King explains that "Joan was the name written on her birth certificate. She began spelling it Joanne, and quietly spelled it that way for the judge at her first-degree murder trial . . ." ("Focus of Slaying Trial" no page number).

13. Much like the publication of "Angela Davis on Black Women" in its August 1972 issue, Davis's decision to publish in such a venue might have been a strategic way to inform *Ms.*'s predominantly white female audience about black women's perspective on rape and their lack of participation in the white feminist and antirape movements.

14. When Davis speaks of the "frame-up rape charge," she is talking about the various fraudulent rape indictments filed against black men for allegedly raping white women, charges that were used as a deterrent to miscegenation or as a way to venerate white womanhood.

15. For more information on Little's supporters, see Genna Rae McNeil's article "'Joanne Is You and Joanne Is Me': A Consideration of African American Women and the 'Free Joan Little' Movement, 1974–75," in *Sisters in the Struggle* (2001).

16. Melhem's statement is actually in reference to Cortez's poem "Drum Everywhere Drums."

17. See Aldon Nielsen, *Black Chant: Language of African-American Postmodernism*.

5. SHE DREAMS A WORLD

1. The Pilgrims also forbade the use of peyote, a drug essential to some Native American religious practices. Peyote enabled Native Americans to use visions (i.e., dreams) as prophecy.

2. In light of Madhu Dubey's research on black nationalism in *Black Women Novelists and the Nationalist Aesthetic,* I argue that "cultural" rather than "revolutionary" nationalism is the mode of black nationalistic thought at work in *The Salt Eaters.* Dubey writes, "An emphasis on class over race is the major factor distinguishing the revolutionary from the cultural nationalists, who give priority to racial over class oppression" (14). Additionally, she argues that the black aesthetic was a literary program developed around the tenets of black cultural nationalism, so much so that one cannot hope to gain a full understanding of the black aesthetic without assessing the "ideological implications of black cultural nationalism" (15).

3. I argue that Bambara sees revolutionary action as a moral and spiritual imperative for African Americans and, therefore, I deem it appropriate to equate the two terms in this instance.

4. *The Salt Eaters* has as its nucleus the theme of wholeness. As I state in my introduction to this project, the theme of wholeness can be found in many African American literary traditions. Wholeness is used as a metaphor for the health and wellness of both the African American body and spirit, as well as that of the racially divided nation-space of the United States.

5. See Houston Baker's *Long Black Song,* C. W. E. Bigsby's "Judgment Day is Coming!: The Apocalyptic Dream in Recent Afro-American Fiction," Susan Bowers's "*Beloved* and the New Apocalypse," Maxine Lavon Montgomery's *The Apocalypse in African-American Fiction,* and John R. May's *Toward a New Earth: Apocalypse in the American Novel* for more complete information about the tradition of apocalypse in African American literature.

6. A pivotal year because of *Brown v. Board of Education,* which ruled segregation illegal.

7. The Neptunian Age and the Age of Pisces are interchangeable. See Brau, Weaver, and Edmands, *Larousse Encyclopedia of Astrology,* for more information concerning both of these ages, as well as the more familiar Age of Aquarius.

8. Dr. Meadows is a biracial man who must not only come to grips with his dual racial identity but must also reconcile his background in traditional Western medicine with that of the non-Western medicines practiced at the town's infirmary. Dr. Meadows's biraciality and his position as an outsider to Claybourne are important to *The Salt Eaters.* Dr. Meadows, like the inhabitants of Claybourne (and like the readers of Bambara's text), must merge his conflicting subjectivities into a harmonious whole.

9. The term "apocalyptic spatiality" comes from Laura E. Donaldson's book *Decolonizing Feminisms: Race, Gender and Empire Building,* in which she explains that apocalyptic spatiality is *not* precisely synonymous with Armageddon, the famed site where the apocalypse is scheduled to occur. Although Bambara suggests that Claybourne is indeed Armageddon, apocalyptic spatiality is also a signifier of a geographic space that epitomizes both the pitfalls and promises of the apocalypse.

10. Eatonville is the birthplace of Harlem Renaissance writer Zora Neale Hurston (1891–1960). A small town located ten miles from Orlando, Florida, Eatonville is credited with being the first incorporated black municipality in the United States.

11. The existence of the neighboring white town suggests that communities similar to Claybourne are cropping up elsewhere and that the coming apocalypse is of concern to others.

12. From *Webster's New World College Dictionary,* 3rd ed., p. 232.

13. For example, Ahiro (Velma's husband's masseuse) advises Obie that in order to cope with separating from Velma he should cry, not necessarily as a release or expression of his pain, but because "[t]he body needs to throw off its excess salt for balance. Too little salt and wounds can't heal. Remember Napoleon's army? Those frogs were dropping dead from scratches because their bodies were deprived of salt. But *too* much" (164).

14. From the videotape *A World of Ideas: Parts One and Two.* In these taped interviews with Bill Moyers, Toni Morrison discusses her characters and the difficulties of writing about the painful subjects that occur in her novels.

15. In her article "Teaching Black-Eyed Susans: An Approach to the Study of Black Women Writers," Mary Helen Washington identifies three types of women in African American fiction written by women, the suspended, assimilated, and emergent woman. According to Washington, the suspended woman leads a life of violence so extreme that her story often ends in death. While the assimilated woman fares better, she nevertheless fails to become self-actualized because she is disconnected from her community (*But Some of Us Are Brave* 212). Washington finally defines the emergent black women as:

> women coming just to the edge of a new awareness and making the first tentative steps into an uncharted region. And although they are more fully conscious of their political and psychological oppression and more capable of creating new options for themselves, they must undergo a harsh initiation before they are ready to occupy and claim any new territory. (*But Some of Us Are Brave* 214)

16. As the name of Velma's healer Minnie Ransom signifies, health and wholeness come at a price—a mini-ransom.

17. For a discussion of the treatment of women in male-dominated organizations of the 1960s, see Angela Davis's self-titled autobiography; Elaine Brown's *A Taste of Power*; Assata Shakur's *Assata*; and Anne Moody's *Coming of Age in Mississippi*.

18. "Daughters of the yam" is Bambara's label for black women from Africa and of the African Diaspora. In her book *Yearning,* bell hooks uses this phrase to refer to the younger generation of women (those of the postsegregationist generation) whom she deems "so modern, so sophisticated, and so lost" (13). However, upon a closer look, the modern women to which Bambara is referring would be of hooks's own ilk.

19. In Christian doctrine, committing suicide is considered a sin and therefore a broken covenant with God, which would prevent a person from entering into the kingdom of heaven. Even in Hinduism, to which Velma's question about reincarnation alludes, suicide is frowned upon because the suicide victim, having never learned the lessons of the present life, must repeat the same cycle in her next life. The narration of the text, however, is not solely dependent upon any religious doctrine

and instead relies on an amalgamation of the moral imperative and innate responsibility to "truth" that most doctrines possess.

20. Newton bases this definition on a May 1970 issue of *Ebony* magazine summarizing Dr. Herbert Hendin's findings of a comparative study of rising suicide rates among black men between the ages of nineteen and thirty-five.

21. The contrast to reactionary suicide is *revolutionary* suicide, which can be seen as more appropriate and moral. Newton explains his use of the term "revolutionary suicide" as follows: "Revolutionary suicide does not mean that I and my comrades have a death wish; it means just the opposite. We have such a strong desire to live with hope and human dignity that existence without them is impossible. When reactionary forces crush us, we must move against these forces, even at the risk of death. We will have to be driven out with a stick" (*Revolutionary Suicide* 5).

22. Here I am, of course, borrowing from Alice Walker's term "womanist"—which I also see to be an apt label for Velma Henry.

CODA

The epigraph is from "An Interview with Farah Jasmine Griffin," p. 878.

1. In 2000, Holland reviews the following texts for *American Literary History*: Jody David's *Negrophobia and Reasonable Racism: The Hidden Costs of Being Black in America* (1997), Lindon Barrett's *Blackness and Value: Seeing Double* (1999), and Hazel V. Carby's *Race Men* (1998).

2. According to Moraga and Anzaldúa, a theory in the flesh is "one where the physical realities of our lives—our skin color, the land or concrete we grew up on, our sexual longings—all fuse to create a politic born out of necessity" (*This Bridge Called My Back* 23).

3. While I am being slightly cheeky in using the term "black ways of knowing" rather than referring to an essentialized notion of black epistemology, I am actually talking about the ways in which black authority is often devalued.

BIBLIOGRAPHY

Abrahams, Roger D. *Positively Black.* Englewood Cliffs, N.J.: Prentice-Hall, 1970.

Abrams, Meyer Howard. *A Glossary of Literary Terms.* 6th ed. Fort Worth, Tex.: Harcourt Brace Jovanovich, 1993.

Adell, Sandra. *Double-Consciousness/Double Bind: Theoretical Issues in Twentieth-Century Black Literature.* Urbana: University of Illinois Press, 1994.

Alwes, Derek. "The Burden of Liberty: Choice in Toni Morrison's *Jazz* and Toni Cade Bambara's *The Salt Eaters.*" *African American Review* 30, no. 3 (1996): 353–65.

Angela Davis Speaks. [Sound Recording] Folkways FD 5401 S., 1971.

Aptheker, Bettina. *The Morning Breaks: The Trial of Angela Davis.* New York: International Publishers, 1975.

Awkward, Michael. *Inspiriting Influences: Tradition, Revision, and Afro-American Women's Novels.* New York: Columbia University Press, 1989.

———. *Negotiating Difference: Race, Gender, and the Politics of Positionality.* Chicago: University of Chicago Press, 1995.

Baker, Houston A., Jr. *Blues, Ideology, and Afro-American Literature: A Vernacular Theory.* Chicago and London: University of Chicago Press, 1984.

———. "Generational Shifts and the Recent Criticism of Afro-American Literature." *Black American Literature Forum* 15, no. 1 (Spring 1981): 3–21.

———. "In Dubious Battle." *New Literary History* 18 (1987): 371–84.

———. *Long Black Song: Essays in Black American Literature and Culture.* Charlottesville: University Press of Virginia, 1972.

———. "There Is No More Beautiful Way: Theory and the Poetics of Afro-American Women's Writing." In *Afro-American Literary Study in the 1990s,* ed. Houston A. Baker, Jr., and Patricia Redmon, 135–63. Chicago and London: University of Chicago Press, 1989.

Baldwin, James. *The Fire Next Time.* New York: Dial Press, 1963.

———. "Going to Meet the Man." In *Norton Anthology of African American Literature,* ed. Henry Louis Gates, Jr., and Nellie Y. McKay, 1750–1761. New York: W. W. Norton & Co., 1997.

———. *An Open Letter to My Sister, Miss Angela Davis.* New York: New York Committee to Free Angela Davis, 1970?

Bambara, Toni Cade, ed. *The Black Woman: An Anthology.* New York: Mentor Books, 1970.

———. *Deep Sightings and Rescue Missions: Fictions, Essays, and Conversations.* Edited by Toni Morrison. New York: Pantheon Books, 1996.

———. *The Salt Eaters.* New York: Vintage, 1980.

———. "Salvation Is the Issue." In *Black Women Writers (1950–1980): A Critical Evaluation,* ed. Mari Evans. New York and London: Anchor, 1984.

———. "What It Is I'm Doing Anyhow." In *The Writer on Her Work,* ed. Janet Sternberg, 153–168. New York: Norton, 1980.

Baraka, Amiri. Introduction to *Confirmation: An Anthology of African American Women.* Edited by Amina Baraka and Amiri Baraka, 15–26. New York: William Morrow, 1983.

———. *Dutchman and the Slave: Two Plays by LeRoi Jones.* New York: Morrow Quill Paperbacks, 1964.

———. *Madheart, Four Black Revolutionary Plays: (All Praises to the Black Man).* Marion Boyers: New York and London, 1998, 80–105.

———. "Statement." In *Nommo: An Anthology of Modern Black African and Black American Literature,* ed. William H. Robinson, 257–58. New York: Macmillan Co., 1972.

Beale, Frances. "Double Jeopardy: To Be Black and Female." In *The Black Woman: An Anthology,* ed. Toni Cade Bambara, 90–100. New York: Mentor Books, 1970.

Berlant, Lauren. *The Queen of America Goes to Washington City: Essays on Sex and Citizenship.* Durham, N.C.: Duke University Press, 1997.

Beverly, John. *Against Literature.* Minneapolis: University of Minnesota Press, 1993.

Bigsby, C. W. E. "Judgment Day Is Coming! The Apocalyptic Dream in Recent Afro-American Fiction." In *Black Fiction: New Studies in the Afro-American Novel Since 1945,* ed. Robert Lee, 149–72. San Francisco: Harper and Row, 1980.

———. *The Second Black Renaissance: Essays in Black Literature.* Westport, Conn.: Greenwood, 1980.

Blitman, Nan, and Robin Green. "Inez Garcia: On Trial." *Ms.,* May 1975, 49–54.

Boan, Devon. *The Black "I": Author and Audience in African-American Literature.* New York: Peter Lang, 2002.

Bond, Jean Carey, and Patricia Peery. "Is the Black Male Castrated?" In *The Black Woman: An Anthology,* ed. Toni Cade Bambara, 113–18. New York: Mentor Books, 1970.

Bone, Robert. *The Negro Novel in America.* New Haven, Conn.: Yale University Press, 1958.

Bonilla-Silva, Eduardo. *Racism without Racists: Color-Blind Racism and the Persistence of Racial Inequality in the United States.* Lanham, Md.: Rowman & Littlefield Publishers, 2003.

Borshuk, Michael. "An Intelligence of the Body: Disruptive Parody through Dance in the Early Performances of Josephine Baker." In *EmBODYing Liberation: The Black

Body in American Dance, ed. Dorothea Fischer-Hornung and Alison D. Goeller, 41–57. New Brunswick, N.J., and London: Transaction Publishers, 2001.

Boskin, Joseph. *Sambo: The Rise and Demise of an American Jester.* New York and Oxford: Oxford University Press, 1986.

Bowers, Susan. "*Beloved* and the New Apocalypse." In *Toni Morrison's Fiction: Contemporary Criticism,* ed. David L. Middleton, 209–30. New York and London: Garland Publishing, 1997.

Bradley, David. Foreword. *A Different Drummer.* By William Melvin Kelley. New York and London, Anchor Books, 1989. Originally published 1962.

Brau, Jean-Louis, Helen Weaver, and Allan Edmands. *Larousse Encyclopedia of Astrology.* New York and London: McGraw-Hill Book Co., 1977.

Brown, Elaine. *The Condemnation of Little B.* Boston: Beacon Press, 2002.

———. *A Taste of Power: A Black Woman's Story.* Norwell, Mass.: Anchor, 1993.

Brown, H. Rap. *Die Nigger Die!: A Political Autobiography.* Chicago: Lawrence Hill Books, 1969.

Brown, Kimberly N. "Of Poststructuralist Fallout, Scarification, and Blood Poems: The Revolutionary Ideology behind the Poetry of Jayne Cortez." In *Other Sisterhoods: Literary Theory and U.S. Women Writers of Color,* ed. Sandra K. Stanley, 63–85. Champaign: University of Illinois Press, 1998.

Brown, Michael K., Martin Carnoy, Elliott Currie, Troy Duster, David B. Oppenheimer, Marjorie M. Shultz, and David Wellman. *Whitewashing Race: The Myth of a Color-Blind Society.* Berkeley: University of California Press, 2003.

Brownmiller, Susan. "Making Female Bodies the Battlefield." *Newsweek,* January 4, 1993, 37.

Brydon, Diana, and Helen Tiffin. *Decolonising Fictions.* Sydney, N.S.W: Dangaroo Press, 1993.

Burks, Ruth Elizabeth. "From Baptism to Resurrection: Toni Cade Bambara and the Incongruity of Language." In *Black Women Writers (1950–1980): A Critical Evaluation,* ed. Mari Evans, 48–57. Garden City, N.Y.: Anchor-Doubleday, 1984.

Butler-Evans, Elliot. "Beyond Essentialism: Rethinking Afro-American Cultural Theory." *Inscriptions* 5 (1989): 120–34.

———. *Race, Gender, and Desire: Narrative Strategies in the Fiction of Toni Cade Bambara, Toni Morrison, and Alice Walker.* Philadelphia: Temple University Press, 1989.

Byerman, Keith E. "Healing Arts: Folklore and the Female Self in Toni Cade Bambara's The Salt Eaters." *Postscript* 5 (1988): 37–43.

Byrd, Ayana D., and Lori L. Tharps. *Hair Story: Untangling the Roots of Black Hair in America.* New York: St. Martin's Press, 2002.

Call and Response: The Riverside Anthology of the African American Literary Tradition. Edited by Patricia Liggins Hill, Bernard W. Bell, Trudier Harris, William J. Harris, R. Baxter Miller, Sandra A. O'Neale, with Horace A. Porter. Boston and New York: Houghton Mifflin Co., 1998.

Chancy, Myriam J. A. *Searching for Safe Spaces: Afro-Caribbean Women Writers in Exile.* Philadelphia: Temple University Press, 1997.

Chandler, Zala. "Voices Beyond the Veil: An Interview with Toni Cade Bambara and Sonia Sanchez." In *Wild Women in the Whirlwind: Afra-American Culture and the Contemporary Literary Renaissance*, ed. Joanne M. Braxton and Andrée Nicola McLaughlin, 342–62. New Brunswick, N.J.: Rutgers University Press, 1990.

Christian, Barbara. *Black Feminist Criticism: Perspectives on Black Women Writers.* New York and Oxford: Pergamon, 1985.

———. "But What Do We Think We're Doing Anyway: The State of Black Feminist Criticism(s) or My Version of a Little Bit of History." In *Changing Our Own Words: Essays on Criticism, Theory, and Writing by Black Women*, ed. Cheryl A. Wall, 58–74. New Brunswick, N.J., and London: Rutgers University Press, 1989.

———. "There It Is: The Poetry of Jayne Cortez." *Callaloo* 9 (Winter 1986): 235–38.

———. "Trajectories of Self-Definition: Placing Contemporary Afro-American Women's Fiction." In *Conjuring: Black Women, Fiction, and Literary Tradition*, ed. Marjorie Pryse and Hortense J. Spillers, 233–48. Bloomington: Indiana University Press, 1985.

Clark, Joanna. "Motherhood." In *The Black Woman: An Anthology*, ed. Toni Cade Bambara, 63–72. New York: Mentor Books, 1970.

Clark, Keith. *Black Manhood in James Baldwin, Ernest Gaines, and August Wilson.* Chicago: University of Illinois Press, 2004.

Clarke, Cheryl. "The Failure to Transform: Homophobia in the Black Community." In *Home Girls: A Black Feminist Anthology*, ed. Barbara Smith, 197–208. New York: Kitchen Table/Women of Color Press, 1983.

Cleaver, Eldridge. *Soul on Ice.* New York: Dell, 1968.

Cleaver, Kathleen. "Back to Africa: The Evolution of the International Section of the Black Panther Party (1969–1972)." In *The Black Panther Party Reconsidered*, ed. Charles E. Jones, 211–56. Baltimore: Black Classic Press, 1998.

Clément, Catherine. *Opera, or the Undoing of Women.* Translated by Betsy Wing. Minneapolis: University of Minnesota Press, 1988.

Collins, Janelle. "Generating Power: Fission, Fusion, and Post-modern Politics in Bambara's *The Salt Eaters*." *MELUS* 21, no. 2 (Summer 1996): 35–47.

Collins, Patricia Hill. *Black Feminist Thought: Knowledge, Consciousness, and the Politics of Empowerment.* Rev. 10th anniversary ed. New York and London: Routledge, 2000.

———. *Black Sexual Politics: African Americans, Gender, and the New Racism.* New York: Routledge, 2004.

"The Combahee River Collective Statement." In *Home Girls: A Black Feminist Anthology*, ed. Barbara Smith, 281. New York: Kitchen Table/Women of Color Press, 1983. First published 1977.

Cook, Ann. "Black Pride? Some Contradictions." In *The Black Woman: An Anthology*, ed. Toni Cade Bambara, 149–61. New York: Mentor Books, 1970.

Cook, Mercer, and Stephen E. Henderson. *The Militant Black Writer in Africa and the United States.* Madison: University of Wisconsin Press, 1969.

Conley, Madelyn. "Do Black Women Need The Women's Lib?" *Essence*, August 1970, 29–34.

Cortez, Jayne. *Coagulations: New and Selected Poems.* New York: Thunder's Mouth Press, 1984.

———. *Festivals and Funerals.* New York: Cortez, 1971.

———. *Mouth on Paper.* New York: Bola Press, 1977.

———. *Pissstained Stairs and the Monkey Man's Wares.* New York: Phrase Text, 1969.

———. *Scarifications.* New York: Bola Press, 1973.

Couser, G. Thomas. *Altered Egos: Authority in American Autobiography.* New York: Oxford University Press, 1989.

Covington, Francee. "Are the Revolutionary Techniques Employed in The Battle of Algiers Applicable to Harlem?" *The Black Woman* (New York) (1970): 244–52.

Craig, Maxine Leeds. *"Ain't I a beauty queen?": Black Women, Beauty, and the Politics of Race.* New York: Oxford University Press, 2002.

Dance, Daryl Cumber. "Go Eena Kumbla: A Comparison of Erna Brodber's *Jane and Louisa Will Soon Come Home* and Toni Cade Bambara's *The Salt Eaters.*" In *Caribbean Women Writers: Essays from the First International Conference,* ed. Selwyn R. Cudjoe, 169–86. Wellesley: Calaloux, 1990.

Davis, Angela. "Afro Images: Politics, Fashion, and Nostalgia." In *Names We Call Home: Autobiography on Racial Identity,* ed. Becky Thompson and Sangeeta Tyagi. New York: Routledge, 1996.

———. *Angela Davis: An Autobiography.* New York: Random House, 1974.

———. "JoAnne Little: The Dialectics of Rape." *Ms.,* June 1975, 74–77, 106–108.

———. *Lectures on Liberation.* New York: New York Committee to Free Angela Davis, 1971.

———. "Rape, Racism and the Capitalist Setting." *The Black Scholar* (April 1978): 24–30.

———, and others. *If They Come in the Morning; Voices of Resistance.* New York: Third Press, 1971.

DeLeon, Robert A. "A New Look at Angela Davis." *Ebony,* April 1972, 53–60.

DeVeaux, Alexis. "A Poet's World: Jayne Cortez Discusses Her Life and Her Work." *Essence,* March 1978, 77–79, 106, 109.

Dickson-Carr, Darryl. *African American Satire: The Sacredly Profane Novel.* Columbia: University of Missouri Press, 2001.

Doane, Ashley W., and Eduardo Bonilla-Silva, eds. *White Out: The Continuing Significance of Racism.* New York, London: Routledge, 2003.

Donahue. "Black Women Writers." Videocassette. Princeton, N.J.: Films for the Humanities, 1992. 28 min.

Donald, Cleveland, Jr. "Cornell in Crisis." *Essence,* June 1970, 23–27, 67–68.

Douglass, Frederick. *The Life and Writings of Frederick Douglass: Early Years, 1817–1849.* Edited by Philip Foner. New York: International Publishers, 1950.

———. *Narrative of the Life of Frederick Douglass: Authoritative Text, Contexts, Criticism.* Edited by William L. Andrews and William S. McFeely. New York: W. W. Norton & Co., 1996. Originally published 1845.

Dubey, Madhu. *Black Women Novelists and the Nationalist Aesthetic.* Bloomington: Indiana University Press, 1994.

Du Bois, W. E. B. *The Souls of Black Folk: Essay and Sketches.* Edited by Henry Louis Gates, Jr., and Terri Hume Oliver. New York: W. W. Norton & Co., 1999. Originally published 1903.

———. Preface. *The Souls of Black Folk: Essay and Sketches.* Jubilee Edition. New York: Blue Heron Press, 1953.

du Cille, Ann. "The Occult of True Black Womanhood: Critical Demeanor and Black Feminist Studies." *Signs* 19, no. 3 (Spring 1994): 591–629.

Dudziak, Mary L. "Josephine Baker, Racial Protest and The Cold War." *Journal of American History* 81 (1994): 543.

Durbin, Karen. "First Person Impersonal." *Ms.*, February 1975, 38–42.

Ellis, Trey. *Platitudes and "The New Black Aesthetic."* Boston: Northeastern University Press, 1988.

Ellison, Ralph. "An American Dilemma: A Review," 1944. From www.teachingamerican history.org.

Fanon, Frantz. *Black Skin, White Masks.* Translated by Charles Lam Markmann. New York: Grove Press, 1967.

———. *Towards the African Revolution.* New York: Monthly Review Press, 1967.

———. *The Wretched of the Earth.* New York: Grove Press, 1963.

Fontenot, Chester J., Jr. "Du Bois's 'Of the Coming of John,' and Toomer's 'Kabnis,' and the Dilemma of Self-Representation." In *W. E. B. Du Bois and Race: Essays Celebrating the Centennial Publication of* The Souls of Black Folk, ed. Chester J. Fontenot, Jr., and Mary Alice Morgan, with Sarah Gardner, 130–60. Macon, Ga.: Mercer University Press, 2001.

Ford, Karen Jackson. *Gender and the Poetics of Excess: Moments of Brocade.* Jackson: University of Mississippi Press, 1997.

Foster, Frances Smith. "Changing Concepts of the Black Woman." *Journal of Black Studies* 3 (1973): 433–54.

———. *Witnessing Slavery: The Development of Ante-bellum Slave Narratives.* Madison: University of Wisconsin Press, 1994.

Fowler, Manet. "Heritage: The Sande Rituals." *Essence,* May 1970, 82.

Gates, Henry Louis, Jr., ed. *Black Literature and Literary Theory.* New York: Methuen, 1984.

———. "'The Blackness of Blackness': A Critique of the Sign and the Signifying Monkey." *Critical Inquiry* 9 (1983): 685–723.

———. "Both Sides Now." *New York Times Book Review,* May 4, 2003, 31.

———. *Colored People: A Memoir.* New York: Knopf, 1994.

———. *Signifying Monkey: A Theory of African-American Literary Criticism.* New York: Oxford University Press, 1988.

Gayle, Addison, ed. *The Black Aesthetic.* New York: Doubleday, 1971.

———. *The Way of the New World: The Black Novel in America.* Garden City, N.Y.: Anchor Press, 1975.

Giddings, Paula. *When and Where I Enter: The Impact of Black Women on Race and Sex in America.* New York: Morrow, 1984.

Gillespie, Marcia, and Ronald Van Downing. "Angela Davis: Black Woman on the Run." *Essence,* November 1970, 50.

Gilroy, Paul. *The Black Atlantic: Modernity and Double-Consciousness.* Cambridge, Mass.: Harvard University Press, 1993.

———. "It's a Family Affair." In *Black Popular Culture,* ed. Gina Dent, 303–16. Seattle: Bay Press, 1992.

Giovanni, Nikki. Foreword to *BlackSpirits: A Festival of New Black Poets in America,* ed. Woodie King, ix–x. New York: Random House, 1972.

———. *Racism 101.* New York: Quill, 1994.

Glaser, Walter D. "Why I Like Black Women." *Essence,* September 1970, 72.

Grayson, Deborah. "Is It Fake? Black Women's Hair as Spectacle and Spec(tac)ular." *Camera Obscura* 36 (1995): 13–31.

Gresson, Aaron David. *The Dialectics of Betrayal: Sacrifice, Violation, and the Oppressed.* Norwood, N.J.: Ablex Pub. Corp., 1982.

———. *The Recovery of Race in America.* Minneapolis: University of Minnesota Press, 1995.

Griffin, Farah Jasmine. "Conflict and Chorus: Reconsidering Toni Cade's *The Black Woman: An Anthology.*" In *Is It Nation Time?: Contemporary Essays on Black Power and Black Nationalism,* ed. Eddie S. Glaude and Eddie S. Glaude, Jr., 113–29. Chicago and London: Chicago University Press, 2001.

———. "Textual Healing: Claiming Black Women's Bodies, the Erotic and the Resistance in Contemporary Novels of Slavery." *Callaloo* 19, no. 2 (Spring 1996): 519–36.

Grimes, William. *Life of William Grimes, the Runaway Slave, Brought Down to the Present Time:* Electronic Edition. Documenting the American South. http://docsouth.unc.edu/neh/grimes55/grimes55.html.

Grosse, Van. "Interview with Harold Cruse." In *The Essential Harold Cruse: A Reader,* ed. William Jelani Cobb, 281–98. New York: Palgrave, 2002.

Guggelberger, Georg, ed. *The Real Thing: Testimonial Discourse and Latin America.* Durham, N.C.: Duke University Press, 1996.

Guy-Sheftall, Beverly. "Commitment: Toni Cade Bambara Speaks." In *Sturdy Black Bridges: Visions of Black Women in Literature,* ed. Roseann P. Bell, Bettye J. Parker, and Beverly Guy-Sheftall, 230–49. Garden City, N.Y.: Anchor Press, 1979.

Hamlet, Janice D. "Understanding African American Oratory: Manifestations of Nommo." In *Afrocentric Visions: Studies in Culture and Communication,* ed. Janice D. Hamlet, 89–106. Thousand Oaks, Calif.: Sage, 1998.

Harlow, Barbara. *Barred: Women, Writing, and Political Detention.* Middletown, Conn.: Wesleyan University Press, 1992.

Harris, Shanette M. "Constructing a Psychological Perspective: The Observer and The Observed in *The Souls of Black Folk.*" In *The Souls of Black Folk: One Hundred Years Later,* ed. Dolan Hubbard, 218–50. Columbia: University of Missouri Press, 2003.

Harper, Phillip Brian. "Nationalism and Social Division in Black Arts Poetry of the 1960s." *Critical Inquiry* 19 (Winter 1993): 234–55.

Harwell, Fred. *A True Deliverance: The Joan Little Case.* New York: Alfred A. Knopf. 1980.

Heath, Louis G., ed. *Off the Pigs!: The History and Literature of the Black Panther Party.* Metuchen, N.J.: Scarecrow Press, 1976.

Hedin, Raymond. "The Structuring of Emotion in Black American Fiction." *Novel: A Forum on Fiction* 16, no. 1 (Fall 1982): 35–54.

Heinze, Denise. *The Dilemma of "Double-Consciousness": Toni Morrison's Novels*. Athens: University of Georgia Press, 1993.

Henderson, Mae G. "Speaking in Tongues: Dialogism and the Black Woman Writer's Literary Tradition." In *Changing Our Own Words: Essays on Criticism, Theory, and Writing by Black Women*, ed. Cheryl Wall, 16–37. New Brunswick, N.J.: Rutgers University Press, 1989.

Henderson, Stephen. *Understanding the New Black Poetry: Black Speech and Black Music as Poetic References*. New York: William Morrow and Co., 1973.

Hobson, Charles. "What Black Men Want From Black Women." *Essence*, September 1970, 38, 40–41.

Hogue, W. Lawrence. *The African American Male, Writing, and Difference: A Polycentric Approach to African American Literature, Criticism, and History*. Albany: State University of New York Press, 2003.

———. *Discourse and the Other: The Production of the Afro-American Text*. Durham, N.C.: Duke University Press, 1986.

Holland, Sharon Patricia. "The Revolution, 'In Theory.'" *American Literary History* 12, nos. 1 and 2 (2000): 327–36.

hooks, bell. *Ain't I a Woman: Black Women and Feminism*. Boston: South End Press, 1981.

———. *Black Looks: Race and Representation*. Boston: South End Press, 1992.

———. *Bone Black: Memories of Girlhood*. New York: Henry Holt and Co., 1996.

———. *Killing Rage: Ending Racism*. New York: Henry Holt and Co., 1995.

———. *Sisters of the Yam: Black Women and Self-Recovery*. Boston: South End Press, 1993.

———. *Talking Back, Thinking Feminist, Thinking Black*. Boston: South End Press, 1989.

———. *Teaching to Transgress: Education as the Practice of Freedom*. New York: Routledge, 1994.

———. *Yearning: Race, Gender, and Cultural Politics*. Boston: South End Press, 1990.

Hubbard, Dolan. "Introduction." In *The Souls of Black Folk: One Hundred Years Later*, ed. Dolan Hubbard, 1–17. Columbia: University of Missouri Press, 2003.

Huggins, Nathan I. *Black Odyssey: The African-American Ordeal in Slavery*. New York: Pantheon Books, 1977.

———. *Revelations: American History, American Myths*. Edited by Brenda Smith Huggins. New York and Oxford: Oxford University Press, 1995.

Hughes, Langston. *The Collected Poems of Langston Hughes*. Edited by Arnold Rampersad. New York: Alfred A. Knopf, 1994.

———. "The Negro Artist and the Racial Mountain." In *Speech and Power: The African American Essay and Its Cultural Content, From Polemics to Pulpit*. Vol. 2, ed. Gerald Early, 88–91. Hopewell, N.J.: Ecco Press, 1993.

Hull, Gloria T. "'What It Is I Think She's Doing Anyhow': A Reading of Toni Cade Bambara's *The Salt Eaters*." In *Conjuring: Black Women, Fiction, and Literary*

Tradition, ed. Marjorie Pryse and Hortense J. Spillers, 216–32. Bloomington: Indiana University Press, 1985.

Hurston, Zora Neale. "How It Feels to Be Colored Me." In *I Love Myself When I am Laughing and Then Again When I am Looking Mean and Impressive,* ed. Alice Walker, 152–55. New York: Feminist Press, 1979.

———. *Their Eyes Were Watching God.* New York: Harper and Row, 1990.

Jackson, Edward M. *Images of Black Men in Black Women Writers 1950–1990.* Bristol, Ind.: Wyndham Hall Press, 1992.

Jackson, George. *Soledad Brother: The Prison Letters of George Jackson.* New York: Coward-McCann, 1970.

Jacobs, Harriet. *Incidents in the Life of a Slave Girl.* Edited by Jean Fagan Yellin. Cambridge, Mass., and London: Harvard University Press, 1987.

Jacques, Francis. *Difference and Subjectivity: Dialogue and Personal Identity.* Translated by Andrew Rothwell. New Haven, Conn.: Yale University Press, 1991.

James, Joy. "The Profeminist Politics of W. E. B. Du Bois with Respects to Anna Julia Cooper and Ida B. Wells Barnett." In *W. E. B. Du Bois: On Race and Culture,* ed. Bernard Bell, Emily R. Grosholz, and James B. Stewart, 141–60. New York and London: Routledge, 1996.

———. *Shadowboxing: Representations of Black Feminist Politics.* New York: St. Martin's Press, 1999.

Johnson, Abby Arthur, and Ronald Maberry Johnson. *Propaganda and Aesthetics: The Literary Politics of Afro-American Magazines in the Twentieth Century.* Amherst: University of Massachusetts Press, 1979.

Johnson, Charles. *Being and Race: Black Writing Since 1970.* Bloomington: Indiana University Press, 1988.

Johnson, James Weldon. "The Dilemma of the Negro Artist." In *Speech and Power,* vol. 2, ed. Gerald Early, 87–92. Hopewell, N.J.: Ecco Press.

Johnson, Randal. "Carnivalesque Celebration in *Xica da Silva.*" In *Brazilian Cinema,* ed. Randal Johnson and Robert Stam. Austin: University of Texas Press, 1982.

Jones, Gayl. "From the Quest for Wholeness: Re-Imagining the African-American Novel, An Essay on Third World Aesthetics." *Callaloo* 17 (Spring 1994): 2507–2518.

Jones, Lisa. *Bulletproof Diva: Tales of Race, Sex, and Hair.* New York and London: Doubleday, 1994.

Joyce, Joyce A. "The Black Canon: Reconstructing Black American Literary Criticism." *New Literary History* 18 (1987): 335–44.

Karenga, Maulana. "Black Cultural Nationalism." *Negro Digest* 13, no. 3 (1968): 5–9.

———. *Introduction to Black Studies.* 3rd ed. Los Angeles: University of Sankore Press, 1982.

Kelley, Margot Anne. "'Damballah Is the First Law of Thermodynamics: Modes of Access to Toni Cade Bambara's *The Salt Eaters.*" *African American Review* 27, no. 3 (Fall 1993): 479–93.

Kelley, Robin D. G. *Freedom Dreams: The Black Radical Imagination.* Boston: Beacon Press, 2002.

Kenan, Randall. *A Visitation of Spirits*. New York: Vintage Books, 2000.

Kester, Gunilla Theander. *Writing the Subject: Bildung and the African American Text*. New York: Peter Lang, 1995.

Killens, John Oliver. "Introduction." In *Black Southern Voices: An Anthology of Fiction, Poetry, Drama, Nonfiction and Critical Essays*, ed. John Oliver Killens and Jerry W. Ward, Jr., 1–4. New York: Meridian, 1992.

King, Deborah K. "Multiple Jeopardy, Multiple Consciousness: The Context of Black Feminist Ideology." In *Words of Fire: An Anthology of African-American Feminist Thought*, ed. Beverley Guy-Sheftall, 294–317. New York: The New York Press, 1995.

King, Wayne. "Focus of Slaying Trial Had Humble Origins: Joan Little." *New York Times*, Tuesday, July 29, 1975.

Koestenbaum, Wayne. *The Queen's Throat: Opera, Homosexuality, and the Mystery of Desire*. New York: Vintage Books, 1993.

Kolmar, Wendy K. "Dialectics of Connectedness: Supernatural Elements in the Novels of Bambara, Cisneros, Grah, and Erdirch." In *Haunting the House of Fiction: Feminist Perspectives on Ghost Stories by American Women*, ed. Lynette Carpenter and Wendy K. Kolmar, 236–49. Knoxville: University of Tennessee Press, 1991.

Krasner, David. *Resistance, Parody and Double Consciousness in African American Theatre, 1895–1910*. New York: St. Martin's Press, 1997.

Lacy, Leslie Alexander. "What Should the Definition of 'Love' Be for People Who Are Oppressed?" *Essence*, May 1970, 6.

Leonardi, Susan J., and Rebecca A. Pope. *The Diva's Mouth: Body, Voice, Prima Donna Politics*. New Brunswick, N.J.: Rutgers University Press, 1996.

Lewis, Ida. "Interview with LeRoi Jones" *Essence*, September 1970, 20–21, 24–25.

———. "Interview with Myrlie B. Evers." *Essence*, November 1970, 24–27.

Lindsey, Kay. "Birth Control and the Black Woman." *Essence*, October 1970, 56–57, 70–71.

———. "The Black Woman as Woman." In *The Black Woman: An Anthology*, ed. Toni Cade Bambara 85–89. New York: Mentor Books, 1970.

———. "Poem." In *The Black Woman: An Anthology*, ed. Toni Cade Bambara, 13. New York: Mentor Books, 1970.

Lorde, Audre. "Feminism and Black Liberation: The Great American Disease." *Black Scholar* 10, no. 9 (1979): 17–20.

Lowe, Lisa. *Immigrant Acts: On Asian American Cultural Politics*. Durham, N.C.: Duke University Press, 1996.

Lubiano, Wahneema. "Standing In for the State: Black Nationalism and 'Writing' the Black Subject." In *Is It Nation Time? Contemporary Essays on Black Power and Black Nationalism*, ed. Eddie S. Glaude and Eddie S. Glaude, Jr., 156–64. Chicago and London: University of Chicago Press, 2002.

Mama, Amina. *Beyond the Mask: Race, Gender and Subjectivity*. London and New York: Routledge, 1995.

Manalansan, Martin F., IV. *Global Divas: Filipino Gay Men in the Diaspora*. Durham, N.C., and London: Duke University Press, 2003.

Mancini, Janet K. *Strategic Styles: Coping in the Inner City*. Hanover, N.H.: University Press of New England, 1980.

Markovitz, Irving Leonard. *Léopold Sédar and the Politics of Negritude*. New York: Atheneum, 1969.

Marshall, Paule. "The Making of a Writer: From the Poets in the Kitchen." *New York Times Book Review*, January 9, 1983, 3, 34–35.

Matthews, J. H. *An Introduction to Surrealism*. University Park: Pennsylvania State University Press, 1965.

May, John R. *Toward A New Earth: Apocalypse in the American Novel*. Notre Dame, Ind.: University of Notre Dame Press, 1972.

Mayfield, Julian. "You Touch My Black Aesthetic and I'll Touch Yours." In *The Black Aesthetic*, ed. Addison Gayle, Jr., 39–46. New York: Doubleday and Co., Inc., 1971.

McDowell, Deborah. *Leaving Pipe Shop: Memories of Kin*. New York: Scribner, 1996.

McKay, Nellie. "An Interview with Toni Morrison." *Contemporary Literature* 24, no. 4 (1983): 413–29.

McLaughlin, Andrée Nicola. "Black Women, Identity, and the Quest for Humanhood and Wholeness: Wild Women in Whirlwind." In *Wild Women in the Whirlwind: Afra-American Culture and the Contemporary Literary Renaissance*, ed. Joanne M. Braxton and Andrée Nicola McLaughlin, 271–80. New Brunswick, N.J.: Rutgers University Press, 1990.

McLaughlin, Thomas. *Street Smarts and Critical Theory: Listening to the Vernacular*. Madison: University of Wisconsin Press, 1996.

McNeil, Genna Rae. "'Joanne Is You and Joanne Is Me': A Consideration of African American Women and the 'Free Joan Little' Movement, 1974–75." In *Sisters in the Struggle: African American Women in the Civil Rights-Black Power Movement*, ed. Bettye Collier-Thomas and V. P. Franklin, 259–79. New York: New York University Press, 2001.

Melhem, D. H. *Heroism in the New Black Poetry: Introductions and Interviews*. Lexington: University Press of Kentucky, 1990, 180–212.

Menchú, Rigoberta. *I Rigoberta Menchú: An Indian Woman in Guatemala*. Brooklyn: Verso, 1983.

Meriwether, Louise. "Black Man, Do You Love Me?" *Essence*, May 1970, 15, 62–64, 81.

Michelson, Peter. *Speaking the Unspeakable: The Politics of Obscenity*. Albany: State University of New York Press, 1992.

Moody, Anne. *Coming of Age in Mississippi*. New York: Delta, 2004.

Moglen, Helene. "Redeeming History: Toni Morrison's *Beloved*." In *Female Subjects in Black and White: Race, Psychoanalysis, Feminism*, ed. Elizabeth Abel, Barbara Christian, and Helene Moglen, 201–22. Berkeley: University of California Press.

Montgomery, Maxine Lavon. *The Apocalypse in African-American Fiction*. Gainesville and Tallahassee: University Press of Florida, 1996.

Moore, Gilbert. "Five Shades of Militancy." *Essence*, May 1970, 16–23.

Moraga, Cherríe, and Gloria Anzaldúa, eds. *This Bridge Called My Back: Writings by Radical Women of Color*. Watertown, Mass.: Persephone Press, 1981.

Morrison, Toni. *Beloved*. New York: Plume, 1988. Originally published 1987.

———. *The Bluest Eye*. New York: Plume, 1994. Originally published 1970.

———. "Memory, Creation, Writing," *Thought* 59, no. 235 (1984): 386–90.

———. *Playing in the Dark: Whiteness and the Literary Imagination*. New York: Vintage Books, 1992.

———. "Rootedness: The Ancestor as Foundation." In *Black Women Writers (1950–1980)*, ed. Mari Evans, 339–45. New York and London: Anchor Press, 1984.

———. "Unspeakable Things Unspoken: The Afro-American Presence in American Literature." In *Modern Critical View: Toni Morrison*, ed. Harold Bloom, 201–30. Philadelphia: Chelsea House, 1990.

———. "What the Black Woman Thinks About Women's Lib." *New York Times Magazine*, August 22, 1971, 4–15, 63–64, 66.

Myerson Michael. "Angela Davis in Prison: An Interview." *Ramparts Magazine*, February 1971, 20, 23, 25.

Nadelson, Regina. *Who Is Angela Davis?* New York: P. H. Wyden, 1972.

New York Committee to Free Angela Davis. *A Political Biography of Angela Davis*. 1971.

Newton, Huey P. "A Letter from Huey to the Revolutionary Brothers and Sisters about the Women's Liberation and Gay Liberation Movements." *Black Panther*, Aug. 15, 1970, 15.

———. *Revolutionary Suicide: The Way of Liberation*. New York: Jovanovich, Inc., 1973.

Nichols, Grace. *I Is a Long Memoried Woman*. Lawrenceville, N.J.: Red Sea Press, 1990.

Nielsen, Aldon Lynn. *Black Chant: Language of African-American Postmodernism*. Cambridge: Cambridge University Press, 1997.

Oliver, Valerie Cassel. *Double Consciousness: Black Conceptual Art Since 1970*. Houston: Contemporary Arts Museum, 2005.

Parker, J. A. *Angela Davis: The Making of a Revolutionary*. New Rochelle, N.Y.: Arlington House, 1973.

Parker-Smith, Bettye J. "Running Wild in Her Soul: The Poetry of Carolyn Rodgers." In *Black Women Writers (1950–1980): A Critical Evaluation*, ed. Mari Evans, 393–410. New York: Random House, 1984.

Patterson, Tiffany Ruby, and Robin D. G. Kelley. "Unfinished Migrations: Reflections on the African Diaspora and the Making of the Modern World." *African Studies Review*. Special Issue on the Diaspora 43, no. 1 (April 2000): 11–45.

Perkins, Margo V. *Autobiography as Activism: Three Black Women of the Sixties*. Jackson: University Press of Mississippi, 2000.

Peterson, Carla L. *"Doers of the Word": African-American Women Speakers and Writers in the North (1830–1880)*. New Brunswick, N.J., and London: Rutgers University Press, 1995.

Poussaint, Alvin, MD. "Black Women are Doubly Subjugated." *Essence,* May 1970, 75.

Quashie, Kevin Everod. *Black Women, Identity, and Cultural Theory: (Un)Becoming the Subject*. New Brunswick, N.J., and London: Rutgers University Press, 2004.

Rabine, Leslie W. "A Woman's Two Bodies: Fashion Magazines, Consumerism, and

Feminism." In *On Fashion,* ed. Shari Benstock and Suzanne Ferriss, 59–75. New Brunswick, N.J.: Rutgers University Press, 1994.

"Radicals: Enigmatic Angela." *Time,* October 26, 1970.

Rainwater, Lee, and William L. Yancey. *The Moynihan Report and the Politics of Controversy.* Cambridge, Mass., and London: The MIT Press, 1967.

Rajiv, Sudhi. *Forms of Black Consciousness.* New York: Advent Books, 1992.

Rampersad, Arnold. "Slavery and the Literary Imagination: Du Bois's *The Souls of Black Folk.*" In *The Souls of Black Folk,* ed. Henry Louis Gates, Jr., and Terri Hume Oliver, 295–311. New York: W. W. Norton & Co., 1999.

Redding, Saunders. Introduction. *The Souls of Black Folk: Essay and Sketches.* New York: Fawcett Publications, 1961.

Redmond, Eugene B. *Drumvoices: The Mission of Afro-American Poetry.* Garden City, N.Y.: Anchor Books, 1976.

Reed, Adolph L., Jr. *Stirrings in the Jug: Black Politics in the Post-Segregation Era.* Minneapolis: University of Minnesota Press, 1999.

———. *W. E. B. Du Bois and American Political Thought: Fabianism and the Color Line.* New York and Oxford: Oxford University Press, 1997.

Reed, Ishmael. *Airing Dirty Laundry.* Reading, Mass., and Menlo Park, Calif.: Addison-Wesley Publishing Co., 1993.

———. *Reckless Eyeballing.* New York: St. Martin's Press, 1986.

Riggs, Marlon T. "Black Macho Revisited: Reflections of a Snap! Queen." *Black American Literature Forum.* Black Film Issue 25, no. 2 (Summer 1991): 389–94.

Rooks, Noliwe M. *Ladies' Pages: African American Women's Magazines and the Culture that Made Them.* New Brunswick, N.J.: Rutgers University Press, 2004.

Rosenberg, Ruth. "'You Took a Name That Made You Amiable to the Music': Toni Cade Bambara's *The Salt Eaters.*" *Literary Onomastics Studies* 12 (1985): 165–94.

Rowell, Charles H. "An Interview with Farah Jasmine Griffin." *Callaloo* 22, no. 4 (1999): 872–92.

Salaam, Kalamu ya. "Searching for the Mother Tongue (Interview)." *First World* 2, no. 4 (1980): 48–53.

Sanders, Fran. "Dear Black Man." In *The Black Woman: An Anthology,* ed. Toni Cade Bambara, 73–79. New York: Mentor Books, 1970.

Santini, Rosemary. "Black Man: White Woman." *Essence,* July 1970, 12–13, 64.

Sapphire. *Push.* New York: Alfred A. Knopf, 1996.

Séjour, Victor. "The Mulatto." In *Norton Anthology of African American Literature,* ed. Henry Louis Gates, Jr., and Nellie Y. McKay, 353–65. New York: W. W. Norton & Co., 1997.

Senghor, Léopold Sédar. *The Collected Poetry of Leopold Sedar Senghor.* Translated by Melvin Dixon. Charlottesville: University Press of Virginia, 1991.

Shakur, Assata. *Assata: An Autobiography.* Chicago: Lawrence Hill & Co., 2001.

Simoes da Silva, A. J. *The Luxury of Nationalist Despair: George Lamming's Fiction as Decolonizing Project.* Amsterdam and Atlanta: Rodopi, 2000.

Simon, Rita J., and Norma Pecora. "Coverage of the Davis, Harris, and Hearst Trials by Major American Magazines." *Studies in Communications* 3 (1986): 111–13.

Singh, Nikhil Pal. "The Black Panthers and the 'Undeveloped Country' of the Left." In *The Black Panther Party Reconsidered,* ed. Charles E. Jones, 57–105. Baltimore: Black Classic Press, 1998.

Smart-Grosvenor, Verta Mae. "Kitchen Crisis." In *The Black Woman: An Anthology,* ed. Toni Cade Bambara, 119–23. New York: Mentor Books, 1970.

Smethurst, James Edward. *Black Arts Movement: Literary Nationalism in the 1960s and 1970s.* Chapel Hill: University of North Carolina Press, 2005.

———. *The New Red Negro: The Literary Left and African American Poetry, 1930–1946.* London and New York: Oxford University Press, 1999.

Smith, Felipe. *American Body Politics: Race, Gender, and Black Literary Renaissance.* Athens and London: University of Georgia Press, 1998.

Smith, Sidonie. "The Autobiographical Manifesto: Identities, Temporalities, Politics." In *Autobiography and Questions of Gender,* ed. Shirley Neuman, 186–212. London and Portland, Ore.: F. Cass, 1991.

———. *Where I'm Bound: Patterns of Slavery and Freedom in Black American Autobiography.* Westport, Conn.: Greenwood, 1974.

Smith, Sidonie, and Julia Watson, eds. Introduction to *De/Colonizing the Subject: The Politics of Gender in Women's Autobiography.* Minneapolis: University of Minnesota Press, 1992, xiii–xxxi.

Smith, Valerie. "Black Feminist Theory and the Representation of the 'Other.'" In *Changing Our Own Words: Essays on Criticism, Theory, and Writing by Black Women,* ed. Cheryl A. Wall, 38–57. New Brunswick, N.J.: Rutgers University Press, 1989.

———. "Gender and Afro-Americanist Literary Theory and Criticism." In *Speaking of Gender,* ed. Elaine Showalter, 56–70. New York: Routledge, 1989.

———. *Self-Discovery and Authority in Afro-American Narrative.* Cambridge, Mass.: Harvard University Press, 1987.

Smitherman, Geneva. *Black Talk: Words and Phrases from the Hood to the Amen Corner.* Rev. ed. Boston: Houghton Mifflin, 2000.

Spencer, Traci. "Midlife Crisis: Is *Essence* Losing its Essence?" http://www.jrn.columbia .edu/studentwork/nyrm/2002/midlifecrisis.asp.

Spillers, Hortense J. Afterword to *Conjuring: Black Women, Fiction, and Literary Tradition,* ed. Marjorie Pryse and Hortense J. Spillers, 216–32. Bloomington: Indiana University Press, 1985.

———. "The Crisis of the Negro Intellectual: A Post-Date." *Boundary 2—An International Journal of Literature & Culture* 21, no. 3 (Fall 1994): 65–116.

———. "Cross-Currents, Discontinuities: Black Women's Fiction." In *Conjuring: Black Women, Fiction, and Literary Tradition,* ed. Marjorie Pryse and Hortense J. Spillers, 249–61. Bloomington: Indiana University Press, 1985.

———. "Mama's Baby, Papa's Maybe: An American Grammar Book." In *Within the Circle: An Anthology of African American Criticism from the Harlem Renaissance to the Present,* ed. Angelyn Mitchell, 454–81. Durham, N.C., and London: Duke University Press, 1994.

Stanford, Ann Folwell. "Mechanisms of Disease: African-American Women Writers,

Social Pathologies, and the Limits of Medicine." *NWSA Journal* 6, no. 1 (Spring 1994): 28–47.

Sudbury, Julia. *"Other Kinds of Dreams": Black Women's Organisations and the Politics of Transformation*. London and New York: Routledge, 1998.

Tally, Justine. "Not About to Play it Safe: An Interview with Toni Cade Bambara." *Revista Carnaria de Estudios Ingleses* No. 1 (November 1985): 133–40.

Takaki, Ronald T. *Violence in the Black Imagination: Essays and Documents*. New York and Oxford: Oxford University Press, 1993.

Tate, Claudia. "Toni Cade Bambara." In *Black Women Writers at Work*, ed. Claudia Tate. New York: Continuum, 1983.

Thiong'o, Ngũgĩ wa. *Decolonising the Mind: The Politics of Language in African Literature*. London: James Currey, 1986.

Timothy, Mary. *Jury Woman: The Story of the Trial of Angela Y. Davis*. Palo Alto, Calif.: Emty Press, 1974.

Tisdale, James E. "Black Women and Drugs: A Losing Combination." *Essence*, September 1970, 54–57.

Traylor, Eleanor W. "Music as Theme: The Jazz Mode in the Works of Toni Cade Bambara." In *Black Women Writers (1950–1980): A Critical Evaluation*, ed. Mari Evans, 165–94. Garden City, N.Y.: Anchor-Doubleday, 1984.

———. "Recalling the Black Woman." In *The Black Woman: An Anthology*. 2nd ed., ix–xviii. New York and London: Washington Square Press, 2005.

———. "*The Salt Eaters*: My Soul Looks Back in Wonder." *First World* 2, no. 4 (1980): 44–47.

Troupe, Quincy, and Rainer Schulte, eds. *Giant Talk: An Anthology of Third World Writings*. New York: Random House, 1975.

Verdelle, A. J. "Paradise Found: A Talk with Toni Morrison About Her New Novel—Nobel Laureate's New Book, *Paradise*—Interview." *Essence*, February 1998, 78.

Vertreace, Martha M. "A Bibliography of Writings by Toni Cade Bambara." In *American Women Writing Fiction: Memory, Identity, Family, Space*. Lexington: University Press of Kentucky, 1989.

Wade-Gayles, Gloria. *No Crystal Stair: Visions of Race and Gender in Black Women's Fiction*. Rev. ed. Cleveland: Pilgrim Press, 1997.

Walker, Alice. *Anything We Love Can Be Saved: A Writer's Activism*. New York: Random House, 1997.

———. *The Color Purple*. New York: Washington Square Press, 1982.

———. *Meridian*. New York: Harcourt Brace Jovanovich, 1976.

———. *The Same River Twice: Honoring the Difficult: A Meditation on Life, Spirit, Art and the Making of the Film The Color Purple Ten Years Later*. New York: Simon & Schuster Adult Publishing Group, 1996.

Walker, Melissa. *Down from the Mountaintop: Black Women's Novels in the Wake of the Civil Rights Movement, 1966–1989*. New Haven, Conn.: Yale University Press, 1991.

Washington, Mary Helen. "'The Darkened Eye Restored': Notes Toward a Literary History of Black Women." In *Reading Black, Reading Feminist*, ed. Henry Louis Gates, Jr., 30–43. New York: Meridian, 1990.

———. "Teaching Black-Eyed Susans: An Approach to the Study of Black Women Writers." In *But Some of Us Are Brave*, ed. Gloria T. Hull, Patrica Bell Scott, and Barbara Smith. New York: Feminist Press, 1982.

Watkins, Mel. "Sexism, Racism and Black Women Writers." *New York Times*, June 15, 1986, 1, 35–37.

Weisbord, Robert G. *Genocide?: Birth Control and the Black American*. Westport, Conn.: Greenwood, 1975.

Whitaker, Charles. "Alice Walker: Color Purple Author Confronts Her Critics and Talks About Her Provocative New Book." *Ebony*, May 1992, 85–90.

Williams, Dana A. *"In the Light of Likeness—Transformed": The Literary Art of Leon Forrest*. Columbus: Ohio University Press, 2005.

Williams, Evelyn A. *Inadmissible Evidence: The Story of the African-American Trial Lawyer Who Defended the Black Liberation Army*. Lincoln, Neb.: iUniverse, 1993.

Williams, Irene. "Women in Dark Times: Three Views of the Angela Davis Trial." *San Jose Studies* 4 (February 1978): 34–43.

Williams, Sherley Anne. *Dessa Rose*. New York: W. Morrow, 1986.

———. *Give Birth to Brightness: A Thematic Study in Neo-Black Literature*. New York: Dial Press, 1972.

———. "Tell Martha Not to Moan." In *The Black Woman: An Anthology*, ed. Toni Cade Bambara, 47. New York: Mentor Books, 1970.

Willis, Susan. *Specifying: Black Women Writing the American Experience*. Madison: University of Wisconsin Press, 1987.

Wolfe, George C. *The Colored Museum: A Play*. New York: Grove Press, 1985.

Wood, Ean. *The Josephine Baker Story*. London: Sanctuary Publishing Limited, 2000.

Wood, Jim. *The Rape of Inez Garcia*. New York: G. P. Putnam's Sons, 1976.

Woodard, Jennifer Bailey, and Teresa Mastin. "Black Womanhood: 'Essence' and its Treatment of Stereotypical Images of Black Women." *Journal of Black Studies* 36, no. 2 (November 2005): 264–81.

Woodard, Komozi. *A Nation within a Nation: Amiri Baraka (LeRoi Jones) and Black Power Politics*. Charlotte: The University of North Carolina Press, 1999.

Woodson, Jon. "Jayne Cortez." In *Afro-American Poets Since 1955*. Vol. 41, ed. Trudier Harris and Thadious M. Davis, 69–74. Detroit, Mich.: Bruccoli Clark/Gale Research Co., 1985.

Wright, Bobby. *The Psychopathic Racial Personality*. Chicago: Third World Press, 1975.

Wright, Richard. *Black Power: A Record of Reactions in a Land of Pathos*. New York: Harper, 1954.

———. "How Bigger Was Born." In *Native Son: The Restored Text Established by the Library of America*. 431– 62. New York: Perennial Classics, 1993

———. *Native Son: The Restored Text Established by the Library of America*. New York: Perennial Classics, 1993. Originally published 1940.

———. *Uncle Tom's Children*. New York: Harper, 1938.

———. *White Man, Listen!* Garden City: New York, 1957.

Wynter, Sylvia. "On How We Mistook the Map for the Territory, and Re-Imprisoned Ourselves in Our Unbearable Wrongness of Being, of Désêtre: Black Studies Toward the Human Project." In *Not Only the Master's Tools: African-American Studies in Theory and Practice,* ed. Louis R. Gordon and Jane Anna Gordon, 107–72. Boulder, Colo.: Paradigm, 2006.

Yette, Samuel F. *The Choice: The Issue of Black Survival in America.* Silver Spring, Md.: Cottage Books, 1971.

Young, Monifa. "High on the Hill." *Essence,* June 1998, 74–76, 156–58, 160–161.

Zamir, Shamoon. *Dark Voices: W. E. B. Du Bois and American Thought, 1888–1903.* Chicago and London: University of Chicago Press, 1995.

INDEX

Abrahams, Roger D., 49
Abrams, M. H., 192
abuse of women, 80
activism: in Bambara's *The Salt Eaters,*
    193, 206, 208, 209, 215; decline in,
    57–58; and literary criticism, 35; and
    patriarchical attitudes, 84; and poetry
    of Cortez, 155; shift away from civil
    rights, 79; women's involvement in,
    93, 99. *See also specific organizations
    and activists such as* Davis, Angela
Adams, John, 137
Adell, Sandra, 35, 36
Adkins, Terry, 25
Africa: ancestral traditions from, 89–90;
    models of gender behavior from,
    81–82, 86; and poetry of Cortez, 160
"Afro Images" (Davis), 113–14
Afros: on *The Black Woman* cover,
    73; chemically processed Afros, 77;
    of Davis, 113; decline of, 231n8; on
    Essence cover models, 73, 75–76,
    231n8; Griffin on, 74
Age of Pisces/Neptunian Age, 198,
    239n70
agency, 17–19, 21, 33, 135
*Ain't I a Woman: Black Women and
    Feminism* (hooks), 79, 171
Airing Dirty Laundry (Reed), 224n9

Algeria, 47, 48, 133
Alligood, Clarence, 174, 175
Altered Egos (Couser), 137
Alwes, Derek, 215–16
*An American Dilemma: The Negro
    Problem and Modern Democracy*
    (Myrdal), 32
Andrews, William L., 237n5
androgyny, 17, 85
Angela Davis: A Political Biography
    (New York Committee to Free
    Angela Davis), 114–15
"Angela Davis: Black Woman on the
    Run" (Gillespie and Van Downing),
    124
"Angela Davis Speaks: The Contro-
    versial Marxist Leader in the Black
    Movement" (radio program), 131
Angelou, Maya, 36, 70
anger, 49–52, 171, 178
Anspacher Public Theatre, 70
anthologies, 110. *See also The Black
    Woman: An Anthology* (Bambara, ed.)
Anzaldúa, Gloria, 157, 220
apocalypse: and the apocalyptic self,
    203–16; and apocalyptic spatiality,
    199–203, 239n9; and chronometrical
    time, 195, 203; as metaphor for revo-
    lutionary change, 187–88, 193–94, 199,

200; theme of, 187–88, 193, 194–99. *See also The Salt Eaters* (Bambara)

Arceneaux, Edgar, 25

Asarté cosmetic ads, 77

Asian and Asian American writers, 62

assertiveness of black women, 82

assimilation, 31, 47, 206, 240n15

Association for Voluntary Sterilization, 100

astrology, 198

audiences: and the black aesthetic movement, 153; connection of divas to, 17, 19; and decolonization, 4, 55; direct address of, 165; and double-consciousness, 9, 55; dual audiences, 37, 53–54; and experiential writing of black authors, 6; and "nommo," 55, 56; and notions of self, 6; and reciprocity, 55, 56; and Sambo/Sapphire, 12, 21; and slave narratives, 7–8, 9, 21, 136–37, 138, 140; and style, 19; uplift of, 19–20; and Walker's castigation, 4; of women-oriented publications, 102–11; writers' relationship to, 55. *See also* black audiences; white audiences

authenticity, 76

"The Autobiographical Manifesto: Identities, Temporalities, Politics" (Smith), 135

autobiographies: autobiographical manifestos, 135; and citizenry, 138; and representativeness, 138–39, 217; shift to, in 1990s, 6; and white audiences, 139; of whites vs. blacks, 236n10. *See also under* Davis, Angela

Autobiography as Activism: Three Black Women of the Sixties (Perkins), 77–78, 116

Awkward, Michael, 6, 44, 91

Ayers, Roy, 96, 233n18

"Back to Africa: The Evolution of the International Section of the Black Panther Party (1969–1972)" (Cleaver), 47–48

back-to-Africa movements, 48, 196

Baker, Houston: on apocalypse, 195–96; on the New World, 195, 196; and Peterson, 37; and "post-integrationist poetics," 46; response to Joyce's criticism, 218, 219

Baker, Josephine, 166–67, 168

Bakhtin, Mikhail, 155

Baldwin, James: on apocalypse, 194, 196–97; and double-consciousness, 36; *The Fire Next Time*, 194, 196–97; "Going to Meet the Man," 50; support of Davis, 130–31

Bambara, Toni Cade: on androgyny, 85, 232n15; apocalyptic theme of, 187–88, 193–94; astrological theme of, 198; and audience, 191; and black nationalism, 189; and *The Black Woman*, 94–95, 103; on coalitions, 202–203; cosmology of, 189–90; criticisms of, 2; *Deep Sightings and Rescue Missions*, 103; and dreaming, 188, 190, 191; on emasculator stereotype, 82, 232n13; and *Essence* magazine, 96; and healing paradigms, 61; and imperative of revolutionary action, 239n3; on Marshall's "Making of Writer," 70; metaphysical themes of, 190, 197; name of, 230n4; "On the Issue of Roles," 84, 85; and patriarchical attitudes, 80, 83, 84–85, 232n15; political consciousness of, 62; as revolutionary diva, 9; on salt as snakebite antidote, 204; on Speaker's Corners, 95, 201; on victimization, 204–205; and Victorian ethic, 115–16; as writer/prophet, 190–91. *See also The Salt Eaters* (Bambara)

Baraka, Amiri (LeRoi Jones): and "African" models of gender behavior, 81–82, 86; and the black aesthetic movement, 58, 59–60, 187; and Black Arts Repertory Theatre/School, 46; and black nationalism, 101; on black womanhood, 182; *Dutchman*, 50–52;

and *Essence* magazine interview, 97; on love poems, 169; *Madheart: A Morality Play*, 80, 231n12; "Statement," 187; and unmasking trope, 50–52; on women's liberation, 90–91

The Battle of Algiers (1966), 95–96

Beale, Frances, 68, 83, 84

beauty standards: and *The Black Woman*, 73–74, 75, 76; and Davis, 113; and *Essence* magazine, 73, 75, 76–79, 231n8; and Morrison's *The Bluest Eye*, 43–45; and skin color, 88

Being and Race (Johnson), 60

bell curve, 31

Beloved (Morrison), 59, 64, 156–57, 158, 225n5

Berlant, Lauren, 118, 119–20, 135

Berry, Halle, 14

Beyond the Masks: Race Gender and Subjectivity (Mama), 225n4

Biggers, Sanford, 25

Bigsby, C. W. E., 33, 46, 53, 54, 60

birth control, 97, 99–100, 233n23

"Birth Control and the Black Woman" (Lindsey), 97

bitchiness, 170–71

black aesthetic movement (BAM), 46–57; audiences of, 4, 153; changing of, 60; compared to other movements, 228n22; and Cortez, 168, 183; criticisms of, 38, 237n1; and critiques of black texts, 35; and Davis's autobiography, 138–39; and decolonization, 9, 47, 48–53; demise of, 57–58, 70; and discourses on racial identity, 34; and double-consciousness, 53, 55; and homosexuality, 168; and integration, 46, 187; and love poems, 169; in Morrison's *The Bluest Eye*, 46; and negritude movement, 228n21; patriarchical attitudes in, 80; period of, 46; and poetry, 150; profanity in, 171; role of female authors in legacy of, 5; and scarification, 183; shift from civil rights and integration to, 46; and the

Southern experience, 234n29; success of, 38, 59, 187; successors of, 22; term, 224n7; violence in, 171; women's marginalization in, 230n33; and women's writing, 9–10

Black and Brown Waves: The Cultural Politics of Young Women of Color and Feminism, 110

Black Arts Repertory Theatre/School, 46

The Black Atlantic: Modernity and Double-Consciousness (Gilroy), 226n11

black audiences: and black aesthetic movement, 9, 49; and decolonization, 4, 9, 55; and Du Bois's *Souls of Black Folk*, 26–27; and *Essence* magazine, 96; importance of, 54; Morrison's targeting of, 56–57; privileging of, 4, 9, 19; and style, 19; and subjectivity, 54; uplift of, 19–20; and Walker's castigation, 4

"Black Cultural Nationalism" (Karenga), 153, 164

The Black "I": Author and Audience in African American Literature (Boan), 35, 36–37

"Black Is the Pursuit of Excellence" (Lewis), 102

"Black Macho Revisited: Reflections of a Snap! Queen" (Riggs), 15

"Black Man, Do You Love Me?" (Meriwether), 89, 107

"Black Man: White Woman" (Santini), 107–108

Black Manhood in James Baldwin, Ernest Gaines, and August Wilson (Clark), 229n29

black men: "castration" of, 80, 89, 91, 92; and feminists, 2; portrayals of, 1–4; reconciliation of black women with, 98; and self-conscious manhood, 38–46; treatment of women, 179–82. *See also* patriarchy; sexism

black nationalism: aims of, 47; in

and theme of violent self-defense, 39, 122, 144, 227n13; "To Our Oppressed Countrymen," 158–59

drag queens, 13, 14–15

Drago, Maria Del, 174–75

dreams and dreaming, 185–87, 188, 190, 216

drug abuse, 100–101

drum imagery, 180–82

"A Drum is a Woman" (Ellington), 181

Drumgo, Fleeta, 119

Drumvoices (Redmond), 152–53

Du Bois, W. E. B.: contact with blacks, 28–29; on "dilemma of the Negro author," 39–40; and dual audiences, 53–54; and gender politics, 33–34; on marginality of African Americans, 203; and popular culture, 26; on price of privilege, 25; and racism, 8, 28, 30, 54; scholarship on, 9, 28–30, 34–35; and "self-conscious manhood," 39–40; veil motif of, 28, 29, 30, 31, 40, 51, 195; and violent self-defense, 42. *See also* double-consciousness

dual-texts, 8–9

Dubey, Madhu, 62, 93, 230n33, 239n2

DuCille, Ann, 67, 222

Dunbar, Paul Laurence, 49

Durbin, Karen, 139–40

Dutchman (Baraka), 50–52

Eatonville, Fla., 48, 239n10

Ebony magazine, 76, 128–29

education, 41, 78

Ellington, Duke, 181

Ellis, Trey, 3, 37

Ellison, Ralph, 32

emasculator stereotype: and "Bullet-proof divas," 10; in *Essence* magazine, 89–90; and the Moynihan Report, 22, 80, 88, 92; reaction of women to, 82; and revolutionary divas, 5

"emergent woman" concept, 206, 209, 240n15

employment, 76

empowerment, 17, 21, 50, 60

entertainment industry, 15

era of the revolutionary diva, 59, 70

erotic empowerment, 21, 225n19

Essence Corporation, 93

Essence magazine: acquired by Time Inc., 109, 235n36; on Angela Davis, 124, 125–26; audience of, 96, 101, 103–11, 234n34, 235n39; and black nationalism, 94, 96, 100–101, 105, 109; competition of, 109–10, 234n34, 235n37; concept of, 103–104; con-tributors to, 108–109; criticism of, 104–105; debut of, 70, 93; epigraph of, 102; The *Essence* Woman, 72, 100, 102, 106; and feminism, 72, 96–100; and hairstyles, 73, 75–76, 231n8; and the Hollingsworth Group, 93, 103–104, 104–105, 234n32; impact of, 71–72; on interracial relationships, 107–109; on Morrison's *Paradise,* 57; and patriar-chical attitudes, 89–92; and *Playboy,* 105; and positive black female ima-ges, 103–104; relevancy of, to black women, 109–10; social context of, 95; as a Speaker's Corner, 95; and stan-dards of beauty, 73, 75, 76–79, 231n8; and talking back to patriarchy, 79

Eurocentric paradigm, 33

European modernism and postmoder-nism, 62

Eurydice, 212, 213

Evers, Myrlie B., 97, 233n19

experiential writings, 5–7

exploitation, 163

families, 80–81, 98

Fanon, Frantz, 52, 156–57, 163, 227n15

fashion, 77–78

femininity: and capitalism, 84; and Cor-tez, 171; and defamation of divas, 12; and matriarchs, 80–81; and militancy, 98; Newton's comments on, 78; rejec-tion of, 85

feminists and feminism: attacks on,

80; and birth control, 99–100; and black aesthetic movement, 58; and black liberation, 62; and black men, 2; and black nationalism, 94–95 (*see also* black nationalist feminism); and *The Black Woman,* 94–95; and *The Color Purple* film, 2; criticisms of, 2, 82, 83, 223n3; and divas, 12–13, 16; and Du Bois, 33–34; and *Essence* magazine, 72, 96–100; and hip-hop, 110; and Josephine Baker, 166; and legacy of *The Black Woman,* 71; negative perceptions of, 57; and poetry of Cortez, 168–84; and racism, 92–93; relevancy of, to black women, 96–97, 98–99; and Watkins on black female authors, 2

fertility, 87

"Festivals and Funerals" (Cortez), 152

The Fire Next Time (Baldwin), 194, 196–97

First Pan African Cultural Festival in Algiers, 48

"First Person Impersonal" (Durbin), 139

"Five Shades of Militancy" (Moore), 97–98

flesh imagery of Cortez, 151, 154–59, 169–70, 183

Fontenot, Chester J., Jr., 41

For Colored Girls (Shange), 70

"For the Brave Young Students in Soweto" (Cortez), 160

Ford, Karen, 168, 171, 172, 179

Forrest, Leon, 58, 59

Foster, Frances Smith, 7, 103, 136–37

Fowler, Manet, 89–90

Franklin, Aretha, 76

Frazier, E. Franklin, 80

Freedom Dreams (Kelley), 154

"From the Family Notebook" (Brown), 234n28

Gaines, Charles, 25

Gaines, Ernest, 229n29

Gallagher, Ellen, 25

Garcia, Inez, 172, 173–75, 176–77, 179

Garvey, Marcus, 48

Gates, Henry Louis, Jr.: and the black aesthetic movement, 58, 237n1; on canonization of African American literature, 218; on double-consciousness, 27, 35; on Du Bois's "Of the Coming of John," 41; on Du Bois's veil motif, 31; and experiential writings, 6; and Peterson, 37; response to Joyce's criticism, 218–19; signification theory of, 219–20; *Signifying Monkey,* 218

Gayle, Addison, 43

Ghana, 47

Gibson, Kenneth, 101, 233n24

Giddings, Paula, 95, 126–27

Gilkes, Cheryl, 67

Gillespie, Marcia, 124, 125–26, 231n8

Gilroy, Paul, 226n11

Giovanni, Nikki: career of, 233n20; as *Essence* contributor, 96; and feminism, 98; on "natural" black women, 185, 186; on options of African-Americans, 203–204; on poetry, 150; and power of female creativity, 187; on style as survival mechanism, 18; and use of profanity, 172

girlfriends, 38

Gittleman, Edwin, 137

Give Birth to Brightness: A Thematic Study of Neo-Black Literature (Williams), 217

Glaser, Walter D., 108–109

Global Divas: Filipino Gay Men in the Diaspora (Manalansan), 16

"Going to Meet the Man" (Baldwin), 50

The Good Negress (Verdelle), 59

Grayson, Deborah, 73, 75

Greece, ancient, 121

Greenlee, Charles, 99

Gresson, Aaron David, 193

Grier, Pam, 75

Griffin, Farah Jasmine: on agency, 221–22; on the autobiographical voice, 217; on cover photo of *The*

sexism: as anti-nation-building, 83; in Bambara's *The Salt Eaters,* 208; and Cortez, 168; and Davis's trial, 134; and female activism, 84; multiple jeopardy of black women, 69; and racism, 83, 92; of white and black men, 79

"Sexism, Racism and Black Women Writers" (Watkins), 2

sexuality, 166–67

"shade," 13, 15

Shakur, Assata, 48, 116, 236n7

Shange, Ntozake: and black aesthetic movement, 70; on black nationalism, 179; criticisms of, 2; on *Donahue,* 1, 5–6, 12; *For Colored Girls,* 70; political consciousness of, 62; *Sassafrass, Cypress, and Indigo,* 59

signification, 13, 220

Signifying Monkey: A Theory of African-American Literary Criticism (Gates), 218

Silvia Dubois, A Biografy of the Slav Who Whipt Her Mistres and Gand Her Fredom (Larison), 227n13

Simmons, Gary, 25

Simoes da Silva, A. J., 63

Simon, Rita J., 128–29

Simone, Nina, 85

Simpson, Lorna, 25

singers, 11, 19

Singh, Nikhil Pal, 47

skin colors, 74, 75, 231n7, 234n28

slave narratives: and citizenry, 138; compared to autobiographies of whites, 236n10; and Davis's autobiography, 140–41; as dual-texts, 9; and individual vs. representative, 136–37; and Peterson's alternate literary tradition, 37; violent self-expression in, 38; and white audiences, 7–8, 9, 21, 136–37, 138, 140

slavery: as basis of American capitalism, 138; and colonization of African Americans, 47; and cultural estrangement, 189; and exploitation of the female slave, 132; and masking, 49; and rape, 98; and scarification, 159; and violent resistance, 122. *See also* slave narratives

Smart-Grosvenor, Verta Mae, 70

Smethurst, James, 46

Smiley, Tavis, 223n6

Smith, Clarence, 103

Smith, Felipe, 40, 45

Smith, Sidonie, 38, 135

Smith, Valerie: on autobiographies, 139, 236n10; on the black aesthetic movement, 48; on the black female body, 67; on subtext of literary criticism and theory, 220

Smitherman, Geneva, 17

Snap! Queen persona, 15, 16

snapping, 14–15

Snead, James, 4

"So Many Feathers" (Cortez), 166–67

social Darwinism, 31

Soledad Brothers, 119, 120, 123–24

Soledad Brothers (Jackson), 132, 236n5

Soul on Ice (Cleaver), 80, 232n12

Souljah, Sister, 59

The Souls of Black Folk (Du Bois): audience of, 26, 227n14; and background of Du Bois, 29; double-consciousness in, 8, 27, 28, 30–32, 37; and dual audiences, 53–54; planned revision of, 30; revered status of, 27–28; significance of, to black readers, 26–27; veil motif in, 28, 29, 30, 31, 40, 51, 195; visiting card episode in, 45

South Africa, 167

Speaker's Corners, 95–96, 201

Specifying (Willis), 215

spectacles, 20–21

Spencer, Traci, 103–104, 109, 234n34

Spielberg, Stephen, 1, 2, 3

Spillers, Hortense J.: on Bambara's *The Salt Eaters,* 192; on the black female body, 67; on black students, 236n4; on "body" as distinct from "flesh,"

whiteness: and the black identity, 32–33; and capitalistic state, 179; counterstereotyping of, 52; and decolonization, 63; deconstruction of, 49, 52; and eradication of double-consciousness, 54; and Harlem Renaissance, 48

wholeness, desire for, 8

Wilkins, Roy, 80

Williams, Dana A., 58

Williams, Irene, 136

Williams, Maxine, 93

Williams, Sherley Anne, 64, 87–89, 217–19, 227n17

Willis, Susan, 214–15, 216

Wilson, Fred, 25

Winfrey, Oprah, 14

Wolfe, George C., 14–15

womanism, 98, 151, 179

"Women in Dark Times: Three Views of the Angela Davis Trial" (Williams), 136

Wood, Ean, 167

Wood, Jim, 174

Woodard, Jennifer Bailey, 72

Woodson, Jon, 160

Woolf, Virginia, 213

words, power of, 14

The Wretched of the Earth (Fanon), 47

Wright, Richard: and black nationalism, 228n18; *Black Power*, 228n18; and double-consciousness, 36; and dual-texts, 9; on failure of black writing, 228n22; "How 'Bigger' Was Born," 42; *Native Son*, 9, 42–43, 45, 49; *on pitying characters*, 42; *Uncle Tom's Children*, 42, 43; *White Man Listen!*, 9

Writing the Subject (Kester), 6

Wyne, Marvin D., 34

Wynter, Sylvia, 57–58

Yearning: Race, Gender, and Cultural Politics (hooks), 200

Young, Whitney, 80

Youngblood (Killens), 227n17, 228n18

Zaire, 47

Zami (Lorde), 65

Zamir, Shamoon, 28, 29–30

KIMBERLY NICHELE BROWN is Associate Professor of English and Director of the Africana Studies Program at Texas A&M University.